Karen Brown's
MEXICO

Dolphin Cove Inn
Manzanillo

MAR 2010

San Diego
Tijuana

UNITED STATES OF AMERICA

Houston

New Orleans

Gulf of California

1

Guerrero Negro

Creel

Chihuahua

Álamos

Loreto

El Fuerte

San Carlos

La Paz

Cabo San Lucas

Mazatlán

2

Zacatecas

Puerto Vallarta

Guadalajara

Manzanillo

Zitácuaro

Mexico City

3

Acapulco

Oaxaca

Palenque

Gulf of Mexico

4

Cancún

Mérida

Cozumel

Campeche

BELIZE

GUATEMALA

HONDURAS

EL SALVADOR

PACIFIC OCEAN

Mexico Overview

Whale Watching in Baja
The Copper Canyon
Colonial Gems
Mexico City & Beyond
Miracle of the Monarch Butterflies
Oaxaca Valley
Mayan Mysteries & A Loop of the Yucatán Peninsula

0   100   200 Kilometers
0   100   200 Miles

UNITED STATES OF AMERICA

BAJA CALIFORNIA

SONORA

CHIHUAHUA

COAHUILA

NUEVO LEON

Gulf of California

BAJA CALIFORNIA SUR

DURANGO

SINALOA

ZACATECAS

TAMAULIPAS

Gulf of Mexico

NAYARIT

SAN LUIS POTOSÍ

1

3

7

4

JALISCO

5 2

8

VERACRUZ

YUCATAN

QUINTANA ROO

9

MICHOACÁN

6

CAMPECHE

GUERRERO

OAXACA

TABASCO

CHIAPAS

BELIZE

GUATEMALA

HONDURAS

EL SALVADOR

PACIFIC OCEAN

Mexico States

Small states numbered as follows:

1. AGUASCALIENTES
2. DISTRITO FEDERAL
3. GUANAJUATO
4. HIDALGO
5. MEXICO
6. MORELOS
7. QUERETARO DE ARTEAGA
8. TLAXCALA
9. COLIMA

0   100   200 Kilometers

0   100   200 Miles

Isla Tiburon

Hermosillo

[1]

[15]

Chihuahua al Pacifico Railroad

Cuauhtemoc

Guerrero Negro

Creel

Laguna Ojo de Liebre

Barrancas

Guaymas

San Ignacio

Santa Rosalia

Ciudad Obregon

Bahuichivo

Cerocahui

Punta Chivato

Navojoa

Alamos

Urique

Copper Canyon

San Ignacio Lagoon

Mulegé

Gulf of California

[15]

[53]

El Fuerte

Loreto

Pacific Ocean

Los Mochis

[15]

[22]

Ciudad Constitución

Culiacan

San Carlos

Bahia Magdalena

[1]

Bahia de la Paz

Mexico Map 1

● Places to Stay

━━ Whale Watching

━━ Copper Canyon

─·─·─ Ferry Route

La Paz

[19]

Rancho Leonero

Todos Santos

[1]

0 25 50 Kilometers

0 25 50 Miles

Cabo San Lucas

San José del Cabo

Los Cabos

Mazatlán

To Mazatlán

Real de Catorce 57

Zacatecas 49

La Quemada

San Luis Potosi 70

15

54

Aguascalientes 85

Tepic

45

Dolores Hidalgo Mineral de Pozos

80

León

Punta Mita

San Sebastián del Oeste

Guanajuato San Miguel de Allende

Bucerias Puerto Vallarta

Guadalajara Valenciana

Majahuitas

Tlaquepaque Querétaro 57

Yelapa

Ajijic Lake Chapala 90

La Cruz de Loreto 80

Tapalpa 15

Quémaro

54

Angahuan Morelia 55

Mexico City Texcoco

Costa Alegre

Cihuatlán San Antonio

Uruapan Pátzcuaro

Colima

Zitácuaro 15 Toluca

Careyes

Cuernavaca

37 Taxco Amacuzac

Isla Navidad Manzanillo

51

200 134

95

Mexico Map 2

Places to Stay
Colonial Gems

0   25   50 Kilometers
0   25   50 Miles

Ixtapa Zihuatanejo

PACIFIC OCEAN

200

Acapulco

Mexico Map 3

- ● Places to Stay
- ♣ Archaeological Sites
- ♣ Sites w/ Places to Stay
- —— Mexico City & Beyond
- —— Miracle of the Monarch Butterflies
- —— Oaxaca Valley

0   25   50 Kilometers
0   25   50 Miles

San Luis Potosi

Ciudad Madero
Tampico

70

85

Dolores Hidalgo

180

Mineral de Pozos

San Miguel de Allende

Querétaro

57

Tula   Pachuca

Poza Rica   Papantla
Tajin

Tulancingo

Teotihuacán

Chincua Butterfly Sanctuary

Morelia

Mexico City

Texcoco

140

Gulf of Mexico

Zitácuaro

Cacaxtla

Tlaxcala

Veracruz

Toluca

Puebla

Malinalco   Cuernavaca

150   Orizaba

Cerro Pelon Butterfly Sanctuary

Xochicalco

Taxco   Amacuzac

51

Coatzacoalcos

134

190

175

180

95

Zihuatanejo

San Felipe del Agua

Teotitlán del Valle

Oaxaca   Yagul

Monte Albán   Mitla

Acapulco

PACIFIC OCEAN

200

135   175

Salina Cruz

Puerto Escondido

Huatulco

Gulf of Tehuantepec

Mexico Map 4

- ● Places to Stay
- ❖ Archaeological Sites
- ❖ Sites w/ Places to Stay
- ━━ Mayan Mysteries & A Loop of the Yucatán Peninsula

0 25 50 Kilometers
0 25 50 Miles

Isla Mujeres
Bahia Petempich
Cancún
Puerto Morelos
Punta Maroma
Playa Xcalacoco
Playa del Carmen
Puerto Adventuras
Xcaret
Xpuha Beach
Cozumel
Xel-Há

Mérida
Xcanatún
Tixkokob
Izamal
Katanchel
Celestún
Rio Celestún Biosphere Reserve
Santa Rosa
Temozón
Oxkintok
Chichén Itzá
Valladolid
Cobá
Tulum
Riviera Maya

Uxmal
Kabah
Labná
Sayil
Balancanoné Caves
Gulf of Mexico
Campeche
Uayamón
Ednzá
Champotón

Dzibanche
Kinchua
Mahahual
Becán
Xpujil
Bacalar
Chicanná
Kohunlich
Chetumal
Costa Maya

180
307
261
180
186

Ciudad del Carmen
Escárcega
Calakmul

Bahia de Campeche
Villahermosa
Palenque
Cascadas de Agua Azul
Yaxchilán
Ocosingo
Toniná
San Cristóbal de Las Casas

190
199
186

BELIZE
GUATEMALA
Caribbean Sea

Contents

Dedicated to the memory of
Steve
Whose love of Mexico and joy of travel
Have been passed down through the generations,
and as always,
To my best friend, Bill

2010 Cover Painting: Dolphin Cove Inn, Manzanillo

Authors: Clare Brown, Karen Brown, and Jane Stevenson Day, Ph.D.

Editors: Clare Brown, Karen Brown, June Eveleigh Brown, Kim Brown Holmsen, Debbie Tokumoto, Terri Jo Woellner, Jane Stevenson Day.

Illustrations: Barbara Maclurcan Tapp.

Cover painting: Jann Pollard.

Color photos: Lake Pátzcuaro (Ben Kong), Mayan Ruins at Río Bec.

Maps: Rachael Kircher-Randolph.

Technical support: Andrew Harris.

Distributed by National Book Network, 15200 NBN Way, Blue Ridge Summit, PA 17214, USA. Tel: 717-794-3800 or 1-800-462-6420, Fax: 1-800-338-4500, Email: custserv@nbnbooks.com

A catalog record for this book is available from the British Library.

ISSN 1540-2983

Foreword

This book is a sentimental journey. My grandfather, Louis Carr Stevenson (Steve), lived part of each year in Mexico, which he called his "second home." Steve had a deep appreciation for the beauty and culture of the country and a genuine love and admiration for its people. By hosting family celebrations there, he instilled in his children and grandchildren his enthusiasm and love for Mexico. We have thought for many years of writing about Mexico, but were concerned that there weren't sufficient hotels of charm and quality to make such a book feasible. How wrong we were! In the past few years, superb inns and hotels have been popping up all over the country—properties that rival in romantic ambiance and service the finest hotels in the world. The idea of a book became too good to resist when my aunt, Dr. Jane Stevenson Day, an archaeologist and renowned authority on pre-Columbian civilizations, retired as chief curator of the Denver Museum of Nature and Science and generously offered to contribute her profound knowledge to our project. This book reflects the efforts of two sisters, Steve's daughters: my Aunt Jane and my mother, Clare, my partner and my best friend. Together, through their writing of *Mexico: Exceptional Places to Stay & Itineraries*, they continue Steve's legacy in sharing his love for Mexico with an even greater audience, our readers. This is truly an exceptional book because of Clare and Jane's extensive research and blended talents: Jane's archaeological expertise and Clare's ability to find the most wonderful places to stay. Consequently, this guide to Mexico is unique in that it has a strong focus on archaeology; while recommending a wide variety of exceptional lodgings, from sumptuous, 16th-century haciendas on vast estates to alluring thatched huts on secluded beaches. Easy-to-follow itineraries encompass a wealth of fascinating attractions—from Whale-Watching in Baja to exploring the country's Colonial heart. Naturally, we include descriptions of Mexico's famous beaches, but our real target is the traveler who wants to have an in-depth experience of this incredible country just "south of the border."

We welcome you to Mexico.

Karen

Introduction

Mexico City, Cathedral

Mexico is an incomparable destination, a stunning country that includes such a wealth of wonders that, whatever your interests, you are bound to have your dreams fulfilled. There are marvelous hotels, archaeological treasures beyond belief, breathtaking beaches, soaring mountains, deep canyons, fascinating 16th-century Colonial towns, cosmopolitan cities, quaint Indian villages, colorful markets, fine golf courses, divine snorkeling, whale excursions, outstanding bird watching, butterfly reserves, tropical forests, dense jungles, superb deep-sea fishing, chic boutiques, cute shops featuring native handicrafts, and, for all of us who love to eat, culinary delights. To add the final touch of perfection, the weather in Mexico is excellent. However, Mexico is not for everyone. If it bothers you when service isn't instant, if you are upset when everything isn't totally tidy, if you are disappointed if your hotel doesn't have internet access, then perhaps you should consider another destination. But the things that may seem like faults to some are, in our estimation, exactly what make Mexico so special. Here you step back into another time where people are not rushed, where friendliness prevails, where cultural differences enrich your travels. We have always loved Mexico. Now, after spending an extended period of time there, we are more captivated than ever by its charms. We know that our readers who are young in heart will share our enthusiasm for this fabulous country with its extraordinarily warm people and amazing culture.

The purpose of this guide is to help you plan your trip. Mexico is an incredibly diverse country with a bewildering selection of sightseeing and hotel accommodations. Our goal is to help you sort out all the options so that you can discover the ideal destination to fulfill your dreams and to choose just the right accommodations so that your holiday will be memorable. There are four sections in the book. This first section, *Introduction,* begins with a bit of history, delving into Mexico's legacy of the past and laying a foundation for what you will be seeing, then follows with practical information that should be useful in your travels. The itinerary section lays out routings that cover the highlights of Mexico; the third section, *Hotel Descriptions*, provides descriptions and pertinent details of recommended hotels; the fourth section contains the index. The color maps in the front of the book pinpoint each hotel's location and outline the routes of each featured itinerary.

Introduction

Archaeology & the Legacy of the Past

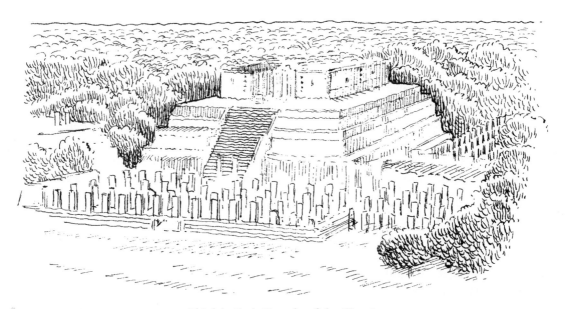

Chichén Itzá, Temple of the Warriors

To visit Mexico without including at least one of its archaeological wonders would be a pity since its history cannot be understood or appreciated without a journey into the past. Mexican archaeology has revealed one of the most fascinating and splendid chapters in all of world prehistory. Mexico has been inhabited for thousands of years, during which time a stunningly sophisticated culture emerged. During the peak of this civilization, awesome cities were constructed, a superb network of roads was built, and massive pyramids emerged in honor of the gods. Today throughout Mexico there are archaeological sites that attest to the profound grandeur of this era. These sites are dotted throughout every part of Mexico and are described in depth in our itineraries. The archaeological and Colonial sites, and various museums recommended here are not in any way a complete inventory. Instead, they are places we consider very special that conveniently blend into our itineraries and are close to excellent accommodations. Note: most museums are closed on Mondays.

The archaeological record in Mexico begins thousands of years ago at the end of the last ice age (c.10,000 B.C.) when Paleo-Indian bands hunted now-extinct animals such as bison and mammoth. However, the great civilizations of pre-Hispanic Mexico have their beginnings about 2500 B.C. with the development of a rich agricultural tradition based on a triad of crops: corn, beans, and squash. Interestingly, this change from hunting to village-based agriculture occurred not only in Mexico, but also all over the world. The establishment of a stable food supply allowed for an increase in population, growth of settled communities, and eventually the development of cities and sophisticated cultures.

The first great civilization of Mexico developed on the hot Gulf Coast around 1500 B.C. among a group of people known as the Olmecs. The majority of traditions and traits that characterize the many succeeding Mesoamerican cultures have their origin with these very early people. In fact, one of the most amazing aspects of pre-Hispanic Mexico is the continuity of these cultural traits across time and space. Most of the hallmarks of pre-Columbian Mesoamerica had their beginnings in the Olmec period, but were still present 3,000 years later among the Aztecs, a civilization well-documented for us by the Spanish conquistadors. Some of these clearly recognizable characteristics are: a dependence on the basic crops of corn, beans, and squash; a preference for green jade over all other materials for royal or ceremonial objects; the making of fine ceramics; the creation of specialized architecture such as stone pyramids, palaces, temples, and ball courts; the carving of massive stone sculptures depicting gods and rulers; the use of solid rubber balls for playing a ritual team sport; a large pantheon of gods whose names, but not necessarily their characteristics, changed over time; and the use of human sacrifice to placate these gods. Perhaps the greatest achievement, however, was the construction of great urban centers containing plazas, pyramids, ball courts, roadways, monuments, and massive stone architecture, all carefully finished with cut stone and white plaster. These amazing ancient cities still survive throughout Mexico and today offer visitors a glimpse of the extraordinary world of pre-Columbian Mesoamerica.

This continued survival of ancient traditions from past into present is one of the most intriguing aspects of a visit to modern Mexico. Travelers to Mexico today become quickly, if unconsciously, aware of this through the food—the basic foods are the same as they were 3,500 years ago. Corn, beans, and squash still form the basic triad of a rural diet and even in sophisticated Mexico City tortillas are preferred to bread. In addition, tomatoes, avocados, chocolate, potatoes, chilies, popcorn, papaya, yams, peanuts, turkeys, and much more are all popular survivors of the pre-Hispanic world. Associated with this are centuries-old agricultural techniques that are still used in rural Mexico. Large-scale agriculture is now more common, but in many small farming communities, fields are still ritually marked out just as they were long ago and a *coa*, or digging stick, is used to plant the corn kernels—three in each hole: one for the gods, one for the birds and one for human needs.

Another modern continuance from the past can be traced to a ritual pre-Columbian game played with a solid rubber ball by two opposing teams. In fact, the actual concept of playing to win as a team, rather than as an individual, and the use of rubber to form a bouncing ball were unknown in the Old World until the Spanish reached Mexico in 1519. On his first return journey to Spain, Cortés took players and rubber balls to play at the royal court of Charles V. The skillful players and the rubber balls amazed the European spectators. Today, ball games played around the world clearly have their origin in this 3,500-year-old team sport with its colorful rituals, stone courts, specialized equipment, and bouncing rubber balls. Happily, no longer is the losing captain sacrificed to the gods!

Also reflecting their pre-Columbian origin are the colorful, local markets you find in Mexico today. Everything imaginable is laid out in its own section of the vibrant, noisy marketplace and an incredible variety of merchandise can be purchased. Shoppers can wander from vendor to vendor to select the freshest produce, strongest baskets, fine jewelry, and even medicinal herbs and the services of the local healer. Today, as in the past, markets are the heart and pulse of daily life. When Cortés arrived in Mexico, he found that markets flourished throughout the country. Riches such as feathers, gold, and jade from far-flung frontiers of the empire were available for purchase, as well as locally produced agricultural crops and goods such as baskets, pots, clothing, and services of all types. Shoppers strolled through colorful rows of fruits, flowers, and vegetables; listened to merchants hawking their wares, and enjoyed a snack amid the noise, odors, and confusion—a scene still typical of Mexican markets today.

Current religious beliefs and activities also hark back to the past, blending ancient pre-Columbian gods with 16th-century Spanish Catholicism. Indeed, the Spanish Colonial churches and cathedrals were often built on the same sacred spot as the original ancient temples and pyramids that preceded them. Pilgrimages are still made to these hallowed places, and the timeless odor of copal incense rises from the altars as the feasts and rituals of past and present blend in the current church calendar.

ARRIVAL OF THE CONQUISTADORS

To understand Mexico today, it helps to be familiar with one of the most dramatic events in all history: the meeting of the Old and New Worlds in the Americas during the early 16th century. Of these many events, the encounter between the Spaniards, under Cortés, and the Aztecs, under Montezuma, is a most astounding, a tale culminating when Cortés's forces finally took over the Aztec capital, Tenochtitlán (now called Mexico City).

The story began on February 18th, 1519, when Hernán Cortés set sail from Cuba to search for gold and glory. He was accompanied by 500 soldiers, 50 sailors, 200 islanders from Cuba, several black servants, and a few Indian women. Also on board his 11 ships were 16 horses, 14 pieces of artillery, supplies of food, and trinkets and clothing for trading. Cortés's ships sailed along the Gulf coast of Mexico. At stops along the way he heard of the power of the Aztecs and of an empire rich in gold ruled by the feared emperor Montezuma. On Good Friday, April 18, 1519, he and his men landed near the site of the modern city of Veracruz.

Cortés's arrival in Mexico on the Aztec calendar date *ce acatl* (one reed) prompted Montezuma to consider that Cortés might actually be the god *Quetzalcoatl,* returning as promised in legend, to reclaim his kingdom in the year one reed. This coincidence of the date of Cortés's arrival, coupled with uncertainty produced by the evil omens, left Montezuma perplexed as to Cortés' identity and purpose. Although originally Montezuma thought Cortés might be a god, it would have been impossible for a few scraggly, Spanish soldiers to have ever been able to defeat the powerful, mighty army of Montezuma without help. Luckily, Cortés had one great windfall—after a successful battle against a Mayan village, the chief presented him with 20 Indian maidens. One of these, La Malinche, was an exceptionally bright, young woman who not only became his mistress, but who also was able to act as translator and advisor. With her aid, Cortés enlisted the assistance of thousands of Tlaxcalan warriors, who were passionate enemies of the Aztecs and joined forces with him.

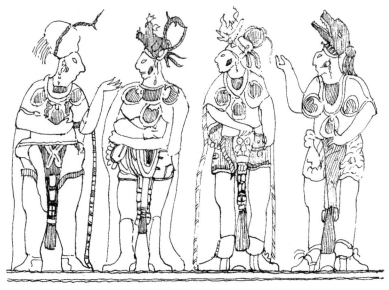

Maya Nobles

By the time Cortés crossed the snows of the last great mountain barrier and descended into the rich valley below, his entourage consisted of several thousand well-equipped Tlaxcalan warriors along with his own still surviving 350 Spanish soldiers. His troops entered Tenochtitlán where the final battle was fought in the great marketplace of Tlatelolco. There the Aztec nobles and warriors, assisted even by the women, according to legend, made a valiant last stand for the city, but the forces of the Spanish and their thousands of Indian allies were too powerful. The end came on August 13th, 1521. Of the 300,000 warriors who had defended the city only 60,000 were left. Mexico had fallen; the glorious city of Tenochtitlán was destroyed and neither the New World nor the Old would ever be the same again.

Once the Aztecs surrendered, the quest for gold was on. The Aztecs and their contemporaries were amazed at the Spaniards' unquenchable thirst for gold. To them objects of rich green jade, with their connotation of rain, water, and fertility, were far more beautiful and valuable than the shiny metal. But the Spanish hungered for the treasure, plundered it, fought over it, and after the fall of Tenochtitlán tortured their captives for information of its whereabouts.

The aesthetic beauty of the gold ornaments created by Aztec artists held little interest for Cortés and his soldiers. Only a handful of the splendid objects described by the chronicles remain today. Most of the magnificent pieces were immediately thrown into the melting pots. Once it was cast into ingots, standardized weights were made to establish the king's fifth, that rich share of New-World wealth that was conscientiously set aside for the Spanish throne. These bars of gold, along with carefully selected examples of the finest jewelry, were sent by ship to Spain where they were displayed with great pomp at the courts of Charles V. In Seville, Valladolid, Brussels, and Barcelona the undreamed-of splendor of Montezuma's gifts to Cortés and the plundered golden treasure of the Aztecs dazzled the world of Renaissance Europe.

The search for treasure exploded. Soon adventurers, priests, bureaucrats, and soldiers flocked to New Spain (Mexico) to look for fame, fortune, and the conversion of souls. A few came to make Mexico their home; some to convert the Indians to Christianity; but most came simply to pillage the wealth of the new land. The population was decimated by disease and bondage. For almost 300 years, the Aztecs and other indigenous peoples lay under the colonial yoke of Spain. Finally, revolutions broke the bonds that tied New Spain to Europe and Mexico rose as a new country, a nation that blended the genes and customs of the Old and New Worlds in a new tradition unique to the Americas.

About Hotels

BASIS FOR SELECTION

This guide does not try to appeal to everyone—it is definitely prejudiced: we visit hundreds of hotels and select only those few we think are special. The place that captivates us might be a 17th-century hacienda surrounded by vast acreage, a simple thatched hut nestled under palm trees, or an appealing beachfront hideaway accessible only by boat, but there is a common denominator—they all have charm. So if you prefer to travel spending your nights in romantic accommodations, this book is for you. For some of you, cost will not be a factor if the hotel is outstanding; for others, a budget guides your choice. What we have tried to do is to indicate what each hotel has to offer and describe the setting, so that you can make the choice to suit your own preferences and budget. We feel that if you know what to expect, you won't be disappointed, so we have tried to be candid and honest in all our appraisals.

BED & BREAKFASTS

Those of you who like the intimate bed-and-breakfast style of travel will be happy to know that this type of accommodation is an increasingly popular concept in Mexico. Some of the ones we feature in this guide are extremely elegant—rivaling the amenities in the finest hotels. Others are more simple, sweet, and appealing. But they all share the same great warmth of welcome and delightful, personal attention.

CHILDREN

Most places in Mexico accept children with open arms. However, in some hotels, especially those that cater to adults who want a romantic get-away, children are not appropriate. Even for the hotels that do welcome children, their policies and stipulations may vary widely: some will accept only infants, some will accept children over 12, some accept children over 16, etc. Therefore, if you will be traveling with your family, be sure to ask the hotel what their policy is concerning children when making reservations.

COMFORT

Read our descriptions carefully to choose the hotel that suits you best—one that not only appeals to your budget, but also your life style. Be aware that our selection of accommodations encompasses an awesome variety, but each place to stay is special in its own way. It should be obvious that a tent camp for whale-watching or a thatched hut on a remote beach can't even remotely compare in comfort to a sumptuous hotel with the finest linens and world class restaurant. But, we have left the selection up to you. Variety is fun.

FINDING YOUR HOTEL

Many hotels in Mexico are difficult to find. In towns, street names frequently change from block to block or the signs continue to use an outdated name that no longer exists— many times you cannot find a street sign at all! If there is no street number, the address reads s/n (which translates "without number"). The situation doesn't improve much in the countryside. Some of the hotels (especially the haciendas on the Yucatán Peninsula and the beach hideaways along the Costa Alegre) are not in any town at all and their addresses only hint at a nearby location. However, some things make finding your hotel easier. In cities, most hotels are marked by signs pointing you in the right direction. In the countryside, your life is made easier if you watch the signs that mark the kilometers along the roads (these are much like the old "milestones" in England). Some hotels use these signs in their addresses, such as "located at km 12," which makes finding the hotel very simple. When making reservations, ask for the closest kilometer sign to the hotel. In all cases, buy a detailed map in advance of your arrival and mark your hotel. To supplement your map, ask the hotel to send exact driving directions and, if possible, a local map.

ICONS

Icons allow us to provide additional information about our recommended properties. When using our website to supplement the guides, positioning the cursor over an icon will, in many cases, give you further details.

We have introduced the following icons in this guide to supplement each property's description. For easy reference, an icon key can also be found on the inside back cover flap. ❋ Air conditioning in rooms, ☺ Archaeological site nearby, ⊥ Beach nearby, ☕ Breakfast included in room rate, ♂ Children welcome, ♨ Cooking classes offered, ▦ Credit cards accepted, ▲ Dinner served upon request, ☎ Direct-dial telephone in room, ⌂ Dogs by special request, ⇟ Elevator, ʸ Exercise room, @ Internet access available for guests, Ⴑ Mini-refrigerator in rooms, ⊗ Some non-smoking rooms, P Parking available (free or paid), ¶ Restaurant, ⚘ Spa (treatments/massage etc.), ≈ Swimming pool, ⚹ Tennis, ▣ Television with English channels in guestrooms, ⚭ Wedding facilities, ♿ Wheelchair friendly, **W** Wireless available for guests, ⛳ Golf course nearby, ⚸ Hiking trails nearby, 🐴 Horseback riding nearby, ⛷ Skiing nearby, ⚓ Water sports nearby, ⚘ Wineries nearby.

PLUNGE POOL

You will notice in the hotel description section that we mention some hotels have "plunge" pools. Several people unfamiliar with the term have asked what this means. This is a term frequently used in Mexico and designates a small pool that was never intended for swimming, but is used for relaxing and dips to cool off while sunbathing. Most of these romantic plunge pools are in deluxe hotels and are private to the room.

RATES

In our other guides we quote room rates in the currency of the country but we have made an exception in the case of Mexico since almost all hotels quote rates in U.S. dollars instead of pesos (though the final bill is calculated in pesos). The rates shown are approximate, based on a double room for two persons in the high season. There might be special surcharges added during Christmas, Easter, or festival times; while sometimes rates are substantially lower during the off season. The rates cover the range of room prices from standard to deluxe but there might be a few special rooms such as a presidential suite offered at substantially higher prices than those shown. Some of the hotels include breakfast in their quoted room rate; some include breakfast and dinner; some include all meals. This is noted in the details for each hotel. When some or all meals are included, you are generally receiving very good value. Some hotels charge extra for parking. We indicate if the hotel has parking available but you will need to ask when you make your reservation if there is a charge.

Be aware that hotel taxes are high in Mexico, varying between 12% and 17%. Some hotels include this tax in their quoted tariff. If not, we indicate that tax is added and the percentage since this is very important when comparing values. Also, be aware that some hotels add an extra service charge to their rates. We find this trend growing, especially in deluxe hotels in popular resort areas. We have noted when hotels add a service charge and the percentage so that you won't be surprised at your final bill.

It is very important to remember the rates shown for each hotel are approximate. Be sure to ask exactly the rate for the period when you are traveling and what the rate includes (such as meals) and what extras are added (such as tax and service charge).

RESERVATIONS

We recommend advance hotel reservations. If you are traveling off-season, you can probably do fine by calling ahead the day you want a room, but don't expect to just stop en route: there are very few choices of places to stay except in major cities or resort areas. There are almost no motels, and hotels off the beaten path are rare and usually offer very basic accommodations. If you are traveling during peak travel periods (Easter, Christmas, and mid-July through mid-August), you will find hotel space very scarce. When you make advance reservations, most hotels will want a deposit; and if you cancel, you might not be able to get your money back. So, when making a reservation, ask what the penalty is. To protect yourself in case you have to cancel due to illness, we recommend cancellation insurance. A link on our website (*www.karenbrown.com*) will connect you to a variety of insurance policies that can be purchased online.

HOW TO MAKE RESERVATIONS

DIFFERENT WORLD: While searching for hotels for the original edition of this guidebook, we were amazed at how many of the gems that we felt so clever to have discovered had already been found by Different World, a company in England that represents a select group of inns in Mexico. Without exception, when we chatted to the owners of the hotels, they poured out accolades of praise for this company, its professionalism, fine service, high standard of excellence, and integrity in terms of their selections. On the same trail as their researcher, our paths often almost crossed, but we never had the pleasure of meeting in person. However, we soon became friends by phone as we shared some of our mutual finds. We are exceptionally pleased to indicate in the *Hotel Descriptions* section (under hotel details) those properties that are affiliated with Different World. Their website is the finest hotel-booking service we have ever seen for its wealth of information and ease of operation.

You can make reservations at many of the hotels in our book that are represented by Different World via the website *www.differentworld.com* or by calling toll free USA (888) 903-9512. Identify yourself as a Karen Brown Traveler by using the code DWKBG2010 and we will ship direct from Karen Brown's Guides a complimentary copy of any one of our titles—your choice, based on availability. Books will be shipped upon completion of your reservation (one copy per customer account, not per reservation). Postage is additional for addresses outside the United States.

EMAIL: If you want to make reservations by contacting the hotel directly, this is our preferred way of making a reservation. Many hotels have an email address, which can be found by going to their webpage from our website, *www.karenbrown.com*. You can link directly to a property (from its page on our website) using its email hyperlink. (Note: Not all hotels choose to be included in our website.)

FAX: If faxing, be aware that even if the hotel has a fax number, the fax machine is sometimes turned off (especially at night) and fax lines are sometimes shared with phone lines, making connections difficult. If faxing from the United States, dial 011 (the international code), then 52 (Mexico code), then the city code and local number.

LETTER: Mail service is slow; letters sometimes take up to one month to be delivered.

PHONE: If dialing from the United States, dial 011 (the international code), then 52 (Mexico code), then the city code and local number.

TRAVEL AGENT: A travel agent can be of great assistance, particularly if your own time is limited. The majority of travel agencies charge for their services.

WHEELCHAIR ACCESSIBILITY

If an inn has *at least* one guestroom that is accessible by wheelchair, it is noted with the symbol &. This is not the same as saying it meets full disability standards. In reality, it can be anything from a basic, ground-floor room to a fully equipped facility. Please discuss your requirements when you call your chosen place to stay, to determine if they have accommodation that suits your needs and preferences.

About Itineraries

Mitla, Vendors in Front of the Church

We have put together itineraries covering Mexico's many fascinating towns, rich archaeological sites, remarkable natural wonders, and delightful beach resorts. These itineraries tie in with suggestions for romantic places to stay. If possible, try to combine one or more itineraries. As an example, top off a week climbing pyramids in the Yucatán Peninsula with several days stretched out on a hammock on one of the unsurpassed beaches of the Riviera Maya. For those who are apprehensive about driving, we begin our selection of itineraries with *Colonial Gems: Charming Towns by Car or Bus,* designed for those who want to get off the beaten path but prefer not to drive. This itinerary gives two ways to get to each destination: one by car and one by bus. Contrary to the situation in Europe, deluxe or first-class bus transportation is the preferred means of public transportation between towns within Mexico.

In addition to Colonial gems, our itineraries cover Mexico City and the surrounding valley, Oaxaca and its nearby archaeological sites, the Yucatán Peninsula with its Mayan ruins, the natural wonders of whale-watching, the Monarch butterfly, and the Copper Canyon. For those whose idea of a holiday is to head for the beach, we also offer itineraries that feature places to play in the sun, including beach resorts on both coasts of Mexico and on the Baja Peninsula.

COMMERCIAL MAPS

If you are driving, you will need to buy detailed maps. The most comprehensive maps for Mexico are called *Guia Roji* or Red Guides, though we have found that even the very latest of these maps do not always show the most recently opened roads (especially on the Yucatán Peninsula). In addition to a map of the country and individual state maps, the *Guia Roji* has an excellent atlas that includes almost all of the towns mentioned in this book.

General Information

CAR RENTAL

Many major U.S. car rental companies operate in Mexico. It is best to stick to well known companies, as many of the lesser-known franchises are not properly supervised. Rental fees are, in general, higher than in the United States, Canada, and Europe. A compact car will cost about $85 per day and the car will probably not be delivered to you with a full tank of gas. You must return the car only to the office where you rented it or an additional fee will be added. Often during high season there are not enough cars to meet demand, so it is best to make reservations in advance.

CREDIT CARDS

HOTELS: Most major hotels accept credit cards but many of the smaller ones will accept payment only in cash. Whether or not a property accepts credit cards is indicated in the list of icons at the bottom of each hotel description by the symbol ▬. We have also indicated the specific cards accepted by using the following codes: AX–American Express, MC–MasterCard, VS–Visa, or simply, all major. Note: Even if an inn does not accept credit card payment, it will sometimes request your account number as a guarantee of arrival.

RESTAURANTS: In large cities that cater to the tourist trade credit cards are generally accepted; however, once off the beaten path, be prepared to pay in cash.

SHOPPING: Large stores usually accept credit cards, but small boutiques and street vendors with whom you negotiate a price usually accept cash only.

SERVICE STATIONS: *Very* few service stations accept credit cards as payment for gas. Since fuel is a major expense while on the road, be sure you have sufficient cash.

TOLL STATIONS: Toll stations do not accept credit cards. The amount adds up very quickly, so be prepared to pay in cash—in pesos. When close to the border, many toll stations will accept US dollars.

DRIVING

BORDER CROSSING: Allow at least an hour to cross the border from the United States into Mexico. On your return from Mexico into the United States, it can take even longer, often several hours. Since September 11, the time has increased due to security. Expect delays, especially during peak hours of the day or holidays, when traffic is more intense. If you are driving across the border, be aware that there are several requirements. These are listed below:

1) Proof of Ownership: A visitor bringing a car into Mexico must have proof of ownership (title or registration). If your car is financed, you must have a notarized letter

from your financing institution on the company's letterhead giving you permission to drive into Mexico. You may not take someone else's car into Mexico.

2) Forms: You need to fill out two forms: a *Temporary Vehicle Importation* permit, and a *Promise to Return Vehicle* form. These forms are available at the border or at AAA club offices in Arizona, California, or Texas.

3) Administration Fee: At point of entry, an administration fee of $29 plus tax must be paid with a credit card. The credit card must be in the registered owner's name and issued by a U.S. or Canadian bank or lending institution. *Cash or checks are not accepted.* A sticker is applied to your windshield after you pay the administration fee. If you do *not* have a credit card, you must purchase a bond valid for 6 months (based on the value of your car) from a bonding company at the border.

4) Mexican Insurance: You must have Mexican car insurance. You can buy insurance at the border or in advance from AAA clubs in Arizona, California, or Texas.

5) Additional documents that must be presented at the border:

Proof of citizenship
Valid driver's license
A tourist permit
Current vehicle license/registration receipt

6) Children under 18 years of age, if traveling with only one parent, must have a notarized letter from the other parent allowing them to travel. If traveling without either parent, children need a notarized letter from both parents allowing them to travel (see Entry Requirements).

After crossing into Mexico, there are two stops where inspectors will check to be sure you have the proper permits and the stickers.

Note that there are certain "free zones" that do not require all the permits listed above. These are generally border towns (within 25 kilometers of the border), the Baja Peninsula, and the state of Sonora. You will encounter checkpoints south of these free zones so do not try to cross without the proper paperwork if you plan to travel farther south.

CUOTA: (TOLL HIGHWAY) Mexico has developed an extensive system of new toll highways, designated by the letter "D" following the route number. Although tolls can be expensive (Mexico City to Acapulco is approximately $125 one way), we recommend taking these toll roads whenever possible. They are very fast and efficient with very little traffic (trucks usually take the free roads). Non-toll roads are usually slow two-lane roads, which might not be in good condition. Toll roads also have the added bonus of solar-powered emergency telephones every 2 kilometers. Most toll roads are four-lane, greatly resembling U.S. interstate highways, though sometimes they have only two lanes. (The roads are privately financed and therefore can vary from region to region.) Tolls are calculated by distance and number of axles on the vehicle and usually only cash (pesos and sometimes U.S. dollars) is accepted. You enter through a control gate and are given a ticket then at various points along the highway you come to toll stations where money is collected. Be sure to keep your receipt—it is your insurance against the cost of road repairs if you get into an accident.

DRIVER'S LICENSE: You need a valid driver's license issued by your home country to drive in Mexico. A Mexican driver's license is not required.

DRIVING AND ALCOHOL: Driving under the influence of alcohol is illegal in Mexico. You can be arrested and taken to jail for drunk driving. If you are involved in an accident and found to be under the influence of alcohol, your insurance will become invalid and you will go to jail.

EMERGENCIES: If you have an emergency while driving, the equivalent of "911" in Mexico is "060." You can also call the Green Angels (see below) for help: (01) 800-903-9200. Toll roads have solar-powered emergency phones for your convenience.

GASOLINE: Gasoline in Mexico is expensive. There are gas stations along all the highways, but be aware that they rarely accept payment by credit card. Also, many gas stations are closed at certain times of the day or on holidays, so be sure you always have plenty of gas in the tank. Gasoline is sold by the liter. Remember to have the attendant "zero" out the pump (meaning starting from zero) to be sure you are not overcharged. It is customary to give the attendant one or two pesos as tip. You should always tip the attendant who washes your window about two pesos.

GREEN ANGELS (*Angeles Verdes*): These are trained, bilingual mechanics traveling the nation's highways from 8 am to 8 pm in 275 green trucks to provide emergency service and first aid. They carry car parts and gasoline and charge only for the parts; their service is free, thanks to Mexico's Tourism Secretariat. Just open your hood all the way and hope one drives by or call their toll-free number (in Mexico only) (01) 800-903-9200 or (01) 55-250-8221, ext. 130. Tips are greatly appreciated.

INSURANCE: U.S. insurance is *not* valid in Mexico—you must obtain insurance from a Mexican insurance company, either on the internet or at the border. Mexican liability insurance is not required by law, but highly recommended. Insurance companies are a wealth of information and can help you with all the paperwork required for crossing the border. Be sure your insurance includes claims adjusters who will come to the scene of the accident and an attorney. Mexican insurance is not valid if you are found to be under the influence of drugs or alcohol. Mexican law follows the Napoleonic Code, which means you are guilty until proven innocent. Also note that theft and vandalism are usually not covered by insurance.

NIGHT DRIVING: We recommend that you avoid driving after sunset whenever possible, unless on a toll road. The danger of driving greatly increases at night due to poor street lighting combined with donkeys, dogs, children, potholes, and unknown objects that are commonly in the road. Also, be aware that it is not unusual for cars to have broken tail lights, etc.

PARKING: When in cities, it is always safest to leave your car in a parking lot with an attendant or in a parking garage. The cost is reasonable and worth the extra expense for peace of mind. If you are driving, when you make your hotel reservation, ask them if they have parking available and the cost. Many hotels have their own parking lot or, if not, they usually have an arrangement with a nearby garage.

RESTRICTED DRIVING DAYS IN MEXICO CITY: In an effort to reduce pollution, vehicular traffic is restricted in Mexico City on certain days of the week. The restriction is based on the last digit of the vehicle license plate (see following page). Since Saturday and Sunday are the only "free" days for access into the city, if you are driving, plan to arrive on a weekend. Note: Our suggestion is *not* to drive into Mexico City at all—wait until the day you leave before picking up a rental car. You will find a car a nuisance while in the city. The best way to get around is to walk or take a private taxi that is recommended by your hotel.

Prohibited Days & Corresponding License Plate Numbers

Monday: no driving if license plate ends with 5 or 6
Tuesday: no driving if license plate ends with 7 or 8
Wednesday: no driving if license plate ends with 3 or 4
Thursday: no driving if license plate ends with 1 or 2
Friday: no driving if license plate ends with 9 or 0
Saturday and Sunday: all vehicles may be driven.

ROAD SIGNS: Road signs are a mix of international picture symbols and signs in Spanish. Signs on smaller roads are often poorly maintained or absent so it is easy to get lost. Make sure you have a good map. The major roads and toll highways will have good signage displaying the highway number, kilometer marker, and mileage for upcoming cities.

SEATBELTS: By law everyone in the car must wear seatbelts.

ELECTRICITY

The standard voltage in Mexico is 110. For those traveling from the United States, no converters or adaptor plugs are needed.

ENTRY REQUIREMENTS

Unless you are traveling to one of the free zones within 25 kilometers of the border, everyone (including children) entering Mexico must now have a passport and a tourist card. A tourist card is required upon entering and leaving Mexico for those visiting for up to 180 days. Tourist cards are free and can be obtained at border crossings, Mexican consulates, and tourist offices, and through most airlines serving Mexico. Be sure to keep your tourist card in a safe place. You may want to write down the number and keep it separate in case you lose it. If you wish to stay longer than 180 days, contact the Mexican embassy or consulate to obtain a visa.

Children under 18 traveling without their parents *must* have a *notarized* authorization letter from both parents giving the adult permission to take their child to Mexico. A child traveling with just one parent needs a notarized letter from the absent parent. You will be turned away at the airport or at the border if you do not have the proper paperwork.

Make sure you can return to the United States with your tourist card and passport. Although some countries require only a birth certificate to enter, United States' law now requires that you have a passport as proof of your U.S. citizenship when you re-enter the United States.

ETIQUETTE

Mexicans are gracious, friendly, welcoming hosts. Business is done leisurely and greetings drawn out, so for those used to rushing through the day, things seem to move at a snail's pace. Probably the reverse seems true to Mexicans: they must wonder why their foreign guests dash about without incorporating the charm of genuine courtesy into their human interplay. So, why not slow down a bit? Savor meeting people. If doing business, don't launch into practical matters immediately—instead, do as Mexicans do: shake hands, look and speak individually to each person, and ask questions about their family and health. Do the same with informal meetings. Don't rush. Display the same courtesy the Mexicans show to visitors and friends: it can't be faulted.

FACTS

BANK HOURS: Most banks are open Monday through Friday from 9 am to 1:30 pm. In larger cities the banks may reopen from 4 pm to 6 pm and open Saturday from 10 am to 1:30 pm. For currency exchange, you usually get a better rate at a *casa de cambio* (money exchange) than you do at a bank, and the transaction is faster.

BUSINESS HOURS: Shops are generally open Monday through Saturday from 10 am to 7 pm. Some smaller stores may close for a few hours' siesta in the afternoon.

CAPITAL: Mexico City, D.F.

CURRENCY: The monetary unit is the peso. The exchange rate as this book went to press was about 11.3 pesos = 1 U.S. dollar. Please note the rate is subject to daily fluctuations.

GOVERNMENT: Federal Republic.

LANGUAGE: Spanish, with some 50 Indian languages and dialects being spoken outside major cities and towns. English is also widely spoken.

POPULATION: 106,203,000 (July 2001 estimate). Mexico City and the surrounding metropolitan area are home to nearly 40% of the nation's population.

FESTIVALS & HOLIDAYS

Festivals and holidays are a time for celebration in Mexico. Frequently music, colorful costumes, dancing and parades can be enjoyed, especially in smaller villages. On the majority of the holidays, banks and commercial offices are closed.

Año Nuevo (January 1): New Year's Day.

Día de os Santos Reyes (Day of the Kings, January 6): This day ends the Christmas festivities. Gifts are exchanged, symbolizing the gifts brought to Jesus by the three wise men. There is usually a party with food, drink, and candy-filled piñatas for the children.

Día de La Constitución (February 5): The commemoration of Mexico's Constitution.

Carnival (February/March): The days preceding the rigors of Lent are celebrated nationally with extravagant parades, floats, confetti, dancing, and the burning of effigies.

Natalicio de Benito Juárez (Birthday of Benito Juárez, March 21): This commemorates the birthday of Benito Juárez, one of Mexico's national heroes.

Semana Santa (Holy Week, March/April, Good Friday through Easter): A very important time that is celebrated all over Mexico. Many parades and passion plays are performed, especially in the southern states and in the Colonial towns.

Cinco de Mayo (May 5): The commemoration of the Battle of Puebla, a Mexican victory over the invading French army in 1862.

Día de La Independencia (Independence Day, September 16): Father Miguel Hidalgo's cry to arms to free Mexico of Spanish rule in 1810 is commemorated all over Mexico. Fiestas take place in every town square on the evening of the 15th, including fireworks, music, and the throwing of eggshells filled with confetti. Children wear national costumes or dress as Independence heroes and many parades take place.

Descubrimento de América (Discovery of America by Columbus, October 12): Commemorates Columbus's arrival in the Americas.

Día de Los Muertos (Day of the Dead, November 1 to 2): Mexico's most colorful fiesta, celebrating the belief that once a year the dead have permission to return to earth and visit friends and relatives. During the Day of the Dead the living welcome the souls of the departed with special foods, flowers, candles, and incense. This is an occasion for gaiety and parties. To celebrate the day, artists often portray death with humor, making rather gruesome yet whimsical skull and skeleton artifacts.

Día de La Revolución (Day of the Revolution, November 20): This day celebrates the Mexican Revolution of 1910.

Fiesta de Nuestra Señora de Guadalupe (December 12): The appearance of Mexico's patron saint in 1531 on the Cerro del Tepeyac hill is remembered in every town and village. Thousands of pilgrims flock to her shrine in Mexico City. In the rest of the country, Las Mañanitas, an early-morning birthday song, is sung at dawn and special church services are attended.

Las Posadas (Christmas Season): This begins December 16 with the reenactment of Mary and Joseph searching for a place to spend the night while Mary is about to deliver her baby. For nine nights people carry lighted candles and figures of Mary and Joseph as they travel between homes begging for a place to lay their heads. They are greeted at each house with gifts of food.

Navidad (Christmas Day, December 25).

GUIDES (LOCAL)

A local guide is of great value. To select a knowledgeable, reputable guide, we recommend asking at your hotel for recommendations and rates. We particularly recommend that you hire a car with an English-speaking driver/guide when you are in Mexico City, because there is a higher incidence of crime there, some involving cabs. But safety isn't the only reason: a guide can greatly enhance your sightseeing experience. If you have several people in your group, then a car and driver is frequently less costly than a package bus tour, and much more personal.

HEALTH

WATER: Because some people get sick when drinking any water that is different from what they are used to at home, we suggest you use bottled water. Many of the deluxe hotels purify their water and if so, it is safe to drink. If your accommodations have a kitchenette, you can always boil water before using it. Almost all hotels serve their drinks with ice made from purified water. If in doubt, ask. When driving, it is a good idea to buy some bottled water to drink along the way. When visiting archaeological sites, be *sure* to carry a few bottles of water with you. It is not always available to buy and you will need a refreshing drink while exploring the ruins and climbing pyramids!

FOOD: Don't buy food at roadside stands. Although you might be tempted because the aroma is usually bewitching, just remember there is little sanitation available at these stands so it difficult to wash hands or utensils to meet high standards of sanitation. Avoid seafood, fruits, and vegetables that you have not peeled yourself or that cannot be cooked. Also avoid unpasteurized dairy products.

INFORMATION SOURCES

If you have questions not answered in this guide, or need special guidance for a particular destination, the Mexican National Tourist Offices can assist you. If you have access to the Internet you may want to visit their websites, *www.visitmexico.com*. The Mexican Tourist Office's general information line, toll-free from the United States and Canada, is

(800) 446-3942. For electronic (print-ready) information, send an email to contact@visitmexico.com.

In an emergency, contact the Mexican Ministry of Tourism's 24-hour hotline: within Mexico, toll-free (91) 800.90.392; from the United States, (800) 482-9832.

MEXICAN TOURIST OFFICES

Los Angeles: Mexican Tourist Office, 1800 Century Park East, Suite 511, Los Angeles, CA, 90067, USA, tel: (310) 282-9112, ext. 23, fax: (310) 282-9116, email: contact@visitmexico.com.

New York: Mexican Tourist Office, 375 Park Ave., Suite 1905, New York, NY 10152, USA, tel: (212) 308-2110, fax: (212) 308-9060, email: contact@visitmexico.com.

Montreal: Mexican Tourist Office, Place Ville Marie, Suite 1931, Montreal, Quebec H3B 2C3, Canada, tel: (514) 871-1052, fax: (514) 871-3825, email: turimex@cam.org

London: Mexico Government Tourist Office, 41 Trinity Square, Wakefield House, London EC3N 4DJ, tel: (207) 488 93 92 or (207) 265 07 05, fax: (207) 265 07 04, email: visitemexico@over-marketing.com

TOURIST OFFICES IN MEXICO: Almost all towns throughout Mexico have a local tourist office. We strongly recommend that, during your travels, you make a beeline for the closest office for current information on local events. The tourist offices, which are generally located on, or near, the central plaza, usually have maps and information on what to see in the town and the surrounding area.

LANGUAGE

Spanish is the official language in Mexico. In cities or popular resort areas, almost all of the hotels have English-speaking staff available to help you. In some of the more remote areas, you might encounter situations where English is not spoken. Under Vocabulary we have given a few common words to help you get along. However, the best bet is to carry a small pocket-sized dictionary and point to some of the words if you need assistance.

There should never be a problem checking into your hotel because the receptionist will have your name if you have a reservation. Carry your confirmation with you to make check-in easier.

MAPS

There is a map section in the front of the guide with the following maps:

OVERVIEW MAP: The first page of the map section shows an overview map with the route of each itinerary indicated in a different color.

MAP OF STATES: This map shows the states of Mexico.

HOTEL LOCATION MAPS: On the top line of each hotel's description there is a map number which corresponds to on of the four numbered maps in the front of the book where towns with recommended hotels are marked in red.

ITINERARY MAPS: Itinerary routings are superimposed on the same maps that show hotel locations at the front of the book. Each itinerary is highlighted in a different color. There are also itinerary maps at the start of each itinerary description.

MONEY MATTERS

The peso is the unit of currency in Mexico. The *nuevo peso* (new peso) was introduced in 1993 and comes in 10-, 20-, 50-, 100-, 500-, and 1,000-peso notes. The symbol for the peso is the same as the dollar sign used in the USA, which can be a little confusing. In the information given for each hotel, the dollar sign represents U.S. dollars. In our other guides, we show the hotel rate in the currency of the country, but Mexican hotels are so geared to the American tourist that their rates are always quoted in dollars.

ATM MACHINES: It is very quick and easy to get money through one of the ATM machines that are found throughout Mexico, often even in small towns. They are usually located at a bank or on one of the main shopping streets. Try to use ATM machines inside banks and avoid using them at night. Note that some U.S. banks are now charging an exchange fee for obtaining money abroad.

MONEY EXCHANGE: Contrary to the situation in many countries, in Mexico you can usually get a better rate of exchange at a *casa de cambio* (money-exchange booth) than at a bank. Also, banks are usually crowded and frequently closed, making the money exchange even more user-friendly. Most hotels will also usually exchange your money, but the rate is generally not as competitive.

MUSEUMS

When planning your itinerary, be aware that most museums are closed on Monday.

PHOTOGRAPHY

In any country one should show common courtesy when photographing people. Blatantly photographing people can be intrusive, and should never be done without asking. However, in some of the remote villages in the state of Chiapas taking photos is more than just impolite: it is actually against the law.

SAFETY

Some people are concerned about safety when visiting Mexico, but we have traveled there several times a year for many years and have had less of a problem with crime than we have had in other countries. Basically, it is a very safe place to visit. However, the same logical safety precautions should be taken as when traveling anywhere. Don't tout your wealth by wearing expensive jewelry. Don't leave valuables within sight in your car. Lock your car and park it in an attended parking lot or parking garage. If traveling by bus, take a first-class (*primera*) or deluxe (*lujo*) bus. When cashing money in a bank or at an exchange or ATM, be discreet and don't flaunt your pesos. When in Mexico City, ask the concierge at your hotel to call you a taxi—don't pick one up on the street. When arriving at airports, never just pick up a random cab, but take one of the taxis or vans that are authorized by the airport. Select one where you can buy a prepaid ticket at the airport transportation counter. Always use a government-approved guide when sightseeing. Keep your valuables locked in the hotel safe or in the safe in your room. Don't keep your wallet in your back pocket. When in tourist areas, always be watchful of your purse and preferably use a purse with a strap over your shoulder and across your chest, or else a pouch around your waist.

Unfortunately, Mexico City has received adverse publicity about safety problems—undoubtedly some of it justified. However, the government is working diligently to make the tourist feel more secure. One of the most recent innovations is the use of policemen who double as tourist "helpers" and not only graciously give advice, but also are at hand in case of an emergency. The one area that we consider a bit "iffy" is the state of Chiapas where political discontent and poverty have resulted in more crime than in other parts of the country. If traveling in Chiapas, be cautious about using public transportation and if you are driving, stay on the major roads and drive only in daylight hours.

SHOPPING

ITEMS TO BUY: Mexican handicrafts are very popular and various regions or towns excel in one or more crafts. These items have often been made for generations and are great gifts to bring home.

Woven goods such as *ponchos* (woolen blankets worn by men), *serapes* (woolen shawls worn by women), rugs, colorful tapestries, and blankets are easy to find in assorted styles, qualities, and prices.

Silver jewelry is sold almost everywhere in Mexico, but Taxco is the most famous town for beautiful designs by skilled craftsmen.

Hand-blown glass is made in Guadalajara, Monterrey, and Mexico City. *Wooden furniture, guitars*, and beautiful *copper items* are commonly found in the Colonial areas. Oaxaca and the Copper Canyon are noted for their *woven baskets* and *leather goods*.

Pottery is one of Mexico's biggest craft industries. The most famous is gorgeous Talavera pottery, which principally comes from two places, Puebla near Mexico City and Dolores Hidalgo near San Miguel de Allende.

Archaeological artifacts: At some archaeological sites, you may find people selling objects they have supposedly found. Refuse these offers. Mexican law states that it is illegal to export antiques or items that can be described as national treasures.

TAXES

Mexico levies a 15% value added tax (IVA) on all goods and services (10% in some areas such as Baja and Cancún). The tax is supposed to be included in the posted price.

TELEPHONES

OVERSEAS CALLS: Making calls from Mexico is not the hassle it once was, but there are a few things to keep in mind. Most hotels have a phone system, but we advise *not* charging calls to your room as charges can quickly soar to over $100. This is not because the hotel is trying to take advantage of you, but because long-distance calls are extraordinarily expensive in Mexico. It is more economical to charge your calls to your AT&T, MCI, or SPRINT calling card (you can request one from your telephone company before leaving home). Each of these companies has a local number in Mexico that will connect you to the USA. AT&T: (01) 800-288-2872 or (001) 800-462-4240; MCI: (001) 880-674-7000; SPRINT: (001) 880-877-8000.

Another option is to buy a Ladatel card. Most public phones are labeled Telemex (the national telephone company) and are part of the Ladatel (long-distance) phone system. You can purchase these cards in different peso denominations at most pharmacies and gas stations or vending machines at airports and bus stations. You swipe the card, enter the access number on the card, and place your call. It is very easy and efficient.

CALLING WITHIN MEXICO: Some hotels may charge for local calls, so you should ask before using the phone in your room. Your hotel concierge may be able to place most calls for you from the hotel's lobby (restaurant reservations, arranging a local tour, etc). Public phones take Ladatel cards for local, as well as long-distance calls. For long-distance calls within Mexico, dial 01 followed by the area code and the number.

TIPPING

In Mexico, it is customary to tip waiters, maids, porters, and guides (make sure that a service charge has not already been added to your restaurant bill). Percentages for hotel and restaurant staff are similar to those in the USA and Canada. Taxi drivers are not usually tipped, except if they have performed some special service. Unlike the United States and Canada, theater ushers and gas station, washroom, and parking attendants all expect to be tipped. In general, calculate $1.50 per person for baggage handlers/porters, $1 per day for chambermaids. Tour guides and drivers should be tipped based on the cost of the tour and the quality of the service. Parking lot attendants and valet parking persons should get about 5 pesos.

TRANSPORTATION

AIR TRANSPORTATION: Most visitors come to Mexico by plane. More than 25 of the world's major airlines service Mexico and there are direct flights from many large cities, such as Los Angeles, London, Miami, New York, Madrid, Paris, and Frankfurt. There are 60 airports in Mexico, 15 of which operate international flights. Mexicana and Aeromexico are Mexico's largest airlines. You can fly to many small towns in Mexico using domestic airlines. Although the distances might look short enough to drive, you may want to consider air travel because travel time by car or bus may be prohibitive.

BUSES: Mexico has the largest bus system in the world, with more than 840 bus companies operating over 44,000 buses. Many Mexicans do not own a car, so buses are widely used and are available to take you to the tiniest town on the map. Every bus company labels their class of service differently, so you need to ask what amenities are offered. We recommend that you use only the two top-category buses: *executive/deluxe/lujo* (the highest class of service offering fully air-conditioned buses with larger reclining seats and leg rests comfortable enough for overnight trips) or *first/plus/primera* (a high-quality bus with restrooms, air conditioning, cassette music). A few tips: Be sure to ask for a direct bus (*directo*), which makes only a few stops, or no stops (*sin escalas*)—avoid ones with lots of stops (*con escalas*). Bus tickets (*biletos*) are always sold one-way, and you will usually not be refunded if you miss the bus. Your departure gate (*sala*) should be listed on your ticket along with your seat assignment if you are traveling on a first- or deluxe-class bus. Buying your bus ticket can be quite bewildering, since you have to find the correct bus station (there may be more than one in town), and then need to know which bus company you want since often more than one offers service to your destination. We suggest that you ask the concierge at your hotel to help you with your reservations. Tickets need to be purchased in advance.

There is an international bus terminal in McAllen, Texas that makes traveling to Mexico by bus from the United States a breeze. At other crossing points, one has to get off the bus at the Mexican border, cross the border by foot, taxi, or local bus, and purchase a new ticket at the Mexican bus station on the other side.

CRUISE SHIPS: Mexico offers three basic cruise experiences. The short three- to four-day northern **Baja cruises** that usually depart from Los Angeles or Ensenada; the seven- to ten-day west coast "Mexican Riviera" cruises, which usually depart from Los Angeles and visit the port towns of Cabo San Lucas, Puerto Vallarta, Mazatlán, and Acapulco; and cruises to the beautiful Yucatán Peninsula with ports of call including Cancún, Cozumel, and Playa del Carmen. Cruise ship companies serving Mexico include Carnival, Celebrity, Princess, Royal Caribbean, Cruise West, Lindblad Expeditions, and Voyager Cruise Line.

FERRIES: Passenger and car ferries leaving from Santa Rosalia and La Paz connect Baja California to Guaymas, Topolobampo, and Mazatlán on the Pacific mainland. On the Caribbean coast, ferries leave from Puerto Morelos (car ferry) and Playa del Carmen (passenger only) to the island of Cozumel. Ferries from Puerto Juárez (passenger only) and Punta Sam (car ferry), both north of Cancún, travel to Isla Mujeres. Another, more expensive ferry leaves for Isla Mujeres from Playa Linda in Cancún four times a day.

TAXIS: Taxis are readily available in most towns and moderately priced. There are only a few things to remember: agree on the fare before getting into the car; if there is a meter, make sure the last fare was cleared; and avoid the green VW bug taxis. If you are in Mexico City, ask your hotel to order a cab for you, as there are many unauthorized cab drivers. If you are looking for a cab from the airport, look for a taxi counter where you prepay your fare and get a ticket before going outside to the taxi station. You do not need to tip taxi drivers unless they provide extra service for you.

TRAINS: The rail service in Mexico has deteriorated in the last few years and, as a means of transportation, we recommend bus over train travel. One delightful exception is the Chihuahua al Pacifico Railroad, which runs through the Copper Canyon (see our itinerary *The Copper Canyon, A Train Adventure to Hidden Mexico*). This train, although frequently off schedule, is definitely first class. Some tour operators, such as Tauck Tours, also offer train trips through the Copper Canyon using deluxe rail cars.

In addition to the Chihuahua al Pacifico Railroad, another exception is the Expreso Maya, a privately owned and operated train that began service in March, 2002, and runs between Mérida and Palenque. There are from one- to four-night deluxe tours offered that include archaeological sites in the Yucatán Peninsula. The Expreso Maya is expensive, but for train buffs, a great way to see the ruins.

VOCABULARY

Most travelers have had a bit of Spanish somewhere along the road of their schooling. If this holds true for you, you will be surprised at how words will pop back into your memory. It is fun to try your hand at speaking, even if only a few phrases. Below we have a few common words and phrases that might be useful. Before your trip, please do practice a few key phrases that are needed for common courtesy. If nothing else, learn to say "good morning," "good night," "thank you," and "please." A smile and a *"please"* and *"thank you"* will work wonders. The Mexicans are exceptionally gracious, and you do not need to be fluent in Spanish to be warmly welcomed everywhere.

COMMON WORDS

Aeropuerto, airport
Almohada, pillow
Autobus, bus
Banco, bank
Centro, center of town
Cuchillo, knife
Correo, post office
Cuchara, spoon
Gasolinera, gas station (Pemex)
Jabón, soap

Malecón, boardwalk on waterfront
Mercado, market
Parada de autobus, bus stop
Plato, plate
Playa, beach
Restaurante, restaurant
Sanitarios, toilet
Servilleta, napkin
Tenedor, fork
Terminal de autobuses, bus terminal
Toalla, towel

Vaso, glass

Zócalo, central square or plaza

PHRASES

Adiós, goodbye

Buenas noches, good night

Buenos días, good morning

Buenos tardes, good afternoon

Cuánto cuesta? how much does it cost?

De nada, you're welcome

Dónde está __? where is __?

Gracias, thank you

Hasta luego, goodbye, see you later

La cuenta por favor, the bill please

Por favor, please

Tiene usted __? do you have __?

FOOD & DRINK

Agua, water

Jugo de Frutas, fruit juices

Almendrado, almond sauce spiced with tomatoes, herbs

Antojitos, snacks

Arroz, rice—staple in diet, served many ways, often with beans

Barbacoa, goat roasted in pit

Burrito, soft flour tortilla, rolled with beans and either meat, seafood, or poultry

Café, coffee

Café con leche, coffee with milk or, often, a glass of hot milk and a jar of Nescafé

Cajeta, caramelized goat milk

Carne, meat

Flautas, small corn tortilla stuffed with beef or chicken, then deep fried

Frijoles, beans—staple of Mexican diet

Cerveza, beer

Ceviche, cocktail of marinated raw fish, with lemon juice, chopped tomato, and onion

Chapulines, tiny grasshoppers fried in oil

Chiles rellenos, poblano peppers stuffed with cheese and/or ground meat then deep fried

Enchiladas, rolled tortillas filled with chicken or cheese, served with green or red sauce

Escamoles, ant eggs, often served with tortillas and guacamole

Flan, baked custard

Fruta, fruit
Guacamole, avocados mashed with onions and tomatoes
Gusanos de maguey, crisp-fried maguey worms
Huevos revueltos, scrambled eggs
Huevos a la Mexicana, scrambled eggs with onions, tomato, and chile
Huevos rancheros, fried eggs on corn tortilla, topped with red Mexican sauce
Jugo, juice
Licuado, fruit shake
Machaca, dried beef, similar to beef jerky
Machaca con huevo, dried beef scrambled with eggs, onions, tomato
Malteada, milk shake
Mantequilla, butter
Margarita, popular drink made of Tequila and lime juice, served in salt-rimmed glass
Masa, ground corn soaked in lime juice—basis of tortillas, staple of diet
Michelada, beer over ice with lime juice
Mixiote, piquant orange-colored sauce used to marinate meat
Mole negro, rich traditional sauce blending chili peppers, peanuts, garlic, and chocolate
Pan, bread
Papa, potato
Pescado, fish
Picadillo, minced meat mixed with tomato and onion
Pimienta, pepper
Pollo, chicken
Postre, dessert
Pozole, thick corn-based soup with variations throughout Mexico
Quesadilla, tortilla folded in half and stuffed with cheese, meat, or chicken
Refrescos, soft drinks or soda
Sal, salt
Salsa, sauce, most frequently a hot sauce either green or red
Sincronizadas, ham and cheese between two grilled flour tortillas

Sopa de limon: chicken-based soup with wonderful lime flavor
Sopa de frijol, black-bean soup with chunks of fresh cheese and tortilla chips
Sopa tarasca, bean-and-tomato soup with garlic, chilies, fried tortilla strips, and cream
Taco, corn tortilla wrapped around choice of ingredients and eaten by hand
Tamales, meat or chicken covered with corn meal, wrapped and cooked in a cornhusk
Té caliente, hot tea
Tequila, alcoholic beverage made from cactus
Torta, sandwich, usually made with a Mexican roll
Tortilla, thin pancake made of corn or wheat, served in many ways and staple of diet
Tostada, fried corn tortilla topped with chicken or beef, cheese, lettuce, and thick cream
Verdura, vegetable
Vino, wine

WATER

When traveling in remote areas we recommend having an ample supply of bottled water. This is absolutely essential when touring the archaeological sites where the weather is often hot and dry and places to buy water are not always available.

WEBSITE

Please visit the Karen Brown website (*www.karenbrown.com*) in conjunction with this book. It provides trip planning assistance, new discoveries, post-press updates, the opportunity to purchase goods and services that we recommend (rail tickets, car rental, travel insurance, etc.), and one-stop shopping for our guides, associated maps and prints. Most of our favorite places to stay are featured with color photos and direct website and email links. Also, we invite you to participate in the Karen Brown's Readers' Choice Awards. Be sure to visit our website and vote so your favorite properties will be honored.

WHEN TO TRAVEL

Spring and fall are lovely times to travel throughout Mexico, but each season has its advantages. At the beach resorts, both on the east and west coasts, the hottest months are September and October. Although the thermometer doesn't read significantly higher than the rest of the year, the days seem muggier since this is the tail end of the rainy season and the humidity has had time to build up. If you want to miss the crowds (and frequently higher hotel costs), avoid traveling during Mexican holidays: Christmas, Easter, and school vacation (mid-July to mid-August). During these periods hotel space is at a premium and the resort areas crowded. November through June is usually lovely at the beach resorts and summer is very nice there also—although you might have some tropical showers, which commonly happen in the late afternoon. The east coast faces the Caribbean where hurricanes occasionally occur between mid-August through October. If your target is one of the major cities, really any time of the year is a great time to travel.

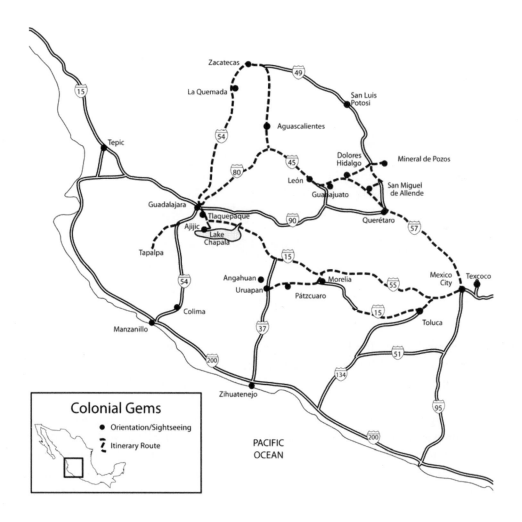

Zacatecas
La Quemada
San Luis Potosi
Aguascalientes
Dolores Hidalgo
Mineral de Pozos
León
Guanajuato
San Miguel de Allende
Querétaro
Tepic
Guadalajara
Tlaquepaque
Ajijic
Lake Chapala
Tapalpa
Angahuan
Mexico City
Texcoco
Uruapan
Morelia
Pátzcuaro
Colima
Manzanillo
Toluca
Zihuatenejo
PACIFIC OCEAN

Colonial Gems

● Orientation/Sightseeing

〜 Itinerary Route

Colonial Gems
Charming Towns by Car or Bus

Guadalajara, Cathedral

The following itinerary covers the trail of the Spaniards, who built a necklace of beautiful towns as they spread their influence throughout the country. There is no better way to experience the romance and history of Mexico than following the path of these conquistadors. When Cortés arrived in Veracruz, he made a bravado gesture, burning the small ships that brought him and his soldiers to the New World. The message was clear— his men were supposed to stay, and stay they did. After the fall of the Aztec capital of Tenochtitlán, the conquistadors spread throughout Mexico, hoping to make their fortunes in the New World. Because precious metals presented the quickest path to wealth, these adventurous men, young and old, fanned out across the country looking for gold and silver. They were quickly followed over the years by newcomers from Spain, almost all looking for fortunes, which is why the majority of Colonial towns you see today had their roots in mining. What makes following the footsteps of these conquistadors especially intriguing is that some of the most beautiful of these early mansions, convents, and haciendas have come to life again as outstanding small hotels that simply ooze with charm.

Mexico abounds with these historic Colonial cities, which strongly reflect the architecture and layout of the towns where the conquistadors were born. As you travel in some of these lovely Colonial towns, you will think you are in Spain. However, the towns possess an extra richness, since when you look closely, a subtle Indian influence is always there—such as an Indian god discreetly worked in amongst the Christian images. Visiting these cities, you are magically transported back three hundred years. You can almost hear the clatter of horses' hooves on the cobbled streets and smell the fragrance of romance in the air.

These towns founded by the Spaniards look much as they did when built hundreds of years ago. The sturdy, handsome buildings, usually made of stone, look a bit stern from the outside, and it is not until you enter through the massive wooden doors that their beauty is revealed, for the Spaniards secreted their delights within. Almost all homes have a central, enclosed courtyard with a lush garden enhanced by fragrant flowers, fountains, and trees. On the ground level is the family living area with dining room, parlors, and kitchen, and a wide, open, stone staircase leading to the floors above. Galleried walkways (with bedrooms opening onto them) wrap around the upper floors and look down into the garden below. Small balconies adorned with black wrought-iron embellish the upper windows overlooking the street, while intricate black wrought-iron lamps embrace each side of the entrance, adding both decoration and light. A huge, thick wooden door with iron braces is typically framed by an arched doorway, which is often surmounted by a carved-stone plaque displaying the original owner's family crest (escutcheon).

Not only the architecture of the buildings looks like "Old Spain," but also the design of the towns. Every town founded by the Spanish, even the tiniest, has a central square (*zócalo*) where the most important buildings and the homes of the wealthy were found. These squares generally have arcaded walkways on four sides, and are like parks with trees, gardens, benches, and paths radiating from a central fountain or bandstand. The larger towns have a series of squares, but there is always a central one that is the most important, usually with a church on one side. Note: Although usually called a *zócalo,* this central square is sometimes called a *plaza* or *jardín* (garden).

Throughout all of Mexico, many cities retain some hint of their Spanish heritage. Some have totally lost their appeal due to the intrusion of modern buildings, but others remain absolute jewels. At first encounter, some of the places we recommend appear to be huge, modern cities (which they are), but have absolutely charming historic centers. Listed below are some of our favorite Colonial cities, many of which are described in this itinerary (others are featured in other itineraries and are so marked). The towns that have an asterisk (*) in front of them are exceptionally romantic jewels with very little from the modern world to spoil their charm.

COLONIAL TOWNS

Alamos (*Copper Canyon*)
Guadalajara
* Guanajuato
Mérida (*Mayan Mysteries*)
Mexico City
Morelia
* Oaxaca (*Oaxaca Valley*)

Querétaro
* Pátzcuaro
* Puebla (*Mexico City & Beyond*)
* San Miguel de Allende
* Tapalpa
* Taxco (*Mexico City & Beyond*)
* Tlaxcala (*Mexico City & Beyond*)
Zacatecas

CHOICE OF TRANSPORTATION

Because these Colonial cities are highlights of Mexico, we designed this itinerary so that it could be used by everyone, including those who prefer not to drive. Therefore, we purposely planned this routing with stopovers in towns that are linked by good bus service, and we explain with each destination how to use public transportation. We give times just as an indication to give you an idea of departure times and length of trip. Please be sure to verify current departure times.

A car offers greater flexibility, but bus transportation also works just fine. If you choose a deluxe line, the buses are excellent. Trains, with a few exceptions, are dreary, rarely on schedule, and much slower than direct bus service. Our introduction has in-depth information on Mexican buses, but here we'll repeat a few of the key factors in planning. Always choose the most deluxe bus company and take only a direct bus. Unless you are fluent in Spanish, ask the concierge at your hotel to arrange a taxi with instructions that you will pay the extra cost for the driver to go into the bus station with you and help you buy your ticket and show you where to board your bus. Some of the bus stations are pretty well organized, but others are quite confusing—so many people milling about and so many ticket counters, many of them seeming to sell tickets to the same destination. It's really hard to know just where to go and which ticket to purchase. Once you have your ticket and know where to board the bus, the only hard part is over. The first-class buses and deluxe and premium buses are very clean, have reclining seats, toilets, reading lights, and often a snack served en route. Frequently there is a television, but this is no great attribute since the program being shown (often quite loudly) is usually nothing that will interest you. The whole scene, though, is fun. When you arrive at your destination, you really do not need much assistance since there are always taxis available outside the station to take you to your hotel. All you need to do is to tell the taxi driver where you want to go. If you don't speak Spanish, you might want to write down in advance the name and address of your hotel to show the driver.

RECOMMENDED PACING: We suggest eleven nights to follow this itinerary, more if you want to savor each destination in a leisurely fashion. With optimum bus connections in mind, we planned this itinerary as a loop, beginning and ending in Mexico City (or if you prefer, beginning and ending in Guadalajara). If you are driving, you could zigzag this itinerary, making it a one-way trip between the two cities. We recommend three nights in Mexico City, three nights in San Miguel de Allende, two nights in Guadalajara, and three nights in Morelia or Pátzcuaro. If you want to shorten the trip, you could skip one of the stops.

ORIGINATING CITY   MEXICO CITY

When you arrive at the Mexico City airport, don't pick up a cab at the curb or barter with hustlers in the lobby trying to entice you to use their cars. These are unregulated vehicles. Instead, go directly to the transportation booth and buy a ticket for your transportation into the city. There is a set price for taxis and minivans so you won't need to haggle over the fee. Just tell the ticket agent your destination; you will be charged accordingly and issued a ticket to give to the driver who will take you to your hotel. Mexico City has a great selection of delightful places to stay in every price range. Note: Because driving is a hassle within the city, wait to rent a car until the day of your departure and use taxis or public transportation until then.

Mexico City with its 22 million inhabitants is the second-largest city in the world, and growing every day. Its importance as a cultural and political center is not new—with its fabulous location on a high, fertile plateau, the site has hosted a great city since long before the Spaniards arrived. The Aztecs had the seat of their flourishing empire here in a magical city they called Tenochtitlán. Set in the middle of a lake, connected to the mainland by causeways and laced with canals, and embellished with palaces and splendid temples, this city was indeed a sight to behold. Even Hernán Cortés, who had seen the wonders of Europe, was overwhelmed by its grandeur.

Three nights will give you two full days to visit some of the city's museums (most museums are closed on Monday), which depict so richly the heritage of the Mexican people, setting the stage for what you will be seeing on your trip. We cover sightseeing for Mexico City in greater depth in the itinerary *Mexico City & Beyond*, but even though it will be duplicating information, we want to mention two places you must not miss: the Museo Nacional de Antropología and the zócalo. Depending upon which hotel you choose, you can either walk or take a cab. Your hotel can arrange a guide or order one of their secure taxis to take you wherever you want to go.

Museo Nacional de Antropología: First, head for the Museo Nacional de Antropología, one of the world's most outstanding museums. We first saw it when it opened in 1964 and now, almost 40 years later, it is even more fabulous, with tremendous improvements made in a massive renovation in 2001. The museum has a stunning architectural style with a spacious, partially enclosed central courtyard. Wrapping around the courtyard is a two-story building with 23 rooms displaying with artful elegance artifacts giving the history of the Mexican nation. Don't miss a single room. Visit them all and read the description in English of what you are viewing. Linger at the dioramas that show the glorious city as it was before Cortés's arrival. Enjoy the rooms that show the everyday life of the Indian people. Study carefully the information on the many archaeological sites and peek below the glass floor to see a royal tomb. Push all the buttons on the video monitors to watch videos of rituals and customs. You could spend an entire day here, which isn't a problem as there is a very good restaurant for lunch.

Zócalo: The second place you must include is a visit to Mexico City's fabulous zócalo (main square). This in an incredible, huge plaza capturing the magic of Mexico's past and present. It is surrounded by handsome Colonial buildings and dominated on one side by a superb cathedral, all built upon, and with the stones from, the mighty Aztec city that previously occupied the site. Wander through the square admiring its majesty and, of course, visit the breathtaking **cathedral**. Be sure not to miss the incredible **Templo Mayor** and **Museo del Templo Mayor**, which are situated on the northeast corner of the square. Scholars knew that a great Aztec city was the foundation for the one built by the Spaniards, but it wasn't until 1978, when workmen accidentally came upon a fabulous statue of the Moon Goddess, that the archaeologists knew where to dig. They excavated in the plaza to the right of the cathedral and unearthed the Templo Mayor, the most important pyramid in the Aztec world. Today you can explore the ruins by a series of ramps and bridges that crisscross above the excavations. To display the wealth of artifacts that were uncovered, the museum was built next door. Within are over 6,000 artifacts taken from the site, superbly displayed, showing the sophisticated culture that flourished here before the arrival of Cortés. Do not miss the model of Tenochtitlán, the Aztec city that was the predecessor of the one you see today. Facing the zócalo is the massive **Palacio Nacional** where you must walk in to admire the bold murals by Diego Rivera. The paintings which adorn the walls of the staircase depict the history of Mexico.

More of our favorite places to visit in Mexico City include: the not-to-be-missed **Museo Nacional de Antropología**, the **Museo Franz Meyer**, the **Museo Dolores Omedo Piña**, the **Palacio de Bellas Artes**, the **Bosque de Chapultepec**, **Chapultepec Castle,** the **Museo de Arte Moderno**, the **Museo Frida Kahlo**, and the **Floating Gardens of Xochimilco**. All of these and more sightseeing options are described in the itinerary *Mexico City & Beyond.*

Your destination today is **San Miguel de Allende**, one of our favorite Colonial towns, which radiates charm and old-world ambiance. Below is a suggested bus schedule in case you opt for public transportation.

BUS OPTION: We offer you two choices here, since if you take the bus, you might prefer to skip the suggested stop in Querétaro (as sightseeing is more complicated when you have luggage) and go directly on to San Miguel de Allende. The bus station for Querétaro is located south of town, not within walking distance of the historic center.

10:05 am	Leave Mexico City, Norte Terminal, ETN bus
2:05 pm	Arrive San Miguel de Allende

or if you want to make a stopover in Querétaro:

9:00 am	Leave Mexico City, Norte Terminal, ETN bus
11:45 am	Arrive Querétaro
3:30 pm	Leave Querétaro, La Central station, ETN bus
4:30 pm	Arrive San Miguel de Allende

Note: If you prefer more time in Querétaro, you can take a later bus at 7:30 pm, arriving in San Miguel de Allende at 8:30 pm.

CAR OPTION: If you are driving, before leaving Mexico City, purchase a detailed map and ask the concierge at your hotel (or the car rental agent) to highlight the best route out of the city heading north to highway 57. You will need all the help you can get because the confusion and congestion getting in or out of the city is staggering.

En route to San Miguel de Allende, stop at Querétaro, a city dating back to the 16th century. In the mid-1700s Franciscan missionaries founded a church here, but its real growth evolved from its strategic position as a stopping point on the main road between Mexico City and the flourishing silver and gold mines farther north.

You come to the **Querétaro** exit from 57 about 130 kilometers after leaving Mexico City. Follow signs to the center of the town. As you drive through its outskirts, Querétaro doesn't look too promising, but persevere since its Colonial heart holds much allure. Once you arrive in the historic center, find a parking lot or garage to leave your car and set out on foot. The center is small and has many pedestrian-only areas that are especially inviting for strolling. As you wander the non-touristy historical center you discover tree-lined lanes, baroque churches, intimate plazas enhanced by fountains, pretty gardens, benches set to enjoy the ambiance, small street-side restaurants, jewelry shops selling semiprecious opals and amethysts that are mined in the nearby hills, and ornate 18th-century mansions.

San Miguel de Allende

Before leaving Querétaro, if the timing is right, have lunch in the courtyard of **La Casa de La Marquesa**—the food is excellent and the ambiance is charming.

Return to highway 57 and continue north in the direction of San Luis Potosi. After about 38 kilometers, turn left and follow signs to San Miguel de Allende. Without a doubt, this is one of the most enchanting of Mexico's Colonial towns, so perfect that it has been designated as a national monument, which adds to its appeal since modern buildings are prohibited and all renovations must strictly adhere to the purity of the original design. If you want to gently immerse yourself in the delights of Mexico without too much of a cultural jolt, nothing is better suited to your first experience of Colonial Mexico than San Miguel de Allende. The town is a delight to the eye, with winding cobblestone streets, splendid 17th-century mansions, fine craft shops, gorgeous courtyards hidden behind thick, wooden doorways, lush gardens, beautiful churches, beckoning art galleries, chic boutiques, and a wealth of appealing, small restaurants.

San Miguel de Allende is a favorite of retired Americans and Canadians, who are lured here by the beauty of the small town, the warmth of acceptance by the locals, and the delightful weather. Many of them have bought splendid old mansions and restored them to their original beauty. The expatriate element is one of the reasons the town is so appealing: without them there probably wouldn't be such a wealth of cute restaurants or so many lovely shops. Many who have discovered San Miguel are artists and writers, and the town has become known as an artists' colony, with the added bonus that boutiques and galleries feature many fine works of original art. The town is also well known for its many language schools, the best known being the Instituto Allende, housed in a once-abandoned, 18th-century hacienda. This has grown into one of the most important schools for fine arts in Latin America, with not only language courses offered, but also year-round classes in fine arts, crafts, and culture.

For the tourist, there is another huge bonus. San Miguel has an abundance of truly outstanding places to stay in every price range that ooze with charm—from intimate bed and breakfasts to exquisite, world-class hotels within 18th-century mansions. Take your choice from the many places we recommend, all of which are either in the center of town or within walking distance. Many have pretty swimming pools nestled in their gardens, making your stay even more enchanting.

The heart of the town is the central plaza, the **Jardín Principal** (Main Garden). Indeed, it is a garden with a festive bandstand in the center, laurel trees, fanciful fountains, and pathways accented by ornate wrought-iron benches. On Sundays and holidays and in the evenings the square is often closed to traffic. It becomes the scene of what seems like a huge party, with everyone greeting friends, stopping to chat, children buying balloons from vendors, young lovers strolling hand-in-hand, and everyone eating snacks. Although there are many tourists, that doesn't in the least diminish the ambiance. It is real. It is unspoiled. By all means join in the fun—find a spot on one of the benches, buy an ice cream cone or a coffee, perhaps have your shoes shined, smile at the children romping about, and just enjoy watching the festivities around you.

Clustered around the square are many handsome stone buildings fronted by 17th-century archways. One side of the plaza is dominated by the town's landmark, **La Parroquia**, the parish church. This fanciful creation is not acclaimed as a masterpiece of design, however, it is a pure delight with a personality of its own. It was built in 1683 by a local stone mason, an Indian named Ceferino Gutierrez who didn't really know what a proper church was supposed to look like—but that didn't stop him. He was enchanted by a postcard he had seen of a European gothic church and decided to use it as his inspiration. The story goes that he sketched his plans in the sand with a stick. Since the postcard showed only the front of the church, he had no idea of how to design the back so improvised with a Mexican style. The result is a fanciful creation enhanced by pink spires that stretch into the blue sky.

San Miguel de Allende, La Parroquia

Of the many churches tucked within the town, my favorite is the **Oratorio de San Felipe Neri**, an extremely appealing church built of pink stone in 1712 by the local Indians. In addition to its many churches, San Miguel de Allende has six patron saints, a delightful excuse for many festivals to honor them. Lining the narrow, cobblestone lanes are splendid mansions built by the wealthy aristocracy of the New World, many of which are still private homes. As you meander, if the thick, wooden doors are open, discreetly take a peek inside to see the many gorgeous inner courtyards secreted within. On Sundays, many of these splendid homes are open to the public. Ask at the tourist office about times.

There is much to see as you stroll the streets including the **Teatro Angela Peralta**, built in 1873, where many famous artists have performed; the **Biblioteca Publica**, a library in a beautiful Colonial building that houses Mexico's second-largest English library; the **Centro Cultural Ignacio Ramirez**, an art institute built within a former convent which has one of the largest interior courtyards found anywhere in the New World; the **Santa Casa de Loreto**, a chapel built to duplicate its namesake in Loreto, Italy; and **Casa de Ignacio Allende**, a mid-18th-century home which was the birthplace of Captain Ignacio Allende, famed hero of the War of Independence.

SIDE EXCURSIONS FROM SAN MIGUEL DE ALLENDE:

Dolores Hidalgo: Although its central square is quite attractive, Dolores Hidalgo is not nearly as pristinely picturesque as San Miguel de Allende, Guanajuato, or Pozos. However it is worth a visit—especially for those fascinated by Mexican history or interested in purchasing Talavera tile. It was in Dolores Hidalgo that **Father Hidalgo** sounded the church bells on the morning of September 16, 1810, calling the townspeople to take up arms against the Spanish king. This was the beginning of the bloody war that would last for 11 years. Unfortunately for Hidalgo, he was soon captured, and then executed, and his head was hung in nearby Guanajuato as a deterrent to liberals wanting freedom. Miguel Hidalgo left his mark in other ways in Dolores Hidalgo. There is a statue of Hidalgo in the central plaza and his simple home is nearby, now the **Museo**

Casa Hidalgo. In an effort to help the impoverished parish, Father Hidalgo taught them the craft of making colorful ceramics and opened the first shop selling Talavera tiles and pottery. The industry thrives and today Dolores Hidalgo, along with Puebla near Mexico City, is one of the major producers of Talavera pottery in Mexico. Connoisseurs consider the pottery made in Puebla to be finer, but what you see in Dolores Hidalgo is beautiful and usually cheaper—the prices for beautiful lamps, dinnerware, vanities, vases, and colorful tiles are incredibly low. Many of the vendors make their own pottery in factories behind their shops, and if you are interested, will show you how the pottery is made and painted, every step done by hand. There are many shops selling the colorful ware in the center of town. Also, the highway that wraps around town is lined with factories and boutiques.

Guanajuato: You can easily stop to see Guanajuato en route from San Miguel de Allende to Guadalajara, however since this quaint, picturesque town deserves more time that a quick visit, we suggest including it as a day's outing from San Miguel de Allende. Because parking is a nightmare here (the streets are in a maze of tunnels beneath the town which is predominantly pedestrian only), we suggest you take a bus from San Miguel de Allende to Guanajuato. In 1559, silver was discovered in the surrounding mountains and Guanajuato became one of the richest cities in Mexico, mining an astonishing one third of all the silver produced in the world. You mustn't miss this perfectly preserved city, which has been designated by UNESCO as a World Heritage Site.

Guanajuato is a photographers' delight, with narrow cobblestone streets, inviting shaded plazas, ornate 18th-century mansions, spectacular churches, and pretty fountains. You can walk everywhere. The town's main plaza, which is in the heart of town, is quite unusual. Instead of being designed as a square, it is a wedge-shaped plaza called **Jardín Union**, affectionately nicknamed Pedazo de Queso (Slice of Cheese). This tiny square is delightfully alluring, featuring an old-fashioned bandstand and pretty tiled walkways shaded by centuries-old trees that form an overhead canopy. In the evening strolling musicians add to the festivity of the scene. Located nearby is my favorite building in town, the **Teatro Juárez**, an ornate theater dating back to 1873 which is fronted by Greek columns adorned by statues of eight muses. Overlooking the plaza is the 17th-century

Church of San Diego, a splendid church with an ornate doorway. Originally part of a Jesuit seminary, the Templo de La Compañia de Jesus is quite impressive, with a dramatic dome that looks like that of St. Peter's in Rome. Guanajuato was the birthplace of Diego Rivera, whose home is open as a museum displaying typical furnishings of the period including the brass bed in which he was born in 1886. Within the house is a collection of his paintings and preliminary sketches for his murals. Also visit the 17th-century **Basilica of Our Lady of Guanajuato**, located on the Plaza de La Paz. Here you find a wooden statue of the Virgin Mary, covered with jewels, that supposedly dates back to 714. King Philip II of Spain sent it to the church as a gift in 1557.

About ten minutes north of Guanajuato in the village of **Valenciana,** you can get a glimpse into how vast the mining industry was. Here you find the Hacienda de San Gabriel de La Barrera, the home of a wealthy mine baron, which has been restored and furnished with antiques and is now open as a museum. On the property are an outdoor restaurant and gift shop. You can also visit the **Valenciana Silver Mine**, dating back to 1558, which is still operational and open to the public. The enormously wealthy Count of Valenciana, owner of the mine that bears his name, spared no expense when he built the dazzling **Church of San Cayetano**, lavishly embellished with gold. Also in Valenciana is one of Guanajuato's most popular restaurants, the Casa del Conde de La Valenciana, which also houses an arts and crafts gallery.

Note: Guanajuato makes a good choice as a place to stay as an alternate choice to San Miguel de Allende.

Mineral de Pozos: About an hour's drive northeast of San Miguel de Allende (just south of the larger town of San Luis de La Paz) is the Colonial town of Mineral de Pozos, affectionately known by all as just "Pozos." In the early part of the 20th century this once wealthy mining town was abandoned and lay dormant until recently rediscovered by an ever growing number of artisans and expatriates who came and fell in love with Pozos' laid back charm. Make it a day's outing and enjoy a delicious lunch in the lovely garden courtyard of the appealing **Casa Montana**, which is also a delightful small hotel. Your hostess Susan Montana (a transplant from New Mexico), will be glad to share her love of the town and advise you what sights to see. Note: The Casa Montana would be an excellent alternate choice for accommodations if you prefer to stay off the beaten path rather than in the tourist center of San Miguel de Allende.

Santuario de Atotonilco: If you are a history buff you might want to visit the Santuario de Atotonilco. From San Miguel de Allende take highway 51 north toward Dolores Hidalgo. About 14 kilometers after leaving San Miguel, turn left and go 3 kilometers farther along an unpaved road to the Santuario de Atotonilco. This is a lovely 18th-century church built by Father Luis Felipe Neri de Alfaro as a place of spiritual retreat. Inside are many sculptures, canvases, and frescoes painted by Indian artists. It was from this sanctuary that Father Miguel Hidalgo took off to join the Revolution in 1810, taking with him the standard bearing the image of the Virgin of Guadalupe, which became the flag and symbol for the fight for independence. People from all over Mexico continue to flock to worship at this shrine.

DESTINATION II   GUADALAJARA

Your destination today is Guadalajara, often called the City of Roses. Below is the bus schedule for those using public transportation.

BUS OPTION: If you are taking the bus, we recommend that instead of stopping en route at Guanajuato (as suggested with the car option), you visit it as a side bus trip from San Miguel de Allende. Ask at the tourist office or at your hotel for the schedules—there is frequent service.

4:15 pm   Leave San Miguel de Allende, La Central station, ETN bus
9:15 pm   Arrive Guadalajara, La Central station

CAR OPTION: When planning your drive to Guadalajara, if you have not already visited Guanajuato as a day excursion from San Miguel de Allende, allow sufficient time to stop en route to have lunch here and enjoy this historic mining town. Otherwise, bypass Guanajuato and join highway 45, and continue toward León. Continue beyond León for 42 kilometers and then head west on highway 80, which takes you directly to

Guadalajara. Buy a detailed city map in advance so that you can find your way to the hotel of your choice.

Guadalajara is a huge, modern, cosmopolitan city with over 5 million inhabitants. It is studded with shady parks, statues highlighting small plazas, tree-lined boulevards, fine museums, world-class restaurants, handsome residential areas, large department stores, and fancy boutiques. However, at first encounter, especially as you drive into the city and experience its horrific traffic, uninspired apartment complexes, and swarm of humanity, you might be a bit less than enthusiastic about what the city has to offer. But hidden within its very heart is the 16th-century Guadalajara, which abounds with historic character. This core of old Guadalajara stretches for seven blocks and is laid out like a cross. At its western end is the **Plaza Guadalajara**, dominated by a stunning **cathedral**; at the southern end of the cross is the **Plaza de Armas**, enhanced by a park with a lacy wrought-iron bandstand where concerts are performed on Thursday and Sunday evenings; at the eastern arm of the cross is **Plaza de La Liberacion**, named in honor of the heroes of the Revolution for Independence; at the northern arm is **Plaza de La Rotonda**, enhanced by a ring of Greek columns in the center of its park. The majority of Guadalajara's Colonial architectural gems face onto this seven-block stretch of plazas.

If you are driving, you can park your car in the underground garage before setting out on foot to explore. Stop first at the tourist office located in an 18th-century mansion at Morelos 102 for general information and a map showing suggested walking tours. You must not miss the 15th-century cathedral, which is marked by two towers that soar 200 feet into the sky. Its interior is beautiful, with rows of columns, eleven altars, and fabulous paintings, some of which were donated by King Ferdinand in thanks for the financial help given during the Napoleonic Wars. Another precious work of art, a beautiful sculpture of Our Lady of the Roses, was also given as a gift; this one by King Carlos V. Across from the cathedral is another impressive edifice, the Palacio de Gobierno, which dates back to 1643. It has great historic importance since it was here in 1810 that Father Miguel Hidalgo, leader of the Revolution for Independence, announced the end of slavery. Within you can see a series of murals by one of Mexico's most famous artists, José Clemente Orozco, whose paintings depict the struggle for independence. A stroll down the block from the palace, in a building enhanced by interior courtyards, you find the **Museo Regional de Guadalajara**, which displays a wealth of exhibits including religious art, paintings, Colonial furniture, portraits, pre-Columbian artifacts, fanciful carriages, pottery, and Indian handicrafts. On Plaza de La Liberación is the stunning **Teatro Degollado**. With its rich red and gold ornate interior and rows of balconies, it is compared by many to Milan's jewel, La Scala. All forms of art are presented here including opera, jazz, classical concerts, and ballet. This theater is also home to the internationally famous dance group, the spectacularly colorful Ballet Folklórico. Ask what is playing while you are in town and try to attend a performance to experience the plush amenities firsthand. Also in the historic center is the Mercado Libertad, a huge indoor marketplace, said to be the largest in the western hemisphere, where vendors sell everything imaginable. For local color, it can't be beat.

In addition to its historic center, Guadalajara has many other attractions for the visitor including many parks. Its largest and oldest, the **Parque Agua Azul**, not only has gardens

but also an orchid house, an aviary, and a butterfly sanctuary, but is also home to the **Casa de Las Artesanias** where some of the best handicraft items made in the state are displayed and sold. There is always something going on here—concerts, outdoor theater, festivals, etc.—and it's a great place for strolling and soaking in the spirit of the city at play.

Mariachi music originated in the state of Jalisco, in which Guadalajara is located, so it is no wonder that you hear so much of it here. "Mariachi" derives from the French word for marriage, and it originated during the brief period when the French controlled Mexico, they often hired local musicians to play at their weddings. This jolly kind of band usually had at least a guitar, a trumpet, and a violin. Today, Mariachis, smartly dressed in spiffy, ruffled shirts, fancy jeans, jackets studded with silver, shiny boots, and large sombreros are called upon to celebrate not only weddings, but almost every festive occasion with their happy, exuberant music. If you want a sound dose of entertainment, go on a Sunday to the **Plaza de Los Mariachis**, where roaming musicians perform (it is customary to tip).

If you want to shop for handicrafts, you can drive or take a taxi out to **Tlaquepaque**, an artists' town located in the suburbs about 9 kilometers from the center of Guadalajara. This once-small crafts village is now all but smothered within the growing sprawl of the city, but at its center Tlaquepaque still retains its old charm with cobbled streets, colorfully painted houses, and picturesque Colonial architecture. The heart of town is El Parian, which has at its core a series of restaurants, cafés, and bars—a favorite place to enjoy a cold beer and watch the activities while strolling musicians entertain. Surrounding El Parian, streets stretch out in every direction, lined with cute restaurants, stunning galleries, fine antique shops, and boutiques selling all kinds of crafts including hand-blown glass, articles made of leather, cheerful pottery, hand-loomed fabrics, embroidered clothing, painted furniture, wrought-iron fixtures, and original art. Usually the wares are artistically displayed and with over 300 stores, you are bound to find a treasure. The popular **El Palomar** pottery, known for its classic, simple design often featuring a dove, is made here.

OPTIONAL SIDE TRIP FROM GUADALAJARA TO TAPALPA

Tapalpa is well worth a couple of nights visit as a side trip from Guadalajara. This small town is highly recommended to those of you who delight in discovering authentic small Colonial villages that have not been spoiled by any modern buildings and still look much as they did several hundred years ago. It is definitely off the beaten path, but in a beautiful rural area of Mexico that otherwise you might never see. This quaint town is one that you can add to your repertoire of memories.

Tapalpa

Although, many sophisticated travelers who know Mexico quite well have never heard of it, Tapalpa is very well known to Mexicans, especially to those who live in Guadalajara. This is a favorite weekend retreat for the "city folks" who love to come here for the sweet fresh mountain air, hiking in the mountains, horseback riding, and the cool weather (since the town sits at a 1,950 meter elevation, it is always cool here). Note: When planning your trip, try to arrive in the middle of the week because not only are the hotel rates often higher on weekends, but also the roads much more crowded. Because it has many local tourists who visit, the town has a surprisingly good selection of places to stay. None are fancy, multi-star hotels, but ones that often have lots of charm and offer very nice accommodations. And a definite bonus to a lesser known destination, the prices are comparatively very low (especially mid-week). Because of the altitude, the nights are chilly—especially in winter. Many of the hotels have fire places in some of the guestrooms to make up for the lack of central heating. Be sure to bring a wrap whether you come in winter or summer.

The Colonial era of Tapalpa dates back to the 17th century. Although, the Spanish architecture creates an exceptionally picturesque ambiance, the town has not yet succumbed to blatant tourism. In fact, there are very few tourist shops—just a few miscellaneous stores selling some local handicrafts or stores offering jars of marmalade and canned fruits from the local produce. It is hard to even find a store selling souvenir T-shirts. The town is so "real" you will often hear clattering and look up to see a farmer on his horse riding through the cobbled streets.

It is definitely not the lure of upscale boutiques or luxurious hotels that bring people here. It is the town itself and its setting that is so appealing. The town is nestled on a high plateau surrounded by densely wooded pine forests. The Mexican government has designated the town as one of the "Pueblos Magicos" (Magical Towns"), a designation that the tourism department gives to towns that exemplify Mexico's culture and tradition. It is well-deserving of this honor.

The town is typical of the area with narrow cobbled streets, white-washed buildings, thick adobe walls, rustic red-tiled roofs, wood shutters and doors, and wrought iron accents. Another detail which adds special personality to the houses in Tapalpa is are the handsome, carved wood balconies that embellish the second stories and are held up by sturdy wood support columns.

The spire of the church will lead you straight to the heart of town where everything is within walking distance. First visit the **Temple de Señora Senora de Guadalupe.** It appears to be quite old, but actually was built in the 1900s. This is an exceptionally lovely church, built entirely of brick. A broad staircase leads up to the front doors. Be sure to go inside. You will be surprised at how beautiful it is. Like most of the churches in town, it was built by the Franciscans.

Close by the Temple de Nuestra Señora de Guadalupe, you find the church called **Apillla La Purisma**. This is one of the oldest churches in town that was also built by the Franciscans.

Just across from the Templo de Nuestra Señora de Guadalupe is another splendid church, the **Antiguo Templo de San Antonio.** This church no longer seems to conduct religious services but is a real beauty. This church was built in the 17th century by Franciscan friars. This beautiful building dominates the central plaza of the town.

Another church built of grey limestone, the **Templo de Nuestra Senora de la Mered,** is located about a 15-minute walk from the town square. It was built in 1859 in the neoclassical style. It has stained glass windows and murals painted on the interior of the dome.

Tapala has still another church worth seeing, the **Hospital Indio de Atacco**, which is located a short distance south of town. The construction of the church was also by the Franciscans who used the church as a hospital where they cared for the native Indians, especially the women, children, and elderly.

You can reach Tapalpa either by bus or car.

BUS OPTION: Tapalpa is about a three-hour bus ride from Guadalajara. The buses leave from the old bus station called Central Vieja. The bus company is "Linea Sur de Jalisco".

CAR OPTION: From Guadalajara follow Av. Lopez Mateos Sur which runs into the Autopista 54 to Colima. Just before you reach the first toll station, there is a turnoff to the right to Barra de Navidad and Tapalpa. Turn right here and take the route called Acatalán de Juárez, continuing to follow signs to Tapalpa. The scenery is exceptionally beautiful—particularly in the fall when everything is very green after the summer rains. The road leads you through the towns of Acatalán de Juárez, Atemajac de Brizuela, Ferreria de Tula and Frontera before reaching Tapalpa. The journey should take around two hours, depending upon traffic.

OPTIONAL SIDE TRIP FROM GUADALAJARA TO ZACATECAS

If you are captivated by Colonial towns, you might want to take a round trip from Guadalajara to **Zacatecas**, which was declared a World Heritage Site in 1993. Squeezed in a narrow valley, high in the barren mountains, this once-famous and thriving mining town was one of the largest producers of silver in Mexico.

Since it is off the beaten path and doesn't fit neatly into any other of our other itineraries, this is your best opportunity for a visit, if you are so inclined.

BUS OPTION: It is a long, six-hour bus ride from Guadalajara to Zacatecas and we don't really recommend the trip since it is so time-consuming. However, for your information, and if you want to try it, the bus company that serves this route is Camions de Los Altos: tel: 333.679.04.55.

CAR OPTION: If you drive to Zacatecas, we suggest making the trip as a loop. Take highway 80 northeast to Lagos de Moreno, then north on highway 45 to Zacatecas, a total drive of about 390 kilometers. On your return, take highway 54 (a two-lane road) south to Guadalajara, about a 320-kilometer drive. En route, stop in La Quemada, mentioned in sightseeing below. Another option would be to drive to Zacatecas after leaving San Miguel de Allende, as a stop before Guadalajara.

The dazzling wealth of this once-prosperous mining town is displayed everywhere you look: opulent mansions, superb churches, ornate theaters, and many museums displaying fine art. You will not want to miss the ornate, pink-stone cathedral, considered by many to be the finest example of baroque architecture in the country. It was built from 1729 to 1752 from the riches of the local mines and its façade, with rows of intricately carved columns framing carved stone statues, is quite unbelievable. Zacatecas had its share of artists, two of whom, brothers Rafael Coronel and Pedro Coronel, donated fabulous museums to the city. One of the most unique museums in town is the **Rafael Coronel Museum** in the beautiful **Monastery of San Francisco**, which displays a staggering private collection of over 5,000 masks and 19th-century marionettes donated by Rafael Coronel.

Not to be outdone, Rafael's brother, Pedro, gave his extensive collection of art to the city and this is housed in the **Pedro Coronel Museum**, an old Jesuit monastery. The museum features not only sculptures and paintings by Pedro, but also works of art by Picasso, Dalí, and Chagall. Adjacent is the fabulous Elias Amador Library where an incredible collection of over 25,000 antique books is magnificently displayed.

While in Zacatecas, take the *teleférico* (cable car), which glides over the city to the **Cerro de La Bufa**, the hilltop that was the site of Pancho Villa's most famous battle. There are monuments on the hill commemorating this event. Also on the summit is a beautiful church. When the cable car returns you to town, ask directions for the short walk to **La Mina Eden**, just a few blocks away. At the entrance to the mine you buy a ticket and a guide leads you through the vast, dimly lit tunnels, hand-hewn by Indian slaves. Along the way you cross suspension bridges over cavernous drop-offs where water has collected. You cannot help being saddened when you see the horrific conditions in which the slaves—men and young boys—worked and died. We were told that not a day ever passed without a fatal accident. At the bottom of the tunnel, your guide leaves you and you board a little train that slowly returns you to a world of light.

About 57 kilometers southwest of Zacatecas on highway 54, there is the interesting pre-Columbian site of **La Quemada**. A visit here can be made as an excursion by car from Zacatecas or as a stop en route from or back to Guadalajara. La Quemada is a fortress-like pre-Columbian site situated on a hilltop overlooking the valley and the route of the ancient traders. The ruins of its massive buildings and stone walls attest to its ancient purpose of protection for traders and the valuable goods they carried. In addition, it probably also served as a warehouse for collection and storage of goods awaiting transfer by Mesoamerica's long trains of porters. Porters were a vital commodity in pre-Columbian Mexico as beasts of burden were not available and most goods moved on the backs of men. Somewhere around A.D. 1000–1200 the site was destroyed, probably by Chichimec tribes from the northern desert.

DESTINATION III   MORELIA OR PÁTZCUARO

Your destination for the next few days is in the heart of the state of Michoacán. This beautiful state, abounding with lush volcanic hills, dense pine forests, rivers, and lakes, is the homeland of the **Tarascan Indians**. This group of indigenous people had a number of characteristics that set them apart from the rest of the natives of Mexico. First of all, they spoke a language unrelated to any other in Mesoamerica. Second, their architecture differed from the style used elsewhere. Third, their design and type of clothing was unique. Fourth, while, like the rest of Mesoamerica, they used gold, silver, and copper for items of jewelry, they also learned to make bronze from which they crafted tools and weapons. Finally, their independent kingdom centered at Lake Pátzcuaro was never conquered by the Aztecs. In fact, these two contemporaneous kingdoms, Aztec and

Tarascan, were constantly at war with each other, skirmishing along an extensive shared border. It may be that the use of superior bronze weapons by the Tarascans prevented them from being overrun by the aggressive Aztec state.

To explore this region, we suggest you stay in either Morelia or Pátzcuaro, two of our favorite gems in Colonial Mexico. Since they are only 55 kilometers apart, choose one or the other to use as your hub while in the area. Each has its individual personality and great appeal. Morelia, a sophisticated, polished city, displays a rich Colonial charm highlighted by splendid buildings; Pátzcuaro, a simple, picturesque Indian village on a lake, has one of the most gorgeous squares in all of Mexico and abounds with authentic charm.

BUS OPTION: There is faster service on a better bus from Guadalajara to Morelia than there is from Guadalajara to Pátzcuaro. So if you are staying in Pátzcuaro, consider changing buses in Morelia, rather than taking the direct service. Whichever town you choose to use as your base of operations, you will certainly want to visit the other location, which is no problem as buses run between the two about every 15 minutes.

9:30 am	Leave Guadalajara, La Central station, ETN bus
1:00 pm	Arrive Morelia (buses leave for Pátzcuaro about every 20 minutes)
or	
11:00 am	Leave Guadalajara, La Central station, Pegasso bus
5:00 pm	Arrive Pátzcuaro

CAR OPTION: From Guadalajara take highway 15 heading southeast toward Mexico City. About 245 kilometers after leaving Guadalajara, turn right when you come to the turnoff for Morelia and continue on for another 24 kilometers to the city. If you are staying in Pátzcuaro, when you come to Morelia, don't go into the center of town but instead follow signs on to Pátzcuaro.

MORELIA

Morelia, the capital of the state of Michoacán, is an attractive, tidy, modern city with many upscale stores and elegant men and women bustling to and fro. If you circumvent the center of town, you totally miss the best part: its fabulous historic center where you step instantly back to the 16th century when Morelia (whose original name was Old Valladolid) was founded by the Spanish. Its heritage, however, goes back to much earlier times for this rich plateau was the ancestral home of the proud Tarascan Indians and their influence is strongly felt in their native handiwork, which makes this area today one of the richest handicraft areas in Mexico.

Before you begin your sightseeing in Morelia, ask at the tourist office or get a map from the concierge at your hotel and mark the places you want to see.

If you are driving, follow signs to the center of town, leave your car in one of the parking garages, and continue on by foot. Wear comfortable shoes because you will be doing a lot of walking. You will be in the vicinity of the main boulevard, Avenida Francisco Madero, which stretches through the center of town and is highlighted by pretty plazas, churches, sculpted gardens, and handsome Spanish-style buildings made of a pastel, pinkish-colored stone. It is immediately obvious that Morelia was a prosperous city, for its buildings are all grand and the boulevards wide. There aren't many tourists in Morelia, so you get the authentic feel of a *real* city.

A convenient spot to start your explorations of Morelia is on the (above-mentioned) Avenida Francisco Madero at the **Plaza de Armas**, nicknamed Plaza de Los Mártires (Square of the Martyrs), in honor of two leaders of the Revolution of Independence who were executed here. This is an especially pretty square accented by a fanciful wrought-iron bandstand. This main plaza is easy to find since it is dominated by Morelia's exquisite **cathedral**, one of the most beautiful in Mexico. Designed and built by Indian artisans, it has a stunning dome embellished with brilliant blue-and-white tile and twin spires that soar over 60 meters into the sky—easily spotted from afar. When you see the immensity of the church, you understand why it took over 80 years to complete. You enter through massive doors covered with intricately tooled leather. Inside there is a central nave with a freestanding altar where an ornate 18th-century silver holder for the Holy Sacrament is displayed. If you happen to be in the cathedral when someone is playing the organ, you are in for a special treat since the music from this 4,600-pipe organ is astounding. Also noteworthy is the statue of la Señora de La Sacristía, made from a claylike paste of dried maize and wearing a gold crown, which was donated in the 16th century by the Spanish King, Felipe II.

Clustered within a few blocks of the cathedral are the following recommended sights:

Palacio de Gobierno (Government Palace): Facing onto Avenida Francisco Madero, catty-corner across from the cathedral, is the 18th-century Palacio de Gobierno. Formerly a seminary that educated many of Mexico's most important statesmen, it has been used as the government building since 1867. Step inside to view the sweeping murals depicting the history of Mexico, painted by Alfredo Zalce, one of Mexico's well known artists.

Museo Regional Michoacán (Regional Museum of Michoacán), corner of Allende and Abasolo: Originally a private mansion where Emperor Maxmillian stayed during his visits to Morelia, this museum displays many pre-Columbian ceramics, Colonial arms, and paintings. Of special interest are Indian codices (most of these rare Indian manuscripts were destroyed by the Spanish). Also of interest is a mural by Alfredo Zalce.

Museo Casa Natal de Morelos (Museum of Morelos's Birthplace), Corregidora 113: The home where Morelia's native hero, José María Morelos, was born in 1765. It is now a library and a museum showing mementos of his life. A torch burns eternally in memory of Morelos.

Museo Casa de Morelos (Museum of Morelos's Later Home), Avenida Morelos Sur 323: This is the home where José María Morelos lived in his later life. This museum shows furniture, personal objects from his life, a wonderful old kitchen, and many displays about the War of Independence, in which Morelos was a hero.

Palacio Clavijero, Nigromante 75: This handsome, baroque building, formerly a 17th-century Jesuit college, is now the tourist office. Stop in here for maps, information on places to see, and events going on during the time of your visit.

Museo del Estado (State Museum), Guillermo Prieto 176: This tiny museum was the home of Ana Huarte, wife of Agustín Iturbide who was briefly Emperor of Mexico after the execution of Maxmillian. The museum displays archaeological artifacts representing pre-Colombian history and jewelry made by Tarascan Indians. You can see didactic displays showing Indian life in the eight regions of Michoacán. The museum also houses a complete pharmacy with a great exhibit of antique apothecary jars.

Templo y Exconvento de San Francisco (Church and Convent of Saint Francis), Fray Juan de San Miguel 129: This church and convent, built in dramatic Spanish-Moorish style, are some of the oldest buildings in Morelia, dating back to 1525. Today the convent houses the Casa de Las Artesania, a museum displaying and selling handicrafts from around the state. As you enter, to your right is a museum with some of Michoacán's finest handmade items on display. A few are for display only, others are for sale. On a galleried upper floor, facing onto the cloister below, is a series of small shops, each representing crafts from Indian villages throughout the state. Sometimes the Indians are working on their crafts as you watch. These shops sell guitars, hand-loomed fabrics, brightly painted lacquerware, copperware, embroidered clothing, and pottery.

Templo y Exconvento de Las Rosas (Church and Convent of the Roses), Santiago Tapia, between Galeana Nigromante and Guillermo Prieto: Facing a small park called Jardín de Las Rosas, the Convent of the Roses was built in the 16th century for Dominican nuns, then later became a school to house and educate poor children. In 1785, it was converted to a music school which has become internationally famous for its Morelia Boys' Choir. If you are lucky, you might be in Morelia when a concert is being performed; otherwise, you might be able to quietly slip in on a weekday afternoon when they practice.

In addition to the above sightseeing, there are a few recommendations that are not clustered around the cathedral. The following sights are still within walking distance, but be prepared for a bit more of a walk—about 4 kilometers round trip from the cathedral to the Santuario de Nuestra Señora de Guadalupe. All can be reached by walking east on Avenida Francisco Madero.

Plaza Villabongin: From the cathedral, turn right onto Avenida Francisco Madero and continue walking for about nine blocks. You will come to a triangular plaza with a park, the Plaza Villabongin, which has a fountain featuring a handsome sculpture of three bare-breasted Indian women holding baskets of fruit and vegetables.

Aqueduct: Just beyond the Plaza Villabongin, you see one of the symbols of Morelia, its aqueduct, built in the late 1700s to supply water from nearby springs for the growing city. It stretches for an impressive 2 kilometers and has over 250 dramatic high arches in excellent condition, which, when softly illuminated at night, are an impressive sight.

La Calzada Frey Antonio de San Miguel: Go under the aqueduct and continue ahead on La Calzada Frey Antonio de San Miguel. The street was named by Father Antonio de San Miguel who commissioned the aqueduct to be built. This pedestrian esplanade is lined by beautiful 18th-century mansions, which during its heyday housed Morelia's elite. This pretty street, which has a parklike causeway running down the middle, adorned with ash trees and ornate benches, is very tranquil except during the celebration of the Virgin of Guadalupe (early to mid-December), when it is very lively and its every inch lined with vendors.

Santuario de Nuestra Señora de Guadalupe (also called Church of San Diego): Continue walking down La Calzada Frey Antonio de San Miguel. The street dead-ends at the Santuario de Nuestra Señora de Guadalupe (Church of San Diego), an 18th-century church that is my favorite in Morelia. The exterior is rather staid and totally belies the treasure within. Step inside and you are surrounded by an interior façade that is awesome. Brilliantly colored plaster rosettes and endless gold totally cover the walls, the ceiling, and the domes. It seems as if you are surrounded by an exquisitely jeweled porcelain egg by Fabergé.

PÁTZCUARO

Pátzcuaro, a small Colonial gem with a strong Indian heritage, is one of our favorite destinations. For the first-time traveler to Mexico wanting to visit just one charming Colonial town, San Miguel de Allende might be a better choice since it is more sophisticated with chic boutiques and upscale restaurants. However, Pátzcuaro gives you the true feeling of being in Mexico, in an authentic Indian village that hasn't been prettied up yet for tourists—it is the real thing. Whereas magnificent 17th- and 18th-century stone mansions embrace the squares, simple one-story whitewashed adobe houses with rustic red-tiled roofs line the surrounding jumble of narrow cobbled streets.

You cannot visit Pátzcuaro without becoming familiar with, and quite a fan of, **Don Vasco de Quiroga**, a 16th-century bishop who is the heart and soul of the town. He not only dreamed of Pátzcuaro becoming one of the most important towns in the New World, but also influenced the lives of the Indians in all the surrounding villages. This gentle yet dynamic priest was sent by the Spanish king to try to make amends for the cruelty rained upon the Indians by one of the most hated of the Spanish conquistadors, Nuño Beltran de Guzman, a lieutenant of Cortés, whose brutality was so extreme and atrocities so profound that finally the Mexican governor ordered him back to Spain to stand trial for his deeds. Don Vasco de Quiroga was a genius with compassion, great organizational abilities, and profound wisdom. He was beloved by all and even today the local Indians affectionately speak of him as "Tata Vasco" (Uncle Vasco) and remember the years he dedicated to preserving their indigenous culture and improving the lot of their people.

What is especially remarkable is how much Don Vasco was able to accomplish in just a few short years. He was already 60 (an age most people think of retiring) when he made the tortuous voyage from Spain to the New World, and then upon his arrival, climbed upon a horse to complete his long journey overland to Pátzcuaro. By the time he died in his 90s, he had accomplished more after the age of 60 than most people could even dream of doing in their lifetime.

SIGHTSEEING SUGGESTIONS

Plaza Don Vasco de Quiroga: If for no other reason, Pátzcuaro would be worth a detour to see its stunning Plaza Don Vasco de Quiroga, in our estimation one of the two most beautiful squares in Mexico (our other favorite is the plaza in Tlaxcala—see *Mexico & Beyond* itinerary). This parklike plaza (also called Plaza Grande) it is a real jewel with

Pátzcuaro, Plaza Don Vasco de Quiroga

huge, centuries-old ash trees shading paths radiating from the center, where a large circular fountain highlights a big, bronze statue of Don Vasco de Quiroga standing on a pedestal. Stone benches are set along the paths so that you can enjoy the beauty of the plaza. Surrounding the square are handsome, stone mansions fronted by arcaded walkways, some of which have been converted into restaurants and hotels. Try to visit this plaza at dawn. It is almost mystical at that time of day with the gentle illumination of the morning light filtering through the trees and tiny, Indian women wrapped in striped, handwoven woolen *rebozos* (shawls) scurrying through the park on their way to work.

Plaza Gertrudis Bocanegra: A block north of the Plaza Don Vasco de Quiroga is another plaza that goes by several names: Plaza Chica, Plaza de San Agustín, or Plaza Gertrudis Bocanegra. This is a bustling square with many shops and commercial buildings around it. The activity really picks up on Friday morning, the big market day when Indians come from far and near to set up their stalls. In the center of the square is a statue of one of the heroines of the Revolution, Gertrudis Bocanegra.

Museo de Artes Populares: Don Vasco wanted to make Pátzcuaro an important religious, cultural, and political center. He decided the town needed a university and so, in 1540, chose a site a block from the main square and founded the Colegio de San Nicolás, which claims to be the second-oldest university in the New World. In 1580 the university was moved to Morelia, which began to surpass Pátzcuaro in political importance. The school now houses the Museo de Artes Populares, a lovely museum with nine rooms opening onto an open courtyard, displaying regional arts and crafts.

Also in the museum is a *troje* with typical furnishings. A troje is a wooden log home used by the Tarascan Indians with a porch in front supported by carved columns. Note: As you stand at the entrance to the museum, look to your right to see a water tank with a niche holding the Virgin Mary. According to legend, Don Vasco de Quiroga struck his staff on the ground here and a spring miraculously appeared to supply water for the town.

Basilica de Nuestra Señora de La Salud: Another of Don Vasco's dreams was to build an extraordinary cathedral, which he designed to be three times larger than the Cathedral of Notre Dame in Paris. With that in mind, he built the Basilica de Nuestra Señora de La Salud on a gentle hill about two blocks from the plaza. Only one nave of the original plan was ever completed, but the simple basilica is appealing. One of its principal attractions is the Virgin de La Salud, a small statue encased in glass on the altar, made by the Indians in 1547 from wild orchids and corn paste. Indians come from afar, especially on feast days, to pay homage and ask miracles from their **Virgin de La Salud** (Virgin of Health).

Casa de Los Once Patios: Not attributed to Don Vasco, but certainly a place you won't want to miss, especially if you are into shopping for crafts, is the Casa de Los Once Patios (House of the Eleven Patios), a 17th-century Dominican monastery just a half block off the Don Vasco de Quiroga Plaza. The original building had eleven interior patios but today only five remain, each of which is lined by small craft shops selling all kinds of native handmade goods such as loomed fabrics, masks, wooden sculptures, embroidered linens, copper, lacquerware, carved furniture, and colorful paper flowers. It is fun to wander from patio to patio to see what new delights await. You will be reminded that this was a living convent when you notice in one of the patios an arch, supported by richly embellished columns sheltering a small niche, where the novices came to bathe.

AROUND PÁTZCUARO

Santa Clara de Cobre: It is great fun to explore the town of Pátzcuaro, but the outlying region holds many places of interest, including towns that blossomed under the tutelage of Don Vasco de Quiroga. To help the Indians make a transition from their pre-Columbian world to the Spanish culture brought by the conquistadors, Don Vasco established special crafts for each small village, based upon the skills they already knew. Each of these villages, even today, continues to thrive on what Don Vasco taught them. These handicrafts included weaving, woodworking, furniture-making, pottery, lacquerware, guitar-making, and embroidery work. Perhaps the most successful venture occurred in the village of Santa Clara de Cobre (the official name of the town is Villa Escalante, but you will rarely hear it called that), where the people were trained in the working of copper. Today this small, out-of-the way village has become a hub for copper craftsmen throughout Mexico—fine artists come to learn the "old ways" of their craft and many stay on to continue working among their peers. You can see the artists and craftsmen at work here and buy wonderful copper objects directly from them. There is a competition each mid-August when all the artisans vie for the finest works of art; the winners' pieces are featured in Santa Clara's National Copper Museum. This is a village that should not be missed on a trip to Pátzcuaro.

Lake Pátzcuaro: This lake is located about 5 kilometers from the center of town. Tourist photos show it as an idyllic expanse of water with a cone-shaped island jutting up in the middle, and fishermen out in rustic, wooden boats fishing with butterfly nets. In our estimation, the beauty of the lake is overrated since the water is polluted, the fishermen rarely fish with butterfly nets (except for the tourists), and Janítzio (the town on the picturesque-looking island in the middle of the lake) is a bit dirty and scruffy-looking once you get up close. That being said, we still think a boat trip on the lake is fun and a very "non-touristy" outing since most of your companions will be Mexicans out for a day of fun. To visit the island in the lake, take a taxi to the wharf (called Melon Grande or embarcadero) where you will see many boats lined up at the dock.

It may be confusing to know quite what to do, but just go to the ticket booth and ask for a round-trip ticket to **Janítzio** (which costs about 30 pesos). Go down the ramp to the boats, show one of the "officials" your ticket, and he will point out which boat to board. The boats seem to leave whenever enough people appear. You shouldn't have to wait too long and, in the meantime, it's entertaining just to watch the action. On weekends and holidays, the boats are full of tourists going to the island to have a meal at one of the many restaurants. During the week, most of the boat passengers seem to be locals, schoolchildren returning home, and women returning from the market. When the boat arrives at the island, disembark, and walk the many steps lined by vendors to the top of the hill, which is topped by a 70-meter statue of José María Morelos (about a 15-minute walk).

Within the statue is a museum with galleries on five floors joined by a rampway, each level covered with huge murals with titles in Spanish. Even if you can't read Spanish, it is pretty obvious that the tale being told is of the cruelty of the Spanish Conquest and the sad plight of the Indians. Walk back down the hill to the village to wait for the next boat back. There are many colorful restaurants on a terrace above the pier.

Butterfly-Net Fishermen at Lake Pátzcuaro

Tzintzuntzan: If you are interested in archaeological sites, you must not miss Tzintzuntzan (translated as "The Place of the Hummingbird"), located on the east side of the lake about 17 kilometers from Pátzcuaro. When the Spanish arrived in the 16th century, more than 40,000 Tarascan Indians lived in this town, which was the capital of their state. This unusual site sits on a rise just above Lake Pátzcuaro, with a splendid view across the water to the islands and fertile fields of this lovely valley in the mountains. Five large *yacatas*, round keyhole-shaped stone structures, stand in a row along a great man-made platform on a ridge facing the lake. Behind the *yacatas* steps lead down into a plaza with remains of a palace, living quarters, and storehouses. While some archaeological excavations have been carried out at the site, very little information has ever been published. It is generally assumed, however, that these finely made round cut-stone bases were once topped with perishable temples dedicated to the major Tarascan gods. In addition, the *yacatas* were used as the burial places of the Tarascan kings. Rich finds from the tombs include magnificent examples of the metalwork for which the Tarascans were renowned as well as skeletons of retainers who were interred with their royal masters in order to serve them after death. Tzintzuntzan is also well known for its intricate straw weavings and there are numerous shops where handicrafts are sold. Note: On the road from Pátzcuaro to Tzintzuntzan you will see factories selling wrought-iron garden furniture, mostly tables and chairs and handsome tall, old-fashioned wrought-iron lamps, at excellent prices. Our choice of these shops, which makes the furniture in a factory behind, is Fundidora Los Fresnos, on the left side of the road as you go toward Tzintzuntzan.

Tocuaro: If you are interested in buying one of the region's popular carved wooden masks, drive along the western edge of the lake to the tiny village of Tocuaro, just a little distance beyond the town of Eroncuariquero. Here you will find a master craftsman, Señor Horta, who creates and sells his pieces of art in his home. His work and skill are so well known that he is frequently invited to the United States to lecture. Once you arrive in the village, anyone you meet should be able to point the way to his home (it has his name on the door).

Cuanajo & Tupátaro: Another skill of the Tarascan Indians is the making of intricately carved furniture. If you are interested in buying some furniture or just want to see how it is made, go to the tiny, nondescript town of Cuanajo. This is an interesting excursion because along the way there is an outstanding tiny church to visit. From Pátzcuaro, take the highway toward Morelia and about 10 kilometers after leaving town, turn right on a small road at a small sign marked to Cuanajo. Soon after leaving the highway you come to the postage-stamp-sized town of Tupátaro, which is not much more that a tiny, beautifully kept plaza enhanced with old-fashioned wrought-iron lamps and bordered on three sides by one-story whitewashed buildings with rustic tiled roofs. Across from the tiny park is an adobe wall enclosing a very old church. Although not in the least ostentatious, this tiny church is truly a gem. Aged shade trees dot the grounds and a rugged stone marks the entrance. Notice as you enter that adorning one side of the doorway is a moon, on the other, the sun—surely not Christian motifs but undoubtedly reflecting the culture of the Indian craftsmen who built the church. The exterior is very simple, making it all the more amazing when you step inside and see the breathtaking gold altar. Be sure also to look up—the ceiling too is quite amazing. Its beams are totally covered with intricate paintings of angels and scenes from the life of Christ, clearly reflecting the style of the early Indian artistic tradition. After seeing the church, continue on to Cuanajo, where it is fun to stroll along the streets to see the vast array of furniture being made of pine wood. Most of the shops (often home fronts) offer intricately carved furniture at incredibly low prices. My favorites are the delicately carved headboards, but these are a bit large to tote home. You might want to consider one of the lovely small carved pine chests, which can be packed up to take on the plane.

Lake Zirahuen: Whereas Lake Pátzcuaro is polluted, Lake Zirahuen, located in the pine-studded hills 22 kilometers southwest of Pátzcuaro next to a town of the same name, is crystal-clear without a hint of pollution. Many Mexicans come here for family outings. If you want to combine sightseeing, dining, and lots of local color, go to Le Troje de Ala restaurant (open on weekends), which is built within a Tarascan-style wooden home called a *troje*. The restaurant faces the lake and has a long wooden pier stretching out into the water. It is possible to drive to the restaurant, but much it's more of an adventure to take a boat. Ask at your hotel for details on how to get there.

Paricutín Volcano: A truly off-the-beaten-path adventure, and one you would probably want to undertake only if you are making an extensive stay in the area, is to the remote village of San Juan Parangaricútiro, which lies covered in ash from the Paricutín Volcano. The volcano erupted in 1943 and for nine years rained ash upon the valley below. What you see today is a field of black lava punctuated by the steeple of the village's 16th-century church, which lies buried below. What makes this trip special is not so much what you see, or don't see, of the buried village, but the jaunt itself, which takes you into a beautiful, lush area of pine-covered hills and tiny villages in a remote area of Michoacán rarely seen by tourists. Here Indians are still living as they have done for countless generations in picturesque *trojes* (log homes with carved columns). Allow a full day for this adventure. From Pátzcuaro, take the toll road west for 60 kilometers to Uruapan, a bustling commercial town that would win no beauty contests but is very important as it lies at the heart of Mexico's vast avocado plantations. Eduardo Ruiz National Park, on the outskirts of town, is a real beauty, with lovely streams, springs, waterfalls, and lush, almost tropical foliage. From Uruapan, go north for about 13 kilometers on highway 37, turn left, and continue for another 20 kilometers to Angahuan. Here you will find plenty of guides eager to rent you horses and guide you to see the covered town (a 6-kilometer round trip). Arrangements can be made also to take you up the volcano, but I think just the round trip to the buried village is enough.

When it is time to end this itinerary, you can return to Mexico City for your trip home, take a flight to one of the beach areas for a few days in the sun, or, if you want to continue your explorations of the countryside, link with one of the other itineraries featured in the guide, such as the *Miracle of the Monarch Butterfly* itinerary.

BUS OPTION: Below we indicate some possibilities for public transportation back to Mexico City.

11:15 am	Leave Morelia, La Central station, ETN bus
3:15 pm	Arrive Mexico City, Observatorio station
or	
9:00 am	Leave Pátzcuaro, La Central station, Autovíos bus
2:15 pm	Arrive Mexico City, Observatorio station

CAR OPTION: If you are driving, return to highway 15 from Pátzcuaro or Morelia and follow signs into Mexico City, a total distance of just a little over 300 kilometers. Note: it can be a little confusing because the highway changes numbers en route from 15 to 55.

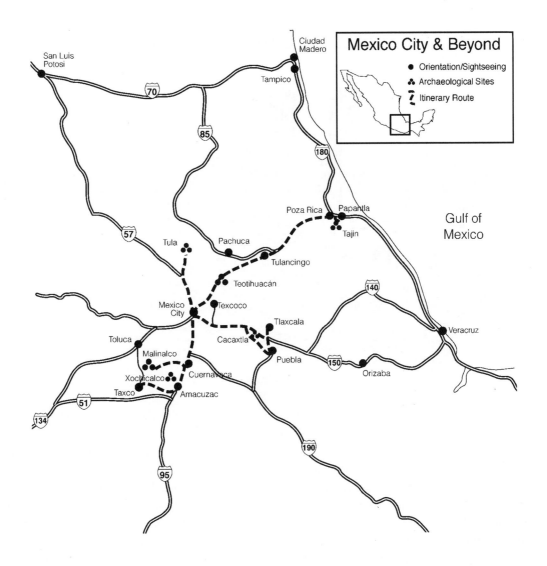

Mexico City & Beyond

- ● Orientation/Sightseeing
- ♣ Archaeological Sites
- ⌇ Itinerary Route

San Luis Potosi

Ciudad Madero

Tampico

70

85

180

Poza Rica

Papantla

Tajin

Gulf of Mexico

Tula

Pachuca

57

Tulancingo

Teotihuacán

Mexico City

Texcoco

Tlaxcala

140

Toluca

Cacaxtla

Veracruz

Malinalco

Puebla

150

Xochicalco

Cuernavaca

Orizaba

Taxco

Amacuzac

51

134

95

190

Mexico City & Beyond

Taxco

This itinerary covers Mexico City (referred to by those who live here as "Mexico") and the high fertile valley that surrounds it. In this valley remains have been found of hunters and the mammoths they pursued, of early village farmers who cultivated the fertile volcanic soil, and of the amazing urban-centered warrior empires that followed them. All of these cultures and empires have left their mark upon the valley itself, and their influence is reflected in many other cultures throughout pre-Hispanic Mesoamerica. The empire builders in this heartland region of Mexico left impressive art and amazing architectural monuments scattered throughout the valley and its environs. Their achievements are monumental, yet like all New World pre-Columbian cultures, these civilizations lacked draft animals such as horses and oxen, knowledge of the wheel, and effective metal weapons and tools. However, in their own way, they were as sophisticated as their European counterparts. Isolated from the Old World, the civilizations of the Americas developed their own architectural styles, political and social structures, agricultural techniques, and religious beliefs. Their accomplishments and their magnificent cities astonished the Spanish invaders of 1519 and continue to amaze visitors in the 21st century.

One cannot fully appreciate a visit to this area without a bit of Aztec history, for the Aztecs built a mighty empire here, long before the Spaniards arrived. The Aztecs were not the first to be lured to this rich valley, but they were the ones that greeted the conquistadors, and whose amazing culture impressed these men from Spain. So, to add more depth of understanding to what you will be seeing, we start this itinerary with some historical background.

THE AZTECS (c. A.D. 1200–1521)

The powerful Aztecs were the last indigenous group to control the Valley of Mexico. They had brought their kingdom to its height when the Spanish arrived in 1519, and they controlled vast territories from their island city of Tenochtitlán, now known as Mexico City. This city was the urban center of an enormous empire that stretched through the Valley of Mexico to both coasts and as far south as Guatemala. The Mexica, as they called themselves, were latecomers to the central Mexican plateau. They were descendents of the Chichimecs, members of barbarian hunting tribes who inhabited the desert frontiers of northern Mexico. Legend relates that they left their mythic homeland of Aztlan (hence the name Aztec) in A.D. 1111 and, led by their fierce tribal god, Huitzilopochtli, wandered for many years searching for a promised homeland. When they finally arrived in the Valley of Mexico (about A.D. 1200) the fertile inland basin was already heavily populated and lack of good agricultural land forced the Aztecs to occupy the undesirable swamps at the edge of Lake Texcoco. For over 100 years the Aztecs served as mercenary soldiers and servants for their more powerful neighbors and it was not until 1325 that they founded their own capital city. According to legend, this settlement was established at a place where they found an eagle with a serpent in its mouth sitting on a cactus, an image still seen today on the Mexican flag. At this sacred spot the Aztecs built a temple to their god and began to construct the city of Tenochtitlán.

Eventually, through political alliances, ruthless warfare, and intermarriages with important families, the Aztecs began their rise to power. Fierce warrior kings eventually extended the empire far beyond the boundaries of the Valley of Mexico, and rich spoils of war poured in from conquered regions. The increasingly powerful military state enforced a tribute system that assured a constant flow of valuable goods such as jade, gold, rubber, food, and slaves into Tenochtitlán. These great riches supplied the Aztec nobility with wealth and the city itself with power and beauty. Tenochtitlán became the urban center of a vast empire but its roots remained entwined in knowledge and traditions derived from earlier civilizations. The Aztecs were cultural heirs of the past and the final powerful flowering of ancient Mesoamerica.

Much of what we know about the Aztecs and the city of Tenochtitlán comes from documents written by Spanish soldiers and priests who were eyewitnesses to the conquest of Mexico (1519–1521). The Spaniards, including their captain Hernán Cortés, were overwhelmed by the beauty and sophistication of Tenochtitlán. They describe this amazing urban center as a city built on islands in the waters of a large lake. Great causeways connected the city with the mainland and aqueducts brought fresh water for its fountains and gardens from the hill of Chapultepec. Edged with beaten-dirt pathways, canals with drawbridges formed the streets of the city. Thousands of canoes plied the lakes and canals daily, carrying people and supplies from one place to another. The city seemed like another Venice to the weary Spaniards.

At the heart of the capital was a walled sacred precinct. Here stood the Templo Mayor, a magnificent double pyramid which held temples dedicated to Tlaloc, the ancient Mesoamerican god of rain, and to Huitzilopochtli, the god of war. Pyramids dedicated to other gods, schools, a ball court, priests' quarters, and great royal palaces were also located there. This was the heart of the empire and the religious focus of the city. Here elaborate ceremonies took place and human sacrifices were offered to the demanding, ever-greedy Aztec gods.

Around the central precinct the Aztec elite dwelt in great palaces with gardens, flowers, and exotic birds. This rich noble class was composed of the relatives of the current ruler and of the many descendents of previous rulers, and was larger than might be supposed as noblemen were allowed to have as many wives and concubines as they could support. Thus elite households contained numerous offspring; reportedly the Emperor Montezuma himself had 150 children.

Beyond this sacred and wealthy center, the rest of Tenochtitlán stretched out into the lake on artificial islands connected by canals and bridges. Here were the *barrios* or neighborhoods where free commoners lived and most of the daily functions of the city took place. Each *barrio* provided the essentials of life for its members: land, schools, markets, local priests and temples, and military training for all men and boys. Farmers, the backbone of Aztec society, lived on the outskirts of the great city on fabricated plots of land called *chinampas*, the basic agricultural unit of the Valley of Mexico. Their carefully planned cycle of crops (often as many as five a year) provided food for the thriving Aztec capital. Unlike the extensive plowed agricultural fields of Europe, *chinampas* provided one of the most intensive systems of horticulture ever developed. As the empire expanded and the population increased, more and more of these islands were created for cultivation by cutting drainage canals through the swampy areas around the lake. Many of these artificial islands, known popularly today as "floating gardens," are still in use and can be visited on small, colorful boats that carry visitors along the ancient canal system. (Excursions to these floating gardens will be described in more detail further on.)

In 1519 over a million people inhabited the Valley of Mexico; at least 250,000 of them lived in Tenochtitlán, making it then, as it still is today, one of the largest metropolises in the world. The stimulation and excitement of the great urban center drew a diverse population from all over the empire into itself like a magnet. Artists came to employ their skills in the service of the king and his nobles. Warriors came to win fame and fortune in battles of conquest. Traders with their burden-laden human caravans carried exotic treasures to the market. Foreign dignitaries paid state visits to the court of Montezuma. Priests and pilgrims visited the sacred shrines and thieves, performers, tourists, and prostitutes all flocked to the city. People came in search of common, everyday necessities or of the rich goods that filled the great marketplace. They listened to the orations of the priests, sought the services of soothsayers and healers, dined on food prepared at market stalls, and visited with friends. As directed by the gods, they participated in the city's rich ceremonial life and watched with awe as human sacrifices were offered on top of the majestic pyramids. This was Tenochtitlán, heart of the Aztec empire.

In the early days of November 1519, Hernán Cortés, with a handful of Spanish soldiers and a multitude of Indian allies from the town of Tlaxcala, wound over a high mountain pass and down into the verdant Valley of Mexico. The seasoned Spanish soldiers who accompanied Cortés were overwhelmed by the beauty and size of Tenochtitlán. Built of stone, adobe and wood, the city had whitewashed stucco walls that shone in the sun like silver; its streets were canals of water, and thousands of canoes could be seen on the lake. The soldiers gazed in wonder at the gardens, palaces, temples, and pyramids rising from the water. With their captain, they waited on the causeway watching with excitement and fear as the elaborate royal litter carrying the Emperor Montezuma approached. The momentous encounter of two different worlds was at hand—this was the beginning of the end for the mighty Aztec empire, and the birth of a new nation.

This itinerary covers not only Mexico City, but also the valley that surrounds it. The first section, *Mexico City*, gives suggestions for what to do and see within the city. The second section, *Short Day Excursions from Mexico City*, highlights some of our favorite archaeological sites that are within a short radius and best seen on a day's outing. *Longer Excursions East of Mexico City* highlights Puebla and Tlaxcala and what to see nearby, while *Longer Excursions South of Mexico City* highlights Cuernavaca and Taxco and what to see nearby.

RECOMMENDED PACING: We suggest a week to cover this itinerary: three nights in Mexico City to give you time to savor its many wonders, then another four days for excursions into the countryside. These side excursions could be done as day trips or else you could spend one or more nights along the way.

Note: If you are apprehensive about driving, you really do not need a car for this itinerary. You *definitely* do *not* want a car while you are in the city since parking is expensive and traffic awful, but you will find that even when you take excursions to the suggested sights outside the city, a car is not necessary. Convenient, deluxe bus service is available to all of the towns mentioned, plus there are excellent tours available that have the added benefit of a guide to add richness to what you see. If this "car-less" option appeals to you, the concierge at your hotel can assist you with bus schedules, tour options, and prices for a private car and driver.

MEXICO CITY

We begin our sightseeing in **Mexico City**, which has always been the heartland of the empire. It lies at an elevation of 2,340 meters and, with its population of 22 million, is the largest city in the western hemisphere. Today, this immense capital serves as the center and hub of modern Mexico. It has a dramatic setting on a verdant plateau surrounded by mountains, including two colossal volcanoes, Popocatépetl and Iztacchíhuatl, whose snowcapped peaks can be seen on clear days.

Be prepared that Mexico City is not a place of pristine perfection. Due to its size and uncontrollable growth, it has many problems, including pollution, crime, ugly buildings, congestion, lack of a good highway network around the city, and mind-boggling traffic within. However, the government is well aware of these troubles and is making great strides in dealing with them. These less-than-perfect aspects of the city should not deter you from visiting it. Here you find at its core not only a magnificent Colonial city, but also some of the world's finest museums, beautiful parks, fabulous restaurants, grand boulevards, splendid modern architecture, chic boutiques, lovely residential areas, and excellent universities. To top it off, there is a wealth of excellent hotels in all price ranges.

SIGHTSEEING SUGGESTIONS

Bosque de Chapultepec (Chapultepec Park): Although Emperor Maximilian ruled Mexico for only a brief period, he left a French influence upon the city, including wide, tree-lined boulevards. One of the finest of these is the Paseo de La Reforma, a 12-kilometer-long thoroughfare, which remains as one of the most important and beautiful boulevards in the city. It crosses through one of the city's highlights, the Bosque de Chapultepec, which dates back to the 16th century. The park is host to many museums, lakes, fountains, amusement parks, statues, theaters, and shaded walkways. It is pleasant to stroll through the park, which is the playground for the city. Here you soak in the local color with parents buying cotton candy and balloons for their children, vendors selling fresh produce, shoeshine men busily buffing shoes, lovers snuggled on park benches, mothers pushing baby carriages, and snack stalls tucked throughout.

Castillo de Chapultepec: On the summit of the highest hill in Chapultepec Park you find the Castillo de Chapultepec (Chapultepec Castle) whose story is rarely reported in American history books. The castle was once the home of Emperor Maxmilian and his wife Carlota and still has furnishings from the era of their reign. After the Revolution, the castle became a military academy for young men. In 1847, during the American-Mexican War, the American army assaulted the castle, which was bravely defended by the young cadets, most of whom died. One gallant youth leapt to his death wrapped in the Mexican flag to avoid capture. These young men were later to become known as the *Niños Héroes*, or Young Heroes. There is a dramatic monument with soaring columns in the park that is dedicated to these young heroes.

Cathedral: This superb structure is the largest cathedral in Latin America and certainly one of its most beautiful. Sadly, today this Colonial monument is slowly sinking into the soft floor of the ancient lake bed that still lies under modern Mexico City, and there seems little can be done to maintain it. The cathedral took almost 300 years to complete and during that time architectural styles from many periods, from classical to baroque, were incorporated into it. Its façade is glorious, enhanced by 67-meter-high twin bell towers with a series of bells on various levels. Between the bell towers is a clock tower, adorned with statues of Faith, Hope, and Charity. In the center of the building there is a huge, gold dome, reminiscent of St. Peter's in Rome. Inside, the magnificence of the richly embellished church continues, with beautiful oil paintings, exquisitely decorated statues, magnificently carved choir stalls, and the Altar de Los Reyes, which is an ornate baroque masterpiece.

Museo de Arte Moderno: The Museo de Arte Moderno (the Museum of Modern Art) is one of the museums that is located in Chapultepec Park. It features 20th-century paintings by Mexican artists.

Museo Dolores Olmedo Piña: The Museo Dolores Olmedo Piña, located in the suburb of Xochimilco, is one of our favorite places to visit in Mexico City. Although it takes about 45 minutes to drive there from the heart of the city, the journey is well worth the effort. Perhaps you have never heard of Dolores Olmedo Piña, but she was an astonishing woman of dramatic beauty, talent, and energy. Born in 1908, she died in 2002, having lived a remarkable 94 years—a life brimming with glamour and wealth. Although travel wasn't simple, she constantly visited exotic destinations throughout the world and seemed to have friends everywhere, from nobility to Popes. Always loving the flamboyant, she built an enormous home in a magnificent multi-acre, walled estate that once housed an Aztec palace. The mansion, surrounded by a large park, is itself worth a visit. Here you can wander through room after room, filled with Piña's furnishings and personal photos, gasping in wonder at her exuberant way of life. But what makes the museum so fantastic is its collection of art. Dolores Olmedo became the last great love and benefactor of Diego Rivera and her home is now a museum, housing one of the greatest collections of his work. This includes Rivera's paintings of her children and sunsets from her estate in Acapulco where he lived for the last few years of his life. Also on display are paintings by many other artists, including an excellent collection of the work of Frida Kahlo.

Museo Franz Meyer: Many visitors to Mexico are unaware of one of our favorite museums in Mexico City, the Museo Franz Meyer Museum, located in the heart of the city on Avenida Hidalgo 45, on the north side of Alameda Park. The entrance is a bit tricky to find since the door is tucked in a courtyard by the side of the entrance to the adjacent church, Iglesia de San Juan de Dios. This museum is elegant and sophisticated with gleaming parquet floors and classical music gently playing in the background. Here you find magnificent Spanish Colonial collections of paintings, furniture, silver, sculptures, etc. Many of the splendid objects reflect the early Conquest Period and form an artistic bridge between Aztec and Spanish artistic traditions. From the outside, the museum looks small, but once within, the rooms extend seemingly forever. Some of the exhibits surround a charming cloister where there is an inviting small café with tables set in the garden.

Museo Frida Kahlo: The Frida Kahlo Museum, located at the corner of Londres and Allende in the suburb of Coyoacan, is of special interest to those who want to know more about Diego Rivera and also gain an insight into the fascinating Frida Kahlo. This intriguing museum was the home of the dark-haired, tempestuous, talented beauty, Frida Kahlo, who was born and died here. She and Diego Rivera lived here after their marriage and the house, set in an enclosed garden, has walls painted in brilliant blue trimmed with red, reflecting their love of vibrant colors and design. Frida, who endured great pain resulting from childhood polio, and later spinal injuries resulting from a bus/streetcar accident, had a turbulent marriage to Rivera lasting 25 years. They must have been quite a pair, the diminutive Frida and the 300-pound Rivera. She was a talented artist in her own right, and her surrealistic paintings and free-spirited approach to life have gained great fame. When Frida died at the age of 47, Rivera left the house, along with the paintings inside, as a museum. The furnishings and personal items are much as they were when she and Rivera shared the home. I had to smile at a gift you will see in one of the rooms, a custom-designed wheel chair and easel, given to Frida toward the end of her life so that she could continue painting. It seemed so incongruous that this thoughtful gift was given to Frida (a passionate communist and champion of the common man) by Rockefeller (an icon of capitalism). If you plan to visit this museum, try to rent a copy of the film *Frida*, a movie released in 2002 depicting her life. Some of the scenes were photographed in this house.

Museo Leon Trotsky: Diego Rivera (a passionate Communist) invited Leon Trotsky to come to Mexico when the political situation changed in Russia and Trotsky's life was in danger. He lived briefly in the home of Diego Rivera and Frida Kahlo. It is rumored he had an affair with Frida, which is perhaps why he and his wife moved into their own house that is now open as a museum. Tragically, his political enemies discovered his whereabouts and assassinated him. The museum is located in the suburb of Coyoacan, about a 45-minute drive from the heart of the city.

Museo Nacional de Antropología: The National Museum of Anthropology, located in Chapultepec Park, is housed in a spectacular modern building containing collections of archaeological objects from all the pre-Columbian cultures of Mexico. There is a large inner courtyard almost totally shaded by a long concrete canopy which protects against the hot sun. The courtyard is embraced by the two-story museum, which displays chronologically and geographically the history of Mexico. These collections provide an excellent introduction to the archaeology of Mexico in an environment that is most pleasing. When the museum opened in 1964, it was considered a masterpiece, displaying a whole new concept of how to make archaeology come alive. Instead of becoming outdated, the museum is more remarkable than ever following extensive renovations in 2001. You move from room to room in an organized way to follow the exhibits in a chronological order and you see many special effects and video displays that explain what you are seeing. Not to be missed are a few highlights such as an incredible funerary mask of jade, which is one of the museum's treasures. In the Aztec exhibit, you cannot miss the Sun Stone with its intricate design showing the sun god in the center surrounded by the Aztec calendar. The mother-of-pearl Toltec Coyote Headed Warrior is another gem. These are but appetizers of the many fabulous pieces you will see—plan to spend many hours here. (There is a very good restaurant on the premises for lunch).

Palacio de Bellas Artes: The Palacio de Bellas Artes is in the heart of Mexico City, bordering onto **Alameda Central**, a delightful park with many shaded paths and pretty bubbling fountains. In Aztec times this was a busy marketplace and still today there are many vendors selling their wares. The Palacio de Bellas Artes, a handsome building made entirely of white Carrara marble, is so heavy that it is slowly sinking into the soft ground. The palace is multi-purpose. A wonderful selection of paintings and artifacts are beautifully displayed on several floors that wrap around a gallery. Also, the building houses the theater where the famous and colorful **Ballet Folklórico** is performed on Sunday morning and Wednesday evening.

Palacio Nacional: The enormous National Palace dominates one side of the Plaza of the Constitution. This is the site where Montezuma had his palace, which was later replaced by the residence of Hernán Cortés. Continuing its heritage, the magnificent structure is today the president's residence. Much of the building is used for government business, but you must go in to view Diego Rivera's stunning murals depicting the history of Mexico. Obviously Rivera had his personal opinion of the struggle of the Indians against the conquistadors, for throughout his murals the cruelty of the Spaniards is clearly embellished. The fact that long before Cortés arrived, human sacrifice, slavery, and brutality were prevalent is lightly downplayed. However, the paintings are even more intriguing because of Diego Rivera's prejudices and his sense of humor in depicting them. You are apt to miss a lot if you don't know what you are seeing, so try to have a guide or do a little reading in advance. Diego's murals depict the faces of real people and those he didn't like received their due at the end of his paintbrush. It is almost like a puzzle to figure out who everyone is. Look carefully and you will see Cortés's mistress, La Malinche, who is often at his side, sometimes holding their son.

Plaza de La Constitución: This main plaza, or *zócalo*, is at the very heart of the city. It was built upon the ruins of the Templo Mayor, described below. It is massive in size and incredibly impressive. This is one of the biggest public squares in the world and one of the most interesting, with handsome Colonial buildings facing onto it. Two of the most dramatic of these are the magnificent cathedral and the Palacio National (see above). One of the best times to visit the plaza to truly capture its magic is in the early morning. At dawn, the colorful Mexican flag is raised on the towering pole in the center of the square, accompanied by music and lots of pomp and ceremony. At this time of the day the square is at its most beautiful, with soft light and few tourists. Later on, the square becomes far more congested with many vendors, lots of tourists, and the noise and bustle of the throng of the city going about its daily activities. This, too, is a fun time to be here and to feel the pulse of the giant square, which was probably as busy during Aztec times as it is today.

Templo Mayor & Museo del Templo Mayor: The Templo Mayor was the heart of the Aztec empire and must not be missed. The site consists of two parts: the outdoor section, encompassing the excavated, stabilized ruins of the great temple complex, which you can view from a series of elevated walkways; and the wonderful Museum of the Templo Mayor, next to the ruins, where the amazing treasures recovered from the temple are stored and displayed. This beautiful museum tells the story of the temple complex through artifacts and clear interpretive text.

In Aztec times, the great Templo Mayor stood in the sacred walled precinct in the middle of Tenochtitlán. Today this sacred area is the central plaza of modern Mexico City, but before the arrival of the Spanish invaders this was the actual and symbolic center of the ancient capital city and heart of the Aztec world. The immense pyramid, topped with two important temples, dominated the skyline of the metropolis. The elaborate temples were dedicated to the worship of the two gods who represented the power sources of the Aztec empire: Huitzilopochtli and Tlaloc—gods of war and rain, of tribute and sustenance.

Archaeologists knew there was a temple located somewhere near the modern plaza in Mexico City, but buildings constructed in Colonial times covered the structures of ancient Tenochtitlán and for centuries the Templo Mayor lay buried. In February of 1978, two electrical workers digging in the central plaza of the city discovered an immense round carved stone (over 3 meters in diameter) and notified the National Institute of Anthropology and History of Mexico. It was soon determined that the stone was carved with a depiction of the dismembered body of Coyolxauhqui, moon goddess and sister of Huitzilopochtli. It had once been situated at the foot of the pyramid steps below the temple dedicated to Huitzilopochtli. This serendipitous discovery of the spectacular carved stone concretely located the position of the great temple and initiated one of the most impressive archaeological excavations ever to take place in Mexico.

The Templo Mayor project focused on the excavation of the magnificent double pyramid complex and the interpretation of its objects. From the excavations it was clear that the great temple had been constructed in seven stages. The first stage related to the earliest temple built in A.D. 1325 when Tenochtitlán was founded and the last to the final reconstruction or building period that produced the temple seen and recorded by the Spanish in 1519. This last temple was almost completely destroyed by the invading Spaniards, both in defiance of the ancient gods and to provide building stones for the Colonial city. The various rebuildings and embellishments of the original small pyramid into the final massive structure were done by a succession of Aztec kings to honor the gods and to enhance their own power and status in the empire. Archaeologists found many precious offerings buried within the walls of the various construction periods of the pyramid. These offerings were dedicated to Tlaloc, the god of rain, earth, and fertility, who was responsible for the success of the crops that fed Tenochtitlán; and Huitzilopochtli, god of war and the sun, who was responsible for the fruits of warfare that sustained the Aztec state. Items representing water, such as green jade beads, shells, mother-of-pearl ornaments, and bones of aquatic animals, reflect the role of Tlaloc as provider of sustenance for humans. Items such as sacrificial knives, weapons, and skulls relate to Huitzilopochtli as provider of sustenance for the empire itself in the form of sacrificial blood and the wealth of conquest.

The iconography of the tall pyramid of Huitzilopochtli and the magnificent carved stone found at its foot refer to an ancient Aztec legend that tells of the birth of the great god Huitzilopochtli on top of the hill of Coatepec and his defeat of his sister, the moon, and his brothers, the stars. The pyramid represents the hill of Coatepec, and the carved stone found at its base is the image of Coyolxauhqui's dismembered body. The defeat of the stars and moon, symbols of darkness and the night sky, by Huitzilopochtli, warrior of the sun, was the epic act that assured the place of the sun in the daytime sky. This legendary drama was reenacted in special ceremonies on top of the pyramid. A victim was sacrificed, his heart torn from his chest, his blood offered as sustenance to the sun, and his body was thrown down the steep "hill" of the pyramid onto the surface of the stone of Coyolxauhqui, thus re-creating the symbolic battle between the sun and moon.

Tlatelolco: Tlatelolco is a section of the ancient city of Tenochtitlán that was once the center of the Aztec market system. In this great plaza, the last battle for Tenochtitlán was fought between Aztec warriors and the troops of Cortés. In 1965, a plaque was installed in the ruins of Tlatelolco to commemorate the momentous events of the first encounters of the Spanish and the Aztecs. Its inscription that addresses the fatal outcome reads:

On the 13th of August in 1521,
heroically defended by Cuauhtemoc,
Tlatelolco fell to Hernán Cortés.
This was neither a triumph nor a defeat,
it was a painful birth
of the mestizo people
who are the Mexico of today.

This site, now known as the Plaza of the Three Cultures, has the excavated ruins of Tlatelolco's main temple in the foreground and a large, very early, Colonial church and convent behind the temple ruins—with the tall buildings of modern Mexico rising in the background. The Plaza of the Three Cultures symbolizes the three cultures that make up Mexico today.

Xochimilco and the Floating Gardens: Before the Spaniards arrived, the Aztec city of Tenochtitlán was an island in the center of a lake, connected to the mainland by causeways. Around the periphery of the city was a maze of floating islands laced by drainage canals that were laid out in an orderly fashion. These weren't really "floating" islands, but began as rafts piled with rich lake mud and then anchored to the bottom of the lake by fast-growing trees with a deep root system. This is where fresh produce and flowers were grown. Today most of these islands are gone, but a few still exist and continue to produce vegetables and flowers for the city, just as they have for hundreds of years. These floating gardens are located in the outlying suburb of Xochimilco, about an hour's drive from the center. There are tours that go here, or you can hire a guide. The way is quite confusing, so we don't recommend driving yourself. We delayed going to these gardens for many years, both because they were off the beaten path and we expected them to be overly touristy. How wrong we were! Yes, the islands are touristy,

Floating Gardens of Xochimilco

but they are also actual remnants of an ancient civilization that remain in use today. The tourists are basically Mexicans who have come for a family outing.

You climb aboard a brilliantly decorated, flat wooden boat with a Venetian-style "gondolier" who steers the craft through the narrow canals. The waterways are jammed with boats with all sorts of passengers: children having birthday parties, school kids on outings; young lovers who snuggle in a boat by themselves, Mariachis serenading, women selling flowers, photographers who want to snap your picture, vendors selling postcards, entrepreneurs with cold drinks, and even boats with kitchens aboard where women in colorful costumes cook up a hot meal. What a jolly experience, especially on a sunny day—the local color just can't be beat.

The sightseeing suggested above is just a taste of what the city has to offer, but should keep you occupied for several days. If you extend your stay, there is a wealth of other places to visit. The tourist office (corner of Amberes and Londres in the Zona Rosa) or the concierge at your hotel can provide you with more suggestions and information.

SHORT DAY EXCURSIONS FROM MEXICO CITY

The sightseeing excursions below usually involve a day trip from Mexico City. You can take a bus tour from the city or hire a car and driver. Check the difference in price because if you have several people in your group, a car with an English-speaking driver/guide might be almost the same price and is definitely more efficient. The concierge at your hotel should be able to assist you with either.

TEOTIHUACÁN (100 B.C.–A.D.750)

Only 40 kilometers northeast of Mexico City is the spectacular site of **Teotihuacán**, the enormous ruins of the great city that was pre-Hispanic Mexico's most important ancient metropolis. Its immense stone pyramids, temples, palaces, streets, and apartment complexes cover over 20 square kilometers and are best seen and enjoyed by walking through the huge, abandoned city. Either before or after a walking tour, make a stop at the **Teotihuacán Museum**, which highlights and displays the most recent excavation and research at the site.

Because Teotihuacán is conveniently located near Mexico City, it is a favorite target for both tour groups arriving by bus, and individuals arriving by car. Therefore, the site usually swarms with tourists. We strongly recommend that you visit mid-week and get up at the crack of dawn in order to be waiting at the gates when they open first thing in the morning (double check, but when we were there the site opened at 8 am). If you do this, you probably will have several hours to enjoy the ruins in blissful solitude. Note: an alternate option for visiting the ruins is to spend the night at the **Villa Arqueológica Teotihuacán**, a simple but very pleasant hacienda-style hotel which is within easy walking distance of one of the main entrances, Gate 8.

Begun about 100 B.C., the magnificent city reached the height of its importance around A.D. 500. It consisted of approximately 600 pyramids and stretched for 4 kilometers. At that time, with an estimated 200,000 inhabitants, it was the sixth-largest city in the world. Unlike in other ancient Mesoamerican cities, these Teotihuacán city dwellers lived in apartment compounds, some built and decorated with great luxury for the royalty and elite of the city, others (obviously tenements) constructed for the lower classes. These communal dwellings were laid out in *barrios* or blocks according to a well-thought-out city plan with streets, plazas, plumbing, and cisterns for collection of rainwater installed before the construction began. The massive stone pyramids of the sun and moon dominate the Avenue of the Dead (main roadway of the city), their awesome size replicating in cut stone the great mountain peaks of the city's skyline. Their powerful architecture, based on the stepped pyramid style of construction, influenced the ceremonial architecture of almost all the cultures that followed. Cities and cultures as far away as the Maya region to the southeast, Tajin on the Gulf Coast, and Monte Albán in the Valley of Oaxaca reflect contact with Teotihuacán. Much of this influence may have traveled along pre-Hispanic Mexico's great trade routes which brought valuable raw materials such as jade, feathers, and cotton into the city's workshops and carried finished products, including tools made of the local obsidian, to the hinterlands. However, strong new evidence now exists that indicates that Teotihuacán rulers were also powerful warriors and thus military conquest may also have been responsible for the spread of Teotihuacán influence into other regions of Mesoamerica. Walking through the site, one sees everywhere traces of the white stucco and painted fresco murals that once covered both the exterior and interior walls of the buildings with imagery of the gods and rituals. Some of these brightly colored frescos still survive and give us a glimpse of the brilliance of the city at its height.

Around A.D. 600 Teotihuacán began to decline and in the early 700s it was sacked and burned. People gradually abandoned the ancient city but the memory of its power and glory and many of its massive buildings survived. Over the years, other empires arose and seats of power shifted in the valley. The Toltec empire flourished from about A.D.

1000 to 1250, its demise leaving a power vacuum, which was eventually filled by fierce Aztec warriors from the north. However, rulers and priests of these later city-states remained in awe of the massive ruins of the ancient city of Teotihuacán. Over many centuries pilgrimages were made to the abandoned site and legend and memory continued to associate it with past glory. It remained as one of the most sacred places in the Aztec world where it was known as the place where the gods were born.

TULA (c. A.D. 1000–1250)

The site of **Tula,** located about 70 kilometers north of Mexico City, was the legendary home of the Toltecs, who were credited by the cultures that succeeded them with being the greatest warriors and artists of ancient Mexico. Whether this was actually the case is uncertain. The site today is considerably smaller and less impressive than one might expect for such a powerful state. However, warrior themes and iconography depicting death, sacrifice, and war dominate the art that remains. The architecture with its step-style pyramids, stone sculptures, platforms, and temples, and a massive central plaza continue traditions established at the earlier site of Teotihuacán.

LONGER EXCURSIONS EAST OF MEXICO CITY

PUEBLA

Puebla is a delight: a very special town that is another of our favorite Colonial destinations. Although it has grown into a sophisticated city—the fourth largest in Mexico, it still maintains the rich cultural traditions of its past and the charm of a small town. Located 123 kilometers southeast of Mexico City, it can be easily reached by taking an excellent toll road, highway 150, or by public transportation. There are convenient buses from Mexico City plus frequent bus service directly from the Mexico City airport.

For several thousand years before the Spanish Conquest, Puebla was the center of worship of the great god Quetzalcoatl and one of the most important pilgrimage sites in

Mesoamerica. Legend has it that when the Spanish arrived in 1519 they found 365 functioning temples in the city, one for every day of the year. After the Conquest it continued as a religious center, with the growing wealth of its leading Catholic citizens supporting rich monasteries and convents as well as numbers of magnificent churches. Until recently many of the beautiful churches were closed as a result of the bitter Revolution. Under the laws of 1857, church lands were sold and convents closed, although many of them continued to function as meeting places for underground religious orders. Today the churches and convents are being refurbished by wealthy patrons to their original richness and beauty. There are over 60 churches in town, many of them centuries old.

Puebla's downtown area, clustered around the central plaza, just oozes old-world ambiance, with nothing unsightly or modern to mar its purity. Some suggestions for places to visit are given below. All are within walking distance of the main plaza and you will find strolling a delight since many of the streets are closed to cars.

SIGHTSEEING IN PUEBLA

Barrio de Los Artistas: If you like to shop, visit the Barrio de Los Artistas, located at 6 Norte, between 6 and 8 Oriente. This is an upscale, fun place to browse and poke around small shops laden with crafts and art. There are also many small stalls selling really nice-quality goods. Many artists have studios here and there are several antique shops nearby.

Catedral de Nuestra Señora de La Immaculada Concepción: Dating back to 1562 and considered by some to be one of Mexico's most splendid cathedrals, the Cathedral of the Immaculate Conception is tremendously imposing with its twin bell towers, massive doorway, and intricately carved façade. The interior is opulent, with soaring vaulted ceilings, elaborately gilded chapels, baroque altarpieces, and fine oil paintings.

Museo Amparo: Don't miss one our favorite museums, the Amparo, housed in an elegant Colonial mansion. The fine pre-Columbian objects displayed here were once part of a magnificent private collection, but now are on view to the public. Don't miss seeing the beautiful pieces once carefully selected by some of Mexico's true connoisseurs of pre-Hispanic art. The museum was named to honor Mrs. Amparo Espinosa-Iglesias, the late wife of the founder of Bancomer who created the museum.

Museo Regional de Puebla & Casa del Alfeñique: Puebla's Regional Museum is housed in an 18th-century baroque mansion which derives its name from the intricate white plasterwork around the windows and roof that resembles an almond paste called *alfeñique*. On the ground floor is an archaeological museum while the second floor exhibits the furnishings of a Colonial home.

Palacio de Gobierno: Standing on the north side of the central plaza you find the Government Palace, which features inside colorful murals depicting the history of Puebla.

Palacio de Justicia: This handsome 16th-century building with an ornate crest above the doorway is located one block south of the Plaza Principal, across from the south side of the Cathedral.

Plaza Principal (Zócalo): As in most Mexican cities, the central plaza is an ideal place to capture the ambiance of the town. The impressively large one in Puebla is a real beauty with fountains, gardens, shade trees, wrought-iron benches, and a lace of paths. At its center is a statue of the Archangel San Miguel, the patron saint of Puebla. The square is faced on three sides by an arcade that stretches in front of handsome Colonial buildings, and on the fourth side is dominated by the Cathedral of the Immaculate Conception.

Santo Domingo Church: Located two blocks from the plaza, this church is famous for its intimate, 17th-century Rosary Chapel, whose ornate plaster walls, ceilings, and altar are covered with gold leaf.

Talavera Tile: Puebla was the first city in the New World to produce the beautiful, Spanish-style Talavera ceramics which included dinnerware, all kinds of pottery, and, of course, colorful tile. The production was closely controlled by the king and only certain families were granted permission to make the pottery. Many buildings in Puebla reflect the importance of the craft, with façades covered by tile. If you are interested in buying some of this beautiful ceramicware, or would just like to see how it is made, visit the Uriarte Factory (Avenida 4 Poniente 911), a stunning building totally faced with colorful tiles, where the same family has been making the pottery since 1827.

TAJIN

Tajin: Tajin, nestled in the jungle about 295 kilometers east of Mexico City in the state of Veracruz, is one of Mexico's most important archaeological sites. This once great city was founded by the Totonacs who were the first Indians that Cortés encountered when he arrived in Mexico. Tajin, which reached its zenith between 800 and 1150 A.D., is an outstanding destination, but until the highway is complete we recommend this excursion only for those passionate about archaeology since the access from Mexico City involves a difficult two-lane highway that twists and turns over the Papanteca mountain range.

The closest town to the archaeological site is Papantla, located 13 kilometers away. The town, although it has a somewhat interesting central square, is not particularly pretty. There are a few hotels, any one of which would be adequate for an overnight stay, but none with much charm.

SIGHTSEEING SUGGESTIONS IN TAJIN

Museum: Before visiting the site, walk into the museum to orient yourself as to what you will be seeing. The museum, which is right at the entrance, contains many artifacts from the site.

Plaza del Arroyo: As you walk into the site, the first group of buildings is found in the Plaza del Arroyo, the oldest part of the city where you find temples, palaces and ball courts. There are 17 **ball courts** found in Tajin, which attest to the importance of the city. Some of the ball courts are still in excellent condition.

Tajin Chico: Take the path up the hill to Tajin Chico (the little city) where the elite built their homes to take advantage of the cooling breezes.

Piramide de Los Nichos: The most impressive building in Tajin is the Piramide de Los Nichos (Pyramid of the Niches). The pyramid derives from the 365 recesses that cover the sides of the structure. Obviously, these niches had some religious significance, corresponding to the days of the year.

Los Voladores: As soon as you arrive at Tajin, ask what time the Los Voladores "The Sacred Flyers" will perform, because you certainly don't want to miss them. (When we visited, there were two performances a day, one in the morning and one in the afternoon). At the entrance to the ruins, there is tall pole with a platform at the top. Five Totonac Indians, dressed in brilliantly-colored costumes representing eagles, climb to the top of the pole. One of men stays on the platform, dancing on the pinnacle and playing a haunting melody; as the others, each attached to a separate rope, step off into space and slowly descend, spinning to the ground as the ropes unwind. A collection is taken for the performers.

Los Voladores

TLAXCALA

Tlaxcala, located 33 kilometers directly north of Puebla, is a treasure. If you are spending time in the area, either Puebla or Tlaxcala would make a superb base of operations; but, whichever you choose, be sure to visit the other. There is a frequent bus service between them; or it is just a short drive, if you have your own car. Many travelers have never heard of Tlaxcala, perhaps because Puebla is so well known and so close. However, it is one of Mexico's jewels—a stunning, small village that retains its Colonial ambiance without any intrusion of modern buildings. Its central plaza is one of the most beautiful in Mexico. If you want to spend the night, or several nights, you can stay in an excellent hotel facing the square, the Posada San Francisco.

Within months after his ships landed in Veracruz, Cortés continued on to Tlaxcala, making this one of the oldest Colonial towns in Mexico. The Tlaxcalans were deadly enemies of the Aztecs, a hatred Cortés played upon in persuading them to join forces with him as he marched forth in pursuit of Montezuma. (Of course, the fact that the choice he offered was either to join him or be killed might have influenced their decision!) Thus Tlaxcala has special significance in the history of Mexico: without the assistance of their warriors, Cortés might never have defeated Montezuma.

Not only is Tlaxcala brimming with charm, but also there is much to see. Following are some of the places to visit.

SIGHTSEEING IN TLAXCALA

Catedral de Nuestra Señora de La Asunción: Our Lady of the Assumption Cathedral, perched on a hill just a short walk from the Plaza de La Constitución, was the first permanent Catholic church in the Americas. Leaving the southeast corner of the plaza, go through the small square and take the pretty, cobblestone pathway lined by trees that leads steeply uphill to the cathedral. As you walk up the path, look down the hill to your right and you can catch a glimpse of one of Mexico's oldest bullrings. When you enter the cathedral be sure to look up at the splendid ceiling studded with gilded stars, a

Moorish style very popular in Spain at the time of the Conquest. It was here that Cortés had king Xicoténcatl, who had joined forces with him, baptized before he and his Tlaxcalan allies set off to conquer Mexico City. In the cloisters of the church there is a museum of pre-Columbian artifacts.

Bullfighting: There are over 40 haciendas nearby that specialize in the raising of fine fighting bulls. There is a very old, picturesque bullring in town that you can see to the right as you climb the path up to the Nuestra Señora de La Asunción Cathedral. Built in the early 1800s, this is one of Mexico's oldest bullrings and although it is now used only during certain festivals, you can take a tour of it.

Museo de Artisanías: The simple Museum of Handicrafts is just a few blocks west of the central plaza. Here you can see how some of the local handicrafts are made plus visit a small shop where you can buy handmade items.

Museo de La Memoria: The Museum of Memory displays fascinating, rare codices (books) that tell the history of the Tlaxcalan Indians.

Palacio de Gobierno: The Government Palace is a handsome brick building with ornate stone trim that dominates the north side of the plaza. On the ground floor and along the walls of the staircase to the upper level is an impressive series of brilliantly colored murals painted by a local artist, Desiderio Hernándes, depicting the early history of the Indians and the story of the conquest of Mexico by Hernán Cortés. These strong, vibrant, 20th-century paintings were done by a local artist, Desiderio Hermández Xochitiotzin.

Parroquia de San José: The Parish Church of San José, facing a small square just off the northwest side of the Plaza de La Constitución, dates back to the 17th century. This is a real beauty with an ornate entrance, a single spire, and a splendid tiled dome. Be sure to go inside—the cheerful yellow-and-green interior is quite unusual. Look carefully for a 17th-century painting of the baptism of a Tarascan chief and see if you can find Cortés standing nearby with La Malinche, his mistress, at his side.

Plaza de La Constitución: Located in the center of Tlaxcala, this enormous plaza is one of the most stunning in all of Mexico. Surrounded on four sides by handsome Colonial buildings fronted by arcades, the park has majestic, centuries-old shade trees, gurgling fountains, trimmed shrubs, wrought-iron benches, beds of flowers, and, center stage, a bandstand given to the city by King Philip III of Spain.

Santuario de La Virgen de Ocotlán: The Sanctuary of the Virgin of Ocotlán is another "must see" and is an easy 20-minute walk from the heart of town. Wear good walking shoes since you must climb a long flight of steps to visit this very holy shrine, built on the site where, so the story goes, the Virgin appeared in 1541 to a very poor Indian, Juan Diego Bernardino—and told him to take water from a stream that had miraculously appeared to cure his people who were ill. She asked him to send monks into the forest, and when they split open one of the pine trees, they found secreted within it a wooden statue of the Virgin Mary, which is now in the church. Since then, many miracles have been attributed to the Virgin of Ocotlán. Within the sanctuary, which was built in the 18th century in an ornate, baroque style that resembles a wedding cake, are scenes depicting the sequence of the events following the appearance of the Virgin.

Shopping: In addition to sightseeing, Tlaxcala is a handicraft town. There is much to buy here including beautiful Talavera pottery, woolen goods, hand-woven rugs, woven baskets, onyx figurines, and woodcarvings.

SIGHTSEEING OUTSIDE OF PUEBLA OR TLAXCALA

Cacaxtla: Another outstanding archaeological site highly recommended, as a side trip from either Puebla or Tlaxcala, is the city of Cacaxtla (A.D. 600–900). If you are in the least interested in delving into the rich accomplishments of the Indians prior to the arrival of the Spanish, this site should not be missed. Wear comfortable shoes because there is a lot of walking involved in this adventure. You can hire a taxi to take you to the ruins or, if you drive yourself, there is a place to leave your car. First visit the museum, which displays many of the original artifacts found in the site plus reproductions of some of the paintings you will see. From the museum it is about a 1-kilometer walk on a well-defined path to the site of the ancient city perched on top of the nearby hill. The site is covered by a gigantic corrugated-steel roof to protect it from the destructive elements of sun and rain. What make this ruin so exceptional are the murals, which rank among some of the best-preserved frescos in Mexico. You can still see huge paintings on some of the walls showing life-sized warriors vividly dressed in jaguar costumes and fancy feather headdresses. These amazing works of art, probably dating back to A.D. 700–900, decorate numerous walls of the ancient city and, to varying degrees, reflect Mayan influence, since similarities are seen between these and the magnificent murals at the site of Bonampak. It is astonishing that the colors are in such excellent condition. This site is truly a treasure.

Cholula: While in Puebla or Tlaxcala you will certainly want to visit the nearby archaeological site of Cholula, lying just on the outskirts of the town. This great pyramid of ancient Cholula (1500 B.C.–A.D. 1521) was the largest in the New World. Originally dedicated to the god Quetzalcoatl, it looks like an immense hill but is really a massive man-made edifice built and rebuilt over many centuries during the pre-Hispanic Period. Today it has a Colonial church, the Santuario de Los Remedios, sitting on top. This massive pyramid and most of the ancient site of Cholula are, like Mexico City, covered by Colonial buildings. However, the ancient pyramid is well worth a visit and while there is little remaining of the site itself, a guide will take you through dark tunnels deep into the bowels of the pyramid, where you will be able to see the evidence of the various building stages and cultural levels connected with this vast structure.

LONGER EXCURSIONS SOUTH OF MEXICO CITY

CUERNAVACA

Cuernavaca, located 90 kilometers southwest of Mexico, is a popular weekend getaway for many wealthy Mexicans, some who have sumptuous second homes here. Due to its excellent climate, Cuernavaca is called "The City of Eternal Spring" and has been a favorite retreat since the time of the Aztec emperors—even Hernán Cortés and Emperor Maxmillian had homes here. The city has a strong Colonial heritage, but traffic congestion and crowded, unkempt streets detract a bit from its ambiance. You will find that most of the mansions and lovely hotels hide away behind high walls, displaying a lush beauty with gardens and inner courtyards once you enter through the thick, wooden doorways. If you want to stay overnight, or indulge in a delicious meal in an exquisite garden setting, one of our favorite hotels, Las Manañitas, is highly recommended.

SIGHTSEEING IN CUERNAVACA

Plaza de Armas: Cuernavaca's main plaza is faced by several Colonial buildings including the Palacio de Cortés and the Palacio de Gobierno, but the Colonial style in the area of the plaza is not pristine since modern buildings managed to slip in before architectural controls were put in place.

Cathedral: Cuernavaca's cathedral is within a walled complex of churches that includes not only the 16th-century cathedral, but also the 18th-century Templo de La Tercera Orden de San Francisco and, the 19th-century Capilla del Carmen.

Palacio de Cortés: The Spanish king bequeathed 30 cities to Cortés, including Cuernavaca, which was supposedly his favorite, and here he built a mansion known as the Palace of Cortés just off the main square. This is now a fine museum displaying many photos of the Revolution, costumes, arms, and splendid murals by Diego Rivera. The exhibitions are well displayed and many have explanations in both English and Spanish.

Museo Robert Brady: This museum, housed in a lovely Colonial home that was owned by Robert Brady, contains over 1,300 diverse pieces of his art. Brady, born in the backwaters of Fort Dodge, Iowa, settled in Cuernavaca in 1960. He was a decorator who loved antiques, sculptures, and paintings and had a fabulous, eclectic collection of art and handicrafts from all over the world. The home is just as he left it. It is on a pretty side street between the cathedral and the Palace of Cortés.

TAXCO

Taxco, which is designated as a national monument, is one of Mexico's quaintest Colonial towns. Being close to Mexico City and on the route to Acapulco, it has many tourists and is a bit more commercial than some other silver towns that are more off the beaten path. Nevertheless, the charm of this small town, squeezed in amongst barren hills, still prevails. The setting is picture perfect, with narrow, cobbled streets twisting up and down the hill, lined by whitewashed buildings topped by rustic tiled roofs. The colorful plaza in the center hugs one of the few level pieces of ground in town. The church is a masterpiece.

One would never expect to find a town in such a precarious setting, but the reason is obvious: silver. Hernán Cortés was constantly on the alert for rumors of gold and silver, hoping to discover mines so that he could please his king by enriching the coffers of Spain. When he learned that the Aztecs traded in silver from the Taxco area, he sent his engineers to investigate and soon mining was under way.

SIGHTSEEING IN TAXCO

Museum of William Spratling: This museum, located two blocks from the Plaza Bora, on Calle Porfirio A. Delgado, features William Spratling's collection of silver and pre-Hispanic art. (Read more about Spratling below.)

Plaza Borda: This small plaza in the center of town is a photographers' delight—the epitome of what one imagines the perfect Mexican square should look like. It is tiny (there isn't much room to spare in Taxco), but as pretty as can be with shade trees, the typical bandstand, whitewashed buildings with tiled roofs, and wrought-iron balconies everywhere you look.

Santa Prisca Church: One would never dream of finding such an incredibly beautiful church as Santa Prisca tucked away in a small mining town, but then most towns didn't have such a wealthy benefactor as José de La Borda. When the word trickled to Europe that silver had been found in the New World, a Frenchman by the name of José de La Borda packed his bags and rushed (as fast as you could rush in the 18th century) to Mexico to make his fortune. Finding nothing, he was about to give up and head for home, when his horse slipped and exposed a rich vein of silver. To thank God for this miracle, Borda built the Santa Prisca church, where his son Manuel became priest. No expense was spared and the church is a jewel. Its twin bell towers and ornate dome have become a landmark of Taxco, repeatedly seen on postcards and posters.

Shopping: It seems every building has its silver shop. You cannot go more than a few steps before finding another one (at last count there were more than 200). Many sell silver items at the same price, and in similar style, to those found in resort shops throughout Mexico, but what is special, and can't be found elsewhere, are the shops where individual pieces are designed. Many of these are exquisite, and not inexpensive. The reason for the prolific number of skilled craftsmen here is partly due to the American ambassador to Mexico in the 1920s, Dwight Morrow (father of Anne Morrow, wife of Charles Lindberg). He was a dedicated statesman who went far beyond the line of duty in trying to improve the lot of the local people. Morrow had a friend, William Spratling, a young professor from New Orleans, who fell in love with Mexico. Morrow persuaded him to stay and set up workshops to teach jewelry design to the artisans in Taxco. This he did, and Taxco is now known worldwide for the skill of its designers.

Silver Museum: Just across from Santa Prisca is a silver museum run by a local silversmith. At first glance it seems more like a shop, but what is interesting is that on exhibit are award-winning pieces of jewelry. It is fascinating to see the superb designs and craftsmanship in these lovely pieces of art.

SIGHTSEEING OUTSIDE OF CUERNAVACA OR TAXCO

Malinalco: Located west of Cuernavaca, the impressive hilltop site of Malinalco (A.D. 500–1521) was inhabited over the years by various groups of people but reached its peak during the final years of the Aztec Period (c. A.D. 1475–1521). The ruins are reached by climbing almost a mile up a winding, well-maintained pathway that offers beautiful views of the valley and the modern town of Malinalco. The location of the site at the top of a defensible hill suggests that over time one of its roles must have been as a military fortress; however, after its capture by the Aztecs in 1476, it seems to have become a sanctuary or ritual home for the Eagle and Jaguar warriors, the elite fighting units of the Aztec military.

There are only a few buildings at the site, the most impressive being an amazing pyramid/temple cut out of the solid rock face. One climbs the pyramid steps and enters the temple through the open mouth of a massive serpent that serves as the entryway to a round, inner chamber. This dark inner room may have been used for secret initiation ceremonies or military rites. Its central altar and semicircular bench are decorated with sculptured stone images of eagles and jaguars. Other buildings in this hilltop complex are thought to have been meeting halls, chambers for ritual events, and storage facilities.

In the modern village below the fortress-like site is an early (1537) Augustinian monastery and church built of cut stone carried down from the archaeological site of Malinalco. This early fortress-church has an interesting open chapel with the Stations of the Cross placed around its large enclosed courtyard.

Xochicalco: To the southwest of Cuernavaca you find the site of the pre-Hispanic city of Xochicalco (c. A.D. 650–900), one of several that rose to power after the fall of the great metropolis of Teotihuacán. The disintegration of that immense city left a power vacuum throughout the region and various smaller city-states, Xochicalco among them, challenging each other for power. The city was situated on a hilltop overlooking the approaches of the ancient trade routes that ran west towards present-day Acapulco, south to the Valley of Puebla, and east to the vast Valley of Mexico. At its height, the city held perhaps 10,000 to 15,000 people and its major function must have been the control of access along the long-distance routes that carried precious goods throughout pre-Columbian Mexico.

The elite precinct built on top of the hill is one of the most recently excavated parts of the site. In this section of the city are found the large storage rooms, ball courts, palaces, and temples of the rulers of Xochicalco. This well-protected precinct was situated to take advantage of the beautiful views across the valley, and the cooling breezes during the hot summer months. It was heavily fortified with thick, fortress-like walls, ramps, and defendable staircases. These massive fortifications can be seen from far across the valley and clearly controlled access to the site.

The commoners lived in the lower sections of the city, where a number of large temple complexes, pyramids, and buildings are found. Here, on an artificially leveled hill, one of the largest ball courts in Mesoamerica is located. In addition, around the site and in the surrounding valley, terraced hillsides indicate the use of intensive agricultural techniques.

The site, like several others of the same time period, appears to have been inhabited or at least strongly influenced by several different contemporary cultures. Most obvious is the Mayan influence, which is clearly seen in the elaborate decoration of the Temple of the Feathered Serpent. This unusual stepped pyramid is carved with a series of Mayan dignitaries each seated within the coils of a great feathered serpent that stretches around the pyramid base. An underground chamber at the site is now recognized as a solar observatory marking the sun's zenith in May and July, dates that were also important in the Mayan calendar, and may reflect further Mayan influence at Xochicalco. A new museum has recently been built at the site and is well worth a visit. It not only exhibits artifacts recovered from the excavations, but also presents the results of the recent research.

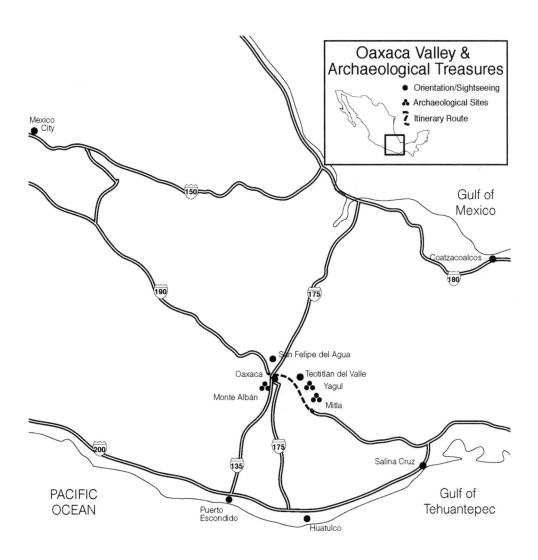

Oaxaca Valley & Archaeological Treasures

Monte Albán, Grand Plaza

Oaxaca, tucked high in a fertile valley 485 kilometers southeast of Mexico City, is one of our favorite places in Mexico. Without a doubt it is one of the most colorful, best-preserved Colonial cities in the country, with the added bonus of a lovely climate year round. It also offers visitors a glimpse of a city and region that truly exhibit three distinct faces of Mexican culture—the ancient archaeological ruins, the wonderful Spanish Colonial art and architecture, and the skilled craftsmen and artists in the surrounding villages. Like the valleys of Puebla and Mexico City, the history and prehistory of the Oaxaca Valley extends far back in time to the end of the last ice age when hunters roamed the area in search of game. In fact, Oaxaca is one of the longest continually inhabited regions in Mexico. Archaeological evidence demonstrates that the ancestors of the modern Zapotec people were contemporaries of the early Olmecs (1500 B.C.–A.D. 400) whose cultural influence spread from the Gulf Coast of Mexico throughout much of Mesoamerica. Today villages in the valley and its surrounding mountains remain the home of the Zapotecs and later arriving Mixtec peoples whose languages, costumes, and traditions are still a significant factor in modern Oaxaca. Amazingly, over half of the population still speaks their own dialect.

An added bonus of Oaxaca is that its wealth lies not only in archaeological sites and fabulous Colonial buildings, but also in the rich selection of places to stay: some of the loveliest hotels and bed & breakfasts in Mexico are found here.

There are direct flights from Mexico City to Oaxaca, as well as deluxe bus service (which takes about six hours). If you are driving, it is about five hours via the toll road. Unless you have your own car, don't bother with a rental car when you arrive. Instead, take a taxi to your hotel and from there, walk to see the sights. One of the joys of Oaxaca is just wandering its quaint streets. The places we highlight within town are close enough to walk to from all of the hotels we recommend, except for the Hacienda los Laureles, which is located nearby in San Felipe del Agua.

RECOMMENDED PACING: We suggest five days in Oaxaca, though a week would be preferable so that you could relax and enjoy the ambiance of this Colonial jewel at leisure. You need three days to explore the city, and two more to take side trips to the nearby archaeological sites and local craft villages. There are truly many wonderful places to visit, both in the city and in the surrounding valley. Detailed below are some of our favorites.

COLONIAL OAXACA

Basilica de Nuestra Señora de La Soledad (Church of the Virgin of Solitude), Avenida Independencia 107: This beautiful 16th-century church, whose ornate façade is studded with statues, is most famous for its shrine containing Oaxaca's patron saint, the Virgin of Solitude. This statue of the Virgin mysteriously appeared in the pack of a mule that died where the church now stands. The statue, which supposedly has special healing powers, is greatly revered and people come from afar to ask for miracles.

Casa de Juárez (Home of Juárez), Garcia Vigil 609: This is the home where one of Mexico's most famous leaders, Benito Juárez, lived as a servant during his youth and the furnishings reflect the style of that period (early 19th century). Benito Juárez, a Zapotec Indian born in the nearby village of San Pablo Guelato, was an outstanding man of great intelligence. Orphaned at the age of 3, he was educated by village priests, who must have done a remarkable job, for he went on to become a leader of Indian rights and, in 1858, Mexico's president.

Oaxaca, Santo Domingo

Museo de Arte Contemporáneo de Oaxaca (Contemporary Art Museum of Oaxaca), Macedonio Alcalá: This collection of contemporary art is housed in one of Oaxaca's most historic buildings, the 16th-century Casa de Cortés, supposedly commissioned by Cortés himself. Here you find paintings of some of Oaxaca's most famous artists including Rodolfo Morales, Francisco Toledo, Rodolfo Nieto, Rufino Tamayo, and Francisco Gutierrez.

Museo de Las Culturas de Oaxaca (Museum of Culture of Oaxaca): This striking museum is connected to and part of the Santo Domingo Church, being housed on two floors of the former monastery attached to the church. (If you have visited Oaxaca previously, do not be confused—it used to be called the Museo Regional.) Here you find a breathtaking collection of artifacts gathered from excavations at nearby archaeological sites. The most spectacular display consists of more than 500 stunning pieces of silver, jade, gold, and turquoise that were found in Monte Albán in just one tomb, number 7. A rich collection of archaeological and ethnographical objects from all over the state of Oaxaca are also exhibited here. One room of special interest is that featuring a collection of pre-Hispanic musical instruments, attesting to the sophistication of the early Mixtec culture.

Plaza de Armas: This tree-studded main plaza in the heart of Oaxaca is truly a gem. For the price of a beer or a cup of coffee you can sit at a café table and watch the colorful world of Oaxaca—with Indian, *mestizo*, Spanish, and gringo faces passing through the busy plaza. You could sit endlessly, time slipping by, with never a boring moment. Totally closed to traffic, the square is always filled with people and is the social center of town. Here you find non-stop action: vendors selling everything imaginable, including huge bunches of brilliantly colored balloons; students on their way to school; tourists basking in the sun; men on their way to work; children splashing in the fountain; roaming mariachis; mothers nursing their babies; shoeshine men buffing shoes to a brilliance; old men snoozing on benches; pretty girls dressed in colorful, native costumes; and, unfortunately, beggars asking for a few coins reflecting the poverty that sadly underlies much of rural Mexico. If you are hungry, you can buy an ice cream from one of the many stalls or if you have a sense of adventure, try one of Oaxaca's specialties, *chapulines* (fried grasshoppers). This lively square is the perfect place to start your sightseeing or to take a break between museums. There are many excellent restaurants overlooking the square.

Rufino Tamayo Museo de Arte Prehispánico (Rufino Tamayo Museum of Pre-Hispanic Art), Avenida Morelos 503: Four blocks from the Plaza de Armas is a museum you must not miss—its stunning archaeological collection is outstanding, with over 1,000 pre-Hispanic works of art beautifully displayed in a handsome mansion. The collection was given to the town by Rufino Tamayo, a famous artist who was born in Oaxaca. Since his death, more pieces of art have been added.

Santo Domingo Church: Santo Domingo, built by the Dominicans in 1670, is a dazzling baroque church. The exterior is handsome with twin bell towers crowned with brightly colored tiles, but there is little hint on the outside of the opulence within. It was here that Pope John Paul II blessed a huge crowd when he visited the city. Like so many Catholic churches in Mexico, its sanctuary and convent were partially destroyed, and its treasures stolen during the days of the Revolution. The interior was particularly badly defaced, and its gold leaf and rich decoration dismantled. However, the church has been restored to its original magnificence with an ornate façade, incredible golden interior, and splendid paintings and murals. The lovely, small chapel dedicated to the Virgin is not to be missed.

SIDE TRIPS FROM OAXACA

When it's time to take your day trips, hire a car with an English-speaking driver who is qualified as a guide (ask your hotel to recommend a reliable person). The cost is not exorbitant—especially when considering you are saving the expense of a car rental—and well worth the convenience and greater appreciation of what you see. The sightseeing on the following pages is highly recommended.

MONTE ALBÁN

Because it is so close to Oaxaca (less than a 30-minute drive) and such a superb site, we suggest a visit to **Monte Albán** (500 B.C.–A.D. 700) as your first taste of the many archaeological sites around Oaxaca.

Monte Albán, Ball Court

Get up early and try to be the first ones there to enjoy the beautiful ruin in the early-morning sun, before the busloads of tourists arrive. This imposing site is one of Mexico's most spectacular ancient cities, and also one of its oldest. Monte Albán sits on top of a mountain, leveled off long ago by the indigenous Zapotecs to serve as a plateau setting for their great city. The view from the top is particularly lovely just after the rainy season when the foliage is green and the flowering trees begin to bloom. This impressive archaeological site has one of the largest plazas in pre-Columbian Mexico, stretching the whole length of the man-made plateau with massive pyramids, temples, and palaces at each end of the immense space and along the sides. In addition, the site has many underground tombs built beneath the patio floors of houses, an observatory, a particularly beautiful ball court, and a fine new museum. The city was founded about 500 B.C. when populations from various smaller sites in the region came together at this easily fortified high point overlooking the valley. Here started construction on a city that, by the early centuries A.D., had become a powerful state that was in contact, probably through trade, with the other civilizations of Mesoamerica.

By about A.D. 700, the site was abandoned and people moved from the mountaintop back to the farmlands in the valley, settling once again in smaller villages. However, the site itself survived, and the Mixtec peoples who followed the Zapotecs as a power in the Valley of Oaxaca used the terraced mountainsides of the older city as a place of burial for their important families. In fact, the richest tomb ever excavated in Mexico was found here in 1970. The golden necklaces, turquoise mosaic masks, crystal cups, and shell jewelry from tomb 7, now in the museum at the Church of Santo Domingo in Oaxaca, indicate that it may have been a royal tomb of the Mixtec kings.

MITLA

Reserve a full day to visit **Mitla** (A.D. 900–1521), since there are places to see along the way. Mitla is located 46 kilometers east of Oaxaca on highway 190, and your first (quick) stop en route is in Santa María del Tule, 9 kilometers outside Oaxaca. Here you find the famous El Tule Tree standing next to the church, just off the road—and what a tree it is! Over 2,000 years old, the cypress has a massive trunk and a sweeping canopy of leaves. Many of the redwoods in California are impressive, but El Tule supposedly has the widest girth of any tree in the world.

Mitla, Design Detail

After a brief stop, continue directly on to Mitla. At the ruins there are rows of stalls with vendors ardently selling all kinds of crafts and souvenirs. There is also a church here that is built from stones taken from the site. These ruins are totally different from those at Monte Albán. Whereas Monte Albán has a glorious setting, in splendid isolation on the top of a hill—Mitla sits in the valley, embraced by the town. The site was built by the Mixtecs who succeeded the Zapotecs as the major power in the Oaxaca region. Mitla was still a flourishing religious and civil center when the Spanish arrived.

There are two main parts of the site to visit. The first is the Church Group, so named because the Spaniards built their church in the middle of the courtyard. This was a clever maneuver since they also pinched the stones from the temples to build the church you see today. Don't spend much time here since the Columns Group is far more interesting. Here you find examples of the special feature of Mitla: its intricate geometric designs. There are 14 geometrical patterns in all, with each building embellished with its own artwork. To create these patterns, small pieces of stone were cut and set into the wall. The zigzag pattern in many of the designs is frequently duplicated in their woven designs.

YAGUL

After leaving Mitla, retrace your way back towards Oaxaca on the same road. After a short distance, at the sign, turn right for about a kilometer to **Yagul**, positioned on the slope of a gentle hill. This is a small site, but really worth seeing. One of its charms is that there are usually few tourists there. If you are lucky, you might be the only ones about. At the top of the ruins is a fortress, below which is a palace with six courtyards linked by intricate passages. Yagul is also noted for its superb ball court, one of the largest and best preserved in the Oaxaca Valley.

TEOTITLÁN DEL VALLE

After leaving Yagul, continue on towards Oaxaca. Watch for the turnoff to the right to **Teotitlán del Valle**, a craft town located about 4 kilometers from the main road. There are many craft villages in the area, but Teotitlán del Valle, which specializes in fine rugs, is one of our favorites. Here not only can you see the weavers at work and buy directly from them, but you can observe the entire process from gathering the wool, then carding and spinning it—to making cochineal, the amazing red dye. This brilliant dye is made from crushing the bodies of thousand of tiny insects that live on nopal cactus leaves. Often you can see children gathering the bugs in containers for the use of the weavers. This process for making cochineal dates way back to the early pre-Columbian years. With the arrival of the Spanish in 1521, the dye remained popular and became in great demand by weavers in Europe. It is one of the continuities that so intriguingly still surround life in Mexico.

If you want to stop for lunch and are in no rush, you might enjoy the **Restaurant Tlamanalli**, located on the approach road into town. The service can be frustratingly slow, but the three sisters (costumed in local dress) who own it and prepare the food are extremely gracious. The fresh corn tortillas for your meal are patted out by hand and cooked on a *comal* (a round, ceramic cooking platter placed over a charcoal fire), while you watch.

If you have the time or inclination to continue your explorations around Oaxaca, there are small ruins tucked throughout the valley plus many towns where you can see and buy excellent crafts. If you are looking for the area's handsome black pottery, San Bartulo Coyotepec is the place to go. For fabulous cottons woven on the traditional back-strap looms, Santo Tomas Jalietza is tops. When it is time to leave, you can return to Mexico City, or perhaps, link with another of the itineraries we suggest.

Balloon Lady in the Park, Oaxaca

Oaxaca Valley & Archaeological Treasures

Mayan Mysteries &
A Loop of the
Yucatán Peninsula

● Orientation/Sightseeing
♣ Archaeological Sites
┇ Itinerary Route

Isla Mujeres
Cancún
Puerto Morelos
Punta Maroma
Playa Xcalacoco
Mérida
Xcanatún
Tixkokob
Izamal
Playa del Carmen
Xcaret
Rio Celestún
Biosphere
Reserve
Celestún
Katanchel
180
Valladolid
Riviera Maya
Chichén
Itzá
Santa Rosa
Temozon
Cobá
Oxkintok
Uxmal
Tulum
Balancanoné
Caves
Cozumel
Campeche
Kabah
Xel-Há
Sayil
Labná
Uayamon
Ednzá
Gulf of
Mexico
Dzibanche
Costa Maya
Champotón
Kinchua
Becán
Bacalar
261
186
Xpujil
Chetumal
180
Ciudad del
Carmen
Escárcega
Chicanná
Kohúnlich
Bahia de
Campeche
186
Calakmul
BELIZE
Villahermosa
Palenque
Cascadas
de Agua Azul
Ocosingo
Yaxchilán
Caribbean
Sea
Toniná
GUATEMALA
199
190
San Cristóbal
de Las Casas

129

Mayan Mysteries &
A Loop of the Yucatán Peninsula

Tulum

In all of Mexico there is no place more enchanting than the **Yucatán Peninsula**, the country's southeast corner that swings up like the tail of a fish with one side facing the Gulf of Mexico and the other facing the Caribbean. Tucked onto this peninsula is a treasure chest of delights: splendid stretches of sugary-fine, white-sand beaches; crystal-clear, turquoise water; the second-largest coral reef in the world; superb snorkeling; incredible scuba diving; deep-sea fishing; expansive nature reserves including remarkable bird sanctuaries; vast jungles; appealing, small islands nestled just offshore; rich Mayan culture evident throughout; women still wearing typical white, gaily embroidered dresses; wonderful crafts including intricate, handmade hammocks; charming Colonial towns; quaint fishing villages; splendid 17th-century haciendas (many converted to stunning small hotels that are featured in our guide); luxurious resorts; romantic, secluded hideaways. And, adding icing to the cake, the area is studded with breathtaking Mayan ruins—an archaeologist's dream.

This itinerary puts great emphasis on the wealth of Mayan sites, cloaked in the mysteries and glories of one of the world's great civilizations, which has faded into memory. It would be a pity to come to this niche of Mexico without visiting at least a few of these once-grand cities. Even if your idea of the perfect vacation is napping in a hammock on the beach (an option explored in our itinerary *Places to Play in the Sun: The Mexican Caribbean*), sneak away at least one day to visit a Mayan site.

There can a bit of confusion when one speaks of the Yucatán, since Yucatán is both the name of the peninsula and also one of the states within it. In total, there are three states that make up the peninsula: Campeche, Quintana Roo, and Yucatán. This itinerary makes a loop, passing through all three, slipping briefly into the adjacent state of Chiapas to visit Palenque, a remarkable Mayan ruin that can't be missed, and the San Crisóbal de Las Casas, a colorful city with a rich Mayan heritage.

Following is some background information about the Mayan civilization and the Yucatán Peninsula to enrich what you will be experiencing en route.

THE MAYAN CIVILIZATION

One of the most advanced cultures of the pre-Columbian World was that of the Classic Maya. Technologically, they were a Stone-Age people, lacking metal tools, draft animals, or knowledge of the wheel; but their artistic and intellectual achievements rank them with the other great civilizations of antiquity. The flowering of their culture encompassed a period from about A.D. 250–900. This span of years is defined for us by dates carved on large stone monuments known as *stele*. These stele are found at numerous Mayan sites and their dates can be read and correlated with our modern calendar. The earliest known so far is A.D. 292 and the last is A.D. 889. These two dates mark the beginning and the end of the 600 years of the Classic Period.

The Mayan people themselves neither begin nor end with this designation of time. For 2,000 years they lived in the jungles and mountain valleys of the region creating a base of art and cultural traditions from which the Classic Period developed. Today over 4,000,000 people of Mayan descent still inhabit their original area, a geographical region that includes all the Yucatán Peninsula, Guatemala, and Belize, portions of Honduras and El Salvador, and parts of the Mexican states of Chiapas and Tabasco. While environment and climate vary widely, the culture itself was remarkably uniform, indicating close contacts and shared values during the Classic Period.

Maya Classic civilization has intrigued scholars and laymen alike since its rediscovery about 150 years ago, but only recently have archaeologists begun to uncover the reality rather than the myth of this ancient culture. For many years the Maya were thought to have been a peaceful group of talented farmers, devoted to religion and led by brilliant, intellectual priests whose primary concerns were astronomy and the recording of time. Recent discoveries now challenge these assumptions. The Mayan elite may indeed have

Chacmool

been the intellectual giants of their era and artistic and religious activities were certainly intimately interwoven in the culture. Realistically, however, the Mayan world was composed of small and large warlike states with constantly changing alliances based on military action and royal intermarriage. Their economic and demographic growth was built on secular activities such as trade and exchange, tribute payments, and military conquest. Even Mayan religious practices were not peaceful, simple ceremonies as previously thought. Instead we now know that they were elaborate costumed rituals, which included blood letting, brutality, and human sacrifices—all dedicated to demanding gods and the rulers who were their earthly representatives.

As evidence of the bloody religious ceremonies practiced by the Maya and other cultures in Mesoamerica, archaeologists found at some Mayan sites an almost life-size sculpture called a *chacmool*. This is a finely carved stone figure reclining on its back with knees drawn up in front. It was here that the heart was cut from the sacrificial victim and probably placed on the stone disk on the chacmool's abdomen as an offering to the gods.

Like many other early civilizations, the Maya had an overwhelming concern with death and the afterlife and they buried their rulers and elite with elaborate gifts of pottery, jade, and stone. These artifacts, along with recent major advancements in reading the Mayan hieroglyphic texts and meticulous archaeological excavations, have done much to expand our understanding of the ancient Maya and their way of life.

There are a number of specific traits and accomplishments of the Classic Period that set it apart from the Pre-Classic and Post-Classic Mayan Periods. Among these are: a sophisticated calendrical system that can be correlated with our modern calendar; a hieroglyphic writing system; the erection of tall stone stele to commemorate actual events in time; the use and possible invention of the concept of zero; the development of an elaborate and complicated style of art; and the construction of monumental stone architecture using a corbel arch.

Architecture is probably the most important, and certainly the most visible form of Mayan art and creativity. While sites on the seacoasts, in the mountain valleys, and on the Yucatán Peninsula are fairly easily seen and visited, massive stone ruins of ancient cities still lie buried deep in the jungle. Structures at almost all Mayan sites include palaces, pyramids, temples, roads, reservoirs, markets, and ball courts—all built of stone and covered originally with a coating of white stucco and bright paint.

Palenque, El Palacio

The magnificent high-stepped pyramids that rise above the landscape were once surmounted by temples dedicated to the Mayan gods, and often hidden within their depths are the rich tombs of Mayan kings. At large sites, these immense pyramids usually dominate both ends of central plazas with lower platforms supporting the palaces and public building associated with them. *Sacbes* (stucco-covered stone roadways) connect regional sites, and were probably used for commerce and trading caravans, movements of troops, and for ritual processionals. A ritual ball game was played on stone courts found all over Mesoamerica. In the Mayan area the game took on cosmic significance relating to the ongoing struggle between the forces of the day and night (the sun and moon, good and evil, etc.). In addition, the actual origin myth of the Maya was based on the outcome of a game of ball. In the Mayan book, the *Popol Vuh*, two young twin ball players descend to the underworld to play a game of ball against the gods of pestilence, famine, and death. They eventually defeated these gods of darkness on the underworld ball court of Xibalba. Their hard-won game assures the victory of light and life over the forces of darkness and death. The ritual sport often ended with the decapitation of the captain of the losing team; numerous depictions of this event are seen on painted and carved pottery, colorful murals, and the carved friezes on the walls of the ball court at the site of Chichén Itzá.

Though architecture may be the most impressive of Mayan achievements, other artifacts also offer concrete evidence of the skill of Mayan craftsmen and artists. These highly trained professionals were probably attached to ruling families or ceremonial centers and held special status in Mayan society. With a few recently discovered exceptions, artists and craftsmen remain anonymous. Most creations were unsigned by their makers and the artist was primarily important as an instrument through which the rulers and gods were honored. These talented artists used various media to create beautiful objects. Stonemasons carved tall limestone stele with figures of rulers wearing the elaborate feather headdresses and jade ornaments that were status symbols among Mayan elite. Scribes carved or painted hieroglyphic texts and calendrical information on stone monuments, walls of buildings and the pages of *codices* (Mayan books). Potters decorated the smoothed surfaces of ceramic vessels with scenes from the underworld, activities of gods and kings, and repetitive hieroglyphics texts. It has been suggested that the primary function of some artists may have been as scribes, craftsmen who painted the codices, which were once abundant in the Mayan world. All but four of these books have been lost due to damp climate and to their intentional destruction by the invading Spanish conquerors. Nevertheless, enough evidence remains to indicate strong resemblances between these lost books and the scenes and hieroglyphs painted on Mayan burial ceramics and on the walls of the ancient buildings.

The Maya were also highly skilled workers in jade, shell, flint, and bone. Jade was the most precious of all materials to the Maya. They were especially fond of the emerald-green or imperial jade and carved it into bead necklaces, masks, pendants, and ear-spools. Gold and other metals were not worked by the Classic Maya, but later when gold was known and used during the post-Classic Period, jade remained the more valued and preferred material. The Classic Maya used the same hieroglyphic symbols to mean jade, water, and precious—indicating the gemstone's supreme value in their life and religious activities.

Other artifacts made of perishable materials are now lost from the archaeological record but can be identified from depictions on ceramics and stone. Finely woven and decorated textiles, paper ornaments, bark-paper books, and many objects carved in wood were documented in this way, but have not survived the damp, tropical climate.

After about A.D. 900, the Classic Maya cities located in the tropical jungle region collapsed. In other Mayan regions, such as the Yucatán Peninsula, Mayan traditions continued, but the magnificent sites of this lowland area were abandoned to the jungle and the great art of the period ceased. Rulers, dignitaries, and priests disappeared and the elaborate religious ceremonies were no longer performed in the temples and plazas created for them. The reasons for the collapse are still unclear. Possibly constant warfare, overpopulation, drought, epidemics, and military invasion may all have been contributing factors. Whatever the causes, the collapse was so complete that some of the lowland tropical areas once occupied by this civilization were only sparsely inhabited until about 50 years ago. Yet this vanished civilization is not truly "lost." Archaeologists continue to work and uncover artifacts and information from the once-forgotten jungle sites. Magnificent works of art still remain to speak to us across the centuries of the culture and people of the Classic Maya world.

THE YUCATÁN

The Mayan cities of the Yucatán Peninsula survived for over 300 years after the fall of the heartland sites. While the Yucatán sites shared fully in the Classic Mayan traditions, their location on important trade routes and an influx of population and new ideas (some no doubt from the collapsed jungle cities), apparently encouraged continuing prosperity.

The Yucatán Peninsula is a limestone shelf. At the base of the peninsula are Mexican jungles and the frontiers of Guatemala and Belize. Much of the Yucatán is devoid of ground water such as springs or rivers, and is dependent for its supply of water on *cenotes* (fallen limestone sink holes which reveal underground rivers) or catchment systems for preserving heavy seasonal rainfall. As might be expected, the major sites of this geographical area occur where fertile soils can be supplied with water by the use of *chultuns* (man-made cistern systems) or where cenotes occur naturally.

Chichén Itzá, El Caracol

During the pre-Classic Period (600 B.C.–A.D. 300) there were a number of important early cities in the Yucatán. These were sites with massive architecture and sophisticated water control systems, such as Calakmul, Edzná, and Dzibilchaltún. They were of major importance in establishing the artistic and intellectual traditions on which Classic Maya culture was built.

Throughout the following Classic Period (A.D. 300–900) some of these Yucatán sites faded but the area still remained a part of the amazing cultural development of such well known Mayan jungle cities as Tikal, Palenque, and Copan. Amazingly, the Yucatán region did not share in the collapse of the sites in the heartland area. Indeed, we now know that the rise of the great Puuc sites, such as Uxmal, Kabah, Sayil, Labná, and the florescence of the magnificent city of Chichén Itzá, occurred as other sites to the south were declining. The emergence of the greatest period in the Yucatán began perhaps as late as A.D. 800, and continued until the fall of Chichén Itzá at around 1250. During these years new ideas and new populations became part of the Mayan civilization, yet lifestyle and world view retained the Classic Maya concepts of culture.

Chichén Itzá was the most important Mayan city on the Yucatán Peninsula until A.D. 1250. It exhibits clear influence from the valley of Mexico at this time. Contacts were probably established by ongoing trading interaction between Central Mexico and the Yucatán, beginning at around A.D. 700. However, influence did not flow one way; Mayan influences can be seen at Cacaxtla and Xochicalco in Central Mexico and people and ideas must have moved freely in both directions. The mechanisms for these exchanges/contacts may not have been direct (e.g. migrations, conquests), but may have been most closely tied to the increasing role of merchants and traders toward the end of the Classic Period throughout Mesoamerica. Archaeological research indicates that the Yucatán was a prime source for the trade of salt, honey, slaves, cotton, and perhaps cacao as well—all major items of exchange in the pre-Columbian world.

Around A.D. 1250, Chichén Itzá fell to a group of competing Yucatán states led by Mayapan but it remained a center of religious pilgrimage and activity until the middle of the 16th century. By that time the Maya/Yucatán region was torn apart by small warring states participating in a complex trading system. This was the situation encountered by the Spanish when they first landed on the Mayan island of Cozumel.

The actual conquest of the Yucatán did not come until 1528, when Francisco de Montejo, under the auspices of the Spanish crown, invaded the region. However, the dispersed states of the peninsula did not succumb easily to the invaders, and fought on until 1542 when a Spanish capital was finally established at Mérida.

Today descendants of the Maya live on in towns and villages of the peninsula. Customs from the pre-Hispanic era dominate much of rural life, and traditions in agriculture, religion, and language still reflect the ancient patterns of the Mayan world.

RECOMMENDED PACING: We recommend 12 nights if you want to follow this itinerary in its entirety. More, if you are a real archaeology buff and want to linger at each site; less, if you want to just choose a section of the itinerary to tag on as a bonus to a holiday at one of the Yucatán's superb beach resorts. We suggest two nights in Chichén Itzá, three nights in the Mérida area, two nights in Palenque, three nights in Río Bec, and two nights along the Riviera Maya.

DESTINATION I   CHICHÉN ITZÁ

Cancún makes a convenient starting point, since its international airport has numerous planes arriving daily from other Mexican cities, the United States, Canada, and Europe. It's hard to believe that only a few years ago there was practically nothing here except long stretches of deserted, white-sand beaches studded with coconut palms. Only an adventuresome few found this hidden paradise until the government, wanting to lure more tourists to Mexico, developed Cancún into a planned resort. Since then, the government has created other tourist destinations, but none have come close to being such a tremendous success.

If your flight arrives late in the day, or if you prefer to relax on the beach before starting out, spend a few days in Cancún. The best hotels are not in the town but line a narrow,

22-kilometer spit of land that wraps around a large lagoon. Here you find an endless row of hotels stretching along the beach. Most of them offer an "all-inclusive package," which includes your airfare (usually a charter flight), your room, your meals, and sometimes even drinks. Most of the hotels are huge high-rises (several with over a thousand rooms) but, by and large, they are of attractive design and high-quality construction. Modern hotels, fast-food restaurants, golf courses, trendy bars, and shopping malls dull the cultural shock of leaving home. If you prefer a more intimate, Mexican ambiance, yet want to be close to Cancún, consider staying at Isla Mujeres, a delightful small island about half-an-hour's boat ride off the coast. If this option interests you, ask about the boat schedule when making your hotel reservations.

After picking up your rental car, continue on to **Chichén Itzá**. It takes about two hours for the 200-kilometer drive via an excellent highway, the 180. The exit to Chichén Itzá is well marked, and it is just a few minutes from the highway to the town. We highly recommend two hotels here, the Hotel Mayaland and the Hacienda Chichén. Each has its own personality; each is exceptional. Both are snuggled right next to the ruins, so you can walk from your hotel to the entrance in minutes.

If you arrive at your hotel in the afternoon, plan to attend the Sound and Light program that is performed each evening (go early to get a good seat). You can rent earphones that translate what you are hearing into English at the ticket counter. These frequently don't work very well but this is no great problem as the story is really self-explanatory. As dusk settles into darkness, the temples are gently illuminated, one by one, and the saga unfolds. One of the stories told is of the decline of this powerful city, which, according to legend, began when the city's emperor stole, the beautiful bride-to-be of his greatest rival, on their wedding day, who retaliated by laying siege to Chichén Itzá.

You will not only enjoy the ambiance of your hotel, but its convenience to the ruins. Chichén Itzá is one of the Yucatán's most popular archaeological sites and attracts hordes of tourists. Being so conveniently close, you can be the first one at the gate in the morning and be able to enjoy the site at its finest in the cool of the morning when the soft light is best for photography—before many people arrive. We suggest you spend several hours exploring the site; then, during the heat of the day, return to your hotel for lunch and perhaps a nap by the pool. In the afternoon, as the shadows lengthen, walk again through the site on your own for a final viewing and wonderful photographs. You will probably be lured to climb up and down many of the pyramids and, even if you don't, you will be walking a lot since the site stretches over almost 10 square kilometers, so wear comfortable shoes. To increase your enjoyment, we suggest you hire a guide. They are available at the gate as you enter, or else your hotel can arrange one for you. Below is a bit of history and information on what to see.

CHICHÉN ITZÁ (A.D. c.700–1250)

The places mentioned below just begin to touch on the rich selection of fascinating places to see within this once-mighty city. They are some of our favorites, and will get you started.

Cenote de Los Sacrificios (Cenote of the Sacrifices): This natural well, reached by a path through the jungle from the central plaza, served not only as a water source for the city but also as a place where offerings were made to the gods. Over the years, a number of archaeological expeditions have recovered artifacts from the bottom of this deep, limestone sinkhole. Golden figurines and disks, jade objects, and ceramic bowls were found along with skeletons, primarily of adolescents and children. All had been offered as sacrifices or perhaps messengers to the gods.

El Caracol (The Snail): Located a bit away from the central plaza and reached by a ten-minute stroll, is a second set of buildings. Be sure not to miss the path, as here you find one of Chichén Itzá's highlights: a fascinating, very unusual domed structure that was obviously used as an observatory. The name "snail" comes from the inner staircase, which, if you stretch your imagination, looks a bit like a snail.

Chichén Itzá, Cenote

Grupo de Las Mil Columnas (Complex of the Thousand Columns): Flanking two sides of the Temple of the Warriors are row-upon-row of stone columns, some carved, some plain. This awesome scene looks like something one would expect to find in Greece, not Mexico. It is surmised that these columns originally supported a thatched roof covering a huge open market. The temple and the columns make a wonderful photograph when taken in late afternoon from the top of the Pyramid of Kukulkán.

Juego de Pelota (Great Ball Court): This dramatic ball court is the largest in Mesoamerica and while there are 12 other ball courts at Chichén Itzá, this one is spectacular. The game was played as a ritual performance, as well as a sport, and is one of the hallmarks of pre-Columbian Mesoamerican culture. At the end of the ball game, the captain who lost was often sacrificed to the gods. This sacrificial scene is realistically carved in a long frieze along both side walls of the court. Look carefully and you will see two rows of ball players standing behind each captain. At the center, these captains face each other across a large rubber ball enclosing a skeletal head. One of the captains stands holding a knife in one hand and a severed head in the other; his opponent kneels and from his headless neck issue seven streams of blood. This graphic scene speaks clearly to the practice of human sacrifice and the offering of human blood to the gods to ensure fertility of crops and the continuity of life.

Pyramid of Kukulkán (Pyramid of Kukulkán): This impressive, 24-meter-high pyramid soars above the other buildings in the complex. Two of the four sides have been restored, and this is a favorite target for schoolchildren who seem to zoom up the 91 steps to the top. You might want to join them for there is a terrific view up there. When you add up the steps on all four sides, plus the platform above, the sum is 365, which clearly links its significance to the Mayan calendar, which had 365 days in its year.

SIDE TRIPS FROM CHICHÉN ITZÁ

If you want to extend your stay in Chichén Itzá, you can take a few side trips. Among the nearby places we suggest are **Izamal**, an early Spanish Colonial town with a church and convent built on top of one of the Yucatán's highest pyramids, and the Sacred Cave of Balankanche, which lies about 7 kilometers from Chichén Itzá. This cave contains chambers which were once filled with hundreds of ceramic incense burners and miniature *metates* (grinding stones) laid out on the cave floors, as offerings to the rain god. Caves were seen by the Maya and most other Mesoamerican cultures as sacred places and as entrances to the underworld. The one is still used by local *shamans* (priests) who continue to regard it as sacred.

Excuse us for not giving an exact location for your next few nights' sojourn, and instead rather vaguely saying your destination is the "Mérida area." After pondering where to suggest you stay, it was impossible to recommend just one place. You can, of course, choose a hotel in the heart of Mérida; but dotting the countryside that wraps around the city is a rich selection of hotels, including gorgeous 18th-century haciendas that have been converted into superb small inns. Here you find the centuries slip away, and you feel like a guest in the home of a wealthy Spanish aristocrat, landlord of a vast sisal plantation. Some of these architectural treasures are listed under Mérida; however, there are other hotels in the area listed by their individual town names. Please look at the map in the front of the book to find all the hotels in this area. Any one of the following properties would make an outstanding choice to use as a base of operation: Hacienda Santa Rosa, Hacienda Temozón, Hacienda San José, Hacienda Xcantún, and the Lodge at Uxmal. Another of our favorites, Hacienda Uayamón (which is closer to Campeche than to Mérida) would also work well as a hub.

The following are some of the places to visit in this region of the peninsula.

MÉRIDA

Mérida, founded by the Spaniards in 1542 upon an earlier Mayan city, is worth a visit to enjoy its rich Colonial heritage. The city is laid out with all streets converging at a large, pretty, central plaza called the Plaza Grande or Plaza de La Independencia. Facing onto this parklike square is the imposing cathedral, the oldest in the Americas. Across the square from the cathedral is the **Palacio Municipal**, enhanced in front by a series of arches and topped by a tall clock tower. A few blocks away is the **Teatro José Peón Contereas**, an elaborate theater that attests to the wealth and sophistication generated by the prosperous sisal plantations nearby.

CAMPECHE

The small port city of **Campeche**, located on the Gulf of Mexico, 178 kilometers southwest of Mérida, makes a great outing. Be sure to include, at the same time, the nearby archaeological site of Edzná (see below). At the heart of Campeche is a colorful small Spanish Colonial town whose stone walls, battlements, watchtowers, and churches still stand. You can stroll through the cobbled streets of the old town and walk along the top of the massive walls that once kept out the English, French, and Dutch pirates who preyed on the rich port cities on the Gulf of Mexico during the 16th and 17th centuries. Few tourists know about Campeche, but it is a jewel, well worth a visit both for its intimate glimpse of the Spanish Colonial period and for its small museums that contain archaeological treasures from the surrounding region. At the south edge of town is a picture-perfect fort, the **Fuerte de San Miguel**, set on top of a hill with commanding views of the sea. Inside is a superb museum, renovated in 2001. Ceramic figurines from the Island of Jaina and steles with carved surfaces and hieroglyphic writing can be viewed here; but, above all, don't miss the incredible jade pieces from rich burials at the ancient site of **Calakmul**. These astonishing items consisting of bead necklaces, large ear spools (large round ear ornaments), and mosaic jade masks are some of the rarest and most beautiful objects remaining from the Classic Period of the Mayan culture.

RÍO CELESTÚN BIOSPHERE RESERVE

On the coast southwest of Mérida you find the small village of **Celestún** where fishermen still pull their boats up onto the wide sandy beach at night as they have done for generations and lining the waterfront are simple restaurants featuring the catch of the day. This is a very laid-back place with few tourists. The main attraction here is a wonderful wildlife sanctuary, **Río Celestún Biosphere Reserve**, an enticing spot for all naturalists, but especially for bird watchers as there are more than 200 species of birds to be seen here. As you drive into town, the road crosses over the estuary and at the far end of the bridge, as you look down to your left, you see many flat-bottomed boats docked with boatmen eager to be your guide. There is a cute little office with a tiny museum where you can buy your ticket (the price is set and varies only according to the length of tour). Most of the tours last about an hour and a half, during which time you go up the shallow waterway. Your guide will point out many birds along the way, but the highlight of the trip is seeing the flocks of pink flamingos that come to the shallow waters to feed. Although at some times of the year they are more abundant than others, you can almost always see them. To avoid frightening the birds away, the boats are not allowed to get close, so it is difficult to get good photographs. On the way back, the boatmen stop at some intriguing *cenotes*—freshwater pools formed by underground springs. These are especially fun because you get out of the boat and walk through the tangle of mangrove jungle on a raised pathway. For those so inclined, there is time to swim in the crystal-clear water. If you really want to get away from the world, we recommend the Hotel Eco Paraíso Xixim, located on the beach within the Biosphere Reserve, about 10 kilometers north of Celestún.

ARCHAEOLOGICAL SITES IN THE MÉRIDA AREA

The history of this part of the Yucatán Peninsula dates far back in time. During the middle to late pre-Classic Period (600 B.C.–A.D. 300) a number of important early cities arose on the peninsula with massive architecture and sophisticated water-control systems. During the following Classic Period (A.D. 300–900) while the cities in the Yucatán shared the amazing cultural development of such astounding Mayan cities in the southern lowland jungles as Tikal, Palenque, and Copan, they remained somewhat on the periphery of the Mayan heartland. It was during the late Classic and early post-Classic Period (A.D. 700–1050), when Tikal, Palenque, and Copan were declining, that the great cities of the Yucatán rose to their height of power and flourished for another 300 years. Below are a few highlights of these sites. You can see any of them by driving yourself, but your experience will be enhanced if you splurge and hire a car with a driver/guide (the concierge at your hotel can help you with arrangements).

UXMAL

Uxmal, 70 kilometers southwest of Mérida, is found in the Puuc Hills, a low range of hills in the southwest region of the Yucatán Peninsula. In this area, the Maya developed a magnificent style of architecture named Puuc, name after the hills in this region and characterized by immense palaces, pyramids, and temples decorated with three-dimensional mosaic stone friezes. Cities here were connected by roads called *sacbes*, which cut through the jungle and entered the towns through beautiful, vaulted archways, many of which can still be seen. The Puuc Hills are dotted with ruins (probably more than 200 are scattered in the area), with Uxmal being the largest and most impressive. Only a small portion of the massive site has been excavated and one wonders what is yet to come.

Cuadrángle de Las Monjas (Quadrangle of the Nuns): Just beyond the Pyramid of the Soothsayer is a broad courtyard surrounded on four sides by large, richly embellished buildings. This large quadrangle reminded the Spaniards of the cloisters of a nunnery, hence its name.

Juego de Pelota (Ball Court): Like most Mayan cities, Uxmal had its ceremonial ball court. Spectators watched from two thick walls, one on each side. This is a particularly well-preserved ball court and shouldn't be missed.

Palacio del Gobernador (Palace of the Governor): This gigantic building (almost 100 meters long, 12 meters wide, and 9 meters high) is one of the finest masterpieces of Mayan architecture. Its exterior is richly embellished with intricate stonework geometric patterns and friezes.

Pirámide del Adivino (Pyramid of the Soothsayer): This is a most unusual, extremely dramatic building with rounded sides, and steps leading up on two sides to a temple crowning the top. From the summit, which is nearly 28 meters high, there is a stunning view.

KABAH

At the height of its glory **Kabah** was one of the largest cities in northern Yucatán. At the entrance to the ceremonial city are the ruins of an arch that marked the start of the great Mayan road connecting Kabah to Uxmal, 23 kilometers to the northwest. Kabah's main attractions include:

Arco Monumental (Monumental Arch): This intricately decorated arch, which frames a high open gateway, is one of the most highly embellished, best-preserved arches in the Mayan world.

El Palacio (The Palace): This 30-room, two-story building standing on a hill was perhaps a palace housing the nobility of Kabah.

Palacio de Los Mascarones (Temple of the Masks): Over 250 intricate stone mosaic masks depicting the rain god, Chac, adorn this entire structure. These grinning faces with trunk-like noses are quite extraordinary.

LABNÁ

Labná, 30 kilometers southeast of Uxmal, is not as large as its neighbor, but has several interesting structures including its magnificent archway, one of the most beautiful in the Mayan World.

SAYIL

We like **Sayil**, which although small, is a particularly appealing site. Its highlight, El Palacio, is a three-story, stone palace with more than 90 rooms. The base structure is crumbling, but the two upper stories are in much better condition. The middle level, by far the most eye-catching, is enhanced by a double row of columns; the lower row alternate with porticos leading into narrow passageways, and the upper row enhanced with ornate carvings.

OXKINTOK

This extensive Mayan site has towering pyramids, palaces, ball courts, and numbers of elaborate causeways. While this Puuc-style city has been mapped and some of its great buildings have been uncovered and preserved, many of its structures are still unexcavated. The site lies somewhat off the beaten track so it attracts only a few tourists, but you can explore the city on your own, climbing the pyramids and walking through the abandoned plazas of this ancient Mayan center.

EDZNÁ

The first major flourishing of the magnificent Mayan city of **Edzná** occurred during the late Pre-Classic period (450 B.C.–A.D. 300). Long before the other Puuc sites were established, this city was home to a large population that tilled the fertile soils of the valley. Its resurgence in the Classic period saw the construction of massive pyramids, public buildings, and palaces. The largest and most impressive of these is a five-story palace/pyramid structure that dominates the large main plaza. From its summit you can look out over this immense ancient center and see the outline of the causeways and canals that once ran through the site, as well as earth-covered mounds that mark buildings yet to be uncovered. Here at Edzná, the Maya built the most extensive hydraulic system in the region, with canals and ponds preserving water for irrigation and the city's needs. At this site the population also raised many steles to honor their kings and commemorate royal events; some are still standing in the plaza, but a number of these can be seen beneath a modern thatched-roof structure at the entrance to the site.

DESTINATION III: PALENQUE & SAN CRISTÓBAL DE LAS CASAS

Palenque and San Crisóbal de Las Casas are found in the State of Chiapas, not on the Yucatán Peninsula. A deviation to explore these jewels is definitely off the beaten path. If your time is limited, after leaving the Mérida area proceed directly on to the next suggested destination, Río Bec. However, if time permits, this side trip is well worthwhile: Palenque is our favorite of all the archaeological sites and San Cristóbal is a fascinating city.

Be sure to get an early start, since this will be a long drive. The amount of time it takes depends upon where you are staying in the Mérida area (to give you an idea, it is about 550 kilometers from Mérida to Palenque). Although the road is good (part of it four-lane) and there is usually not much traffic, expect the drive to take most of the day. From Mérida, take highway 180 south toward Campeche, bypassing the town and continuing on to Champotón. Here the road splits and you continue on 261 to Escárcega, a scraggly town that you go through before joining highway 186 in the direction of Villahermosa. Before reaching Villahermosa, the road passes very briefly into the state of Tabasco and then into Chiapas. After crossing over the river that marks the border into Chiapas, it is about 35 kilometers to where you turn left on 199, continuing for 22 kilometers to Palenque. Remember, you will need to a minimum of two nights here.

PALENQUE

Palenque, one of the most beautiful ancient cities discovered in the Americas, is tucked in the jungle where the Usumacinta River drainage meets the coastal plain of the Gulf of Mexico. Due to the interest and dedicated scholarship of a number of talented epigraphers and art historians, the history of Palenque is better known than that of any other Mayan site. The rich hieroglyphic texts carved on stone panels, buildings, and monuments have brought to life the story of the rulers of Palenque, their names, dates, and historic events.

You need at least one full day to explore this lovely Mayan ceremonial city. Get up early and be ready to buy your ticket as the gates open. Not only do you want to arrive before countless busloads of tourists pull into the parking lot, but morning is a magical time. The mists from the mountains hang over the ancient buildings, lending an air of mystery to the magnificent city. Stone structures of amazing beauty rise on every side as you walk among the ruins of the great *castillo*, the immense palace, temples, and ball court. The pyramids, crowned by temples, cluster around plazas, each temple decorated with finely

Palenque, Temple of the Count

inscribed panels and tall, soaring roof-combs of open-stone fretwork. There are guides available who will enhance your explorations, though all of the buildings have plaques describing them in Spanish, English, and Mayan. There is a treasure of wonders to see here and to get you started, we mention below a few of our favorites.

Templo de Las Inscripciones (Temple of the Inscriptions): This towering pyramid that dominates the landscape is named for the stone hieroglyphic panels found within. In 1948, a Mexican archaeologist, Alberto Ruz, discovered a steep hidden stairway leading from the floor of the elevated temple deep into the heart of the tall pyramid. At the bottom of the stairway, under 400 tons of rubble which were removed by hand, he found a royal crypt occupied by Pacal, the most important ruler of Palenque. He had been buried with great splendor, and was accompanied by magnificent jade jewelry and an elegant jade mosaic mask. His sarcophagus was topped by an elaborate lid carved with figures and a hieroglyphic text tracing his dynastic descent from the gods, assuring his royal presence and rebirth in the afterlife. The discovery of this tomb was of major importance to Mayan archaeology because it definitively established that many of the massive Mayan pyramids were the sites of royal burials. Note: To the right of the entrance you will see the tomb of Alberto Ruz, who wanted to be buried next to the temple where he made his remarkable discovery.

El Palacio (The Palace): This huge, imposing complex is quite unlike others in the Mayan world. It looks more like a structure one might expect to find in Europe, with a slender, tall watchtower, a labyrinth of intricate rooms, a series of inner courtyards, galleries faced by columns, and exquisite stucco designs. This building is thought to have been the dwelling of royalty, since steam baths and bedrooms were found here. What is especially interesting about this building is that many of the rooms still have roofs, making it easier to visualize what life here might have been like. It is fun to explore this maze of rooms via dimly lit passageways. El Palacio is the building that the intrepid explorer, John Lloyd Stephens, and his talented artist colleague, Frederic Catherwood, chose to make their home when visiting Palenque. These two men explored this fascinating region between 1839 and 1841, laying the groundwork for later archaeological expeditions. Before heading off to Mexico, borrow Stephens's book, *Incidents of Travel in Yucatán*, *Volume II*, from your local library. It is enthralling to gaze at Catherwood's wonderful illustrations, and see what Palenque looked like before being rescued from its slumber of many years within the jungle.

Templo del Conde (Temple of the Count): This temple is named for Jean Frederic Maximilien de Waldec, an eccentric German count who lived here for a year in 1832 in a small temple tucked at the top of this high pyramid The count brought along his mistress, who must have been quite madly in love with him to camp high atop a pyramid in the middle of a steaming jungle without running water or air conditioning—modern amenities that today might make such a romp quite fun. No doubt the views were romantic, but the steps up and down each day must have been quite arduous.

When visiting this gigantic complex, it is intriguing to realize that only about a third of this awesome city has been uncovered. It is interesting to walk along the paths lacing the dense jungle, watching teams of archaeologists going about their meticulous work.

To complete your day, before returning to the hotel, be sure to stop by the fine Museum of Palenque, which you passed on the right side of the road as you drove into the site. This museum contains many objects of jade, stone, and pottery excavated at the city. In addition, in a building next to the museum is an exceptionally attractive gift shop that handles not only books and replicas of objects, but also wonderful ethnographic materials such as textiles and carvings made by modern Mayan artists.

SAN CRISTÓBAL DE LAS CASAS

If your time is limited, after spending a couple of nights in Palenque return to the Yucatán Peninsula and continue on to Río Bec (see the next destination). However, for those interested in anthropology and delving into the rich culture of the Mayan people, then San Cristóbal de Las Casas is well worth a detour. This should be done as a round trip from Palenque, with a minimum three-night stay in San Cristóbal.

Agua Azul: Leave Palenque early in the morning, allowing time to stop en route to visit the waterfalls at Agua Azul. Ask the hotel to pack you a lunch and plan to have picnic here (there are also many open-air restaurants available if you are the adventuresome type). If the weather is warm, you might want to bring your swimsuit for a dip in the river. Although the distance is only about 60 kilometers, it takes over an hour to get there since the road is winding and there is usually a lot of traffic. To reach Agua Azul, from Palenque go south on highway 199. After 9 kilometers the road splits. At the junction, keep to the right on 199 toward **Ocosingo** and **San Cristóbal de Las Casas**. As the road climbs into the lush mountains, you need to watch the road markers—at about marker 87, turn to the right at a sign to **Cascadas de Agua Azul**, a favorite spot for Mexican families. If you are into "local color," this is it! A river rushes through the rich foliage, forming rapids and waterfalls that drop into tranquil pools of turquoise water. On holidays and weekends the place is positively packed with people: children splashing in the crystal-clear water; babies napping in the shade, women preparing tables laden with food, grandmothers asleep in hammocks stretched between the trees, men chatting while enjoying cold beers, lovers strolling hand in hand, youngsters climbing steep paths to the top of the waterfalls. Note: Don't even think about visiting Agua Azul during the rainy season, which turns the clear turquoise waters into a muddy river.

San Cristóbal de Las Casas: After your visit to the waterfalls at Agua Azul, return to highway 199 and continue south. The road climbs ever higher as you travel on for 145 kilometers into the pine-covered hills until you reach San Cristóbal de Las Casas, nestled in a 2,100-meter-high valley wrapped by pine covered mountains. Founded in 1528 by

San Cristóbal de Las Casas

the Spaniards, the town strongly reflects a classic Colonial heritage. There are opulent churches, tree-studded plazas, cobblestone streets, red-tiled roofs, and secreted garden courtyards. However, it is the rich culture of the Mayan people that makes a visit here so special. The clock seems to have stopped, and the indigenous people, descendents of the Maya live much as they have for hundreds of years throughout the hills and jungles of Chiapas. Although colorful to see, this untouched way of living is problematic: Chiapas, tucked right on the border with Guatemala, seems to be a "forgotten" state and its poverty level has ripened political unrest, as evidenced by the Zapatista uprisings in the mid-1990s. There is still unrest, particularly in the countryside, but you have little sense of any hostility in San Cristóbal de Las Casas, a town named for Bartolomé de Las Casas, a benevolent Spanish priest who came to minister to the Indian people in the 1500s and became their compassionate protector.

San Cristóbal is one of the most colorful towns in Mexico, not only because of its Spanish influence in style of architecture, but even more so because you see the indigenous people wearing colorful attire. Each surrounding village has not only its own dialect, but its distinct costume with hand-loomed, colorfully embroidered clothing. The girls marry very young, and all seem to have a baby, snugly wrapped in a shawl, tucked on their back. Many of the men are dressed in vests of brilliant colors and hats decorated with ribbon streamers. You will need at least three nights in San Cristóbal, giving you a minimum of two days to explore in town and the nearby villages. You can walk to all of the places within the city, but for the outlying towns, take a tour. Your hotel can arrange either a private guide or an organized group tour.

Note: Be aware to use extreme caution when taking photographs. Throughout Mexico it is always polite to ask permission before taking pictures of people, but in the state of Chiapas it is not only the proper thing to do, but photographing people is forbidden by law. When in San Cristóbal, it is almost irresistible to snap a photo of the colorfully dressed people. However, this problem can be solved. Frequently the street vendors will ask you to buy some of their trinkets and will add, "Take my picture?" It is a small price to pay. Sometimes, if you buy some of their wares, the photo is free. Other times, there might be a surcharge, but it is well worth it to have them willingly pose for you. However, the situation is much more stringent in the outlying villages where photographing the indigenous people is strictly forbidden. Your film can be confiscated and you can be arrested.

PLACES TO VISIT IN SAN CRISTÓBAL DE LAS CASAS

Plaza Principal: Your first sightseeing target should be the main square (*zócola*) which is located in the heart of the city. For later sightseeing, note that the streets all change names as they pass through the square. Sit on one of the benches in the plaza and watch the colorfully garbed people come and go. In the center of the plaza there is an unusual two-story gazebo where you can get a snack. A main pedestrian-only street, filled with boutiques and restaurants, borders the west side of the square and stretches for several blocks north and south of the plaza. To the south of the square, the street is called

Plaza Principal

Avenida Miguel Hidalgo, to the north, Avenida 20 de Noviembre. To help you find your way, the following sightseeing is referenced in relation to the Plaza Principal.

La Catedral: The cathedral, dating back to 1528, is tucked on the northwest corner of the Plaza Principal. Father Bartolomé de Las Casas, for whom the city was named, was the church's first bishop. The exterior is brilliantly painted in bright yellow with coral-colored trim. The interior is ornate with many paintings and carving. The small chapel to the left, as you enter, is particularly beautiful. **Iglesia de San Nicolás**: The Church of San Nicolas is also on the Plaza Principal, located on the northeast corner.

Palacio Municipal: The Municipal Palace stretches across the entire west side of the Plaza Principal. This dramatic, long, two-story yellow building, fronted by a parade of colonnades, was built in the late 19th century as the government house. Today, many of the festivities of the town take place in the square directly in front of the palace.

Templo de Santo Domingo: You must not miss this spectacular 16th-century ex-convent, which is located about five blocks north of the Plaza Principal. The baroque façade of the pale peach-colored church is richly embellished with intricately carved stonework. If you like photography, arrive in the late afternoon when the church glows in the warm light of the sun. It is a stunning sight.

Textile Market: On the west side of the Templo de Santo Domingo is a remarkably interesting craft market. Here the local villagers come to display their handicrafts. The array of colorful wares to buy is overwhelming. Beautiful shawls, hand-embroidered blouses, hand-loomed purses, jackets of natural wools, colorful skirts, belts, lovely table clothes, and wall hangings are but of few of the incredible selection of things to buy.

Mercado: About two-blocks behind the Templo de Santo Domingo is a huge, outdoor city market, open every day of the week, filled with vegetables, fruits, herbs, medicines, dry goods, hardware, chickens, pigs—just about anything you could possibly want! This is the place where the local people come to buy and sell. It is very authentic, very colorful.

Templo de Santo Domingo

Mayan Mysteries & A Loop of the Yucatán Peninsula

Museo Na Bolom: Located ten blocks northeast of the Plaza Principal, is the Na Bolom Museum, which was the home of Frans Blom, a Danish anthropologist, and Trudy Duby, a Swiss photographer and journalist. They came to San Cristóbal de Las Casas in the mid-1900s and became passionate protectors of the indigenous people, working tirelessly to maintain their culture and environment. The Bloms have passed away, but their home is open to the public. It is now a non-profit foundation and houses a museum with many of the fascinating photographs taken by Trudy, as well as many religious artifacts and archaeological treasures they discovered. The museum can only be visited on a tour (when we visited, English tours were given at 4:30 pm, but be sure to check the time). Na Bolom is also a hotel—the favorite choice of accommodation for archaeologists, artists, and anthropologists. Na Bolom means the Jaguar, and there is a gift shop by the same name across the street from the museum where you can buy souvenirs and craft items. If you are not staying at Na Bolom, you can make a reservation for dinner (the meal is served family-style with the guests sitting at one large table).

Museo del Ambar: San Crisóbal de Las Casas is famous for its amber, and about four blocks west of the Plaza Principal, there is an excellent Amber Museum ensconced within an old convent. There are many examples of jewelry, but my favorite pieces are the exquisite amber carvings. Throughout town, you can buy beautiful pieces of amber jewelry at excellent prices. Don't buy amber from street vendors as their selection of jewelry could be acrylic.

VILLAGES TO VISIT OUTSIDE OF SAN CRISTÓBAL DE LAS CASAS

San Juan Chamula & Zihacantán: There are many Mayan villages near San Cristóbal. The two most popular are San Juan Chamula (12 kilometers northwest of San Cristóbal) and Zihacantán (9 kilometers west of San Cristóbal). Both are fascinating; you feel that you have stepped back 500 years in time. Although the villages are only a few kilometers apart, each has its own mode of dress and dialect.

San Juan Chamula: The main sight in San Juan Chamula is its church, dedicated to St. John the Baptist. Here, in a simple white church with turquoise-colored trim, you find the pagan beliefs of the indigenous Mayan people intermingled with the Catholic faith. You step into the dimly lit church where you see families in colorful costume huddled in small groups on the floor, praying behind an assortment of candles. The church is illuminated by the soft glow of hundreds of candles. The odor of incense hangs heavy in the air. Occasionally you hear the squawk of a chicken that is being sacrificed to the gods. It is almost unbelievable to believe that such old customs still exist. The scene is real—it is in no way a tourist presentation. In fact, all photographs are strictly forbidden.

San Juan Chamula

Zihacantán: Your second stop is in the even smaller village of **Zihacantán** to visit its church. Here the worshipers sit on chairs, not on the floor as they do in San Juan Chamula. The mens' garb is exceptionally colorful with brilliantly embroidered vests. As in San Juan Chanmula, the pagan beliefs of the indigenous people creep into their religious ceremonies with clay animals (similar to those worshipped in the Pre-Colombian times) used as candle holders. Again, photography strictly forbidden.

RETURN TO PALENQUE

When it is time to leave San Cristóbal de Las Casas, it is too far from the Yucatán Peninsula to make the journey in one day. Therefore, you will need to stop for another night in Palenque. However, you can squeeze in a bit more sightseeing en route at another wonderful archaeological site, Toniná.

Toniná: When leaving San Cristóbal, get an early start and head north on highway 199 in the direction of Palenque. After 98 kilometers, just before the town of Oscingo, turn right on the toad marked to Toniná. This is a relatively small archaeological site, but well worth a visit. To add to the magic, you might be the only tourists there. Toniná was one of the last functioning Classic Mayan cities, surviving almost 100 years beyond the demise of the others. To enrich your explorations, browse through the museum before meandering through the site. Excavations are still underway but there is plenty to see including ball courts, carvings, and an exceptionally impressive, 80-meter-high pyramid, supposedly the tallest in the Mayan World.

From Toniná, return to Ocosingo, then continue north on highway 199 for 109 kilometers to Palenque.

DESTINATION IV   RÍO BEC

When it's time to leave Palenque, retrace your way to highway 186 then turn right toward Escárcega. Go through Escárcega and continue east on 186, following signs to Chetumal. Dotting this stretch of highway between Escárcega and Chetumal is a group of fabulous Mayan ruins in an area called **Río Bec**. These are some of our favorite archaeological sites in Mexico—not only because they have awesome structures, but also because you are frequently the only person about, a truly magical experience.

We suggest two hotels in the Río Bec area: the Chicanná Ecovillage across from the ruins of Chicanná, and The Explorean Kohunlich near the ruins of Kohunlich. Although approximately 70 kilometers apart, either makes an excellent hub from which to visit the various sites. We highly recommend both hotels, although they are quite different. The Chicanná Ecovillage has simple rooms in attractive two-story thatched-roofed bungalows that look like something out of *Robinson Crusoe*. The super-deluxe Explorean Kohunlich

Río Bec, Becán

has beautifully decorated rooms in cottages overlooking dense jungle as far as the eye can see.

The Río Bec style occurs in a series of important archaeological sites that reached their zenith from A.D. 600 to 900. Some of these are incredibly well preserved. Until recently, access to these ruins was appalling, with four-wheel drive needed to maneuver the potholed roads. All that has changed—the government has improved all the roads and now access is easy. Some of the sites, that tour books said even recently were five-hour drives from the highway are now within an easy hour's drive. However, news of these huge improvements has not yet leaked out, leaving a visit to the archaeological sites a sublime experience. Nowhere else can you visit such outstanding Mayan monuments in such blissful isolation. But don't wait too long because tourists will surely soon be flocking here. When we explored all of the ruins described below, we usually had the place to ourselves. Another bonus here is that the signs are excellent, and each building is clearly labeled in English, Spanish, and Mayan, so that you know what you are seeing. Below are descriptions of the various cities we suggest seeing, arranged according to their location along highway 186, starting with Calakmul as the most western site, and Dzibanche as the most eastern site. There is no way that you can see all these in one day: you will definitely need two, since Calakmul alone will take a day. Study the recommendations below. If your time is limited, you might like to know that our personal favorites are Calakmul, Becán, and Kohunlich.

CALAKMUL

If you have time to visit only one ruin, choose **Calakmul**. It is stupendous, and although rarely visited, ranks in grandeur with its greatest rival, Tikal, which is somewhat alike in layout and architecture. It is not surprising that they share similarities, since although Tikal is in Guatemala, the border is only 30 kilometers away. This site is farther off the highway than any of the others that we mention in the Río Bec area. After leaving the main road, it takes about an hour to drive there, with most of the distance along a single-lane road. However, the road is straight and has little traffic. Best of all, you pass through the Calakmul Biosphere Reserve (established in 1989 to protect the natural rainforest) where you are likely to spot many species of exotic birds and some wild animals. In the spring, wild turkeys, resembling colorful peacocks, are common. The city spreads over a huge area of 25 square kilometers, and it is estimated that at the height of its grandeur (A.D. 400–800) as many as 200,000 people lived here. It is fascinating to wander along the jungle paths, coming across grand structures rising from the tangle of trees, including the highest pyramid ever built by the Maya, which soars 53 meters into the sky and has a base of 5 acres. As found in other sophisticated Mayan sites, Calakmul had an observatory for charting the movements of the stars. Other places of interest include a huge market and ball courts. The site is still in the process of being renovated. (Plan to make Calakmul an all-day outing.)

CHICANNÁ

From Calakmul, go back to highway 186, turn right, and continue for 44 kilometers to **Chicanná**, located on the right side of the highway, just across from the Chicanná Ecovillage Resort. This is the third-largest of the Río Bec cities and is known for its stunning architecture. Its special feature is Temple 2, called the Earth Monster. Its doorway is a giant mouth through which the high priests entered to communicate with the underworld. You can clearly see the eyes, the nose, and the menacing teeth, which hang down above the door.

BECÁN

Leaving Chicanná, it is only 2 kilometers on 186 to **Becán**, which is on the left side of the highway. Although intimate in size, this is a real gem. You find here a series of courtyards surrounded by huge pyramids, so steep that a rope is provided to give you leverage as you ascend. Some of the buildings have deep tunnel-like staircases that lead to nowhere. Fun to explore, but be aware that you need to back out the same way you entered. Also of interest is a giant mask on one of the temple walls, covered by glass to protect it against the elements. The ubiquitous ball court is here too, of course. The city was originally surrounded by a 2-kilometer moat crossed by seven bridges. The moat is now dry, but you can clearly see its remains.

XPUJIL

The next ruin is **Xpujil**, only 6 kilometers beyond Becán on 186 on the left side of the highway. This site isn't as impressive as the others you have visited, but is worth a stop to see the three crumbling towers, which must have been quite splendid when originally built. Notice the picture that depicts what the towers probably looked like in their prime.

KOHUNLICH

Leaving Xpujil, it is 62 kilometers farther east on 186 until you see the turnoff to the right to **Kohunlich**, which is about a 15-minute drive off the main highway. The special features here are an impressive pyramid, the Temple of the Sun (also called Temple of the Masks), whose steps are flanked on each side with eight, huge, stone masks, some of which show traces of their original red paint. These quite fearsome faces have bulging eyes and protruding ears. Kohunlich covers a vast area, and it is fun to wander the paths that wind through the jungle. You will come across a ball court and also a large plaza which was the marketplace.

DZIBANCHE & KINCHUA

From Kohunlich, return to highway 186 and continue east. In about 2 kilometers, you come to a turnoff to the left marked to **Dzibanche** and **Kinchua**, located about half-an-hour's drive off the highway. These are two individual sites, but so close together that one entrance fee covers both. Don't bother going to Kinchua unless you have an interest in seeing what archaeological sites look like before restoration. Dzibanche, however, is beautiful, not so much for its structures but for its setting. You walk through a splendid forest with the path meandering through lovely glens when suddenly in a clearing before you, a giant pyramid appears. The setting is mystical.

DESTINATION V   RIVIERA MAYA

Your next destination is the Riviera Maya, a stunning coastal stretch of white-sand beach lying between Cancún and Tulum. This once-sleepy area is booming with huge hotels and condominium complexes secreted behind high walls with security guards at the gates. These developments aren't intrusive, however, because they are far apart and hidden from the road. In addition to these hotels, there is a rich selection of fabulous smaller places to stay in every price range, from luxurious hotels with every imaginable amenity to simple thatched-hut bungalows tucked on secluded beaches. Any one of the places we recommend would make a suitable hub to explore the archaeological sites featured below.

When it's time to leave the Río Bec area, drive east on 186 to **Chetumal**, the capital of the state of Quintana Roo, located on an estuary of the Río Hondo, which divides Mexico from Belize. Chetumal has little of historic architectural interest since in the 1950s, when most of the buildings were destroyed by a hurricane. At the entrance to the town is a powerful sculpture of **Gonzalo Guerrero** standing proudly next to his wife and children. Guerrero was one of the first two Spaniards to land in the Yucatán, as a result of being shipwrecked offshore in 1511. Guerrero married a Mayan princess and fathered the first *mestizos* (persons of mixed Spanish and Indian blood) to be born in Mexico. The other sailor who survived the shipwreck was **Jerómimo de Aguilar**, who played a key role in the conquest of Mexico. When **Cortés** landed in the Yucatán, he persuaded Jerómimo de Aguilar (who by then spoke fluent Mayan) to come along as an interpreter. A little later, when Cortés arrived in Tabasco, he was presented with a gift of 20 maidens, one of whom was La Malinche, who not only became Cortés's mistress and bore him a son, but also helped to make the conquest of Mexico successful. She quickly learned Spanish, and with the combined dialects of **La Malinche** and Jerómimo de Aguilar, Cortés was able to forge alliances with Indian groups against the Aztecs. La Malinche was of particular help, not only because of her interpretive skills, but also because of her knowledge of the ways of the people. When Cortés returned to Spain, he "gave" La Malinche to one of his captains.

The town of **Chetumal** is not special, but its **Museo de La Cultura Maya** (Museum of Mayan Culture) is stunning—small, but exquisite and tasteful, and no expense seems to have been spared to create a jewel. The floors are made of gleaming green marble and classical music plays softly in the background. The museum is designed around three floors (connected by ramps) representing the underworld, the human world, and the celestial world. Throughout the museum are excellent exhibits and video presentations enhancing what you see. The most dramatic visual display is along one wall where a huge screen features a constantly repeating movie that takes you flying over the great Mayan cities in a small plane.

Leaving Chetumal, head north on highway 307 in the direction of **Cancún**. The highway traces Lago Bacalar (Lake Bacalar), a narrow but very long lake stretching for 104 kilometers. It is fed from underground *cenotes*, so its water is crystal-clean and quite remarkable in color, shading from dark blue to turquoise.

Chichén Itzá, El Castillo

Continue north on 307 to Tulum, which is about 260 kilometers north of Chetumal. Rather than doing more sightseeing, call it a day and settle in at the hotel of your choice along the Riviera Maya. All of the hotels we recommend are on the sea, so take a swim in the warm Caribbean water and perhaps a walk on the beach. The next day begin your sightseeing, for which we suggest the following:

TULUM (A.D. 1000–1521)

Tulum is one of the loveliest small Mayan sites on the Yucatán Peninsula and due to its convenient location just off the main highway, it is heavily visited by tourists. The ruins open at 8 am. It is best to go as early as possible to avoid the extremely hot sun and the flood of tour buses that visit the site each day. The ruins are on a lesser scale than in most other areas of the Mayan world, and you will notice that the pyramids are smaller and the buildings somewhat sloppily constructed. However, this is one of Mexico's most picturesque spots, one captured endlessly on calendars and tourist brochures, and there is an incredible view from the site's magnificent headland overlooking the Caribbean. Originally Tulum was a port for long-distance trading canoes, and its defensive walls can still be seen along with a fine watchtower looking out to sea. The beach at the foot of the cliffs was once used to pull large seagoing trading canoes from the sea, and if you bring your swimming suit, you can enjoy a swim in the warm, clear, turquoise water. Tulum, and the Island of Cozumel, just across from it, were the first Mayan sites visited by Cortés on his initial voyage to Mexico in 1519. Unlike most pre-Columbian sites, they continued to flourish into the Colonial period.

COBÁ (A.D. 200–1000)

The large ruined city of **Cobá** lies about halfway between Tulum and Cancún, and is situated 40 kilometers inland from the coast at the end of a good road. It is built around a group of five small lakes that once provided water for a region of perhaps 50,000 people. The presence of lakes and an abundance of water are rare in this area and sustained Cobá as a major Mayan center until its conquest in about A.D. 1000 by a group of militant Mayan traders known as the Itzá. It has immense pyramids, a ball court, and palaces, but it is best known for its many *sacbes*, the raised causeways or roads that connected the site with other great Mayan centers of the Classic period. These roads also run through the city itself, connecting various clusters of buildings, and where they have been cleared, visitors can quite easily walk to the majestic, towering pyramids whose tops rise above the trees. If the idea of staying next to the ruins appeals to you, we recommend a very pleasant small hotel, Villa Arqueológica Cobá. From here you can take an early-morning walk through the jungle to the ruins, a very special way to see this ancient city.

CENOTES

The surface of the land in this part of the Yucatán Peninsula that lies in the state of Quintana Roo is basically a limestone shelf, beneath which flows a network of underground rivers. Occasionally the limestone collapses, exposing the water below and forming natural wells, which the ancient Maya called *cenotes*. The location of these cenotes determined the location of many of the Mayan cities, where they not only provided a source of pure water, but also served for religious ceremonies. Today these cenotes are popular places for the tourist to visit. Some people like to swim in the crystal-clear, turquoise water, while others don scuba gear and enter a cenote at one point, swim underground in the river, and pop up at another cenote. Large theme parks, such as Xel-Ha and Xcaret, have developed to highlight natural wonders in the area and include underground rivers in their list of attractions. These places are fun, especially if you are traveling with children, but extremely commercial, and we definitely prefer the secluded, lesser-known cenotes. Ask the concierge at your hotel to recommend one nearby—they are dotted throughout the landscape.

When it is time to return home, you can quickly travel from the Riviera Maya to Cancún airport, completing your loop of the Yucatán Peninsula.

Ladies in Typical Mayan Dresses

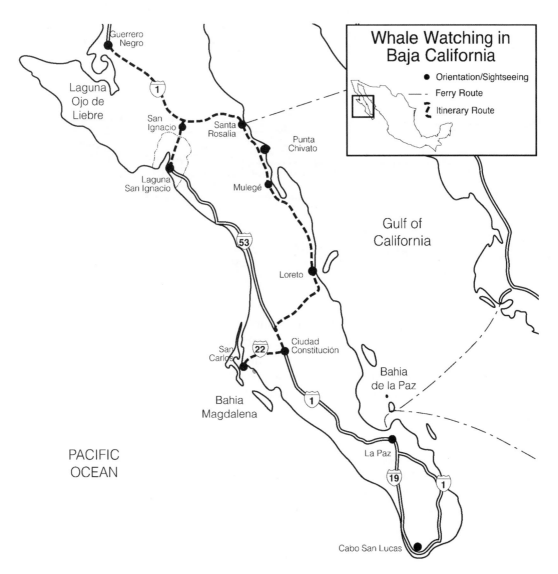

171

Whale-Watching in Baja: The Gentle Giants

One of the world's most awesome adventures must surely be visiting the incredible gray whale (*la Ballena Grise*) in its natural habitat. Each year these gentle giants, which can weigh up to 35 tons and can measure up to 15 meters, leave the cold Arctic waters off Alaska about October when the frigid waters begin to freeze, signaling it is time to begin their 8,000 to 9,000 kilometer journey south (the longest known migration of any mammal). It takes about 3 months for them to travel from the Bering and Chukchi Seas to the warm breeding lagoons of Baja California Sur.

The female whales are larger than the males—it is thought their greater size is to accommodate the huge calf in their abdomen. The females enter into one of three lagoons located along the west coast of Baja California (Bahía Magdalena, Laguna Ojo de Liebre, or San Ignacio Lagoon) to give birth to their calves. Usually the males do not enter the lagoon, but linger in the deeper waters at its mouth. Most species of whales have their babies in the open ocean, but the gray whale chooses the warm, shallow water of these protected lagoons as its nursery. At birth the winsome calves weigh in at over a ton (the size of a small car) and are approximately 5 meters long. Then, in the space of a few months, thanks to their mothers' rich milk, they more than double their weight (gaining about 150 pounds a day) and by the time they are ready to start the long journey back north, they have grown to about 6 meters in length. The life span of the whale is over 40 years (some scientists speculate they can live 60 years or more). In a female's lifetime she will usually have about three babies with a span of three years between each pregnancy, which has a gestation period of 12 months. The calves usually stay with the mother for about a year and are then sent off on their own.

In the course of researching and detailing our own trip, we struggled with conflicting information and recommendations of just what to see, where to go, and how to pace it. Based on our own travels and experiences, we now feel confident in sharing with you what to consider when planning your journey.

WHERE TO GO: You can spot many different types of whales all along the coast of Baja, but since the bays and lagoons have a defined space, they offer a superb opportunity to view a high concentration of gray whales up close. Plan to visit one or more of the three bays where the gray whales migrate each winter. These three bays are **Bahía Magdalena**, **Laguna Ojo de Liebre** (nicknamed Scammon's Lagoon for the whaling captain who discovered the bay), and **San Ignacio Lagoon**. Of these three bays, Laguna Ojo de Liebre and San Ignacio Lagoon offer by far the best whale-watching. The two most accessible bays are Bahía Magdalena and Laguna Ojo de Liebre. Although Lagoon San Ignacio requires a difficult two-hour drive along a bumpy, ill-kept road from the town of San Ignacio, this is our personal favorite place for whale-watching because the boats are smaller, the journey through the lagoon to where the whales can be seen is shorter, and the experience is more personal (staying at a tent camp is rather like a house party—you quickly make friends with your fellow guests). Nevertheless, San Ignacio Lagoon is not recommended for everyone: it is less accessible and has no hotels. The only accommodations are in a few tent camps, and these would appeal only to the more adventuresome traveler who doesn't mind roughing it. Very important: It is a bit confusing when you read advertisements for whale-watching. Several companies offer whale-watching tours or boat trips that leave from La Paz and explore the Sea of Cortez. Indeed, these are fun trips that enable you to see an incredible amount of wildlife (including whales), but be aware, if you *really* want to see the whales, you must go to one of the three bays mentioned above, where the gray whales come to have their babies.

LOCATION OF THE BAYS: Bahía Magdalena (closest town, San Carlos) is the most easily accessible place to watch whales if you are flying into La Paz. It is about a two-and-a-half-hours' drive northwest of La Paz or about a two-hour drive southwest of Loreto (both La Paz and Loreto have international airports). Laguna Ojo de Liebre (Scammon's Lagoon) is located near the town of Guerrero Negro, on the main Highway 1, about a five-hour drive northwest of Loreto or about a ten-hour drive south of Tijuana, the border town with the USA. San Ignacio Lagoon is located approximately midway between Laguna Ojo de Liebre and Bahía Magdalena. The closest town is San Ignacio, on Highway 1, but it takes two hours to reach the lagoon from the highway because the gravel coastal access road is extremely rough.

WHICH BAY TO CHOOSE: All three bays mentioned above provide wonderful whale-watching opportunities and no experience can ever be duplicated or guaranteed—so, which to choose? Laguna Ojo de Liebre and San Ignacio Lagoon are considered to offer the best likelihood to see mothers and babies up close. It is a tossup which of the two is better—both are excellent. On the other hand, Bahía Magdalena has the advantage of being the closest destination to see the whales if you are staying in La Paz. Our advice: if you have the luxury of unlimited time, visit all three bays. If time is limited, just include Bahía Magdalena and Laguna Ojo de Liebre, since access to San Ignacio Lagoon is more difficult. If you want to concentrate on just one bay, we recommend Laguna Ojo de Liebre, because it has an abundance of whales (50% of all the babies are born here) and it is easily accessible by a good road.

WHEN TO SEE THE WHALES: The whales can be visited from January through mid-April. The optimum time to see them is in February and March.

HOW TO SEE THE WHALES: Although whales can be spotted from the shoreline, without a doubt the best way to see them is by boat. It would be a waste of money to go so far to see this marvel of nature, and then not be able to enjoy the adventure to its fullest. There are several ways to view the whales—we have listed below some of the options, information on closest towns to the whale-watching areas, and recommended pacing.

ESCORTED TOURS BY CHARTERED PLANE: There are several tour companies that operate chartered flights in February and March from the United States to see the whales. One of these, Baja Discovery, offers tours that depart by bus from San Diego, California, cross the border to Ensenada, where the trip continues by a charter plane to an airstrip near San Ignacio Lagoon. Another, Baja Expeditions, offers tours using a charter flight from San Diego to San Ignacio Lagoon with a stop en route for customs. A third company, Baja Ecotours, arranges charter flights for groups leaving from San Diego. Baja Ecotours also accepts guests at their tent camp who arrive by their own private plane or car. For more details, visit *www.karenbrown.com*.

Usually these tours spend four nights at a tent camp near the lagoon, returning on the fifth day to San Diego. Days are spent whale-watching, hiking, bird watching, and kayaking. See our website, *www.karenbrown.com*, for more information.

INDEPENDENT ARRANGEMENTS BY BUS: If you are on a tight budget, the least expensive option for whale-watching is to take a Greyhound bus from San Diego to Tijuana, and then a take a first-class bus (ABC Bus Line, Tres Estrelles de Oro, or Transportes Aguila) from Tijuana to Guerrero Negro where you can visit the whales in the Laguna Ojo de Liebre. Call the Tijuana Bus Terminal for schedules and rates (664-626-7101). Before arriving in Guerrero Negro, make a reservation at the Hotel Malarrimo. The Achoy family, who own the hotel, also operate whale-watching trips, so when you book your room, reserve a place on one of their tours, which leave the hotel by bus at 8 am or 11 am. After a few days in Guerrero Negro, you can either return home or continue on by bus to San Ignacio where you can arrange a whale-watching tour to San Ignacio Lagoon (about a two-hour drive from town by a rough road).

INDEPENDENT ARRANGEMENTS BY CAR: Another choice of transportation is to drive your own car south from San Diego on Highway 1, but this is a long, arduous journey best suited to those with lots of time. Much easier than driving down the long Baja Peninsula is to take a commercial flight from Los Angeles or San Diego to Loreto and rent a car. There are good hotels in Loreto, but no exceptional places to stay in any of the towns close to where the whales congregate. Of the three lagoons where whales can be visited, the most convenient is San Carlos (Bahía Magdalena), which you can easily visit as a day trip out of Loreto, but the whale-watching here cannot compare with either Guerrero Negro or San Ignacio Lagoon. The town with the best accommodations is Guerrero Negro, near Laguna Ojo de Liebre. Once you arrive at any of the three lagoons, you can book an organized tour to see the whales. It is extremely important during the height of the season (especially in February) to make an advance reservation for whale-watching excursions, since they are sometimes sold out a year in advance. Another option is to drive to one of the coves and hire one of the licensed guides (often local fishermen) who linger nearby with their boats, called *pangas*, to take you out into the lagoon or bay. Note: There is no guarantee that there will always be someone available to take you out without a prior reservation.

TOURS ORIGINATING IN MEXICO: In Loreto the hotel Posada de Las Flores offers packages to see the whales. These tours vary in length from three to eight days and one, their five-day "Kiss the Whales" tour, is very similar to the routing we suggest in our itinerary. What makes this tour so hassle-free is that one phone call can wrap everything up—when you book a room at the Posada de Las Flores, you can also reserve a tour. If none of the packages offered are quite right for you, request a quote on what it would cost to have a tour designed to suit your needs. Another possibility is Baja Ecotours, which offers a flexible program of group tours or individual travel arrangements to San Ignacio Lagoon. Baja Ecotours, tel: USA (877) 560-2252, email: info@bajaecotours.com, website: *www.bajaecotours.com*.

CRUISE SHIP: During the whale-watching season, cruise lines sometimes offer whale-watching itineraries. Most of these ships have a naturalist aboard, adding greatly to the experience. However, before signing up, read the brochure carefully to be sure the ship is going to one of the three lagoons mentioned above where the babies are born. Also, be sure that the cruise offers the option of excursions on small boats that go into the bay because you can't see the whales up close from a cruise ship. Note: Some of the ships (especially those from La Paz) go only into the Sea of Cortez, and this is not where you find the greatest concentration of whales.

INFORMATION ON GUERRERO NEGRO (LAGUNA OJO DE LIEBRE): **Guerrero Negro**, a salt-mining town, is the closest town to Laguna Ojo de Liebre (Scammon's Lagoon). There are two points of departure for whale-watching in the lagoon. Area 1 is used by most of the tour operators in town, and the cost of the tour includes round-trip transfers to the pier from which the boats depart. It is about half an hour's drive in each direction, passing through the salt mine production area. There are two tours a day: one leaves town at 8 am and the other at 11 am. The tour costs about $45 per person and includes lunch. One of the major tour operators in town is Malarrimo Eco Tours, a professional and very dependable tour company owned by the Achoy family, entrepreneurs who also operate a restaurant, gift shop, and a simple hotel (tel: (615) 157-0100, email: malarimo@telnor.net). Enrique Achoy was the first tour operator licensed by the National Ecology Institute of Mexico to conduct guided excursions to Scammon's Lagoon. Area 2 (used mostly by people who have their own car or camper) is located at the end of a 27-kilometer dirt road that turns off the highway to the south of town. A cooperative called Ejido Benito Juárez has the concession, located right on the beach. There is a building with a restaurant and an office where you can sign up for a whale excursion. When the tide is low, you need to wade out to the boat, so come equipped with water sandals. The cost of a boat ride from Area 2 is about $25 per person, which does not include transfers from town or lunch. The maximum time any boat can be out among the whales in Scammon's Lagoon is two and a half hours, a time limit set by the government to protect the whales. Private boats such as kayaks, sailboats, motorboats, or rafts are not allowed into the lagoon when the whales are in residence.

INFORMATION ON SAN CARLOS (BAHÍA MAGDALENA): Local tours are available from the town of San Carlos on the edge of **Bahía Magdalena**. One of these is Mar y Arena, owned by Fito Glez, who gives a short history of the area before taking you out into the shallow water of the bay. They have recently acquired a glass-bottom boat, which should be wonderful for when the whales swim underneath—which they often do! (Reservations and information: Mar y Arena, Zona Portuaria Int. API de B.C.S., Pto. San Carlos, B.C.S., Mexico; tel. and fax: 613-136-0076 or 613-136-0453, email: fitoglez@yahoo.com.mx).

INFORMATION ON SAN IGNACIO: Underground springs make **San Ignacio** one of the most verdant spots in Baja California. Date palms and flowering shrubs are a welcome sight after hours of driving through a beautiful but starkly barren desert whose vegetation consists mostly of towering cacti. This tiny town has a small central square dominated by the Misión San Ignacio, which was founded in 1728 by Jesuit priests. The attraction of San Ignacio is that it's the closest town for visiting the whales in San Ignacio Lagoon (about a two-hour, rough drive beyond the town). There are no hotels on the lagoon, only tent camps. There are four **tent camps** on the lagoon. All are without electricity or private bathrooms. They only provide very basic communal bathrooms and showers (with limited warm water). Two of the camps, one owned by Baja Discovery and the other by Baja Expeditions, cater to clients on charter airline tours from San Diego. Two other camps, one owned by Ecoturimo Kuyima and the other by Baja Ecotours, are available for the independent traveler. Ecoturismo Kuyima has an office on the square in San Ignacios opposite the church and offers single or multi-day whale-watching tours (email: kuyima@prodigy.net.mx, website: *www.kuyima.com*). Baja Ecortours offers tent accommodations at their Campo Cortez with a minimum stay of two nights and has an office in California for making reservations (tel: USA (877) 560-2252, email: info@bajaecotours.com, website: *www.bajaecotours.com*). In addition to independent travel, Baja Ecotours can also arrange tours originating in San Diego or Loreto.

RECOMMENDED PACING: To follow this itinerary we recommend eight nights. For those traveling independently, we suggest flying into Loreto and spending two nights there, giving you time to explore the town and then travel south to view whales at Bahía Magdalena. From Loreto, drive north to Guerrero Negro, where we recommend a stay of three nights in order to have two full days to take several whale-viewing outings. We then suggest driving south and settling in at Punta Chivato for three nights so that you have an entire day to look for shells along the beach and enjoy the beauty of the setting, and another full day to travel to Mulegé to explore the prehistoric caves. Depending on your departure from Loreto, it might be possible to drive directly from Punta Chivato to the Loreto airport (approximately two hours), or you might want to consider an overnight in Loreto, if you have a morning departure.

Note: If you have a tendency for seasickness, before your departure, you might want to ask your doctor about the advisability of purchasing Transderm patches, as the sea can be rough.

ORIGINATING TOWN   LORETO

The town of **Loreto**, the oldest town in Baja California, its first capital and home to its first mission, enjoys a spectacular setting on the Sea of Cortez looking out to the Coronado Islands, with a backdrop of the magnificent Sierra de La Giganta mountain range. It is an easy trip into town from the small airport, with taxis readily available. Tourism has developed to accommodate both seasonal whale-watchers and fishermen who claim that Loreto has some of the best marlin fishing in the world.

The first mission in Baja California, **Misión Nuestra Señora de Loreto**, was founded in Loreto in 1697 by an Italian Jesuit Padre, Juan María Salvatierra. The first structure, a tent, was replaced by a permanent building, and by 1752, the lovely church, as you see it today, was completed. This mission served as hub for the exploration of the entire Baja Peninsula and was the starting point for Padre Junipero Serra's expedition to establish a chain of missions northward into Alta California (he is well known as the priest who founded many missions in the San Francisco area).

Misión Nuestra Señora de Loreto

Loreto was destroyed by a hurricane in 1829, although the mission church survived. Fear of another hurricane motivated the move of the capital from Loreto to La Paz. After this the town remained dormant for many years, until it gained life again in the mid-1800s when a small band of English settlers came to the area (evidence of this can still be seen in the many local British names). The town didn't really grow again until the 1950s when sports enthusiasts, looking for unspoiled waters, discovered this fishing paradise. In 1997, Mexico President Zedillo declared the 60 kilometers of coastal waters off Loreto a marine park, forbidden to commercial fishing.

Loreto is a small town and easy to explore on foot. The town square is across from the **Posada de Las Flores**, and it is an easy stroll up the cobbled street to the Misión Nuestra Señora de Loreto. Loreto also boasts an interesting museum, the **Museo de Las Misiónes**, one block west of the plaza. The museum features paintings and displays showing the life of the early Jesuit priests who played such a large part in the development of not only Baja California but of "our" California (Alta California), which used to be part of Mexico. Loreto has a number of shops selling pottery, baskets, embroidered dresses, T-shirts, and blankets, and it also has the only bank in the region with an ATM machine (opposite the Posada de Las Flores). We were surprised how few people accepted credit card payment, so we needed more cash than we normally travel with. However, it is not necessary to convert to pesos as everyone seems quite comfortable accepting U.S. dollars, giving you change in pesos or sometimes in dollars. It is always handy to have $1 bills ready for tipping.

We recommend two nights in Loreto. On the day of your arrival, explore the heart of the historic town and the waterfront promenade. On your second day, take a side trip to see the whales at Bahía Magdalena.

Loreto

To reach Bahía Magdalena, leave Loreto traveling south on Highway 1, which hugs the coastline. The drive along the coastline from Loreto is spectacular, with Isla Coronado, Isla del Carmen, and the gorgeous blue waters of the bay on your left, and dramatic, jagged mountain peaks rising on your right. There is a turnout at Nopoló with a gorgeous view of water and mountains. Soon after the vista point, the road travels inland, banded by desert, cacti, and high mountain peaks. The road then climbs to a plateau as it crosses over to the west coast of Baja and overlooks a river valley. It takes approximately two hours to reach the town of San Carlos, the departure point for tours of Bahía Magdalena.

You will know when you've arrived, as the terrain changes dramatically from rocky desert to sandy inlets on the approach to town.

In San Carlos, Mar y Arena Tours, situated next to the tourist office, offers whale-watching excursions. It is just a short drive from their office to the pier next to a thatched-hut complex that is home to an international whale-study foundation. The two-hour tour goes to the center of the bay, where it is easy to see whales because of the shallow water and the white sandy bottom; but we suggest taking the three-hour trip, which takes you closer to the mouth of the bay and deeper waters. The return includes a stop by the buoys to see the barking seals, and a landing on a white stretch of beach backed by spectacular, high drifts of sand dunes.

If you are hungry and want a bite to eat before the drive back to Loreto, ask Fito Glez, owner of Mar Y Arena Tours, for restaurant recommendations—this is a wonderful region for seafood such as lobsters, shrimp, and clams.

DESTINATION I   GUERRERO NEGRO

Today's agenda is to travel the distance north from Loreto to **Laguna Ojo de Liebre** at **Guerrero Negro**, a journey that should take approximately five hours. Upon leaving Loreto, the road travels inland from the Sea of Cortez, cutting a path through desert forested by cacti and then a mountain canyon, which opens up on the other side to the gorgeous turquoise waters of Bahía Concepción, a huge bay protected by a long, jutting peninsula. During the winter, the beaches are lined with campers and trailers, since this is a paradise for northerners escaping the cold. Bahía Concepción is designated as a nature reserve, and you find here an amazing variety of marine life, birds, whales, dolphins, and shellfish.

As you continue, Highway 1 goes through the town of **Mulegé** (approximately two hours from Loreto), which is just up the coast from Bahía Concepción. It is worth a stop to visit **Misión Santa Rosalia de Mulegé**, a simple, old stone mission crowning the hillside above a grove of palm trees. Note: Mulegé is also the departure point for visiting the prehistoric wall paintings and etchings, which we take you to later in this itinerary.

Mulegé, Misión Santa Rosalia de Mulegé

Santa Rosalia, a copper-mining town and the departure point for ferries across the bay to Guaymas, is located another twenty minutes north of Mulegé. Soon after Santa Rosalia, the road turns inland and cuts a path through volcanic mountains. Past the volcanic peaks, the terrain levels, and the road is banded on either side by a vast expanse of flat desert colored only by cacti and tumbleweed, with the dramatic peaks of the Sierra San Francisco in the distance. San Ignacio is located 3 kilometers off this road, and it is perhaps worth the detour to see the small town square and its lovely old mission.

The drive between San Ignacio and Guerrero Negro is monotonous as you travel through dry, flat desert, and the scenery becomes even more desolate as you approach Guerrero Negro. If you want to include a whale-watching expedition this afternoon, before you reach Guerrero Negro, turn left on a road marked with a sign *Laguna Ojo de Liebre* and *Whales*. This dirt road goes for 27 kilometers through a 33,000-acre easement of land owned by the salt company, and you have to stop for registration soon after leaving the highway. As you approach the bay, there is another entry point where you are required to pay a 30 peso or $3 entrance fee. The skeleton of a large whale is on display in front of the only restaurant, which is also where you sign up for a whale-watching excursion ($25 per person). It was here we learned the sad story behind the name *Laguna Ojo de Liebre*

(Eye of the Jack Rabbit)—apparently the bay looked like the red eye of a jack rabbit when its waters were stained with blood during the whale slaughter of the 1800s.

Boats are tethered as close to the shore as possible, but how far you have to wade out depends on the tide. In any case, we recommend that you don waterproof shoes or go barefoot; as the sand is very sticky and claylike, and will destroy shoes. The boats (accommodating up to ten people) depart from 8 am to 4 pm and the trip lasts for about two hours.

After the tour, return to the main road, and complete the short journey farther north to the town of **Guerrero Negro**. Soon after entering town, turn right into the parking area for the Malarrimo family operation. This is the headquarters for Malarrimo Eco Tours and also the Malarrimo hotel, restaurant, and gift shop. Check in with Enrique Achoy Jr. in the tour office (on the right side of the parking area) to secure your reservations and tickets for tomorrow's whale-watching tour. Departures are at 8 am and 11 am. Although afternoon trips can provide an absolutely fantastic experience; in general, the mornings are considered the best for viewing whales, as the winds and tides are calmer and afford easier sighting through the waters. Catty-corner from the Malarrimo Eco Tours office, you find the hotel and restaurant. Elena, Enrique's sister, is in charge of the gift shop and has a tempting selection of T-shirts, jewelry, and pottery. In addition to offering the best accommodations in Guerrero Negro, the simple Hotel Malarrimo is very convenient since it is the starting point for your whale-watching tour. You can enjoy a leisurely breakfast knowing that you are just steps from the bus, whose departure is announced by the courtyard bell.

Your tour price for the whale-watching expedition includes a box lunch so there is no need to pack food or drink, but you most definitely want to wear sunscreen and dress in layers, as the winds can affect the temperature dramatically. The bus ride through the salt factory property to the boat launch takes about half an hour, passing by the bird sanctuary; where from the bus, you can spot herons, sandpipers, seagulls, egrets, and the dramatic osprey guarding their enormous nests perched on man-made pillars, constructed to facilitate their migration. It is quite fascinating to pass by piles of salt so huge that they look like mountains of snow.

At the boat launch, you board a *panga* (motor boat), which then travels quickly for about 15 minutes, bouncing across the water to where the gray whales are most easily seen. There is no doubt that you will see whales—it is just a question of how many and how friendly they will be.

Every whale-watching outing is different and one never knows how many whales will be seen. Tides and winds impact the situation dramatically. On our first trip (the 11 am departure), the boat slowed and lingered in what seemed a quiet location, and within minutes, we were literally surrounded by whales that kept diving under and around our boat—they truly seemed as curious about us as we were about them. It was endearing to see the mothers and calves swimming and diving side by side, and while whales seemed to come and go, a few of them (we could recognize them by their markings) stayed with us for more than an hour. They would *spy hop* (poke their heads out of the water), seemingly to better study us. Then they would playfully whip their tails right at the side of the boat (without question trying to splash us in fun), and would breach and blow spray just a few feet from the boat. A few particularly friendly whales rose right at the boat's edge, lingering for us to touch them. It was an incredible, once-in-a-lifetime experience.

Our second excursion (the 8 am departure) was also exciting, and had we not had the experience of the day before, we would have been thrilled. Our boat captain motored to a number of locations, and at each, we would be visited by whales who would stay awhile and then move on—curious but seemingly not as friendly as the day before. One or two came right up to the boat to look us over, but did not stay long. Our captain explained the tides were strong and the whales were having trouble lingering at the boat's edge.

While our first experience was incredible, we saw lots of whales on both excursions, both at the boat and swimming in the distance, and loved seeing them leap completely out of the water—but always a great distance away. Be sure to pack lots of film—it seemed everyone underestimated how many photos they would take. Whereas when viewing whales in U.S. waters, boats by law may not get up close to the whales; in Mexico no such rules prevail. However, there is absolutely no fear that you are intruding upon their privacy. When the boats stop in the water, these gentle giants take the initiative and they seem to come up to the boats just to say hello.

Other than the whale-watching tours and walking through the bird preserve, the town of Guerrero Negro has very little to offer the tourist. It is basically a simple, little town with one main street lined by basic, rather bland motels. The production of salt and whale-watching during season is the means of its existence. But since this is the most accessible town to outstanding whale-watching, and its lagoon, Laguna Ojo de Liebre, is considered one of the best two in Mexico for spotting these gentle giants, we recommend staying three nights in order to have two full days for whale-watching.

DESTINATION II   PUNTA CHIVATO

Retrace the drive back from Guerrero Negro, past San Ignacio, to the coast at Santa Rosalia. About twenty minutes south of Santa Rosalia, at the town of Palo Verde, there is a sign for the Posada de Las Flores (sister hotel to the one in Loreto) directing you to turn left and travel 18 kilometers down a rugged dirt road. You will be rewarded at its end as the hotel is gorgeous, sitting right on the water's edge in Punta Chivato. (See our description in the next section of the guide.) Because of its isolation and incredible setting it is not surprising to learn that this was once a getaway for movie stars. Recently renovated by its new owners, the hotel is more beautiful than ever. La Posada de Las Flores serves as a base for whale-watching trips, and yet guests come here all through the year just for the beauty of the hotel and its remarkable setting (it is actually possible to watch the sun both rise and set over the bay)—it is truly an oasis and destination in its own right. After getting settled in your room, take a stroll along the expanse of white-sand beach with its incredible bounty of beautiful shells. If you enjoy beachcombing, this beach is paradise.

If you are interested in prehistoric drawings, we recommend taking a day trip from Punta Chivato to Mulegé to see the **cave paintings**. The paintings, located on a private ranch, **Rancho La Trinidad**, approximately half-an-hour's drive along a rugged dirt road, can be visited only with a private guide. Salvador Castro Drew, one of the two authorized tour guides, has as his base of operations (until he builds his own office) the Hotel Las Casitas in the center of Mulegé. The hotel is easy to find but, for an additional fee, Salvador will pick you up at the Posada de Las Flores in Punta Chivato. Wherever you rendezvous with Salvador, you will have to stop in town at the government offices as they require that individuals register and show proof of identification before being

Canyon at Rancho Trinidad

allowed to access to the caves. You also have to pay a small fee per camera (30 pesos at the time of our visit). For this excursion, you wear comfortable shoes and pack binoculars and bottled water.

Rancho La Trinidad, Cave Paintings

Salvador offers a variety of tours of different lengths. We recommend that you request the abbreviated version of his full-day trip—four hours should be ample. Your first stop is at an organic citrus farm, then you enter the boundaries of the Rancho La Trinidad, which encompasses 5,500 beautiful acres and produces goat and cattle for cheese, milk, beef, and leather products. The next stop is to explain and identify the various plants and cacti (some of which are incredibly 400 years old) before continuing on to where, seasonally (April through September), you can observe goat cheese production, as well as the making of lassos and whips, and the process of tanning leather. A final stop is at the caretaker's cottage where you must register once again. Then it is just a short distance to where you park and begin a hike on a trail that climbs up over boulders and the barriers of an old dam into the beauty of the red-rock canyon. In about 20 minutes, you come to an open cave where the paintings date back to the Neolithic period—some 1,500 to 4,500 years B.C. This area was later home to the Cochimies Indians.

It is incredible that these prehistoric paintings are unprotected, left just as they were when first discovered—the only restriction is that one stand at least 3 meters from the paintings. Salvador provides an interesting narration of the history and explanation of the various paintings and their significance. You see fish, deer, children's handprints, and warriors painted in hues of red, black, and white. It is possible from here to journey farther up the canyon to view more cave drawings (although the first are considered the best) and even swim in a high mountain reservoir, but we suggest returning to the van and using the time to see some rock etchings. Salvador will point out to you the first of what turns out to be many etchings—fish, turtles, warriors, animals—carved in boulders above a dry riverbed. Salvador Castro Drew can be reached directly at P.O. Box No. 9, 23900 Mulegé, B.C.S., Mexico; tel: (615) 153-0232. Price for a four-hour tour is about $50 per person.

Note: There are other caves to visit, many which are found in remote canyons through the sierras of Baja, and many of which were discovered by the famous naturalist, Harry Crosby. Said to rival the paintings of Lascaux in France and Altamira in Spain, one of the most stunning is the huge mural at Cueva La Pintada in the overhanging rocks in the Cañon de Santa Teresa. Ten meters high and stretching for over 160 meters, the mural is of mystic animals and stylized people with hands extended into the sky. You might also want to consider traveling to San Ignacio, which is central to the majority of the cave paintings. Pictographs are found in caves and arroyos north of San Ignacio. It is possible to arrange tours from Guerrero Negro to an area called the Sierra de San Francisco, named as a World Heritage Site by UNESCO in 1993. In each case the access is rugged—not for the casual archaeologist—and you must always have a guide and a permit, a government regulation designed to protect these precious relics of the past.

From Mulegé, we recommend returning to the luxury of Posada de Las Flores in Punta Chivato. From there, it is an easy two-and-a-half-hour drive back to Loreto.

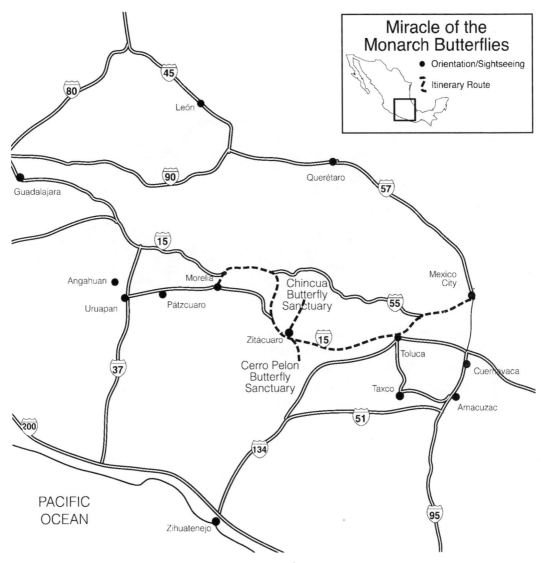

PACIFIC
OCEAN

191

Miracle of the Monarch Butterfly

It is not only the gray whale that embarks on an incredibly long journey each fall to enjoy the warmth of Mexico: the **Monarch butterfly** (*Mariposa Monarca*) makes a similar trip south. But what a difference! The gray whale weighs up to 35 tons, whereas the dainty Monarch is so light that it feels like a feather when it lands on your wrist. For years, we read about the Monarch migration, and had heard from friends that it was quite an amazing sight. However, it wasn't until we saw it for ourselves that we could really appreciate this truly breathtaking event. This wonder of nature far exceeded our expectations and provided one of those magical moments that will linger long in our memories. As the itinerary unfolds below, you will see that you need to be in good health, rather sporty, and game to walk long distances at high altitudes and ride a horse to take advantage of this experience. However, if you enjoy the outdoors, you will be totally captivated.

Every winter, hundreds of millions of brilliant black-and-orange-colored **Monarch Butterflies** brave their way through incredible hardships and flutter all the way from Canada and the northern reaches of the United States to one of about a dozen known wintering sites in the Sierra Madre mountain range in the state of Michoacán. In September, when chill hits the air, swarms of butterflies start to gather (mostly in Canada) then, when they decide that the time is perfect, they take off in flocks heading south on a long, two-month flight to warmer climes. World-renowned naturalists who have studied this migration in depth generally think that their departure is based on the slant of the sun and that once they are in flight, they are then guided by built-in magnetic compasses. They fly in daylight for six or seven hours a day at an average speed of about 12 kilometers an hour. After traveling over 4,000 kilometers, across lakes, deserts, and mountains, by November of each year (regular as clockwork), they all arrive at the same destination—an utterly remote, almost inaccessible, 3,000-meter-high mountainous area heavily forested with fir trees. The target is not large—an area of just 30 by 60 square kilometers, secreted in a cloud forest about 130 kilometers northwest of Mexico City. An estimated 100 million of these delicate creatures settle in the fir forests, accumulating in such staggering numbers that some of the sturdy tree limbs have been known to break under their weight.

This feat is even more astonishing when you realize that the butterflies that make this incredible journey have never been in Mexico before. Unlike the salmon who return to their spawning grounds, this generation taking to the air is made up of the great-great-grandchildren of ancestors who spent the previous winter in Michoacán.

For many years, no one knew where the butterflies were headed. It wasn't until 1975 that the mystery was solved when a Canadian zoologist, **Fred Urquhart**, rediscovered the wintering grounds of the Monarchs. However, the local Indians had always known about the phenomenon and were depicting butterflies in their drawings long before the arrival of Columbus.

After the rediscovery of the wintering grounds, conservationists were extremely worried that the habitat would be destroyed as more and more forests were being cut down for lumber, but thankfully, the Mexican government has wisely designated a large area as a Monarch butterfly sanctuary. Most of the land had been owned by *ejidos* (local communities of farmers who were granted the land after the Revolution of 1910) whose members were compensated for their loss of revenue from logging. Today most of these *ejidos* make money by acting as guides to the sanctuary.

Although extensive areas of forest in Mexico have now been set aside as safe havens for the butterflies, there is still fear that someday they might become extinct because of the threat to the milkweed plant on which they feed and lay their eggs. This flowering weed used to be ubiquitous throughout the butterflies' route, but now with subdivisions sprouting up everywhere, the milkweed is disappearing fast at the hands of the developers. The milkweed is in itself another strange story. This plant, which is the Monarch's staple diet, exudes a milky substance that is deadly to their enemies, but which is harmless to the butterflies.

Plan your trip to view the Monarchs between late November and late March. The butterflies start arriving in Michoacán in early November, but the sanctuaries where you go to view them frequently don't open until almost December. Then, as April approaches, the butterflies flutter up from the fir trees where they have spent the winter and begin their long journey north. Their arrival coincides with one of Mexico's premier festivals, the Day of the Dead (*Día de Los Muertos*) and old Indian legends say that the returning butterflies carry their ancestors' souls. There is usually more activity in February and March as the butterflies fly about, mating. The later you go in the season, the better chance there is for warm weather and better viewing. Sometimes there is a frost in January, at which time the butterflies stay clustered for warmth in the branches of the trees and don't fly about. However, there can be a cold spell at any time, so we recommend staying several days so you can pick the best day for your adventure. When scheduling your itinerary, try to avoid visiting the butterflies on a weekend since the sanctuaries are much more crowded with busloads of tourists.

The sanctuaries are tucked in the forests of Michoacán, located between Mexico City and Morelia. There are organized one-day bus tours during the butterfly season leaving from

Mexico City, Morelia, and Pátzcuaro—all places that are wonderful destinations in their own right and described in depth elsewhere in our guide. Any of the hotels where you stay should be able to steer you to a company that offers these bus tours, which leave very early in the morning and return in the evening—usually about a 12-hour trip. If you are traveling with friends and have your own small group, we recommend that you hire a guide with a car instead of taking a bus tour. If you have several people in your party, the cost isn't much greater (maybe even less) and it is a far more personal way to make the trip, as you can plan your own schedule. Again, your hotel can put you in touch with a reputable guide. If you are on a really tight budget, and yet want to splurge on a butterfly spree, this too can be done. There are first-class buses from Mexico City to **Zitácuaro** and from there, a local bus can take you to Angangueo, which is about an hour's ride beyond. Once your bus arrives in Angangueo, you can overnight at one of the very basic hotels in town and arrange a trip to see the butterflies from there. Guides are readily available.

For a more leisurely way to see the quite remarkable Monarch butterfly migration, we offer the following suggestions:

RECOMMENDED PACING: Instead of just one day, we highly recommend spending at least three nights in the area, so as to have a choice of two days (for better weather) to visit the butterflies, and also a chance to see other places of interest in this beautiful and interesting niche of Mexico, so frequently missed on the normal tourist route.

ZITÁCUARO

The closest town to the best known of the butterfly sanctuaries is **Angangueo**, a tiny town squeezed in a narrow, mountain valley where silver was mined from 1792 to 1992. The village has just one cobbled road cutting through the middle and leading up to the 3,000-meter mountaintop. Although Angangueo is the nearest town to the most popular sanctuaries, we recommend you stay instead in **Zitácuaro**, which is about a 45-minute drive away. There are three reasons we suggest you stay in Zitácuaro: The first reason is that Zitácuaro is centrally located for visiting not only the **Chincua Butterfly Sanctuary**, but also the lesser known, recently opened, **Cerro Pelon Butterfly Sanctuary**. The second reason is that Zitácuaro is a convenient base for other sightseeing possibilities (see descriptions below). The third reason is that Zitácuaro offers a delightful small hotel, the **Rancho San Cayetano**, located in a parklike setting just outside of town. This intimate inn, owned and managed by Lisette and Pablo Span, has much to recommend it: the lovely Lisette Span, who is French by birth, is a fabulous cook and oversees excellent meals, while her husband, Pablo, is exceptionally knowledgeable about what to see and do in the area and will be glad to help you plan your day.

From Morelia, the fastest way to reach Zitácuaro is to take the toll road 15 marked toward Mexico City. Exit at Maravatío and follow the signs toward Ciudad Hidalgo and Zitácuaro. It is about a two-hour drive from Morelia to Zitácuaro. A good detailed map is necessary, since once you leave the highway, the roads are not well marked. From Mexico City, take the toll road 15 west to Toluca and continue north for another 100 km. on road No. 15 (which after Toluca is no longer a four-lane highway) to Zitácuaro. It is about a two-hour drive from the outskirts of Mexico City to Zitácuaro.

Zitácuaro, Rancho San Cayetano

The Rancho San Cayetano is about 3 kilometers south of town on the 51 to Huetamo. When making reservations, ask for detailed driving instructions.

Miracle of the Monarch Butterfly

The first day you arrive, after settling into the inn, we suggest a walk that takes about 20 minutes up a cobbled, narrow street to visit the precious little **San Pancho parish church**, which faces a postage-stamp-sized square in the tiny hamlet of the same name. The church has a rustic interior, stone walls, and a simple, yet beautiful altar. If you are lucky and the charming Italian priest, who has worked tirelessly to restore the church, is there, he can enrich your experience by telling you about this 16th-century church's history.

CHINCUA and CERRO PELON BUTTERFLY SANCTUARIES

Most of the literature about Monarchs says that the best place to see them is the Rosario Butterfly Sanctuary. This is the best-known sanctuary since it was the original site, but it is *not* the place to go. The Rosario Sanctuary involves a 45-minute ride in an open truck over hopelessly bumpy roads, after which it is a long walk to the site. In addition, the Rosario Sanctuary is far more congested and more commercial than the ones we suggest, either the Chincua Butterfly Sanctuary or the Cerro Pelon Butterfly Sanctuary.

Chincua Butterfly Sanctuary: After a leisurely breakfast, head off from Rancho San Cayetano for your butterfly adventure. There is no need to rush because midday, when the temperature is the highest, is the best time to view the butterflies, which cluster in huge masses on the limbs of the trees to keep warm. They don't begin to fly about until the sun warms the air, so arriving early in the morning is of no advantage.

To reach the Chincua Sanctuary, follow the road on your map that leads north from Zitácuaro through Ocampo and on to the tiny town of Angangueo. You might want to stop briefly in Angangueo to see its churches, the main plaza, and visit the **Casa Parker Museum** that describes the mining history of the town. Just up the block from the central church is an historic **mural** that covers both sides of the walls of a narrow, block-long alleyway.

Go through **Angangueo** and continue for about 8 kilometers as the road climbs up ever higher into the mountains. You will see guides along the way trying to catch your attention and entice you to let them take you to see the butterflies. Don't stop, just keeping going. Soon, on the right, you will see a sign with a picture of a large Monarch butterfly and here you turn left off the road into the sanctuary, paying at the entrance for parking.

As you drive on, you soon come to the parking lot where you leave your car. It is a little confusing from here on, since everything is delightfully laid-back and non-commercial, but just head toward the horses for hire and you will be approached by some of the guides. The price is set, so you don't need to worry about negotiating—everyone charges the same and included in the price is someone (usually a young boy) who will lead your horse. As well as a horse for each person in your party, you want to hire an extra guide to accompany you all the way to the butterflies, beyond where you leave your horse.

Miracle of the Monarch Butterfly

Once you are on your horse, the adventure begins. The path, dappled with sunlight filtering through the towering trees, winds up through a beautiful pine and fir forest. The altitude is over 3,000 meters, so although you can walk, it is very strenuous—and the horses are great fun!

After about a 40-minute ride, you come to the "horse parking lot" and continue on foot for about another half hour, led by your guide. A narrow path twists downward through the fir and pine trees, and occasionally gaps appear in the dense foliage through which you catch glimpses of beautiful faraway valleys. You will be glad you have a guide, for not only does the path sometimes split, but also it's tricky to know when you have arrived. Several times we came to small clearings filled with butterflies and we thought we were "there." However, you will *know* when you are at the site. A gentle hum in the air signals you are close. At first the hum is almost unnoticeable, but becomes louder as you approach and then, all of a sudden, the air is filled with butterflies. You can hardly see the sky through what looks like confetti in the air. You would think that there could be no more until you glance at the trees whose limbs are smothered with huge clumps of butterflies huddled together for warmth, looking like enormous nests. It's very much like being in a cathedral: the ambiance is almost ethereal and you cannot help being humbled by the experience. You will probably want to spend at least an hour here, soaking up the sublime display of nature. This is a photographer's dream, so bring lots of film to capture the magic of the moment. Note: Flash photography is prohibited.

It will be difficult to leave this unforgettable scene, but you can't stay forever. When it is time to go, retrace your way back to your horse and the parking lot. In addition to paying the set fee, tip your guides well. They make very little money and now that logging (once their main source of income) has been halted, their yearly subsistence is dependent upon the short tourist season when the butterflies come to Michoacán.

Cerro Pelon Butterfly Sanctuary: Either instead of, or in addition to, the Chincua Sanctuary the Cerro Pelon Sanctuary makes for a superb adventure. This sanctuary, located about a 40-minute drive southeast of Zitácuaro, is tricky to find; but if you are staying at the Hotel Rancho San Cayetano, Pablo Span can help you with directions.

There are three access points: El Capulin, Macheros, and El Campamento. The one we chose was the Macheros entrance. The overall quest is quite similar to the approach to the Cerro Pelon Sanctuary: You drive through the entrance, park your car, arrange for a horse and hire a guide to lead you up the mountain. The difference is that at the Cerro Pelon it takes longer by horseback to reach the butterflies (about a 2-hour ride) and the way is much more difficult. This excursion would not be suitable for children or those not experienced with horseback riding. Even if you are familiar with horses, you might feel more comfortable to have a guide lead your horse since the path is narrow and very steep. Nevertheless, the Cerro Pelon Sanctuary holds many rewards. Not only does it have awesome views, but also has the enormous advantage that the site is little known.

Whichever sanctuary your choose, on returning to Zitácuaro ask Pablo Span if he will show you his excellent video about the butterflies. This will answer most of your questions about the migration and reinforce your experience of the day.

Miracle of the Monarch Butterfly

MORE SIGHTSEEING

There so are many places to visit in this part of the state of Michoacán that if you have the luxury of time, we highly recommend at least an extra day or more here. Another advantage of spending at least two full days is that if the weather is unseasonably cold (at which time the butterflies stay clustered on the branches of the trees), you can reverse this itinerary and do your sightseeing on the first day, then go to see the butterflies on the second day, when it might be warmer. Some of the places to see in the area are the following:

Enandio Waterfalls: This 100-meter spectacular waterfall is located south of Zitácuaro on the highway to Huetamo. At the 21-kilometer marker, turn right to reach the town of Enandio, a distance of 2 kilometers. Stop in this village to visit the church and its 17th-century Saint Isabel of Hungary statue. In front of the church, ask for a guide to show you the way to the waterfalls (there are no signs). You drive along a 3- to 4-kilometer dirt road, park the car, and take the 45-minute downhill walk on a path to a pool suitable for swimming. Be careful—the last 25 meters are steep and slippery.

Ocampo: The small town of Ocampo is located about 10 kilometers south of Angangueo. Its attractions include the Templo del Santo Niño, the Hacienda de Trojes, and items by local artisans who specialize in handworked wood.

San Felipe de Los Alzati: Nine kilometers west of Zitácuaro, the town of San Felipe de Los Alzati has a beautiful 16th-century church that is well known for its atrium and monolithic cross.

Los Alzati: If you are interested in archaeological sites, particularly those off the beaten path, Los Alzati is a treat. Here, in a deserted field, you find the ruins of once-mighty stone pyramids This was an Otomi ceremonial center with beautiful sweeping views of the valley below, best seen in the afternoon before sunset. It is especially fun to visit this site since you will probably be the only person about.

There are in addition day trips to other attractions that include natural hot sulfur springs, caves, and the warm-water springs in San José Purua. Information is available from Rancho San Cayetano.

Miracle of the Monarch Butterfly

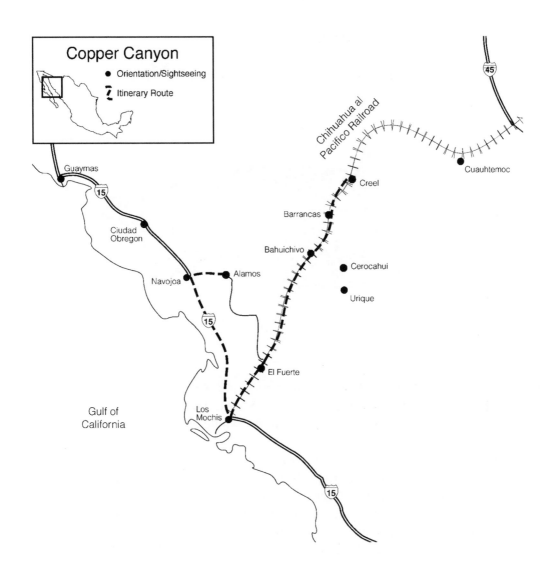

Copper Canyon

- ● Orientation/Sightseeing
- ⌇ Itinerary Route

Chihuahua al Pacifico Railroad

Cuauhtemoc

Guaymas

Creel

Barrancas

Ciudad Obregon

Bahuichivo

Cerocahui

Urique

Navojoa

Alamos

El Fuerte

Gulf of California

Los Mochis

Copper Canyon
A Train Adventure to Hidden Mexico

Mexico's well known **Copper Canyon** (*Barranca del Cobre*) boasts statistics more impressive than the Grand Canyon in the United States. The Copper Canyon is deeper and, if you include the six canyons that make up the whole, covers more than four times the area. However, in our estimation, although the Copper Canyon's figures are more dramatic, the Grand Canyon still wins the prize for beauty and grandeur. Nevertheless, the Copper Canyon is well worth visiting. Not only is the canyon very pretty, but there are also other reasons to make the journey: you have the opportunity to take a train ride that is lots of fun, you have the chance to stay in a hotel with a breathtaking perch on a cliff overlooking the canyon, and you have the rare privilege of seeing the reclusive Tarahumara Indians whose way of life has changed little in over a thousand years.

You can make the trip any time of the year, but many prefer the fall when everything is very green and the waterfalls are gushing after the summer rains. Spring too is a lovely time to make the journey. If you go in winter, be sure to take warm clothing since the weather can be very cold and it can snow. In summer, if you hike down to the floor of the canyon, the weather is very hot and humid. Just remember, the canyon area is made up of two distinct climate zones, with the weather ranging from Alpine at the top of the canyon to subtropical at the floor.

The only easy access to the canyon is by train, which gives you various options of where to leave from and where to stop along the route. In the itinerary below we have outlined a way to have the ultimate experience in a short length of time.

RECOMMENDED PACING: We suggest two nights in El Fuerte (one before your train trip and one at the end of the train trip), and two nights in Barrancas at the Posada Mirador—a minimum of four nights total.

ORIGINATING TOWN   EL FUERTE

The Copper Canyon is so remote that for many years it was inaccessible to tourists. Only a few rugged individuals made their way by foot or on horseback to enjoy the spectacle of this masterpiece of nature. The situation changed dramatically in 1961 when the Chihuahua al Pacifico Railroad was completed, connecting the towns of Los Mochis (about 20 kilometers from the coast) on the west and Chihuahua on the east, a total distance of about 660 kilometers. You can take the **train** from either direction, but since the most beautiful part of the ride is that on the west side of the Continental Divide, we recommend making a round-trip journey from the west instead of going all the way to Chihuahua since the last part of the trip is a bit bland.

Because the train leaves early in the morning, you will need to spend the night before your departure at your originating town. Many passengers board the train at Los Mochis, where the train originates. However, we suggest spending the night instead in the small Colonial town of **El Fuerte**, which offers several advantages: El Fuerte, founded in 1564 along the El Fuerte River by the conquistador Don Francis de Ibarra, is much more charming than Los Mochis; you can sleep in later since the train leaves Los Mochis at 6 am whereas it leaves El Fuerte at 7:40 am; and El Fuerte offers the Posada del Hidalgo (featured in our guide), which has far more old-world ambiance than anything in Los Mochis.

View of the Copper Canyon

You can take a bus from Los Mochis to El Fuerte, although it is easily accessible by car on a good road. Once you arrive in El Fuerte, follow signs to the large, central square, where you easily find the Posada del Hidalgo sitting just off one corner. If you get lost, ask anyone to point the way. Note: Although the official address of the hotel is Calle Hidalgo, the entrance is around the corner on Cinco de Mayo.

One enormous advantage of booking a room at the Posada del Hidalgo is that it is owned by the Balderrama family, pioneers of the Copper Canyon tourist industry. They were the first family to see the need for hotels and tours in the canyon area and now own most of the best hotels and offer most of the tours. They also sell train tickets, so with one telephone call to their central office (800-896-8196 from the U.S.), you can book not only hotels, but also train tickets and transfers to the train station (which is about 7 kilometers from town). You might be able to call your own cab and also purchase the train tickets for less money on an individual basis, but why do it? It is so satisfactory to have everything arranged and know in advance that everything is confirmed. Work out your dates for the Posada del Hidalgo, the **Posada Mirador** (second and third night on the itinerary), and the trains—and book it all at once. When you arrive at the Posada del Hidalgo, they will give you vouchers for the hotels, transfers, and train tickets. Also, when you make the reservations for the hotel, ask about leaving your car at the Posada del Hidalgo while you are away for the several days of your canyon trip.

After settling in at the hotel, take a stroll around the charming, small, historic town with its attractive, central plaza studded with palm trees and narrow cobblestone streets ornamented by 17th-century buildings.

DESTINATION I   BARRANCAS

Today your train adventure begins. The official time for the train to leave El Fuerte for the Copper Canyon is 7:40 am, but the train is rarely on time. Request a wake-up call at the reception, and ask what time you need to leave for the train. When you make your reservation, request the entire "package"—your hotels, train tickets, and round-trip transfers to the station.

It is about a 15-minute drive to the small train station. You will probably have to wait a while for the train to come, so bring a good book or postcards to write. The train, known as the **Chihuahua al Pacifico**, is amazingly nice. Not lavish, but far better than we had expected. It is air-conditioned, the seats are comfortable, everything is neat and tidy, and there is a bathroom in each rail car. In addition, there is a cute bar on one of the cars where you can enjoy a drink, and a good restaurant with attentive service where you can get breakfast or lunch. The best views of the canyon are on the right side of the train but if you find that your seats are on the other side, you can often switch since the train is not usually full.

At first the train travels through the rather arid lowlands before gradually beginning the ascent into the Sierra Madre Mountains, where it loops and turns its way up. As you climb ever higher through the pine forests, there are views of the canyon far below. The train bridges high ravines, traces surging rivers, climbs to 2400 meters, and tunnels through the mountains. Altogether, there are 86 tunnels, 37 bridges, and one 270-degree turn. The track runs mostly through the forests rather than hugging the rim of the canyon, but stay alert since stunning canyon views frequently pop unexpectedly into view. However, the very finest views await at the hotel where you will be spending the night.

Officially, the train is scheduled to arrive at your stop, Barrancas, at 1:30 pm. It will probably be much later than this when the train slowly comes to a halt, at what is no more than a tiny little station and a cluster of buildings. There will be a bus waiting to take you to your hotel, the Posada Mirador, which is only about a five-minute drive away. The Balderrama family, owners of the Posada Mirador, also have another hotel, the Posada Rancho, just a few steps from the train station. Although this hotel is pleasant, when making reservations be *sure* to specify the Posada Mirador, since it is the one with the incredible setting.

If you visit the Copper Canyon, you just *must* stay at the **Posada Mirador**. The hotel seems as if it is pasted onto the steep canyon walls and has views more stunning than any you will see on your train ride. Not only is the location spectacular, but also the hotel itself is a real winner. The salmon-colored stucco building looks like a large, rugged, Indian adobe dwelling. As you approach, you will see Indian women, with their children playing beside them, sitting on the steps of the hotel weaving and selling their baskets. The craftsmanship of their wares is outstanding.

Posada Mirador

Once inside, you find a charming, lodge-like ambiance. Low, beamed ceilings, a huge stone fireplace, tiled floors, enormous murals showing the canyon and the Indians, leather and wood furniture, woven rugs, brightly painted walls, and native crafts create a delightful, rustic atmosphere. One wall of the lounge/dining room is a wall of glass and opens onto a huge deck suspended over the canyon. The views are breathtaking. The restaurant encompasses one part of the central lounge where long tables are set up family-style to serve the many tour groups, as well as individual travelers. Don't expect gourmet dining—instead, you have just good, simple cooking appropriate for serving a lot of people quickly and efficiently. The waiters are friendly and there is plenty to eat.

Plan to stay two nights at the Posada Mirador—more if you want to do a lot of hiking. Your room at the inn has its own balcony, where you could easily sit all day soaking up the panoramic view that unfolds below. However, there are all kinds of activities to enjoy from the hotel, such as hikes down to the canyon floor, visits to Indian villages, horseback riding, and jeep excursions. You can ask at the reception desk for information on the possibilities of what to see and do here, and the staff can help you with all arrangements.

This is the perfect spot to explore the Copper Canyon and there are several things you just must not miss. Be sure to take the trail that leads steeply down the canyon wall to visit a complex of Indians who are living as their ancestors have for countless generations. Their homes are perched on a narrow shelf of the canyon wall, half cave, half home. It is almost unbelievable that anyone is living like this in the 21st century. Longer walks take you deeper into the canyon, where you find more Indian dwellings. Also, be sure to take the trail that makes a loop below the hotel—the views are lovely, so stop along the way to savor them. There are a few observation points en route, but whenever you pause and look down, the vista is beautiful.

One of the highlights of a visit to the Copper Canyon, in addition to experiencing the canyon itself, is the opportunity to learn more about the gentle **Tarahumara Indians** (also called the Raramuri), who share a common ancestry with the fierce Aztecs who settled farther to the south. They are really your hosts, having dwelled in this remote, almost inaccessible part of Mexico long before any tourists arrived. This is their home and you will be introduced to them from the beginning of your train trip, since the women, colorfully dressed in their native costumes, are at all the train stations and hotels where they sit quietly weaving their **baskets**, which are always for sale. They bring their children with them—infants, warmly wrapped in blankets, sleep beside their mothers, while older children romp and play nearby.

Tarahumaran Women and Children

Be sure to buy a few baskets—they are beautifully made and reasonably priced. The Tarahumara Indians are renowned as long-distance runners and if you walk the paths twisting along the canyon walls at what you think is a brisk pace, you will be amazed at how quickly you are passed by women and children whose speed will far surpass yours. It is said the men were able to chase deer tirelessly, following them for days at a time until their prey collapsed from exhaustion. The Tarahumara Indians used to occupy the entire state of Chihuahua. However, in the 17th century when the Spaniards arrived and began to enslave the Indians to work their mines, the Tarahumarans moved ever deeper into the remote, hidden valleys of the canyons. In winter, when the weather can be very cold due to the high elevation, they move to the floor of the canyons where the climate is almost tropical. In summer, they move to higher elevations. They live in **cliff dwellings** in the side of the canyon or log huts, or a combination of both. Due to their isolation, their way of life, dress, food, and traditions have changed little. They are a shy, independent people, who seem to treasure their way of life. Although the government has tried to make their life easier, they seem to prefer living as they do protected against the influence of modern civilization.

DESTINATION II   BACK TO EL FUERTE

You can continue on the train, taking it to the final destination, Chihuahua. However, the scenery gets less dramatic as the train goes east. There are a few stops en route to Chihuahua that are somewhat interesting. One of these is **El Divisadero,** where the train stops for 15 minutes so that passengers can enjoy the view from a scenic overlook and buy souvenirs from Indians selling at small stalls (though the view can't surpass that of the Posada Mirador!) Another stop farther east is at Creel, a small, bland country town, popular as a base for those embarking on hiking trips into the canyons.

Our suggestion is to head back west, the same way you came (the seats on the left side of the train provide the best views). Although repeating your journey, the scenery always looks different approached from the opposite direction. The train is supposed to depart from the Barrancas station at 1:20 pm and arrive back at El Fuerte at 6:15 pm. However, the train rarely runs to schedule, so ask at the Posada Mirador what time the train is expected and what time the bus leaves for the short trip to the train station.

When you arrive back at El Fuerte, there should be a taxi waiting to take you back to your hotel, the Posada del Hidalgo, in time for dinner in their cozy restaurant.

The next morning, you can continue on your way or, if you want to extend your stay in El Fuerte, there are more things to see including nearby ancient petroglyphs, a local market, Indian villages, and a river float trip.

Cliff Dwelling of Tarahumaran Indians

OPTIONAL EXTENSIONS TO ITINERARY

The above itinerary covers the basic highlights of the Copper Canyon, giving you time to enjoy its major attractions. However, for those who would like to spend more time in the area and enjoy further adventures, we suggest you expand your stay to include one or all of the following extensions.

CREEL, SIERRA LODGE: About two hours east of Barrancas, the train stops in **Creel**. The town is not especially attractive, but the surrounding area is lovely. About half-an-hour's drive from the train station, you can stay in the Sierra Lodge, a small hotel built on a rise just above the river. Here you feel a part of this primitive, beautiful environment. The hotel has no electricity and no phones—at night the rooms are lit by kerosene lamps and warmed by pot-bellied stoves. Wholesome, hearty meals are included in the room rate and served family-style in a charming, rustic dining room with a large, open fireplace. The building, made of logs and stucco and topped by a corrugated tin roof, looks like an old-fashioned motel—a long strip of rooms with a porch stretching across the front, where rocking chairs are set for relaxing and enjoying the vista. The hotel is very primitive in many respects, but you are not really roughing it at the Sierra Lodge. Although the price is unbelievably low, the simple accommodations are very pleasant, with hot water in the bathrooms, comfortable beds, plenty of warm blankets, fluffy bath towels tied with ribbons, and even bathrobes in the rooms.

CEROCAHUI, HOTEL MISIÓN: Owned by the Balderramas, who own most of the hotels and organize most of the tours in the Copper Canyon, the Misión adds a whole new dimension to your canyon experience. As with the other Balderrama properties, a stay here is very easy to set up since one phone call to the head office (800-896-8196 from the U.S.) completes all the needed arrangements including hotel, train, and transfer to the hotel. Spending the night here, either before, or after going to the Posada Mirador, works in well with the above itinerary. About four hours after the train leaves El Fuerte, it stops in Bahuichivo. Balderrama Tours arranges the transfer to the hotel, which is located about an hour from the train station along a very bumpy road to Cerocahui, a hamlet in a high, fertile river valley of orchards surrounded by the Sierra Madre mountains. The hotel, named for the old Jesuit mission, exudes charm. The guestrooms are cozy with beamed ceilings, carved wooden furniture, terracotta floors, and brightly colored hand-woven fabrics. You can take guided horseback rides, trek to the lovely Huicochi waterfall (five hours round trip), explore the many nearby trails, take a bus to the old mining town of Urique where there is a lookout with sweeping canyon views, and visit the Jesuit mission across from the hotel. The mission was founded in 1694 by Juan María de Salvatierra, a Jesuit priest from Italy who was the first European to reach the floor of the canyon, and who later founded the first mission in Baja California in Loreto.

ALAMOS, HACIENDA DE LOS SANTOS: We cannot resist mentioning a side trip to Alamos. Although not located in the Copper Canyon, **Alamos** is a Colonial jewel very much like El Fuerte and shares a similar heritage. The **Hacienda de Los Santos**, a remarkably charming, beautifully decorated hacienda abounding with antiques and exquisite gardens, is one of our favorite places to stay. The town is tucked into the hills about a three-hour drive north of El Fuerte, making it a convenient stopover for a few days, either before, or after your Copper Canyon adventure. If you have the time, go to Alamos and enjoy the spa, the food, the superb accommodations, the gardens, the swimming pools, and the tender personal attention.

Alamos, Hacienda de Los Santos

Cerocahui, Hotel Misión

Places to Play in the Sun
An Overview

Mexico has long beckoned tourists to its beautiful coastal resorts where one can play in the sun and enjoy excellent weather, beautiful beaches, splendid accommodations, and wonderful food. The quality of the resorts available is unsurpassed anywhere in the world. One need not go all the way to the South Pacific for sublime secluded beaches studded with palm trees, or to Penang for a gentle warm sea, or to the Seychelles for pristine, white-sand beaches. These can all be found in Mexico. To make these beach resorts even more alluring, you find here some of the finest hotels in the world—not just super-expensive, lavish, world-class resorts (although there are plenty of these), but also charming little inns on secluded beaches. There are even several places to stay that have no road access but can be reached only by boat. How much more exclusive can you be?

We have divided the beach areas into three geographical parts: the Pacific Coast, Baja California Sur, and the Mexican Caribbean. Each of these areas has its own personality.

The Pacific Coast abounds with wide, golden-sand beaches and wonderful swimming. Here you find a great variety of resorts including Mazatlán, Puerto Vallarta, Manzanillo, Zihuatanejo, Ixtapa, and Huatulco.

At the tip of the Baja Peninsula, the ultra-chic Los Cabos area is becoming more popular every day. With its gorgeous golf courses, superb lavish hotels, and excellent sport fishing, it offers something for everyone. Here you find the colorful towns of San José del Cabo and Cabo San Lucas, joined by a strip of some of the most expensive real estate in the world, called simply The Corridor.

The eastern coast of Mexico has just one main beach resort—but what a resort this is! The Mexican Caribbean on the east coast of the Yucatán Peninsula offers some of the most astounding white-sand beaches in the world, made all the more beautiful by the turquoise water that laps upon the shore. To add the finishing touch of perfection, this is the world of the Maya and you can combine visits to superb archaeological sites with your time lazing on the beach.

To help you decide where to go, in the following itinerary we give the special attributes of each area along with sightseeing possibilities. Once you decide where you want to go, there are many fabulous places to stay.

Places to Play in the Sun
The Pacific Coast

Puerto Vallarta, Cathedral

Along the Pacific Coast, dense jungles sweep down to meet the deep-blue Pacific, providing spectacular backdrops for modern resort cities and smaller coastal villages. Pristine beaches stretch for miles, and in some areas are snuggled in coves embraced by high bluffs. In other spots, the mountains drop right down to the sea where the surf pounds against the rocks. The waters of the Pacific are not as crystal-clear or as turquoise-blue as you find in the Caribbean, but the golden-sand beaches are some of the best in Mexico and usually safe for swimming. A profusion of modern hotels, easy air access, and a growing array of activities have transformed this region of Mexico into one of the country's premier resort areas. Although the landscape may be similar all the way along this western coast of Mexico, with wide sweeps of beaches dotted with palm trees and mountains rising just inland, the resorts here couldn't be more varied in personality. From high-energy seaside cities to pristine, primitive coves, this is the Mexico that first lured vacationers from around the globe.

Spanish conquistadors frequented the Pacific Coast, lured by its numerous sheltered coves and protected bays from which to set sail for the Far East. Years later, Mexico's first tourists found the same elements appealing and began to come for holidays.

The following beach resorts are listed geographically, starting with Mazatlán in the north and ending with Huatulco in the south.

MAZATLÁN

Mazatlán, "land of the deer" in the ancient Nahuatl language, offers 20 kilometers of sandy beaches. Hosting more than one million visitors each year, it is definitely geared towards tourists looking for casual, value-packed vacations. Most of the hotels here are high-rise and offer inexpensive, all-inclusive packages that include airfare, room, and meals. More than any other beach resort, it probably best represents the golden beaches, fresh seafood, and inexpensive vacation accommodations that launched Mexico's appeal to travelers. Most of the resorts are located on the Zona Dorado (Golden Zone) with its long expanse of shoreline, trendy restaurants, and endless tourist shops. There has been much development over the past few years and Mazatlán has become a favorite for college students at spring break.

The downtown area has an old Colonial section. Here you find the splendidly restored **Teatro Ángela Peralta**, named after a famous Mazatlán-born opera singer, and the **cathedral**, which has a gothic exterior and a baroque interior. Both buildings date from the late 19th century. Several of the buildings around Plaza Machado have been restored and converted into artists' studios, galleries, and restaurants. The renovation of the Teatro Ángela Peralta has done wonders for the historic section, which had become rather ramshackle. The surrounding area is upgrading and becoming constantly more attractive.

Mazatlán, Beach Scene

Mazatlán is famous for its carnival. With its pre-Lent festivals including parades, coronation parties, street dances, fireworks and floats, Mazatlán claims that this is the third-largest celebration in the world after Rio de Janeiro and New Orleans.

Bullfights are also a passion in Mazatlán and are usually held in the late afternoon on Saturdays from mid-December to April in the Plaza de Toros Monumental. The city is one of the best places on the west coast to watch a bullfight.

Several day trips are possible from Mazatlán. You can take a boat tour to the islands just off the coast for viewing wildlife and enjoying secluded beaches. You can also take a drive into the mountains or to the towns of Concordia or Copala, both about 65 kilometers away. Concordia is famous for its leather goods and furniture shops, and Copala is an old mining village with whitewashed adobe homes draped with bright pink bougainvillea. Copala has been declared a national historic site and many United States citizens have retired here.

PUERTO VALLARTA

Puerto Vallarta has a scenic location on the sea with the Sierra Madre foothills behind it, and the ornate crown of the **Church of Our Lady of Guadalupe** serving as a photogenic landmark. It is a quaint, picturesque town with cobblestone streets, Colonial buildings, traditional Spanish red-tile rooftops, and brilliant flowers. This is the second most-visited resort in Mexico (behind Cancún), boasting 43 kilometers of golden-sand beaches with many private coves accessible only by boat, great dining and nightlife, accommodations for every budget, entertainment, art galleries, shopping, world-class golf and tennis, activities and excursions galore, and fun: all this in the atmosphere of a traditional Mexican village.

In 1963, Ava Gardner and Richard Burton starred in *Night of the Iguana*, filmed in Puerto Vallarta. Burton and his new love, Elizabeth Taylor, had a wild romance during the filming (even though they were both married to others at the time). The international *paparazzi* arrived, and this small seaside village was never the same again. Now with a population of over 250,000, Puerto Vallarta continues to grow as new hotels are constantly being built north of town. However, the old town retains its original, typical Mexican charm, since there can be no further building—Puerto Vallarta town is bound by hills, leaving no room for expansion. In fact, there are just two main, one-way streets (usually very congested with traffic) leading through town, one going north and one south.

The majority of Puerto Vallarta's hotels are not in the town center, but just to the north. Here the hills are farther back from the coast, and you find a long sweep of wide beach bound by a continuous strip of high-rise, modern hotels. Other hotels are located in small coves just south of town, where the hills drop right into the sea, forming intimate, sheltered coves.

The newest tourist area is north of Puerto Vallarta, just across the border in the state of Nayarit in an area of spectacular beauty called **Punta Mita**. The stunning Four Seasons was the first hotel to be built here, but more are soon to follow. For some reason the beaches here are of superb white sand, surpassing by far those usually found along the Pacific Coast, where the sand is coarser and golden yellow.

Puerto Vallarta offers all the usual beach-resort activities, but the river is also popular for kayaking. Also offered are expeditions along the jungle trails that lead into the mountains, which are popular for mountain biking and horseback riding.

There are many boat excursions available. During the season, whale and dolphin expeditions are popular, while another excursion involves a trip south in a boat that hugs the splendid coast to **Yelapa** (a private beach accessible only by boat). The town isn't special, but the trip down is lots of fun.

COSTA ALEGRE

Costa Alegre, considered one of Mexico's greatest undiscovered treasures, is becoming a favored hideaway both for celebrities and the wealthy seeking seclusion in a natural paradise. Alternatively referred to as Costa Alegre (Happy Coast) or Costa Careyes (Turtle Coast) after the many sea turtles that nest here annually, it encompasses a 240-kilometer stretch of coast that runs from Puerto Vallarta in the north to Manzanillo in the south. This entire coastal area is magical, with endless, untouched coves and secluded beaches tucked between folds of dense jungle stretching to the edge of the sea. Today the Costa Alegre is home to an eclectic array of the most unique, captivating, and exclusive places to stay, with a choice of activities including championship golf and polo. We have listed the hotels under "Costa Alegre" in the *"Hotel Descriptions"* section of the book with their specific town name following as many of these small towns are tucked along the coast in secluded areas that might not show up on a map.

The two-lane highway 200 connecting Puerto Vallarta and Manzanillo runs a bit inland, rarely giving a glimpse of the sea. The road is safe, but has no lighting and curves through mountains, so it is best to make the drive during daylight hours. Along the way, you pass through a few nondescript villages, but the hotels are secreted within vast jungles and can be reached only by narrow lanes. Some of the hotels have built their own access roads, but others have as their only access the original dirt roads. It seems as if you are in the middle of nowhere but when you arrive, what a marvelous surprise awaits!

Costa Alegre

These resorts are tricky to find (and some are so isolated that the only approach is by boat) so it is vital that you have prior reservations and obtain detailed instructions to the hotel of your choice. The best maps, even though supposedly up to date, are not accurate. Also, many of the hotels do not want "drop-ins," so have few or no signs, and once you arrive at the entrance, you find a guard and a security gate. You will be amazed at the ultimate luxury available in such a totally remote area.

MANZANILLO

Manzanillo? Never heard of it? Except to the Canadians, who come in droves during their bitterly cold winter, Manzanillo is a relatively unknown destination. It's located on the west coast of Mexico, about 250 kilometers south of Puerto Vallarta. Manzanillo doesn't have the pizzazz of Puerto Vallarta's quaint cobbled streets or Acapulco's non-stop nightlife: its allure lies in its pristine beaches, near-perfect winter weather, and lack of commercialism. Here you feel you have found the *real* Mexico, not one prettied up for show. Downtown Manzanillo is a busy port for large cargo ships and has little appeal although an effort has been made to spruce up the central square and the promenade along the waterfront. The popular resort hotels are not in town, but located to the north.

In the winter, there is rarely rain, just day after day of sunshine. Summertime is also popular, especially with Mexican families. Frequently there are thunderstorms, but these usually occur in the afternoon or at night. If you enjoy swimming in warm water, you'll be thrilled to learn that in summer the temperature of the ocean hovers at 90 degrees. Absolute heaven!

Manzanillo is famous for its superb golf and is quickly emerging as a key golf destination: two of its courses were listed in the top ten of *Golf Digest* magazine. Another draw for sportsmen is deep-sea fishing. Designated the "Sailfish Capital of the World," Manzanillo is considered by many to have some of the best deep-sea fishing in Mexico.

If you want to combine a bit of archaeology with your beach holiday, you can drive about an hour east of Manzanillo up into the lush mountains to Colima. This is a clean, attractive working city with a pretty Colonial plaza where you find the excellent Museum of Archaeology. Originally, this exhibit of magnificent pre-Columbian objects was a private collection housed in a rather rundown building. At the owner's death the collection came under the auspices of the Mexican National Institute of Archaeology and History, and today a beautifully executed, small museum displays in great style this immense collection made over a lifetime by the original owner. The pieces, mostly of ceramic, came from burials throughout the state of Colima. Most were found by local farmers in the course of working the land and were brought to Colima for sale. Details of origin are lacking for most of the items, but the artistic value is obvious and the museum enables visitors to see a wide range of objects and styles of ancient indigenous craftsmen.

ZIHUATANEJO-IXTAPA

Zihuatanejo and **Ixtapa** are really two resorts in one. Ixtapa, 10 kilometers northwest of Zihuatanejo, is a modern resort full of luxury high-rise hotels set along 7 kilometers of curving beach, **Playa Palmar**. Zihuatanejo, in contrast, with low-rise buildings only, sits in a scenic sheltered bay (much visited by cruise ships and private yachts) and still has the intimate feel of a small fishing community. Both offer great fishing and some of the best scuba diving on Mexico's Pacific Coast. They are both also convenient starting points for exploring the spectacular deserted beaches along the surrounding coast. This dual destination tends to cater towards adults and couples, rather than families (some places are off limits to those under age 16).

Zihuatanejo (which means "place of the woman" in the native Nahuatl tongue) has grown to 80,000 inhabitants, but still retains the ambiance of a small village with a lot of local color. Along its cobblestone streets are a number of cozy restaurants, grocery stores, rug shops, art galleries, and artisan markets, and you can find all levels of accommodations, though you won't find any high-rise mega hotels. The city has mandated a four-story limit to buildings in an effort to maintain its charm and village appeal. The downtown area, El Centro, is great for walking and browsing, as is the Paseo del Pescador, a brick-paved beachfront promenade along Playa Principal.

Zihuatanejo is famous for its great fishing, diving, and water sports. The area's three beaches invite all kinds of sports, and the local waters are famed for their abundance of game fish, including sailfish, marlin, and roosterfish. Because it lies on a relatively small bay, the excellent beaches have clean water and are safe for young swimmers. For further recreation, do what the locals do—take a

La Casa Que Canta, Zihuatanejo

boat from the town pier and go to Los Gatos beach for a day of swimming and eating. There are no "great buys" these days, but shopping can be fun. Bargain at the artisan market, and you might come away with a very nice silver bracelet or a pretty hand-painted plate or vase.

Ixtapa is a modern, world-class resort that was created from the ground up beginning in 1968 by Fonatur (Mexico's National Tourism Development Fund). In contrast to Zihuatanejo, Ixtapa is a modern resort town with high-rise hotels along the beachfront, which is backed by a palm-lined promenade with restaurants, nightclubs, and shops. This is a good place for souvenir shopping (T-shirts and Mexican crafts). Ixtapa also offers 14 unspoiled beaches, golf courses, tennis courts, and a yacht marina. Launches explore the turtles, fish, and pelicans at El Morro de Los Pericos, and boat excursions tour Ixtapa Island, which served as the location for the film *Robinson Crusoe*. The town sits on a wide bay dotted with small rocky islands inhabited solely by sea birds. Here you find excellent beaches with clean water (although the water is a little rougher than in Zihuatanejo). The beach in town, Playa del Mar, a 3.5-kilometer stretch of white sand, gave Ixtapa its Nahuatl Indian name, "the white place." A very special experience is to swim with dolphins at the new Dolphinarium.

ACAPULCO

Acapulco was one of Mexico's first beach areas to become popular. It is no wonder these early tourists were captivated, since Acapulco has a stunning natural setting. Today, the aura of secluded bliss in the downtown area of Acapulco has faded behind rows of high-rise hotels (many of which have seen better days) and fast-food restaurants. Nevertheless, the views of Acapulco Bay, framed by mountains and beaches, are still breathtaking day or night. The towering Sierra Madre mountains are beautiful; they seem to reach right down to the shoreline. At night, the bay is magical and romantic with millions of lights reflecting in the water like stars.

The more recently built hotels, many of them real beauties, are not in town, but tucked along the coast, away from the hustle and bustle. Here golden-sand beaches, blue sea, and waving palm trees create an idyllic setting. Acapulco is non-stop, 24-hour-a-day energy. The perfectly sculpted bay is an adult playground full of water skiers and wave runners. Golf and tennis are popular, but the real attraction is the nightlife!

The nightlife scene begins at 1 or 2 am and doesn't stop until daylight. The beaches are generally wide and clean, but the ocean is polluted, although it is cleaner than in years past. In the 1990s, a program was instituted to clean up the water, and whales have recently been sighted offshore for the first time in years. If you do decide to swim in the sea, be aware of the strong undertow and riptides (at least two swimmers drown each year).

One of the largest and most decadent of Mexican resort towns, Acapulco leapt into the international spotlight when movie stars made it their playground in the late 1930s, but it has fallen out of favor with international visitors in the last decade.

Acapulco, Cliff Divers of La Quebrada

Today, the vast majority of visitors are Mexicans from Mexico City and Guadalajara, who pour into town in huge numbers to spend a vacation by the sea.

A visit to Acapulco would not be complete without seeing the famous cliff divers of La Quebrada who have been jumping from the rocks (about 35 meters up) into a small crevasse of ocean since 1934. Get there in time to see the spectacular sunsets and watch the divers as they plunge into the cliffs holding flaming torches. Visit the small shrine where the divers pray prior to their performances (Elvis said a few prayers himself there during the filming of *Fun in Acapulco*).

For those looking for a sightseeing excursion, a day trip can be made to the spectacular mountainside town of Taxco, although it is a rather long trip. However, if you are driving to Mexico City, Taxco makes a good stopover along the way. (For more information on Taxco, see our itinerary *Mexico City & Beyond.)*

HUATULCO

Commonly referred to as the Bahías de Huatulco (Bays of Hautulco), **Huatulco** is based around nine bays and 35 kilometers of beaches. After the tremendous success of Cancún, the Mexican government looked for an equivalent site to start a new tourist destination on the Pacific Coast, and started building this resort in the 1980s. Located 130 kilometers south of Puerto Escondido, Huatulco is slowly building a name for itself as Mexico's authentic tourism haven. It has an 18-hole golf course and luxury resort hotels, and it also offers a growing array of ecotourism adventures that include bay tours, diving, jungle hiking tours, river rafting, and rappelling. Both dining and nightlife are limited here, but it is a beautiful and relaxing setting, and the nine bays include 36 beaches and countless inlets and coves for exploring. The clear, blue water and golden beaches are enough of an attraction for many visitors. Its most important quality is the fact that it still isn't plagued by mass tourism, thus ensuring that your stay will be truly pleasant. (It is not easy to get to Huatulco—there are not many direct flights and it relies heavily on charter service from the United States and Canada.)

Places to Play in the Sun
Baja California Sur

The Rocks, Cabo San Lucas

The Baja Peninsula is a long, very narrow strip of land that juts like a finger down from California, creating the Gulf of California, which separates Baja from the mainland of Mexico. Until recently, because of a lack of roads, gasoline stations, sources for food, and accommodations, only a daring few in four-wheel-drive vehicles dared to venture into this desolate area. Although the road is still not top-notch, you can now drive down Highway 1 for 1,765 kilometers from Tijuana at the northern border all the way down to Cabo San Lucas at the southern tip of Baja. Most of the peninsula is like an untouched frontier, with few places for tourists to stop along the way. However the barren desert landscapes display a remarkable, austere beauty. In just about its midsection, the 28-degree parallel intersects the peninsula: to the north of the line is the state of Baja California and to the south is the state of Baja California Sur. This itinerary features Baja California Sur, highlighting the extremely popular resort area that has mushroomed along its southern tip. The government picked this area to develop as a tourist destination in 1976, due to its natural beauty and setting, and their venture has indeed been enormously successful.

In 1535, an officer under the command of **Hernán Cortés** became the first European to land in Baja California. The reports he brought back, particularly in respect to the existence of pearls in the Gulf of California, were so tantalizing that a year later Cortés himself led settlers to the present site of La Paz. The poverty of the land and the fierceness of the Indians forced Cortés to abandon the area a few years later. The conquistadors became busy with other parts of Mexico, and all but forgot about Baja. It was not until 1697 that a permanent settlement was established: a Jesuit mission and a presidio at Loreto, 366 kilometers north of La Paz. Throughout the 18th century, the Indians in this barren land were ministered to by the Jesuits, who founded the first missions. When the Jesuits were banished from Mexico in the 1760s, the Franciscans and the Dominicans followed. But along with churches, the Spaniards brought disease and smallpox, which almost wiped out the population by the 19th century. Meanwhile, primitive settlements began to appear, but for many years the only means of access between them was by boat or on foot. Loreto remained the most important town and capital of Baja, until 1829 when a hurricane leveled the town. The capital was then moved to La Paz.

One can reach Baja California Sur by plane, car, or ferry—the most popular means of transportation being by plane. There is an airport at La Paz, but since the boom in tourism in the past few years, the airport at San José del Cabo has expanded and has become the most popular access point with many flights arriving daily, especially from Los Angeles. You can also take a ferry across the Gulf of California to or from La Paz, connecting to the mainland towns of Los Mochis or Mazatlán. If you plan to take a car or reserve a private cabin on the ferry, advance reservations are needed. Even the "deluxe" accommodations are pretty basic and if you want to take your car, there are long delays and mountains of paperwork to be filled out. Even so, the ferry is definitely faster than driving all the way north and driving back down the entire peninsula.

CABO SAN LUCAS, SAN JOSÉ DEL CABO & THE CORRIDOR

The southern tip of Baja has long been popular with wealthy sportsmen, such as the late Bing Crosby, who fly down in their private planes for deep-sea fishing. Happily, what used to be almost a private playground for the super-rich is now available for everyone. However, the area still caters to the more affluent traveler: the superb hotels and world-class golf courses here are not cheap.

This tip of the peninsula, commonly referred to simply as Los Cabos, basically consists of twin towns: **Cabo San Lucas** (to the west) and **San José del Cabo** (to the east). The 33-kilometer strip of land joining the two towns is called **The Corridor**, a once-barren area transformed into a verdant paradise with superb hotels perched on cliffs overlooking the brilliant blue sea, championship golf courses, colorful gardens, and dramatic beaches with waves crashing against the shore. A fine, four-lane, divided road called the Transpeninsular Highway traces the coast, joining the two towns. The resorts that have sprung up along Los Cabos are exceptional. Each seems to vie with the other for originality and quality of design, gorgeous landscaping, and splendid amenities. There is nothing tacky about this area—it is obviously one of money and impeccable taste.

Because flights are so easy from Los Angeles, it has almost become a weekend retreat for Californians, and many of them have built homes here.

Although the two towns are often grouped together, they are really quite different. Cabo San Lucas became famous for sport fishing and, with a population of 25,000, is the bigger and faster-growing of the two cities. It is much more commercial and Americanized. Many people think the official language here is English!

San José del Cabo, with its pastel cottages and narrow streets, is more sedate, more charming, and still retains the feel of a small Mexican town. However, San José del Cabo has become famous by association with its neighbor and is now also growing rapidly.

Los Cabos offers some of Mexico's finest golf and great sport fishing, with the majority of visitors now coming for the world-famous championship golf courses. With a few exceptions, the sea here is not safe for swimming since the surf is often fierce and the undertow strong. Most people are content to use the beautiful swimming pools at the hotels and reserve the gorgeous beaches for walking. The contrast of the stark desert landscape with the dark blue of the sea is magnificent. Other big attractions here include kayaking, surfing, snorkeling, horseback riding, windsurfing, whale-watching, and an active nightlife!

Los Cabos tends to be more expensive than other Mexican resorts and, unlike most of the other beach resort towns, the weather in Los Cabos does vary by season, although it is predictable. It is hot and sunny in the summer and can be fairly cool and windy in the winter; however, it is usually warm enough for water sports year-round and the average temperature throughout the year is 75° F. With 300 days of sunshine annually, there isn't much rain, and any rain usually comes during the month of September.

You should consider renting a car here because it is nice to be able to drive between the two towns and to explore The Corridor (taxis are expensive). Note: The coastal highway is not lit at night.

DAY TRIPS

LAND'S END & LOVE BEACH: Take a boat trip to the southern tip of the Baja Peninsula, where the Pacific and the Sea of Cortez meet. Towering granite monoliths lie along the coast, including the most dramatic and famous, **El Arco**, a rock arch that has been carved by the waves over millions of years. The Arch is a marine refuge for hundreds of species of fish. One can often spot dolphins, sea lions, and whales (in the winter). Land's End is also a popular dive spot with underwater canyons, believed to be as deep as the Grand Canyon, and famous sandfalls or cascades, discovered by Jacques Cousteau. Diving is unpredictable given the weather and rough seas. Bring plenty of film. Many tours will also drop you off at Playa del Amor (Love Beach) where you can picnic and choose between swimming in the cool waters of the Pacific or the calm, clear waters of the Sea of Cortez.

LA PAZ: Located 183 kilometers north of Cabo San Lucas, **La Paz**, where Cortés landed in 1535, means "peace" and this port town does indeed have a peaceful feel. A rather large city with 200,000 inhabitants, La Paz is the capital of Baja California Sur, with a library, anthropology museum, and a theater with performances by local and visiting artists. All of the action and tourist attractions run along the main street, Obregón, where you find restaurants, boutiques, and hotels. There is a relaxed, laid-back, old-fashioned demeanor to the town—a far cry from the trendy upscale ambiance of Los Cabos. Except for a few locals, no one much uses the narrow beach in town: the water does not look too appealing and the beach is not too clean. If you want to swim, on the road to the port where the ferries and freighters arrive, there are a few inviting coves wrapped by cactus-studded hills where the water is clear. However, most people come to La Paz for sport fishing, which is world-famous, or to take a ferry to the mainland.

TODOS SANTOS: If you want a side excursion, it is fun to take a trip to the quaint town of **Todos Santos**, an artists' colony located on the west coast about 70 kilometers north of Cabo San Lucas. This tiny town, dating back to the 1800s, exudes a Colonial ambiance with its central plaza, narrow cobbled streets, and whitewashed houses enhanced by rustic tiled roofs. Many expatriates, including many artists, have discovered the charm of this small town off the beaten path, and have settled here to open appealing boutiques, excellent restaurants, art galleries, and a few hotels. The town is located a bit inland from the ocean, but nearby you find beautiful secluded beaches. However, swimming is frequently treacherous due to pounding surf and strong undertows. If you want to come for a few nights, instead of making Todos Santos just a day trip, we recommend two hotels here, Todos Santos Inn in the heart of town, and Posada La Poza just a few kilometers from town on a coastal nature reserve.

WHALE-WATCHING: Between January and March, the gray and humpback whales are frequently seen along the coast of Baja. At this time, many tour operators offer excursions out to see these majestic creatures. However, if you prefer a more in-depth experience and want to see many more whales, you need to go to the calm lagoons farther north where the gray whales come each winter to have their babies. For this experience, refer to our *Whale-Watching in Baja* itinerary.

Places to Play in the Sun
The Mexican Caribbean

There is nowhere in the world where you can find beaches that surpass those of the Mexican Caribbean. If you are looking for warm, crystal-clear turquoise water and endless stretches of soft white-sand beaches, this part of Mexico is paradise. This coast of rare beauty is found in the state of Quintana Roo, on the eastern shores of the Yucatán Peninsula, stretching from Cancún in the north to Chetumal in the south. What is quite extraordinary is the wide range of both hotels and styles of resorts found here. There is an intriguing selection of places to stay in every price range, from super-deluxe to very simple. You can also choose between secluded beaches, where the activity of the day is walking out to your hammock, and modern bustling resorts such as Cancún, where the activity is non-stop. And, in addition to the coastal resorts, the beautiful islands of Isla Mujeres and Cozumel lie just offshore, offering a further dimension of holiday possibilities.

Another tremendous bonus of the Mexican Caribbean is that the coast is protected by the Great Mesoamerican Reef, the largest coral reef in the western hemisphere. As one would expect, scuba diving and snorkeling are immensely popular and a dazzling array of fish can be seen. Adding icing to the cake, the area abounds with Mayan ruins, allowing you to easily combine a holiday in the sun with the delight of seeing some of the most stunning archaeological sites in the world, including the sensational Chichén Itzá, Tulum, and Cobá.

The resort area along the Mexican Caribbean is divided into two parts. The most developed and the larger of the two is called Riviera Maya, which begins in Cancún and stretches south to Tulum. The second area of this coast, Costa Maya, runs from Tulum south to the border with Belize. The Costa Maya is just beginning to develop tourism and we hope to be able to offer some hotel selections here in our next edition.

From whichever hotel you choose as your base along the Riviera Maya, there are many places to visit and things to do. Listed below is information on places where we recommend hotels that you can use as your "hub," followed by sightseeing suggestions.

CANCÚN

For a no-hassle beach vacation where you can fly in, soak up the sun, eat at the Hard Rock Café, and never speak a word of Spanish or even have to exchange your money into pesos, **Cancún** is the place. If you want to experience some Mexican culture on your visit, you can visit a number of exceptional Mayan ruins (see "Sightseeing Suggestions" below). One of the top vacation destinations in the world, Cancún basks under year-round warm sun. This action-packed government-built Mexican resort offers pleasure seekers gorgeous white-sand beaches and clear turquoise water. There are water sports galore, as well as vigorous entertainment until the wee hours of the morning. Add excellent accommodations, gourmet restaurants, and outstanding shopping, and you've got the ultimate escape.

Cancún was just a deserted, sun-drenched spit of land off the northeast tip of the Yucatán Peninsula until the 1970s when the government chose the site to build a huge resort, offering visitors over 25,000 hotel rooms with all levels of accommodations. These hotels are located on a narrow strip of land that loops around a large lagoon, which is ideal for sailing and water sports. This 22-kilometer-long beach is lined with hotels, American restaurant chains, nightclubs, movie theaters, and shopping malls. The hotels here mostly cater to tour groups and package holidays with airfare, hotel, and food included. Although most of the accommodations are in huge, modern, high-rise hotels, they are usually ones that are well-built and of imaginative architectural design. If you prefer a vacation with non-stop action, Cancún is an excellent choice. If you prefer to be away from the crowds, choose one of our other hotel recommendations along the Riviera Maya or on the islands of Cozumel or Isla Mujeres.

Cancún's beaches are excellent. The water is placid along the upper shore facing the Bahía de Mujeres, while beaches facing the Caribbean are subject to choppier water and crashing waves on windy days.

COZUMEL

Located just 20 kilometers off the coast from Playa del Carmen, **Cozumel** is Mexico's largest island (measuring 52 kilometers long and 15 kilometers wide). This still-unspoiled island remains only moderately developed; the rest is wild jungle populated by iguanas, foxes, deer, and other wildlife. However, it isn't the terrestrial scenery that draws visitors back year after year, it's the water. The turquoise water is so clear that visibility can reach up to 76 meters, with aquatic scenery that includes black coral and millions of exotic fluorescent fish. Cozumel's chains of coral reefs along its southwestern shore make it one of the world's best scuba-diving and snorkeling spots. During the 17th and 18th centuries, Cozumel became a favorite hideout for pirates, who ambushed and sunk many cargo ships off the island's shores, further enhancing the diving experience. What is especially remarkable here is that due to the clarity of the water, you do not have to be a diver to enjoy the underwater views. Simply put on a mask and snorkel and jump in—it will seem as if you've dropped into a tropical fish tank!

Until Cozumel was established as a major resort, the island's economy was based on chicle (used in making chewing gum), coconuts, and seafood. It remained more or less undiscovered until Frenchman Jacques Cousteau recognized the marvels of Cozumel's waters as a divers' haven in the 1960s, declaring it one of the most beautiful scuba-diving areas of the world. To protect the delicate balance of its fantastic coral reefs and abundant variety of tropical fish, in 1996 the National Marine Park of Cozumel Reefs was created, home to over 500 species of fish. Within the marine park is a saltwater lagoon called Chankanaab Nature Park where you can not only snorkel, but also watch trained dolphins perform at the dolphinarium. You can also pay to swim with the dolphins, if you so desire.

The people native to Cozumel are of Mayan descent. The Maya ruled the Yucatán for over 2000 years before the arrival of the Spanish explorers in the 16th century. The legacy of their culture survives in the ruins of the huge cities that they built during their reign. On Cozumel, you can find one of the lesser-known, but interesting, sites, San Gervacio, which was once a sacred place where Mayan women journeyed to worship Ixchel, the goddess of fertility.

There are many direct flights to Cozumel or you can take the island-hopper plane from the Cancún airport. You can also travel by air-conditioned bus (about one hour) from Cancún to Playa del Carmen, walk from the bus station to the pier, and take the 45-minute ferry over to the Island. The ferries shuttle constantly between the mainland and the island.

ISLA MUJERES

Only 13 kilometers offshore and easily accessible by ferry from Cancún, **Isla Mujeres**, just 8 kilometers long and 4 kilometers wide, is a laid-back reprieve from Cancún's conspicuously commercialized action. This is an island of white-sand beaches and turquoise waters, complemented by a town filled with Caribbean-colored clapboard houses and rustic, open-air restaurants specializing in the bounty of the sea. Most tourists come just for the day, but there are wonderful places to stay on this small island. So if you favor a quieter, slow and easy-going vacation pace, we recommend you stay here rather than in Cancún.

Francisco Hernández de Córdoba gave the island its name, which means "island of the women," when he landed here in 1517 and found figurines of partially-clad females along the shore. These are now believed to have been offerings to the Mayan goddess of fertility, Ixchel, and the presence of these figurines indicates that Isla Mujeres was sacred to the Maya. Next to the lighthouse on the southern tip of the island are the ruins (not much more than a pile of rocks) of a small pyramid, which was an observatory built to the moon and goddess Ixchel.

While on the island, spend time at El Garrafón National Underwater Park, located at the southern tip of the island. This is an excellent spot for snorkeling. At the northern tip you find Playa Norte, the island's best public swimming beach.

You can take a take a ferry from Cancún's Embarcadero Pier at Playa Linda to Isla Mujeres. You might need to ask where the pier is located, since it is hidden within a shopping arcade and, therefore, not easily visible. You can also take a ferry from the port of Punta Sam, just outside Puerto Juárez. This ferry is less expensive, but not nearly as convenient since the dock is north of town.

PLAYA DEL CARMEN

Playa del Carmen

Playa del Carmen is located on the Riviera Maya about an hour's drive south of Cancún. Many tourists' first introduction to the town is when they take a bus from Cancún that drops them off at the bus terminal from where they walk through town to the pier. This part of Playa del Carmen is congested and lacking in charm, giving the impression that the town does not have much to offer. However, this is misleading. The nicest part of Playa del Carmen is not near the port, but a few blocks north where the main street, Quinta Avenida, parallels the sea. This pedestrian-only area, several blocks long, between the Quinta Avenida and the beach, is the most attractive part of town. Here you find shops, restaurants, hotels, and lots of local color. The wide strip of beach here is outstanding, with beautiful white sand that seems to go forever. Facing this sensational beach is a string of hotels, most of which are nice, but usually quite simple, catering to travelers on a limited budget. As you go farther north along the beach, the hotels become more expensive.

All in all, Playa del Carmen gives the impression of being a relatively sleepy seaside town with a relaxed atmosphere. The town is small enough for you to walk anywhere. Save one day for an excursion to Cozumel.

SIGHTSEEING SUGGESTIONS

CENOTES

In addition to its beautiful beaches and ocean swimming, the Riviera Maya area is well known for its underground rivers that honeycomb the porous limestone of the Yucatán. In some places the limestone collapses, forming *cenotes*. A cenote is a spot where the underground river comes into view. Sometimes collapsed walls form a deep well, at other times the river runs through a cave. Because the water in these cenotes is usually pure and clear, many people come to swim in them, and the really adventurous even don wet suits and follow the underground path of the river from one cenote to the next. There are major eco-theme parks, such as **Xcaret** and **Xel-Ha**, where you can swim in cenotes, but our favorites are the lesser-known ones that are far less commercial. Since these cenotes dot the countryside, ask the concierge at your hotel to suggest some nearby favorites.

COBÁ

The archaeological site of **Cobá** is located about 45 kilometers inland from the sea, on a road that turns west from the coastal highway 307 just south of Tulum. Cobá has very interesting and significant ruins built around a group of lakes in the middle of a jungle. Be prepared for some walking and climbing, especially if you want to see the staggering view from the top of the highest pyramid. Because it is a bit off the beaten path, there are fewer tourists here than at many other sites, making this a very rewarding excursion for those who make the effort to come. If you want to spend the night, we recommend the Villas Arqueologicas Cobá, a simple but very pleasant small hotel near the lake, within walking distance of the ruins.

CHICHÉN ITZÁ

A favorite day trip from anywhere along the Riviera Maya is to the Mayan site of **Chichén Itzá** with its massive pyramids. This is one of the most-visited archaeological sites on the Yucatán Peninsula and a memorable experience, from the dizzy heights of the Pyramid of Kukulkán to the mysterious depths of the Sacred Cenote. Allow plenty of time here and be prepared for walking and climbing in the heat. If possible, visit early in the morning. There are good facilities, including bookshops and refreshments, available at the site. If you want to spend the night, we recommend two outstanding hotels: the Hacienda Chichén and Hotel Mayaland. Both are within easy walking distance of the park, which is especially convenient if you attend the Sound and Light show, which takes place at dusk each evening when lights play upon the ruins, and stories of its rich history are narrated in Spanish.

ECO-THEME PARKS

There are a few natural aquariums formed by interlocking lagoons off the ocean that mix fresh and salt water, which is perfect for viewing wildlife and snorkeling. These "eco-theme parks," including **Xcaret** and **Xel-Ha**, are more "theme parks" than "ecological" parks—they are a bit like Disneyland and very popular, especially with families traveling with children. They also offer swimming with dolphins.

SIAN KA'AN BIOSPHERE RESERVE

Just a few kilometers south of Tulum, this 1.3-million-acre reserve was established in 1986 to preserve tropical forests, savannas, mangroves, coastal and marine habitats, and 115 kilometers of coastal reefs. Access is restricted and the best way to visit the area is on an excursion. Guided tours are available with biologists who can point out the amazing variety of birds and animals resident in the reserve, including crocodiles, pumas, flamingos, herons, and turtles. An unforgettable experience!

TULUM

Tulum, a Mayan fortress built in the 10th century, has a stunning position high on a cliff above the sea, overlooking the clear turquoise water of the Caribbean below. The setting is incredibly romantic and pictures of the fortress are frequently depicted on travel posters and calendars. Until the arrival of the Spanish, this was a Mayan seaport whose inhabitants traded with Cozumel, Isla Mujeres, Guatemala, and central Mexico.

Tulum, Castle

Although immensely popular with tourists because of the spectacular setting, the ruins at Tulum are not large or particularly important archaeologically. The famous *castillo* (castle) overlooking the sea, used both as a fortress and a temple, is the most impressive building at the site. Try to imagine what it looked like in its heyday when covered with stucco and painted. If you want to stay near Tulum, we recommend the Cabañas la Conchita, a very primitive but charming hotel nestled on a small, secluded beach just a few kilometers south of the ruins.

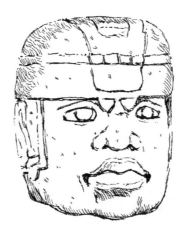

Hotel Descriptions

Set on a hillside with beautiful views of the deep-blue water of Acapulco Bay, Las Brisas offers a romantic getaway. Add the fact that most guestrooms have their own small swimming pool tucked on the terrace (the other guestrooms share a pool between two rooms) and you are in for a special treat. When we first stayed at Las Brisas over 30 years ago, we could not imagine that the brochure could be accurate: that our room would have its own private pool—we had to see it to believe it. Now other hotels have copied this extremely imaginative concept, but Las Brisas was the first with the idea and remains known worldwide as a honeymoon retreat. The guestrooms are in contemporary-style pink casitas terracing down the hillside on the 110-acre property, which spreads both above and below the main highway. The bedrooms and the Bella Vista Restaurant (a delightful place to dine with an outdoor terrace with an unbeatable view of the bay) are high on the hill. On the lower side of the highway, Las Brisas has its own private La Concha Beach Club with an informal restaurant and several swimming pools nestled on a terrace above the sea. The property is so spread out that it's a long way from the guestrooms to the waterfront, but should you decide to leave the privacy of your terrace, just call and one of the hotel's jaunty little jeeps will whisk you down to the Beach Club. *Directions:* On the main road into town, about 15 minutes from the airport.

❄ ☕ 🛎 💳 ☎ 🍴 @ ⍭ P ‖ ⚓ ≋ 🏄 🏖 ⛵ 🎿 🚶 🐎 🚣

LAS BRISAS
Manager: Francisco J. Garcia
Carretera Escénica 5255
Acapulco, Guerrero, 39868, Mexico
Tel: (744) 469-6900, Fax: (744) 446-5332
263 Rooms, Double: $330–$1690*
*Service: $20/day in lieu of all tips, *Tax: 17%
Open: all year, Credit cards: all major
Different World
Region: Beach–Pacific Coast

Crowning a gentle hill in an exclusive residential area called Punta Diamante, the Quinta Real exudes perfection in every detail. From first glance, the hotel (whose entrance is flanked by two stone guardian angels) is splendid—obviously no expense was spared to create a masterpiece. The thatched roof, open-air reception area sets the mood of elegant informality. The decor is outstanding, with creamy, pastel colors blending in a quietly elegant fashion with the handsome carved furniture. All of the bedrooms, sumptuous yet comfortable, have a view of the sea and some suites even have their own private plunge pool. Ultimate luxury prevails with marble floors, bathrobes, and private balconies or terraces. The hotel is built into the hillside with pathways through the gardens leading down to the sea. For those who prefer to save their energy, an elevator will whisk you to the lowest level, where you find several gorgeous swimming pools snuggled in the gardens, palapa-style restaurants, bars, and an expanse of lush lawn stretching to a beautiful beach. If you have previously rejected the idea of a holiday in Acapulco, thinking it is a bit dated and overbuilt, consider again. You cannot help but love the Quinta Real where you are secluded in your own private paradise, yet just a short drive to the center of the city. *Directions:* About a five-minute drive from the airport heading toward the center of Acapulco on the Carretera Escénica.

QUINTA REAL ACAPULCO
Manager: Juan Rivas Seledon
Paseo de la Quinta, 6
Fracc. Real Diamante
Acapulco, Guerrero, 39907, Mexico
Tel: (744) 469-1500, Fax: (744) 469-1516
74 Rooms, Double: $348–$1440, Cottage: $100*
*Breakfast not included, *Tax: 17%
Open: all year, Credit cards: all major
Different World
Region: Beach–Pacific Coast

In the '60s, Acapulco was the resort of royalty and Hollywood stars. For many celebrities, Villa Vera was the favorite place to stay. Elizabeth Taylor, Elvis Presley, Frank Sinatra, Lana Turner, Rita Hayworth, and Julio Iglesias all chose it as their hideaway. It is rumored to have had the very first swim-up pool bar—if it was to happen anywhere, Acapulco was certainly the place. Villa Vera continues to be the choice of many who are looking for a great getaway in one of Mexico's most exciting cities, especially for nightlife. Villa Vera is an oasis within the city, sitting high on a hillside overlooking the boulevard and the bay. There are both suites and individual houses available on the property, and although the hotel is not on the beach, that is not a problem as it has 17 swimming pools! The main terrace features a multi-level swimming pool with a waterfall flowing into the main pool, overlooking Acapulco. Top-notch facilities include a racquet club and a fully equipped spa and gym, which is one of the finest in town. Throughout the resort are lush gardens with wonderful trails and walkways to enjoy at any time of day. *Directions:* In Club Deportivo residential area, five minutes from beach.

VILLA VERA HOTEL
Manager: José Eduardo Gómez
Lomas del Mar 35
Acapulco, Guerrero, 39690, Mexico
Tel: (744) 484-0333, Fax: (744) 484-7479
59 Rooms, Double: $165–$1200*
*Breakfast not included
*Tax: 17%
Open: all year, Credit cards: all major
Region: Beach–Pacific Coast

The charming Casa del Sol is located in the heart of Ajijic, a retirement haven for Americans and Canadians who have chosen this picturesque village for its equitable climate, pleasant setting on Lake Chapala, and proximity to Guadalajara. Your exceptionally gracious hostess, Cathy Roberts, fell in love with Ajijic while visiting friends. She decided to stay, bought a house located just a short walk to the plaza, and opened Casa del Sol to guests in January 2007—fulfilling her dream of a lovely place to stay where guests are warmly welcomed like friends of the family. Casa del Sol offers the personal attention usually associated with B&Bs, but it is really more like an intimate inn with its expansive areas for guests including a spacious lounge, breakfast area, cute bar, and a gorgeous swimming pool nestled in a lush garden. The inn is imbued with the flavor of Mexico with the generous use throughout of bold colors, wrought iron fixtures, hand-made Talavera tiles, antique accents, and handicrafts by local artisans. All of the nicely-decorated guestrooms (my favorites are those overlooking the garden) have top notch linens, comfortable mattresses, and very nice bathrooms, each with its own pretty tile pattern. Bouquets of fresh flowers abound throughout, adding to the home-like ambiance. Perched on the top level is a delightful terrace where guests can relax with a good book and enjoy views of the lake and mountains over the red-tiled rooftops.

CASA DEL SOL B&B INN
Owner: Cathy Roberts
Javier Mina #7
Ajijic–Lake Chapala, Jalisco, 45920,Mexico
Tel: (376) 766-0050, Toll Free: (866) 403-9275 USA
10 Rooms, Double: $80–$100
2 Casitas: $110-$150
Open: all year, Credit cards: none
Region: Central–Colonial Town

The Hacienda de los Santos is an absolute dream. If you are anywhere near the Colonial village of Alamos (a wonderful old mining town that in its heyday produced more silver than any other location in Mexico), this hotel is a must. Even if you don't have plans to be in the area, make a special trip. The Hacienda is a place to experience utter relaxation, to dine superbly, to enjoy the facilities of a lovely spa, and, best of all, to be pampered by an attentive staff. This beautiful inn is the creation of your gracious hosts, Nancy and Jim Swickard, who fell in love with Alamos, bought a 17th-century mansion, and converted it to a jewel of a private home for themselves. It has now evolved into a fantastic small inn with 27 guestrooms, splendid gardens, four swimming pools, two fabulous restaurants (plus a third for private parties), intimate dining rooms, a fun cantina serving over 500 kinds of tequila, an exercise room, a spa, and if you arrive by private plane (as 50% of the guests do) there is even a hanger for your plane. High walls enclose the entire property and guestrooms face various romantic patios. All the rooms exude the same superb taste— even the standard rooms are gorgeous and have their own fireplaces. If you want to splurge, request one of the suites, all are breathtaking. At the Hacienda de los Santos you enjoy the facilities of an ultra-deluxe hotel while feeling like a guest of the family—a rare combination. *Directions:* Ask for specific directions.

❄ ☕ 🚴 💳 ☎ 🏋 @ W ⌾ P ⑪ 🚭 ♨ ≈ 🐾 ♿ 👫 🐴

HACIENDA DE LOS SANTOS
Owners: Nancy & Jim Swickard
Calle Molina 8, Alamos, Sonora, 85760, Mexico
Tel: (647) 428-0222, Fax: (647) 428-0367
13 Rooms, Double: $155–$255*
12 Suites: $195–$960*
*Tax: 17%
*Includes full breakfast & 4 course dinner
Open: all year, Credit cards: all major
Different World
Region: Central–Colonial Town

The lovely Hacienda San Gabriel de Las Palmas, which was the headquarters of Emiliano Zapata during the Mexican Revolution, adjoins a magnificent church that was built in 1529 at the order of Hernán Cortés. You would never guess from its nondescript surroundings that such a delightful hotel is secreted within the tall, thick concrete walls that enclose the property. It is not until you pass through the gated entrance that the charming vine-covered buildings, cobblestone promenades, giant palms and expansive lawns are revealed. Each guestroom is uniquely designed and decorated, primarily with Mexican antiques. In the main hacienda, our favorite accommodations are not the suites, but rather the standard rooms (such as Vitral or Capitán). If you prefer a deluxe room, request one of the beautiful, newly renovated, suites (such as Cieba) tucked near the acqueduct. The hotel's spa overlooks a little park near the remains of a picturesque old mill, romantically overgrown by jungle. The restaurant, nestled under tall trees next to the swimming pool, serves delicious cuisine that presents the rich flavors of the region. Part of the delight of the hacienda is its laid back charm and the genuine gentle, naïve hospitality of the staff. *Directions:* The Hacienda is about a 30-minute drive from Cuernavaca, just off the road to Taxco. The hotel can arrange to pick you up at the Mexico City airport. If you drive, ask for a detailed map.

HACIENDA SAN GABRIEL DE LAS PALMAS
Manager: Juan Fenton
Km 41.8 Carreterra Cuernvaca-Chilpancingo
Amacuzac,Cuernvaca, Morelos, 62642, Mexico
Tel: 52 (751) 348-0636, Fax: 52 (751) 348-
0113, Cell: 52 (777) 113-0331
*8 Rooms, Double: $180–$220**
*10 Suites: $250–$285**
**Breakfast not included*
Open: all year, Credit cards: all major
Region: Central–Colonial Town

Rancho Encantado nestles right on the edge of Laguna Bacalar, a beautiful, crystal-clear lake almost at the Belize border. This is not your standard hotel, but rather a complex of cottages tucked in amongst the trees and a large, inviting, open-air restaurant with dining tables covered with brightly colored linens, reflecting a typical Mexican motif. Breakfast and a three-course set dinner are included in the room rate. In front of the restaurant, a pier stretches out into the turquoise lake, with kayaks and canoes nearby that guests can rent. The guestrooms are in individual casitas, some in the garden and others facing the lake. In the rates shown below, we have priced only the five newer rooms facing the lake (9 through 12 and the Laguna Suite) since these are far superior to the others and well worth the relatively small difference in price. Each has a private porch in front with hammocks. Inside, you find a very spacious room, really a suite, with a separate sitting area and bedroom divided off by shelving. The décor is very pleasing, with red-tiled floor, hand-loomed bedspreads, a beautiful palapa ceiling, rattan furniture, brightly colored curtains, murals of Mayan design, and fresh flowers artfully arranged. Best of all, these lakefront units have large, louvered windows on four sides, allowing the breezes to flow through the room (there is also an overhead fan). *Directions:* On the road between Cancún and Chetumal, 2 km north of Bacalar.

RANCHO ENCANTADO
Owners: Susanna Star & Raymond Childers
Km 3, Hwy 307
Bacalar, Quintana Roo, 77930, Mexico
Tel: (983) 831-0037, Toll Free: (800) 505-6292 USA
13 Rooms, Double: $180–$285*
*Tax: 10%
*Includes breakfast & dinner
Open: all year, Credit cards: all major
42 km south of Chetumal, 3 km north of Bacalar
Region: Yucatán Peninsula–Laguna

The Riviera Maya is legendary for its immense hotel complexes where hoards of action-seeking tourists descend each week to eat, drink and make merry in the sun. A far cry from this is the ultra sumptuous Paraiso de La Bonita, an intimate hotel attracting guests who look for privacy, world class amenities, a glorious beach, fine food and excellent wines, the ultimate in service, and exceptional comfort. The security of the front gate might give the appearance of a formal hotel, but once you enter, magically the formality vanishes and you feel like a cherished guest in a superb home. The staff is incredible, from the superb manager, Lionel Álvarez (who mingles with and personally greets guests) to the waiters, bartenders, bellboys, and maids whose smiles are infectious. From the inside, walls open to gorgeous, impeccably manicured gardens and dazzling sea views. In décor, it is a virtual showplace of museum-quality antiques from around the world collected by the owners to decorate their hotel. Guestrooms are huge suites, each totally different in décor with themes of romantic, far-away places. The greatest asset of the Paraiso de La Bonita is the service. The staff anticipates your every whim—be it a romantic dinner in the wine cellar, a helicopter hop to archaeological sites, or an overnight yacht excursion. *Directions:* The hotel can arrange pickup at the airport; otherwise, ask for detailed instructions when making reservations.

ZOETRY PARAISO DE LA BONITA
Manager: Lionel Álvarez
Carretera Cancún-Chetumal, Km 328
Bahia Petempich–Riviera Maya, 77500, Mexico
Tel: (998) 872-8300, Fax: (998) 872-8301
90 Rooms, Double: $839–$2074
Open: all year, Credit cards: all major
Different World
Region: Beach-Caribbean Coast–Riviera Maya

Hotel Descriptions   255

When the Hacienda Puerta Campeche opened in 2004 it added a new jewel to the superb group of hacienda hotels located on the Yucatán peninsula. Its four "sister" hotels (Hacienda Santa Rosa, Hacienda Temozón, Hacienda Tixkobob, and Hacienda Uayamón) are haciendas that have been converted into deluxe, intimate hotels. The Hacienda Puerta Campeche, unlike the others, is a not hacienda nor is it secluded in the countryside. Instead, the hotel is ensconced within the walls of a series of colorfully painted, 17th-century houses, blending so cleverly with the others on the street you would never dream a hotel is secreted within. Until you walk around the corner and find the discreet entrance, you might well think you had the wrong address. Once you step inside the magic begins. The hotel is like a work of art with the rooms created masterfully from the original small houses. Each spacious guestroom has deep-hued walls setting off handsome furniture. Each bathroom is exceptionally large and splendidly appointed. Adding to the perfection, skillful maids decorate the towels, bathrobes, bed linens, and vanities with intricate designs of fresh flowers. The guestrooms and dining room enclose an inner garden courtyard where another surprise awaits: Interconnecting stone walls of what once were homes, form a stunning swimming pool where you can swim through the doors from one room to the next. *Directions:* Located facing the Puerta de Tierra.

HACIENDA PUERTA CAMPECHE
Calle 59, No. 71 (between Calle 16 & Calle 18)
Campeche, Campeche, 24000, Mexico
Tel & Fax: (981) 816-7375
15 Rooms, Double: $272–$572*
*Breakfast not included
*Service: 5%
Open: all year, Credit cards: all major
Different World
Region: Yucatán Peninsula-Archaeological Area

Campeche is an exceptionally alluring port town with a rich history. Adding to its appeal are narrow streets lined by brightly painted houses, a picturesque plaza, excellent museums, and an old fortress. In addition, there are great archaeological sites nearby, making this a wonderful destination for tourists. If you are looking for a larger, remarkably well-priced, really nice place to stay with a great location, the Hotel Plaza Campeche, which opened in 2004, is an excellent choice. On one side it faces onto a small park, on the other side is the Circuito Baluuartes, a main boulevard that wraps around the city. Although the hotel is not within the once-walled historic center, it is literally steps away. Once you cross the street, you are in the most attractive part of the old town and within two blocks of the cathedral and the plaza. Although newly built, the mustard yellow façade, accented by white trim and wrought iron balconies, melts right in with its centuries-old neighbors. Inside you find a very attractive, immaculate, nicely furnished hotel. The dining room and one section have large windows, framed by handsome swag draperies, looking out to the swimming pool. The spacious guestrooms offer every modern comfort and all the amenities that business travelers crave including a business center onsite. *Directions:* From the cathedral go west for two blocks on Calle 10 and you will see the hotel.

HOTEL PLAZA CAMPECHE
Manager: Sara Cesar
Calle 10, No 126-A
Campeche, Campeche, 24000, Mexico
Tel & Fax: (981) 811-9900
83 Rooms, Double: $90–$200*
*Breakfast not included
Open: all year, Credit cards: all major
Region: Yucatán Peninsula-Archaeological Area

In Cancún, where almost all the hotels are enormous (some offering over 1000 guestrooms), the intimate, 33-room Casa Turquesa is one of the few small luxury hotels in Cancún. The white, Mediterranean-style, three-story building is decorated formally, with Mayan accents. The lobby has French-style chairs with paisley upholstery, yet the native accent is strongly evident. Colorful, large murals and stone Mayan temple carvings (reminiscent of those seen at nearby archaeological sites) enhance the walls in the sunlight -filled lounge. The bedrooms are appointed with every modern amenity and all have a terrace or balcony with a view of the sea. All have king or queen beds, vanity mirrors, mini-bars, 90 cable-TV channels, and private, outdoor Jacuzzi tubs. The marble bathrooms are exceptionally outstanding: enormous, and beautifully outfitted. Although small, Casa Turquesa has the luxury of three restaurants: the Belle Vue offers international cuisine, El Gazebo serves breakfast overlooking the sea, and the Celebrity (temporarily closed for renovation) specializes in beef and fresh fish. The hotel's highlight is a large pool, which extends to a bluff overlooking the turquoise-blue waters of the Caribbean. Steps lead down to a beckoning, pristine, white stretch of sand, one of the few semi-private beaches in Cancún. The staff of the Casa Turquesa is friendly and very professional. *Directions:* Located on Blvd. Kukulkan at 13.5 kilometer marker.

❋ ✁ 🖻 🏠 ⅄ P ⑪ ≈ ⚲

CASA TURQUESA
Managers: Cynthia Valdes & Alberto Cuautli
Km 13.5, Boulevard Kukulkan
Cancún, Quintana Roo, 77500, Mexico
Tel: (998) 885-2924, Fax: (998) 885-2922
33 Rooms, Double: $175–$450*
*Breakfast not included
*Tax: 17%
Open: all year, Credit cards: all major
Region: Beach–Caribbean Coast

If you really want to discover a hideaway far off the beaten path and surrounded by remarkable natural beauty, then the Eco Paraiso Xixim makes an outstanding choice. The Eco Paraiso Xixim began as a dream to preserve a long stretch of unspoiled coastline and, to make this project financially feasible, an intimate, small hotel was built along 5 kilometers of virgin beach, with 15 rooms in thatched-roof cottages tucked in amongst the sand dunes overlooking the sea. Each cottage mimics the simple style of homes built by the Mayans for over 1,000 years, but inside the similarity ends. All the delightfully spacious bedrooms are nicely decorated and extremely comfortable with two queen-sized beds, a sofa, and a desk; and in front there is a large covered porch. All the cottages have the same configuration and décor and all face the sea, but by far the best views are in 2, 4, 6, or 8. Breakfast and dinner are included in the room rate and served in an attractive dining room with a terrace overlooking the water. Activities here include excursions to visit the spectacular flocks of brilliant pink flamingos who come to feed in the nearby lagoon, kayaking, hiking, observing the sea turtles in season, fishing, and swimming in the ocean or the hotel's pool. *Directions:* When you arrive in Celestún, continue straight and one block beyond the square turn right at the last street before the sea. Continue for 10 km, following signs to the hotel (beware—this gravel road is like a washboard!).

HOTEL ECO PARAISO XIXIM
Manager: Jaime Solis Garza
Km 10 de la Antigua Carretera a Sisal
Celestún, Yucatán, 97000, Mexico
Tel: (988) 916-2100, Fax: (988) 916-2111
15 Rooms, Double: $152–$220*
*Includes breakfast, dinner, taxes & tips
Open: all year, Credit cards: all major
Different World
Region: Yucatán Peninsula–Eco Resort

The Hotel & Bungalows Mayaland, with over 100 acres of parklike grounds, has an unsurpassed setting, right on the grounds of Chichén Itzá, one of Mexico's premier archaeological sites. The ruins are so close that some of the ancient temples can be seen rising above the jungle. The Mayaland is a large hotel and, because of its strategic location, attracts many sightseeing buses that bring hundreds of guests for lunch. However, it is amazing that this activity really doesn't distract from the aura of the hotel. Excellent management efficiently handles the day visitors while protecting the privacy of overnight guests. You will really feel pampered and away from the crowds if you splurge and request a room in one of the clusters of bungalows (named after famous archaeologists) that nestle in the lovely gardens. Once you are in your room, the Mayaland has the intimate feeling of a much smaller hotel. The guestrooms are very attractively decorated and there are various swimming pools on the grounds, conveniently located so that you don't have far to walk to enjoy a refreshing dip. The joy of staying at the Mayaland is that you can stroll over to the ruins before the hordes of tourists arrive in the morning, and again in the evening to watch the Sound and Light show. Many dignitaries have stayed at the hotel, including Pavarotti, for whom one of the cottages is named. *Directions:* Located short walk from entrance to ruins.

❄ 🛵 📇 ☎ ⛾ P ⫼ ≈ 🖼 🛎

HOTEL & BUNGALOWS MAYALAND
Manager: Anna Harcourt
Chichén Itzá, Yucatan, 97751, Mexico
Tel: (998) 884-4512, Fax: (998) 884-4510
92 Rooms, Double: $98–$490*
*Breakfast not included: $10.50
*Tax: 17%
Open: all year, Credit cards: all major
Different World
Region: Yucatán Peninsula-Archaeological Area

The ruins at Chichén Itzá are spectacular—absolutely not to be missed if you are the least bit tantalized by the mysteries of the Mayan world. However, during the tourist season, some of the magic is lost if you are viewing these ruins along with hordes of other tourists, so an excellent plan is to stay at the Hacienda Chichén, right on the grounds of the site, where you can stroll through the jungle in the early morning to savor the romantic beauty of the remains of this ancient Mayan city in relative solitude. The Hacienda Chichén is an excellent choice for accommodations, especially if you want to feel part of the history of the exploration of these ruins, because it was in this very hacienda that the archaeologists stayed when doing their original research. This nostalgic, very authentic, old hacienda and the charming gardens remain much as they must have been in their prime. You can sip a gin and tonic or have a cup of tea on the veranda after a day of exploration and just feel the excitement the explorers must have felt so long ago. The guestrooms, tucked about the property in houses built of concrete blocks, are really nice—not fancy at all, just very comfortable and tastefully decorated. My favorite was the cottage named for Dr. Thomason, who was in charge of the original dig. *Directions:* Located within walking distance of the ruins. Follow signs from main road.

HACIENDA CHICHÉN
Owner: Doña Carmen Barbachano
Km 120, Carretera Mérida Puerto Juárez
Chichén Itzá, Yucatan, 97000, Mexico
Tel: (999) 924-2150, Fax: (999) 924-5011
28 Rooms, Double: $160–$225*
*Breakfast not included: $8
*Tax: 17%
Open: all year, Credit cards: MC, VS
Different World
Region: Yucatán Peninsula-Archaeological Area

"Villas Arqueológicas" is a group of hotels that are located close to most of the major archaeological sites in Mexico. These cater to the more adventurous travelers who want to explore Mexico's archaeological riches. Villas Arqueológicas are always well priced and offer clean, simple, nice guestrooms; but the one within walking distance of the rich Mayan site of Cobá stands out as a very appealing place to stay in its own right. This one-story, bright-yellow, stucco hotel with white trim is as pretty as can be. You enter into an interior courtyard, around which are shops, a library, office, and reception. Beyond is a second courtyard, enhanced by a tropical garden and swimming pool, with an open-air restaurant on one side of the quadrangle and guestrooms on the other three. The bedrooms are quite small, but tidy and nicely decorated. There are plenty of public areas in which to relax, so the size of the bedrooms should not be a problem except for long stays. A sign in the village saying "beware of crocodiles" explains why swimming in the lake is discouraged! *Directions:* From Cancún take Highway 307 to Tulum then connect to Highway 5 and continue to Cobá. The drive is 99 miles and takes about 2 hours.

VILLA ARQUEOLÓGICA COBÁ
Manager: Jerome Lemmier
2 Poniente N° 601
San Andrés, Cholula Puebla
Cobá, Quintana Roo, 72810, Mexico
Tel: (222) 273-7900, Fax: (222) 247-1508
43 Rooms, Double: $94*
*Tax: 17%
Open: all year, Credit cards: all major
Region: Yucatán Peninsula-Archaeological Area

For those who relish discovering super-deluxe hideaways far off the beaten path, the Hacienda de San Antonio is the perfect choice. This splendid property, originally a tobacco plantation, is really isolated, nestled beneath the shadow of a majestic volcano about a 20-minute drive into the hills from Colima. Guestrooms open off a garden courtyard, the first floor being surrounded by a colonnaded walkway and an upper gallery repeating the arched colonnades. You really don't need to choose a suite to achieve luxury, since all the antique-filled rooms are spacious and decorated with great taste. The decor has a richly masculine feel, with strong colors, tapestries, hand-woven carpets, and hand-loomed draperies. All the suites have fireplaces, terraces or patios, and beautiful bathrooms. The public rooms are vast and as you pass from room to room it seems as though you are stepping back in time and are a guest in a private home. You walk through a terraced, formal garden with reflecting pools and fountains to a gorgeous, incredibly large swimming pool. The Hacienda makes a wonderful retreat if you want to be alone and away from the world for a while but if you want activity, horseback riding, bird watching, nature walks, and bicycling on the 4,000-hectare property are all options. *Directions:* Colima airport is 30 miles away. If driving, ask for directions.

❄ ☕ ⚓ 💳 ☎ P ⑂ ⚘ ≈ 🚶 🏇

HACIENDA DE SAN ANTONIO
Manager: Viviana Dean
Municipio de Comala
Colima–San Antonio, Colima, 28450, Mexico
Tel: (312) 316-0300, Fax: (312) 316-0301
25 Rooms, Double: $650–$1200*
*Service: 10%, Tax: 17%
Open: all year, Credit cards: all major
Different World
Region: Inland–Pacific Coast

If you take the train through the Copper Canyon, be sure to include a night at the Posada Mirador which offers incomparable views of the canyon. The hotel, built into the walls of the canyon, seems to be glued against the rocks that plummet straight down to the canyon floor. The tangerine-colored adobe-style building blends the feel of an old Spanish mission and a lodge. Although individual reservations are accepted, you will notice many groups since this is a favorite stop for tours. The interior décor exudes a rustic ambiance with terracotta floors accented by Indian rugs, rough-hewn beams, richly painted thick stucco walls, large murals, stone fireplaces, chairs accented by bright cushions, Indian pottery, and hand-woven baskets. However, the artful décor can't compete with the stunning panoramic view from the windows of the dining room, cozy bar, spacious lounge, and guestrooms. A large deck in front of the dining room and lounge extends out over the edge of the canyon. At night walk out onto the private balcony of your bedroom—the stars look so close that it seems you can reach right up and pull one down. If you desire more exclusivity, ask for one of the guestrooms in the new addition that is perched on the hillside above the hotel. It is a bit of a walk up the hill and you are further from the dining room, but it is quieter and the views are even more breathtaking. *Directions:* A hotel van will pick you up at the train station.

POSADA MIRADOR
Owners: Vilma & Roberto Balderrama
Copper Canyon–Barrancas, Chihauhua, 81200, Mexico
Tel: (668) 816-7046, Fax: (668) 812-0046
65 Rooms, Double: $100–$120*
*Tax: 17%
Open: all year, Credit cards: all major
Region: Copper Canyon

Hotel Misión adds a new dimension to your Copper Canyon adventure. You leave the train at Bahuichivo (about four hours west of El Fuerte) and take a bumpy 14-kilometer ride down into the canyon to the tiny village of Cerocahui, nestled in a beautiful fertile valley. Here you find the Hotel Misión, surrounded by apple orchards and a vineyard that produces table wines for the restaurant. The Balderrama family, who originated Copper Canyon tourism, owns the property and when you book your room, they can also arrange for train tickets, transfers, and sightseeing tours—making everything very easy. Across the street from the hotel is a beautiful Jesuit mission founded in 1694 by Salvatierra (the first white man to reach the bottom). This is not a luxurious hotel, nor was it ever meant to be; however, it exudes a cozy, rustic, inviting, lodge-like ambiance, appropriate for its setting, and the food is amazingly good for such a remote hotel. The guestrooms are cozy with beam ceilings, carved wood furniture, terracotta floors, large chandeliers, and brightly colored hand-woven fabrics. My favorite guestrooms are those that face onto the vineyard. While you stay here you can take guided horseback rides, trek to the lovely Huicochi waterfall, explore the many nearby trails, or take a tour to the old mining town of Urique where there is a lookout with sweeping canyon views. *Directions:* Transfer needed from Bahuichivo, a train stop along the Copper Canyon.

HOTEL MISIÓN
Owners: Vilma & Roberto Balderrama
Copper Canyon–Cerocahui, Chihauhua, 81200, Mexico
Tel: (668) 818-7046, Fax: (668) 812-0046
42 Rooms, Double: $248*
*Includes all meals
Open: all year, Credit cards: MC, VS
Region: Copper Canyon

The Sierra Lodge, nestled against the side of a small pine-scented valley in the Copper Canyon, is about as far off the beaten path as you can get. Here you'll find no electricity, no telephones, no TVs, no radios. The closest town is Creel, 20 minutes' drive away. The Lodge is built like a long, low, old-fashioned log cabin with a corrugated tin roof. All of the guestrooms open onto a long, tiled, front porch, with rustic wooden chairs outside each door so, guests can sit and look out at the Cusarare River, which twists and winds its way through the valley below. Although rustic in nature, the spacious guestrooms are all surprisingly attractive with rich-red-tiled floors, white walls, Indian carpets, attractive homespun cotton bedspreads and matching drapes, beamed ceilings, Indian prints on the walls, nice bathrooms with hot water, and even bathrobes! The gentle glow of the gas lamps lends romance. Each room has a wood-burning stove to keep you warm. All meals are included in the incredibly low price and the simple, hearty food is perfect after a day of hiking. Guests dine together in a large but delightfully cozy room with a giant stone fireplace, a wonderful Indian mural, antique prints on the walls, and varnished tables. *Directions:* Take the Copper Canyon train to Creel and then a taxi to the hotel (about $30 each way).

COPPER CANYON SIERRA LODGE
Owner: Hoteles Sierra Madre
Copper Canyon–Creel, Chihauhua, 31000, Mexico
Tel: (800) 776-3942 (USA), Fax: (635) 456-0036
20 Rooms, Double: $184*
*Includes all meals
Open: all year, Credit cards: none
Region: Copper Canyon

If you want to take the train going east to visit the Copper Canyon, you can board at either Los Mochis or El Fuerte. Our preference is to begin the journey in El Fuerte since you don't have to get up as early to board the train and, more importantly, it is a much quainter town. One of the best choices for accommodation is the Posada del Hidalgo. This isn't a deluxe hotel, but it offers quality and old-world ambiance. Built in the Colonial style, it has inner courtyards, fountains, wrought-iron gates, beam ceilings, lush tropical gardens, tiled floors, shuttered windows, and some antique furnishings. There is even a small swimming pool tucked on the terrace adjacent to the cute bar. The restaurant, which caters to tour groups, has colorfully painted wood chairs, dark walls, a huge antique mirror, and a cascade of brilliantly hued paper flowers and piñatas hanging from the beamed ceiling. The guestrooms are built around various courtyards. My favorites are the 16 newer "Zorro" guestrooms that face onto a pretty garden highlighted by a stature of Zorro. If you make your reservations in advance, the room cost is a bit more than if you just pop in, but it is really comforting to have your accommodations secured, especially since the train leaves early in the morning. When making room reservations you can also book the train. *Directions:* Located on the northeast corner of the square. The address says Calle Hidalgo but the entrance is around the corner on 5 de Mayo.

POSADA DEL HIDALGO
Owners: Vilma & Roberto Balderrama
Hidalgo 101
Copper Canyon–El Fuerte, Sinaloa, 81820, Mexico
Tel: (698) 893-1194, Fax: (668) 812-0046
68 Rooms, Double: $125*
*Tax: 15%
Open: all year, Credit cards: MC, VS
Region: Copper Canyon

One of the most beautiful bays along the Mexican Pacific coastline is located a few hours south of Puerto Vallarta called Costa Careyes since it was home for this variety of turtles, this bay also hides one of the most beautiful and exclusive hotels in the area "El Careyes Beach Resort." Guestrooms vary depending on the category, but all are classically decorated with the Mexican coast style, some might have a jacuzzi or living room and kitchenette but all are situated around an incredible meandering pool which snakes its way through lush tropical gardens. Its private beach is perfect for swimming, snorkeling or kayaking while sailing and deep sea fishing is available nearby. For land-based fun you can practice tennis or exercise in the gym followed by a relaxing massage at the spa. Horse back riding and bikes are also available and a fun way to explore the area. However, a favorite activity is simply lounging and reading on the huge cushions at the Camas Careyes during sunset where the staff makes sure your every need is met. The beach front restaurant offers a wide variety of choices and the cuisine is excellent. *Directions:* Take the coast highway south from Puerto Vallarta for about 2½ hours. You'll come to clearly marked signs and the entrance will be on your right-hand side.

❄ ⚷ 🖬 ☎ 🍸 @ ⅋ P ⚟ ⊘ ⚓ ≈ 🕴 🖼 ⚲ ⌗ 👫 🏇 ⚓

EL CAREYES
Manager: Miguel Rivero
Km 53.5 Carretera Barra de Navidad
Costa Alegre–Careyes, Jalisco, 48970, Mexico
Tel: (315) 351-0000, Fax: (315) 351-0100
53 Rooms, Double: $268–$1379*
31 Suites: $339–$669*
*Breakfast not included: $19
*Tax: 17%
Open: all year, Credit cards: all major
Different World
Region: Beach–Pacific Coast

From the moment I saw it from afar, I immediately fell in love with the Casitas de Las Flores. This cluster of adorable, brightly painted casitas—tucked on a wooded hillside overlooking a beautiful small bay—doesn't look like a hotel at all, but more like a charming, tiny, picturesque village. There are from one- to three-bedroom, bougainvillea-draped casitas available. The larger ones all have a small private plunge pool on the terrace. Although this is technically not a hotel, you enjoy all the services that you would find at a fine boutique hotel. A steep path from this "village" leads down to an incredibly picture-perfect cove with a palm tree-studded private beach called Playa Rosa. Here you find additional accommodations in three romantic bungalows set directly on the beach where you can just open your door and walk across the sand for a dip in the crystal clear sea. Also on the beach there is a charming, casual, open-air thatched restaurant that is a favorite gathering spot, not only for guests of the hotel, but also for yachtsmen who come ashore to enjoy a delicious meal. In addition to the casitas and bungalows, there are also sumptuous, ocean-view villas (some with eight bedrooms) that can be rented. Each of these stupendous homes has its own swimming pool, along with many incredible amenities, as well as chefs and servants available to make your stay extraordinary. *Directions:* The entrance is off the coastal highway 200 at Km 53.5.

CASITAS DE LAS FLORES & VILLAS
Manager: Tayde Manghisi
Km 53.5, Carretera Barra de Navidad
Costa Alegre–Careyes, Jalisco, 48980, Mexico
Tel: (315) 351-0240, Fax: (315) 351-0246
35 Rooms, Double: $180–$5000*
*Breakfast not included: $15
*Service: 5%, Tax: 17%
Open: all year, Credit cards: all major
Region: Beach–Puerto Vallarta

Do you ever dream of a romantic hideaway where you might be the only person on the beach of a secluded cove fringed by palm trees? Happily, you don't need to travel to the South Pacific—just such a tropical paradise awaits you at El Tamardino. It is not surprising this hotel is so special—it is part the prestigious Yellowstone Club World (YCW), a super exclusive private club that caters to the rich and famous who expect the ultimate in beauty, luxury, privacy, and service. The hotel is secreted away from the main highway via an 11-kilometer-long cobbled lane which meanders through a dense jungle. Along the way you catch glimpses of the brilliant-green fairways of the hotel's superb 18-hole golf course. The road ends at the reception building where you will be greeted and taken to one of the brightly-hued, thatched-roof, individual cottages that dot the property. Some are nestled in the trees, others are ocean-front. Their rustic appearance is only skin-deep: inside, each of the bungalows provides the ultimate in luxury with the finest amenities, and is beautifully decorated in a casually elegant style. To top it off, each has its own tiny plunge pool plus a lazy hammock for dreaming. It seems unbelievable that such a luxurious resort with 10 kilometers of private coast could be tucked in the middle of a remote tropical jungle. *Directions:* About 45 minutes north of Manzanillo airport on the coast highway at Km 7.5 marker.

❄ 🖋 💳 ☎ 👨‍🍳 @ 🍸 P ⑪ 🌸 ≈ 🎿 🖼 ⚓ ⚓ 🏹 🏃‍♀️ 🐎 🌊

EL TAMARINDO
Manager: Rui Reis
Km 7.5 Carretera Melaque-Puerto Vallarta
Costa Alegre–Cihuatlán, Jalisco, 48970, Mexico
Tel: (315) 351-5031, Fax: (315) 351-5070
29 Rooms, Double: $425–$1100*
*Breakfast not included
*Service: 10%, Tax: 17%
Open: all year, Credit cards: all major
Different World
Region: Beach–Pacific Coast

Hotelito Desconocido is undergoing a major renovation and is scheduled to reopen in May 2010. We look forward to seeing the upgraded facility. For those looking for a natural paradise, this unusual hotel, elegant in its simplicity lures guests back year after year for utter relaxation and pampering by the gentle, caring staff. Hotelito Desconocido is an environmentally friendly hotel—it has no phones or electricity and uses biodegradable products. This unique hotel is the dream of Marcello Murzillo, a well-known Italian fashion designer, who fell in love with this remote bit of coast and bought 100 acres bordering a nature preserve with miles of remote beach. The complex mimics a simple fishing village of rustic thatched cottages. Delicious meals are served in a thatched, Tahitian-looking, open-air restaurant perched over the water. At night, when the restaurant is illuminated by candlelight, the ambiance is sheer magic. The nicely decorated guestrooms tucked around the property have colorful furnishings and fine linens. Boats are available for guests who want to row across the small estuary to the beach, which is great for walking, turtle viewing, and bird watching, but not recommended for swimming. The hotel is open all year, but our choice would be to avoid the hot, rainy summer season. *Directions:* About 100 km south of Puerto Vallarta. Four-wheel drive is needed. An airport transfer is recommended.

HOTELITO DESCONOCIDO
Owner: Marcello Murzillo
Tomatlán, Costa Alegre–La Cruz de Loreto
Jalisco, 48360, Mexico
Tel: (322) 281-4010, Fax: (322) 281-4130
24 Rooms, Double: $510–$950*
*Service: 10%, Tax: 17%
Open: all year, Credit cards: all major
Different World
Region: Beach–Pacific Coast

Las Hadas hotel in Manzanillo, the dream of Bolivian billionaire tycoon Antenor Patiño, is world renowned, but only a lucky few know that Patiño's granddaughter, Isabel Goldsmith, created her own jewel, Las Alamandas, a charming hotel located to the north along the gorgeous Costalegre. Her hotel offers the ultimate in accommodations, yet exudes a natural, understated elegance. There are no signs along the road to identify Las Alamandas: absolutely no hints that a paradise exists at the end of the narrow road through the jungle. This is not an oversight. Guests who arrive (many by private plane onto the hotel's own landing strip) cherish their privacy and Las Alamandas has become a favorite hideaway for many celebrities seeking seclusion. A beautiful beach, bound by a lush lawn studded with coconut palms, stretches in front of the hotel. There are only fourteen suites within six villas. No matter whether you have the Presidential Suite or one of the Garden View rooms, you will be pampered by the staff who seem to take great pleasure in catering to your every need. Nothing you want seems to be too much trouble, whether it be a romantic lunch served on a secluded beach or a special request for dinner. The resort is surrounded by 1,500 acres of ecological reserve with pristine beaches, exotic trees, hidden lagoons, and a myriad collection of birds. *Directions:* Located off Hwy 200 at Km 83, midway between Manzanillo and Puerto Vallarta.

LAS ALAMANDAS
Manager: Miguel Andres Hernandez
Hwy 200, between Puerto Vallarta & Manzanillo
Costa Alegre–Quémaro, Jalisco, 48980, Mexico
Tel: (322) 285-5500, Fax: (322) 285-5027
*14 Rooms, Double: $371–$2070**
*Breakfast not included
*Service: 15%, Tax: 17%
Open: all year, Credit cards: all major
Different World
Region: Beach–Pacific Coast

The Playa Azul, right on one of Cozumel's best stretches of beach, is a small, moderately priced, family-run, beautifully managed hotel offering excellent value. At first glance it seems similar to many hotels built in the '50s and '60s, with a swimming pool dominating a courtyard surrounded on three sides by a four-story, pink-stucco complex, forming a "U" that opens to the ocean. The bedrooms look toward the turquoise-colored sea and all have at least a partial ocean view. However, once you enter your bedroom, the caring touches that make the Playa Azul so very special and distinguish it from others in its class quickly become evident. You cannot help smiling when you find the beds adorned with white towels whimsically shaped into swans and hibiscus blossoms everywhere. The theme of fresh flowers extends into the bathroom and vanity areas, again with towels shaped in artistic designs. All of the guestrooms are air-conditioned, although frequently it is cool enough to just open the sliding glass doors and sleep to the melody of the waves. All of the rooms have a spacious balcony or terrace with either a direct or partial view of the sea. The beach beckons with lounge chairs shaded by thatched palapas. A delicious breakfast is included as well as free golf at the Cozumel Country Club (cart not included). The hotel's lovely spa facility has created another sanctuary of serenity. *Directions:* Located on the beach, about 3 km north of town.

PLAYA AZUL GOLF.SCUBA.SPA
Owners: Martha Nieto & Fernando Beristain
Carretera a San Juan Km 4
Zona Hotelera Norte
Cozumel, Quintana Roo, 77600, Mexico
Tel: (987) 869-5160, Fax: (987) 869-5173
50 Rooms, Double: $185–$272*
12 Suites: $287–$317, 1 Cottage: $325*
*Room rate includes golfing green fees
*Service: $5.00 USD, *Tax: 12%
Open: all year, Credit cards: all major
Different World
Region: Beach–Caribbean Coast

If you are looking for deluxe accommodations on the charming island of Cozumel, we suggest the Presidente Inter-Continental. Although not small like most of the other properties we recommend, it stands out from the other large hotels that line the beach, most of which cater to groups looking for all-inclusive holiday packages. A sweeping drive leads up to the main part of the hotel, which opens to gardens and the sea. The reception area and lounges have a modern decor enhanced by many flowers and greenery. Some of the guestrooms are in this five-story section but I prefer the rooms in two wings stretching along a kilometer of beach. Ask for a room on the ground level with its own private terrace leading onto the beach for the pleasure of opening your doors and stepping straight outside for a swim. Rocky escarpments divide the beach into smaller, gentle swimming areas of soft white sand, giving a secluded feel. Small piers also stretch out from the rocks for swimming access. The heart of the hotel is its enchanting, open-air, palapa-style, thatched-roof restaurant, which stretches to the edge of the water—an idyllic place to dine. Most guests seem to gravitate to the crystal turquoise sea to swim but for others there is a giant pool tucked next to the beach. Sports enthusiasts enjoy world-class snorkeling, tennis courts, and a nearby Nicklaus-designed 18-hole golf course. *Directions:* Located on the beach, about 6.5 km south of town.

PRESIDENTE INTER-CONTINENTAL
Manager: Javier Rosenberg
Km 6.5 Carretera a. Chankanaab
Cozumel, Quintana Roo, 77600, Mexico
Tel: (987) 872-9500, Fax: (987) 872-9522
253 Rooms, Double: $290–$3900*
*Breakfast not included
*Tax: 17%
Open: all year, Credit cards: all major
Region: Beach–Caribbean Coast

For location, the Casa Colonial just can't be surpassed. The pink-stucco building faces onto a small street that is right in between Cuernavaca's prime sites: the Cortes Palace and zócalo are just a few minutes' walk in one direction, while the cathedral is almost next door. Another favorite, the Robert Brady Museum, is practically across the street. Netzahualcoyotl, the street that the hotel is on, is very quiet and also much more attractive than most. The hotel was at one time a private mansion and still reflects the personality and ambiance of a home. You enter through the foyer into a small reception area where you register at an antique desk. Open, arched doorways lead into a garden highlighted by a large swimming pool. Beyond is a luxuriant garden with a sweeping expanse of lawn enhanced by mature shade trees and bordered by lush beds of flowers and shrubs. Artistically placed stone sculptures add further to the appeal. The entire mood is one of outdoor living, for which Cuernavaca (nicknamed "The City of Eternal Spring") is famous since its weather is so mild. The garden is definitely the heart of the hotel and all of the rooms open onto it. The living room and cozy breakfast area are both windowless, with just stone columns supporting an overhanging red tile roof. There are seventeen guestrooms: all are tastefully decorated with rustic antiques and Mexican-style fabrics. *Directions:* Located between the Cortes Palace and the cathedral.

CASA COLONIAL
Manager: Angela Alvarez
Netzahualcoyotl, 37
Cuernavaca, Morelos, 62000, Mexico
Tel: (777) 312-7033, Fax: (777) 310-0395
15 Rooms, Double: $185–$275
Open: all year, Credit cards: MC, VS
Region: Central–Colonial City

Las Manañitas fills a very special niche in my heart. My mother and father spent many happy winters in this bit of paradise, ensconced in one of the inn's loveliest suites, and I was fortunate to visit them on many occasions. Nothing much has really changed in the nearly 30 years since I first stayed there—it remains one of Mexico's most exquisite hideaways. Not only is this a superb, intimate hotel, but it is also renowned as one of Mexico's finest restaurants; people line up daily at lunchtime to dine. The entrance is most unassuming. The magic doesn't begin until you walk out into the courtyard where you are greeted by an exquisite garden with lush foliage and expansive lawns decorated with sculptures, a lily pond with a water fountain, and peacocks wandering freely throughout the property. On one side, the restaurant offers both terrace and inside dining and overlooks the gardens. To the left, is a very comfortable lounge and bar (primarily for hotel guests), which comes to life in the evenings. The guestrooms are very spacious, especially the garden suites, and come completely outfitted with all amenities. The corridors leading to the rooms are adorned with fine art of well-known Mexican artists and large bouquets of fresh flowers. The hotel is located just outside the historic central area, close enough to walk there, but far enough away from the hustle and bustle of the street noises. *Directions:* Five blocks from center of town.

LAS MAÑANITAS
Owner: Rebeca K. de Bernot
Ricardo Linares 107
Cuernavaca, Morelos, 62000, Mexico
Tel: (777) 362-0000, Fax: (777) 318-3672
25 Suites: $224–$501*
*Service: 5%, Tax: 17.5%
Open: all year, Credit cards: all major
Different World
Relais & Châteaux
Region: Central–Colonial City

Reposado is not only an intimate, three-bedroom hotel, but a wonderful restaurant (open Wednesday through Sunday) and a cooking school (called La Villa Bonita). Strolling down the splendidly located Netzahualcoyotl Street, you could easily walk right by the hotel's massive wooden doors without knowing a hotel exists within—only a discreet sign on the exterior wall gives a hint that guests are welcomed. The Robert Brady home (now a fascinating museum) is across the street and Helen Hayes used to own the villa next door. The Reposado is the creation of a talented, hard-working young couple, Robb and Ana Garcia Anderson. Having come to Cuernavaca to polish his Spanish, Robb met his future wife, Ana, an accomplished chef. They bought a splendid, centuries-old home, renovated it, and opened the doors to guests in the spring of 2000. You come into a foyer from which a staircase leads up to the three, simply-furnished guest rooms. Beyond the entryway is a delightful small, inner courtyard enhanced by a dramatic antique statue of an Indian woman. A few more steps bring you to an intimate dining room that looks out to a walled garden highlighted by a swimming pool. Although rooms are available on a nightly basis, most guests come for a six-night package that includes three days of sightseeing and three days of hands-on cooking lessons given by Ana in her colorful, Mexican-style kitchen. *Directions:* Located between the Cortés Palace and the cathedral.

REPOSADO
Owners: Ana Garcia & Robb Anderson
Netzahualcoyotl 33
Cuernavaca, Morelos, 62000, Mexico
Tel: (777) 169- 7232, Toll Free: (800) 505-3084 (USA)
3 Rooms, Double: $85–$125*
*Breakfast not included
*Tax: 17%
Restaurant open Wed through Sun
Open: all year, Credit cards: all major
Region: Central–Colonial City

Hotel Descriptions   277

Guadalajara is a huge, bustling metropolis, but secreted within a few blocks of its heart is a section with a rich Colonial heritage. This Centro Histórico is the highlight of Guadalajara, and if you want to be within steps of its architectural wonders, the Hotel de Mendoza makes a good choice for accommodations. With a prime location next to the beautiful 16th-century Santa María de Gracia Church, the Mendoza attracts tourists from around the globe. This is a simple hotel that offers a genuinely warm welcome and pleasant facilities. From the canopied entrance, you enter an old-fashioned lobby accented by a bronze, multi-tiered chandelier and large oil paintings. To the left is a raised area with tables and chairs in a parlor-like setting. A hallway to the right leads to La Forja restaurant. The hotel is built around an inner courtyard, with an inviting swimming pool as the center of attention. Some of the guestrooms overlook this courtyard, but my favorite is number 308; a smaller bedroom than many of the others, but with a romantic view overlooking the Santa María de Gracia Church. All of the bedrooms are simply furnished and have a traditional hotel look with built-in headboards. They all have good lighting, air conditioning, color cable television, and marble bathrooms. *Directions:* Follow signs to the Centro Histórico. Once there, you need a detailed city map to find the small side street where the hotel is located.

HOTEL DE MENDOZA
Manager: Raul de la Brena
Calle Venustiano Carranza #16
Centro Histórico, Guadalajara, Jalisco, 44100, Mexico
Tel: (333) 942-5151, Fax: (333) 613-7310
87 Rooms, Double: $110–$129*
*Breakfast not included: $8
*Tax: 17%
Open: all year, Credit cards: all major
Different World
Region: Central–Colonial City

If you want to be within walking distance to the picturesque heart of Guadalajara (called Centro Histórico), the moderately-priced Hotel Morales makes an excellent choice for accommodations. It is located just three blocks from one of the city's treasures—its 16th-century cathedral. The hotel was originally a private mansion, built in colonial style with galleries surrounding an inner courtyard. In the early 1900s two additional stories were added and the home was converted to a hotel that became an instant success—it was the place to see and be seen. All the celebrities flocked here including Mexico's legendary bull fighters, renowned artists, illustrious movie stars, and prestigious politicians. But this Golden Era ended and the structure was abandoned for more than 30 years. After a two-year renovation the hotel reopened in 2005 and is now the prime place to stay in the historic part of the city. During the restoration care was taken to respect the hotel's original classic ambiance as verified by a charming stone fountain highlighting the atrium and a series of arches leading into comfortable sitting areas and the restaurant. However, all modern amenities were added to the attractively decorated guestrooms such as top notch bathrooms, free high-speed internet access, satellite TV, air conditioning and coffee maker. For meals, the hotel offers the Ruedo Restaurant (Bullring Restaurant). There is also a rooftop garden with views of the city.

❄ 🏊 💳 ☎ 🛗 🍴 @ W P 🍴 🚭 🖼 👤 🏇

HOTEL MORALES HISTORICAL & COLONIAL
Manager: Alberto Fornos
Av. Corona # 243, Centro Histórico
Guadalajara, Jalisco, 44100, Mexico
Tel: (333) 658-5232, Fax: (333) 658-5239
*64 Rooms, Double: $78–$96**
*3 Suites: $142–$148**
**Breakfast not included: $8*
**Tax: 17%*
Open: all year, Credit cards: all major
Region: Central–Colonial City

For many years we searched throughout Guadaljara for the perfect hotel, but sadly never found it. Happily, all that has changed, and dramatically so. With the opening of the Quinta Real, Guadalajara now has a hotel that is an absolute jewel: one that instantly captured our hearts. Conveniently located about a 15-minute taxi ride from the city's historic center, in the upscale hotel zone, the hotel is appealing at first glance. From the street you pass under the canopied entry into an elegant atrium highlighted by a 250-year-old elephant tree and galleried walkways above adorned with greenery. Off to the right is an indoor-outdoor garden restaurant, a real beauty, which is a favorite spot for local families to bring their children for Sunday brunch. The heart of the hotel is its inner courtyard where fountains, trees, sculptures, and immaculately groomed gardens create a magical scene. The owner of the hotel is especially fond of angels, and if you look carefully you will see tiny angel statues and ornaments tucked into the lush garden greenery. Also in the garden is a splendid swimming pool. As you'd expect, the guestrooms are elegantly appointed and top-notch in every respect. Although the Quinta Real has fabulous amenities, its crowning glory is its superb, well-trained staff who strive to make every guest's stay a happy one. *Directions:* Two blocks from the Minerva Fountain at Avenida Lopez Mateos and Avenida Mexico.

❋ ⛷ 💳 ☎ ♈ P ♨ ≈

QUINTA REAL GUADALAJARA
Manager: Alfredo Aguilar
Av. Mexico 2727
Guadalajara, Jalisco, 44680, Mexico
Tel: (333) 630-1797, Fax: (333) 615-0000
76 Rooms, Double: $228–$992*
*Breakfast not included
*Tax: 17%
Open: all year, Credit cards: all major
Different World
Region: Central–Colonial City

Villa Ganz is situated close to the historic central area of the city. Many of the homes here are colonial mansions that have been wonderfully restored as shops and upscale office space, or in this case, as a boutique hotel. Villa Ganz opened its doors in 2001 after undergoing a complete renovation. The result is a charming hotel that makes you feel right at home from the minute you walk through the front door. The rooms and suites are spacious and detailed, each uniquely designed and decorated. The garden at the rear of the property is a welcome escape from the busy boulevard out front, with a lounging area that's complete with a fireplace. In the mornings, this is where a buffet breakfast, made up mostly of fruits, cereals and yogurts, is served. Villa Ganz will serve lunch or dinner upon request, or there are many restaurants and cafes nearby. Copies of their menus are available at the reception. The central salon is full of books in multiple languages and there's always hot coffee or snacks in the morning and chilled wine from 6 to 8 pm each evening. Villa Ganz delivers comfort and character with style, and is a welcome starting point for exploring Guadalajara or one of the many neighboring towns. *Directions:* In the heart of the city's commercial, restaurant and financial center. One street over from main Vallarta Avenue, near the intersection with Chapultepec, near downtown and historic center.

VILLA GANZ
Owners: Klix Kaltenmark & Sally Rangel
Lopez Cotilla 1739
Colonia Lafayette
Guadalajara, Jalisco, 44140, Mexico
Tel & Fax: (333) 120-1416
Cell: (333) 105-0875
10 Suites: $200–$280*
*Service: 5%, Tax: 17%
Open: all year, Credit cards: all major
Region: Central–Colonial City

When visiting Guadalajara you must not miss Tlaquepaque, an artisans' village with fabulous shopping (famous for its handicrafts and colorful pottery) on the outskirts of the city. Though urban sprawl has grown up around it, Tlaquepaque keeps its small-town identity with a central plaza enclosed by an arcaded promenade. If you choose to stay overnight in Tlaquepaque and prefer B&Bs, the Casa de Las Flores, located four blocks from the heart of Tlaquepaque, makes an excellent choice for accommodations. Located in a simple neighborhood, the lovely house stands out from all its neighbors. Inside, you enter the private home of your extremely gracious, capable hosts, Stan Singleton and José Gutiérrez. Their house wraps around an enclosed inner courtyard enhanced by a flower-filled garden, lovingly tended by José (a native of Guadalajara) who spends several hours every day keeping the gardens perfect. Stan, who relocated from northern California, is both an artist and an accomplished cook whose talents are evident in the breakfast served and the tasteful decor of the guestrooms. The guestrooms are appealingly fresh and pretty, exuding artistic good taste with hand-painted tiles, handmade brick and marble floors, and furnishings by local artisans. Casa de Las Flores is constantly being improved for the guests. *Directions:* Located just on the edge of the pedestrian zone. The one-way streets make driving tricky, so ask Stan for directions.

CASA DE LAS FLORES
Owners: Stan Singleton & Jose Gutierrez
Santos Degollado No 175
Guadalajara–Tlaquepaque, Jalisco, 45500, Mexico
Tel & Fax: (333) 659-3186
7 Rooms, Double: $95–$105*
*Tax: 17%
Open: all year, Credit cards: MC, VS
Region: Central–Colonial City

Quinta Don Jose is an ideal place to stay if you prefer a hotel outside of Guadalajara in Tlaquepaque—famous for its picturesque plaza and excellent shopping. Its quaint cobbled pedestrian streets are lined with stores that abound with colorful things to buy, most of which are made by local artisans. The Quinta Don Jose started out as a simple B&B, but over the years, as more guestrooms and amenities were added, it evolved into a small boutique hotel. Your exceptionally charming young hosts, Estela and Arturo Magaña (both born in California of Mexican parents) add the final touch of perfection. While visiting family in Tlaquepaque, Arturo realized the need for accommodations and later opened the Quinta Don Jose. Its location is perfect—just a couple of blocks from the main plaza with its rich selection of restaurants, art galleries, museums and boutiques housed in 18th-century buildings. The hotel faces directly onto the street with a simple façade that belies the oasis found within. Its meticulously-kept reception room, lounge, restaurant, and cute bar all lead to the heart of the hotel—a lush walled garden with manicured beds of flowers, a splendid swimming pool, stone fountains, and hideaways where you can laze the day away in a hammock. All of the attractively decorated guestrooms offer amenities such as wireless internet, direct dial telephone, and air conditioning. *Directions:* Call for directions. Free airport pickup for a 3-night stay.

QUINTA DON JOSE
Owners: Estela & Arturo Magaña
Calle Reforma #139
Guadalajara–Tlaquepaque, Jalisco, 45500, Mexico
Tel: (333) 635-7522, Fax: (333) 659-9315
15 Rooms, Double: $80–$140
Open: all year, Credit cards: all major
Region: Central–Colonial City

Dating back to 1862, the Hotel Posada Santa Fe is one of Guanajuato's most historic hotels. (The city's name was originally Santa Fe, hence the name of the hotel.) It faces onto the Jardín Unión, by far the prettiest plaza in the city—in our estimation, by far the choicest place to be. Just in front of the hotel is a park with a bandstand, fountains, a pedestrian-only walkway of colorful tiles, and marvelous trees that are trimmed to form a dense canopy to screen the sun. Reminiscent of a Paris scene, a line of cafés with jaunty umbrellas stretches along the street, one of these being the Posada Santa Fé's restaurant-bar, La Terraza, a prime place to sit and "people watch." The lobby lounge has a rather dark, old-fashioned, faded elegance that reflects an era of days long past. The hotel is almost like a museum, with walls enhanced by colorful murals reflecting the legends and traditions of Guanajuato. An intricate wrought-iron staircase with a delightful skylight of stained glass leads up to the guestrooms. Request one of the best rooms (such as 2, 5, 7, 8, or 9). These rooms have small balconies overlooking the plaza and are far superior to the standard rooms, which are smaller and darker. However, be aware that there is much festivity in the cafés below, with music lasting until the wee hours. *Directions:* Guanajuato, with its underground maze of streets, is almost impossible to navigate—ask the hotel for directions. The hotel has free valet parking.

🍺 🛵 💳 ☎ @ W P 🍴

HOTEL POSADA SANTA FÉ
Manager: Gerardo Herrera Garcia
Plaza Principal, Jardín Unión 12
Guanajuato, Guanajuato, 36000, Mexico
Tel: (473) 732-0084, Fax: (473) 732-4653
40 Rooms, Double: $90–$130
8 Suites: $150–$232
Open: all year, Credit cards: MC, VS
Different World
Region: Central–Colonial Town

Guanajuato is a national treasure, offering numerous examples of the rich colonial lifestyle at the time when the city was one of Mexico's leading producers of silver. Its winding, narrow streets, some actually under the city itself using the abandoned mine tunnels and the well-preserved buildings make the city wonderful for exploring Mexico's past. A good choice for a place to stay here is Quinta Las Acacias, a family-managed small hotel located just above the downtown area, next to a dam that was once the water source for the city. It is possible to walk down into town, but since the road is steep, a taxi is best for your return. This small inn is one of the many mansions in this neighborhood that have been renovated and is a quaint and comfortable place to rest and relax after enjoying Guanajuato. The entrance/reception area, decorated with antiques and family mementos, is very inviting. There is a small dining room on the main floor where breakfast is served and on the second floor you find a library and sitting area for guests. The guestrooms in the main house exude a Victorian formality, but my favorites are those in an annex behind the hotel where there are pretty terraced gardens and a pool. These accommodations not only offer plenty of privacy, but also have a charming Mexican décor. *Directions:* Very tricky to find—ask for detailed directions.

QUINTA LAS ACACIAS
Manager: Ana Pérez Ordaz
Paseo de la Presca 168
Guanajuato, Guanajuato, 36000, Mexico
Tel: (473) 731-1517, Fax: (473) 731-1862
9 Rooms, Double: $185–$280*
*Breakfast not included
*Tax: 17%
Open: all year, Credit cards: all major
Region: Central–Colonial Town

An alternate to staying in the center of the exceptionally picturesque city of Guanajuato is to take a 10-minute drive into the historic hillside suburb of Valenciana and stay at the charming Casa Estrella de La Valenciana. The owners, Sharon and Jaye, are friends who worked together in Long Beach, California, before deciding to open a small inn. Guanajuato was a natural choice since Sharon's husband's family immigrated to California from there. Sharon is your gracious hostess at the inn, while Jaye takes care of reservations in California. The inn, nestled on the hillside above the Valenciana mine, has a panoramic view of the city as well as the famous Church of San Cayetano, a lavish church built in the 18th century by the Count Alococer whose enormous wealth came from the nearby silver mines. A 5-minute walk from the hotel leads to nearby plaza. Casa Estrella opened in 2003 after extensive remodeling and offers a quieter alternative to stayiing in the center of town as well as offering the finest modern comforts without losing one iota of Mexican charm. A casual elegance prevails with terracotta floors, abundant use of colorful Talavera tiles, beautiful lamps, hand-loomed carpets, fine linens, and excellent Mexican art. Tucked into the garden below the inn is a beautiful swimming pool where guests love to relax after a day of sightseeing. The hotel also rents a lovely large 2 bedroom house, Casa Estrellita. *Directions:* Ask for directions.

🍴 ⚡ 💳 🐕 @ W P ≋ 🖼 ♿ 🚶

CASA ESTRELLA DE LA VALENCIANA
Owners: Sharon Mendez & Janet (Jaye) Johnson
Callejon Jalisco 10
Guanajuato–Valenciana, 36240, Mexico
Tel & Fax: (473) 732-1784
4 Rooms, Double: $185–$235*
2 Suites: $235–$265*
Casa Estrellita: $425/night*
*Tax: 17%
Open: all year, Credit cards: all major
Region: Central–Colonial Town

Soon after entering the town of Guerrero Negro you can't miss the Malarrimo complex where you find the headquarters of Malarrimo Eco Tours, as well as the Hotel Malarrimo, gift shop, and restaurant. Guestrooms are found in separate buildings, painted deep red with white trim. The theme of whales is dominant in the décor, with headboards and chests in some of the rooms carved as whales. The guestrooms are very simple in décor and appointments, but clean and comfortable. Our first choice would be one of the three guestrooms in the newest wing (numbers 16, 17, and 18), which are a bit more spacious and have more modern bathrooms. There are four rooms that are a little larger than the others and offer a sleeping loft, which would be handy if you're traveling with children. The restaurant boasts some of the best seafood in the area and we enjoyed abalone, lobster, and scallops—all reasonably priced and delicious. Although the Hotel Malarrimo is a very basic hotel, reminiscent of old-fashioned motels that used to dot the highways in the USA, it offers the best accommodations in town and we really liked it a lot. The staff is very accommodating and it is also very convenient to stay right at the point of departure for your whale-watching tour. We enjoyed a leisurely breakfast knowing we were just minutes from the bus and only had to be summoned by the courtyard bell. *Directions:* You will see the hotel to the right, just as you enter town.

HOTEL MALARRIMO
Owner: Enrique Achoy
Boulevard Zapata
Guerrero Negro, Baja California Sur, 23940, Mexico
Tel & Fax: (615) 157-0100
22 Rooms, Double: $45–$49*
*Breakfast not included
Open: all year, Credit cards: none
Region: Whale Watching-Baja California

Staying at Agua Azul La Villa is like being a guest in a lovely private home. Located just one bay (five minutes by car) away from the bustling Tangolunda Bay "strip" of Huatulco, the house is snuggled into the hillside above Conejos Bay—one of nine that the area is known for. This small B&B is a marvelous value and offers six air-conditioned bedrooms, each overlooking the bay below from private, hammock-bedecked terraces. Your gracious Canadian hosts, Brooke and Rick Gazer, designed the Pacific Coast-style villa, combining stucco, palm thatch, and wood—successfully achieving an intimate inn tucked in a garden-like setting. The attractive main salon hosts an ample Continental breakfast each morning. The bedrooms are simply decorated with a fresh, uncluttered appeal and feature built-in tile headboards and side tables, terracotta floors, and richly hued blue bedspreads of hand-loomed Guatemalan fabric. Tasteful use of blue-and-white tile livens up the bathrooms and wood wall units with cubbies and hangers serving as closets. For the most spacious guestroom, ask for Orca, which has two beds. The others, each with a queen bed, are smaller. The appealing, two-tiered pool in the back garden is ringed by flowering foliage and features a waterfall and wonderful view. A three-minute walk down the hill takes you to an idyllic, golden crescent of a semi-private, beach. *Directions:* Ask for specific driving instructions.

AGUA AZUL LA VILLA
Owners: Brooke & Rick Gazer
Huatulco, Oaxaca, 70989, Mexico
Tel: (958) 581-0265
6 Rooms, Double: $119–$139*
*Tax: 12%
Minimum Stay Required
Open: all year, Credit cards: MC, VS
Region: Beach–Pacific Coast

Spread throughout 27 verdant acres, 19 buildings, and 3 levels overlooking Tangolunda Bay, the traditional white-stucco Camino Real Zaashila is an excellent choice for a family getaway to Mexico's Pacific Riviera. The property boasts a quarter-mile of exclusive, wide golden beach and what must be the largest (450 feet) and loveliest sculpted pool in Huatulco's nine-bay area (request poolside accommodation if you want to minimize stairs). Fully a third of the rooms feature a 196-square-foot private pool, and every room has a small, furnished balcony with a view of the bay and the blue expanse of the Pacific beyond. The rustic, off-white stucco bedrooms have green-painted ceilings and Italian-marble floors, and are large enough to accommodate a reading chair and small writing/eating table. Verdigris wrought-iron and Mexican-style pale-mahogany and rattan furniture are tastefully combined to create a light and airy ambiance. The bathrooms and closets are surprisingly spacious—a blessing at a beach resort where an extended stay is likely. Once you've undergone the bustle of check-in at the bottom of the hill, and oriented yourself to your room amidst the gardens and walkways, you'll be able to relax utterly and savor totally the natural beauty of the landscape, a myriad of water sports, tennis, nearby golf, and all the benefits of a full-service resort hotel. *Directions:* Located overlooking Tangolunda Bay.

CAMINO REAL ZAASHILA
Manager: Juan Francisco Perez Breton
Boulevard Benito Juárez #5
Huatulco, Oaxaca, 70989, Mexico
Tel: (958) 581-0460, Fax: (958) 581-0461
*145 Rooms, Double: $157–$660**
**Breakfast not included*
**Tax: 17%*
Open: all year, Credit cards: all major
Different World
Region: Beach–Pacific Coast

Truly a grand-class resort on an intimate scale, the Quinta Real is the jewel in the tiara of hotels that crowns Oaxaca's Riviera. If you're seeking an experience wherein every desire is anticipated by a staff that outnumbers the guests two to one, and every detail of your accommodation fantasy is realized, this should be your destination. From the welcoming fountain in the open-air lobby to the gorgeous tiered pool and tempting strip of private beach far below (shuttle service provided for those wishing to avoid stairs), the place caters without pretension to guests accustomed to excellence and elegance. The sumptuous, oversized rooms seem suffused with golden light during the day and each includes a roomy sitting area and covered terrace with lounging couch, hammock, table, and sea views. Arabian royalty would feel at home amidst the stone pillars and tables, creamy domed ceilings, niched walls, and white cement floors polished to a soft sheen and inset with dark, smooth pebbles. The decor features pale, sun-colored textiles, armoires from Michoacán hand-painted in a tropical motif, and framed original art and weavings. Spacious bathrooms contain family-size Jacuzzi tub, shower and WC in separate curtained alcoves, and every amenity you could possibly need. And, finally, the superb restaurant is justifiably proud of its regional and international cuisine, beautifully served inside or out. *Directions:* Located overlooking Tangolunda Bay.

QUINTA REAL HUATULCO
Manager: Federico Roth
Boulevard Benito Juárez Lote 2
Huatulco, Oaxaca, 70989, Mexico
Tel: (958) 581-0428, Fax: (958) 581-0429
28 Rooms, Double: $218–$1575*
*Breakfast not included: $12
*Tax: 17%
Open: all year, Credit cards: all major
Different World
Region: Beach–Pacific Coast

The Hotel Playa La Media Luna makes no pretense at being a super fancy, trendy hotel, but is a real winner for those seeking a friendly, family-run, moderately priced place to stay in Isla Mujers, just steps from its shops and restaurants. In spite of the reasonable rates, there is no compromise in quality or location. Guests enjoy a continental breakfast at the hotel; but for other meals, stroll into town (just a few blocks away) where there is a rich selection of places to eat. You reach the hotel by a private alleyway that leads to a white-sand, moon-shaped beach called Playa la Media Luna (Half Moon Beach). Once you enter the buff-colored building, you realize its excellent position: all of the guestrooms (each with a private, palapa-shaded terrace with comfy hammock) face the sea. The rooms are pleasantly furnished and offer all the amenities you really need such as modern marble bathrooms, air conditioning, comfortable mattresses, and mini-bars. Prime rooms are king-bedded suites with especially large terraces with marvelous views and Jacuzzi tubs. The hotel overlooks a pretty, free-form swimming pool that stretches to the edge of the secluded beach. There is also a small pool for children. For those who want more action than the quiet Half Moon Beach in front of the hotel, Isla Mujere's bustling, famous North Beach is just a few minutes' walk away. *Directions:* Take a ferry from Cancún or Puerto Juárez to Isla Mujeres, then a taxi to the hotel.

❄ ☕ 🏊 🚤 CREDIT ☎ ⛻ P 🚭 🏊 🖼 ⚓ ♟ 🎣 ⛷

HOTEL PLAYA LA MEDIA LUNA
Manager: Kin Lima
Lotes 9 & 10 Punta Norte
Isla Mujeres, Quintana Roo, 77400, Mexico
Tel: (998) 877-0759, Fax: (998) 877-1124
18 Rooms, Double: $120–$200*
*Service: Add 10% if paying by credit card
Open: all year, Credit cards: all major
Different World
Region: Beach–Caribbean Coast

If you are looking for a small, deluxe hotel in a prime location that is very secluded, yet just a few minutes' walk to shops and restaurants, the Hotel Secreto is a superb choice. We fell in love with this tiny, privately owned and managed hotel whose motto is 'Intimate, Elegant, and Tranquil' describing perfectly what makes the Secreto special. However, the hotel has much more to offer: a powdery white beach, a spa, lovely furnishings, stunning views, quality linens, nice bathrooms, exceptionally friendly service, top-notch quality throughout, rooms that all open to the sea, and a great swimming pool. The hotel exterior makes an architectural statement with its white walls, tall narrow windows, and accents of towering palm trees. As you step inside, the contemporary, fresh look continues with an uncluttered, soothing decor—the walls are all painted white, most of the upholstery on chairs and lounges is white, and the furniture of light wood. The dazzling white color scheme is the ideal background for the views of the turquoise sea, lovely gardens, and swimming pool. Splashes of color appear in bouquets of flowers and colorful paintings on the walls. The hotel, which is constantly upgrading, closed in the summer of 2005 to reopen in time for Christmas, with new gifts for its loyal guests: a new restaurant, more deluxe rooms, and a spa. *Directions:* Take a ferry from Cancún or Puerto Juárez to Isla Mujeres, then a taxi to the hotel.

HOTEL SECRETO
Owner: Scott Boyan
Sección Rocas Lote 11, Punta Norte
Isla Mujeres, Quintana Roo, 77400, Mexico
Tel: (998) 877-1039, Fax: (998) 877-1048
12 Rooms, Double: $225–$400
Minimum Stay Required: 2 nights, Christmas: 5 nights
Open: all year, Credit cards: all major
Region: Beach–Caribbean Coast

The magic of the Villa Rolandi begins when you are met in Cancún and whisked across the turquoise-blue water in the hotel's private catamaran to Isla Mujeres. The magic continues when you enter the hotel's impressive lobby richly embellished with dramatic marble columns, domed ceiling, and fresh flowers, with its distinctly Italian ambiance spiced with a tantalizing Mexican-Caribbean flavor—not surprising, as the owners hail from southern Switzerland, just at the Italian border. The Villa Rolandi has a fabulous, romantic restaurant with a deck extending right over the water and steps down to a pier where in season private yachts dock, bringing the rich and famous to dine. The suites are all similar in a modern style, with leather headboards, excellent reading lights, a separate sitting area, and private terrace or balcony sporting a Jacuzzi tub. The marble bathrooms are especially outstanding, with state-of-the-art amenities like double marble showers with dual showerheads, Jacuzzi-style sprays, and a steam-bath option. Guestrooms all look out to the hotel's private beach with its soft, pure-white sand extending to the turquoise sea. For those who prefer a pool, there is an exquisite, large, swimming pool with a waterfall dropping down to a pond below. Be sure to make time for a spa treatment during your stay too. The wonderful staff here seems to take joy in pampering all of the guests. *Directions:* No need to worry about finding the hotel—you are picked up in Cancún.

❄ ☕ 🍴 CREDIT ☎ @ W ♈ P ❚❙ ≈ ⚓ ⚓ 🚶 ⚓ 🍸

HOTEL VILLA ROLANDI THALASSO SPA
Manager: Giancarlo Frigerio
Isla Mujeres, Quintana Roo, 77400, Mexico
Tel: (998) 999-2000, Fax: (998) 877-0100
34 Rooms, Double: $290–$620, 1 Suite: $880*
* Service: $3 to $6 daily, Tax: 12%
*Includes breakfast & dinner
Open all year, Credit cards: all major
Different World
Region: Beach–Caribbean Coast

Isla Mujeres is a small island just offshore from Cancún, yet here you feel far removed from the bustling commercialism of its famous neighbor. An excellent choice for accommodations on the island is the Villa Vera Puerto Isla Mujeres, which caters to yachtsmen whose sumptuous boats glide into the hotel's private marina. The hotel attracts not only wealthy sportsmen who come for a month at a time and use the resort as a hub for fishing, but also guests from around the world who come to relax and enjoy the fine accommodations. The spaciousness of the beautifully kept property sets a mood of quiet seclusion. A stunning circular swimming pool is the centerpiece around which the guestrooms are clustered in cream-colored, two-story buildings with Spanish-style red-tiled roofs. All of the rooms are suites with separate sitting areas and individual terraces. In addition to the suites, there are villas available with private plunge pools and kitchenettes. These make ideal accommodations if you are traveling with children (who stay free under the age of 12). A Continental breakfast is delivered discreetly to a little cubbyhole in the wall hidden by a cute painting. Canals wrap around the property and, any time you want, a speedboat will whisk you in five minutes to the hotel's splendid white-sand beach with its own swimming pool and palapa-style restaurant. *Directions:* Complimentary boat transfers from Cancún.

❄ ☕ ✂ 🚐 🛎 @ 🍸 P 🍴 🌿 ≋ ⛵ 🏊 ⚓ 🕴 🚤

VILLA VERA PUERTO ISLA MUJERES
Manager: Javier Silva
Puerto de Abrigo, Laguna Macax
Isla Mujeres, Quintana Roo, 77400, Mexico
Tel: (998) 287-3340, Fax: (998) 287-3345
24 Rooms, Double: $290–$385*
*Tax: 12%
Open: all year, Credit cards: all major
Region: Beach–Caribbean Coast

If you yearn for unspoiled nature and fascinating archaeological sites, yet don't want to sacrifice creature comforts, look no further than The Explorean, where sensual delights combine with superb, understated, casual elegance. That such superb luxury can be found so far off the beaten path is quite miraculous. The complex is designed in the style of a traditional Mayan village, but there the similarity ends. The reception area, bar, and restaurant, all open to the air under a high, thatched roof, look out to a stunning terrace—an architectural masterpiece. A long, fairly narrow swimming pool and a Jacuzzi hot tub stretch across the terrace, lined by white lounge chairs and umbrellas. What makes this extraordinary is that as you look out over a green expanse of lush jungle, the only structure you can see, if you look very closely, is the top of one of the pyramids of Kohunlich peeking out of the sea of green. Paths meander through the rich foliage, leading to the guestrooms, which are in thatched cottages tucked about the property. These are exceptionally spacious and beautifully furnished in elegant simplicity and all have a private terrace with sofa and hammock. As you might expect, such luxury isn't cheap, but you do get value since the rate includes all meals, taxes, tips, drinks, cocktails, and even sightseeing excursions. *Directions:* From 186, between Escárcega and Chetumal, turn at the sign for Kohunlich. The hotel is on your left after about 6 km.

❄ ☕ ⚒ CREDIT ☎ P ⅋ ⚘ ≋ ⛱ 👫

THE EXPLOREAN
Owner: Antonio Arroyo
Zona Arqueologica de Kohunlich
Kohunlich, Quintana Roo, 77981, Mexico
Tel: (555) 201-8333, Toll Free: (877) 397-5672 (USA)
40 Rooms, Double: $520–$800*
*Includes all meals, drinks & activities
Open: all year, Credit cards: all major
Region: Yucatán Peninsula-Archaeological Area

El Ángel Azul (The Blue Angel) is a delightful Bed & Breakfast that is made even more special by your Swiss hostess, Esther Ammann, a truly a remarkable young woman. While on an extensive road trip exploring the United States, Esther was saving money by sleeping in her car at night. When winter arrived, the nights turned cold so she headed south to sunny Mexico to surf. She ended up in Southern Baja, fell in love with La Paz, and decided to stay. It was a destination made in heaven for her. Since childhood she had been passionate about whales and cacti—both in abundance here. With more bravado than money, she acted on a whim and made an offer to buy an abandoned 19th-century courthouse in the heart of town. To her amazement, her offer was accepted and she became the owner of one of the few historic buildings in La Paz. With determination and a huge amount of her own labor, she beautifully renovated the building and planted in the interior courtyard a fabulous cactus garden. In 1999 she opened the doors to her first guests. A Mexican ambiance prevails with arcaded walkways, wrought iron accents, hand-loomed fabrics, local artifacts, and brilliant colors used throughout. Breakfast is served in the courtyard, which is also a favorite niche for a margarita before heading out to a nearby restaurant for dinner. *Directions:* Located on the corner of Guillermo Prieto & Independencia, five blocks to the malecon (along the waterfront).

❄ ☕ CREDIT ☎ @ W ⊗ ⚓ 🍴 ⚓

EL ÁNGEL AZUL B&B
Owner: Esther Ammann
Independencia 518/ corner Guillermo Prieto
La Paz, Baja California Sur, 23000, Mexico
Tel & Fax: (612) 125-5130
9 Rooms, Double: $100–$120*
1 Suite: $165*
*Service: $5.00, Tax: 13%
Open: all year, Credit cards: all major
Different World
Region: Beach-Baja California

La Paz is a paradise for avid fishermen who come in search of the marlin and sailfish, which ply these deep-blue waters from May to November. Although the largest city in southern Baja, La Paz still has a sleepy, small-town ambiance, especially along the waterfront. Facing the sea wall is where you find most of the restaurants, shops, and hotels, including our favorite, Posada Santa Fé, a small hotel whose architecture reflects the town's early Spanish heritage (Cortés landed here in 1535). The rosy-pink, stuccoed hacienda-style building faces onto the street and it is not until you go through the wrought-iron gate that the charm of the inn is revealed. You come into an inner courtyard with a tiny, pretty, turquoise-colored swimming pool tucked into the corner, complete with tiled fountain against the far wall. Clusters of tall palm trees and potted plants enhance the scene. Steps lead up to a higher terrace, where you find a guest lounge and an outdoor patio where breakfast is served overlooking the water. There are ten guestrooms, some on the lower level facing the swimming pool and others on the top floor with balconies looking out to the ocean. All are attractive and tastefully decorated, with tiled floors, colorful bedspreads, Mexican paintings, and hand-carved wooden furniture. This intimate inn is not only very well priced, but offers quality and charm. *Directions:* On Paseo Alvaro Obergón, at the corner of Via Guerrero.

POSADA DE LAS FLORES
Owner: Giuseppe Marcelletti
Paseo Alvaro Obergón 440
La Paz, Baja California Sur, 23000, Mexico
Tel: (612) 125-5871, Fax: (619) 872-0781
5 Rooms, Double: $150*
3 Suites: $250*
*Tax: 12%
Open: all year, Credit cards: MC, VS
Region: Beach-Baja California

The Inn at Loreto Bay, located in a tourist development just south of Loreto, nestles between the beach and a golf course. Designed to resemble a mission, architecturally the complex is simple, with high stucco walls on three sides embracing a large, open, central courtyard, pool, and terrace bar-restaurant, leaving the fourth open to the gray sand beach. Only the bell tower pierces the horizontal lines of the complex. The reception is on the right as you enter the complex, with a boutique and restaurant opposite, and a flight of stairs leading up to the bell tower and an open terrace bar. Guestrooms are found in two wings stretching from the reception and out to the beach. The rooms' décor is similar throughout, with warm earth tones selected for the paints and tiles. Standard rooms are comfortable but the suites are a bargain for the difference in luxury provided. Junior suites have a single outdoor terrace off the bedroom while master suites enjoy a two-tiered terrace and outdoor spa tub. The Inn at Loreto Bay is a large hotel and seems a bit functional in design but we recommend it as an alternative to the charming Posada de las Flores in the heart of Loreto, which might often be full, and as a good location if you are traveling with children. The grounds are expansive, with an excellent large swimming pool, private beach, and two restaurants. *Directions:* Located 7 km south of Loreto on the beach.

❄ ⚞ 🖭 ☎ 'Y' P ¶¶ ≈ ⚓

INN AT LORETO BAY
Manager: Pedro Lisarga
Paseo de la Misión s/n
Fraccionamiento Napoló
Loreto, Baja California Sur, 23880, Mexico
Tel: (613) 133-0010, Fax: (613) 133-0020
155 Rooms, Double: $140–$258*
*Breakfast not included
*Tax: 12%
Open: all year, Credit cards: all major
Region: Beach-Baja California

On a cobbled street in the heart of Loreto, Baja California's oldest town, the charming, Italian-owned, Posada de las Flores has a prime position facing the Plaza Salvatierra, one block from the mission. This handsome, two-story, Spanish Colonial-style building has a rich sienna-red exterior enhanced by arched windows framed by stone. Wrought-iron lamps and potted plants in front add to the appeal. A massive door affords a glimpse into the interior garden courtyard featuring a stone fountain, many potted palms, Talavera ceramic pots, and groupings of overstuffed chairs. Above, heavy beams support the glass bottom of a small swimming pool found on the upper terrace. From this interior patio a wrought-iron spiral staircase winds up to the pool and an informal, very attractive restaurant looking out across the rooftops to the mission. All of the guestrooms are named for flowers. The suites are spacious and afford a prettier view, but can be noisy due to activities on the square. The smaller, quieter standard rooms face the courtyard and have colorful (although not well-soundproofed) bathrooms with hand-painted Mexican tiles. Posada de Las Flores has two sister hotels on the Baja: one in La Paz and the other in Punta Chivato, both with the same name. All three hotels are lovely and offer superb management. *Directions:* Facing the square in the historic center of town.

❄ 🍴 ⚙ 💳 ☎ ⛾ 🍴 ≈ ⚐ ⚓ 🎿 ⚓

POSADA DE LAS FLORES
Owner: Giuseppe Marcelletti
1 Madero / Salvatierra
Loreto, Baja California Sur, 23880, Mexico
Tel: (613) 135-1162, Fax: (613) 135-1099
15 Rooms, Double: $150–$290*
*Tax: 12%
Restaurant closed for dinner Tue
Closed: Sep 9 to Oct 10, Credit cards: MC, VS
Region: Beach-Baja California

Casa Bella is an exceptional, moderately-priced, boutique hotel in the heart of Cabo San Lucas—within steps of the colorful marina, endless boutiques, cute restaurants, and lively bars. The hotel is literally quite amazing—walking down the street you would never dream such a jewel could exist right in the center of town. The attractive white-stuccoed exterior, which is accented by arched doorways and wrought iron balconies, stands out from the bland buildings surrounding it. However, it is not until you step inside that the true wonder of the property is revealed. Magically, you find a lovely old-world-style hacienda surrounding a spacious inner courtyard. The courtyard features a beautifully-kept garden, pretty fountains, potted plants, palm trees, roses, bougainvillea, a whimsical gazebo, and a splendid swimming pool. Large comfortable bedrooms face the courtyard and are attractively furnished—many with family antiques. The bathrooms are particularly nice. Most have huge walk in showers made of colorful Talavera tiles. For many years Casa Bella was the home of the Ungson family who converted the hacienda into a charming small hotel in 2004. The daughter, Barbara, now manages the hotel for her family. It was her great grand father, who began the dynasty. In the 1800s, he left China as a boy of 16 to escape the Opium Wars and ended up in Mexico. *Directions:* Located in center of town, facing the town square.

CASA BELLA
Owner: Barbara Ungson
Hidalgo 10
Los Cabos–Cabo San Lucas
Baja California Sur, 23410, Mexico
Tel: (624) 143-6400, Fax: (624) 143-6401
12 Rooms, Double: $145–$185*
*Service: 10%
Open: All year, Credit cards: all major
Region: Beach-Baja California

In 2002 Esperanza joined the glamorous scene of sumptuous resorts in Los Cabos. The hotel, located within a 17-acre property in Punta Ballena (Whale Point), is perched on a gentle bluff over looking dramatic rock formations that enclose two picturesque sandy coves. Thatched casitas that resemble a small Mexican village form the heart of the hotel. Here you find open air restaurants, bars, lounge areas, and a two-tiered swimming pool embraced by a series of terraces leading down to the beach. The hotel's 57 suites are in a series of three-story buildings. All the guestrooms are beautifully decorated with handcrafted furniture and offer only the finest amenities. A unique feature is that when the glass door facing the sea slides fully open, the bedroom becomes one with a spacious private terrace—many of which have their own plunge pool. Every detail has been planned to indulge the guests. There is even an option to choose which original art you wish to decorate your room while in residence. The restaurants at the hotel are excellent and meals are served outside by candle-light are exceptionally romantic. Although the hotel is super luxurious, it is in no way austere—there is a charming, friendly casual ambiance throughout. For those who want to be especially pampered, the hotel boasts a world class spa. *Directions:* From the Los Cabos Airport take the highway toward Cabo San Lucas. At the 7 Km marker follow signs to the hotel.

❄ 🛥 🖦 🍴@W Ⓨ P 🍴 🚫 🌿 ≈ 🖼 ⚓ ⛷ ⛵ 🎿 🏄

ESPERANZA
Manager: Severino Gomez
Carretera Hwy, Km 7
Los Cabos–Cabo San Lucas
Baja California Sur, 23140, Mexico
Tel: (624) 145-6400, Fax: (624) 145-6499
57 Rooms, Double: $475–$1875*
7 Suites: $1350–$7000*
*Service: 15%, Tax: 13%
Minimum Stay Required
Open: all year, Credit cards: none
Different World
Region: Beach-Baja California

Los Milagros is a small, reasonably-priced place to stay in the heart of Cabos San Lucas. Sandra Scandiber, your gracious hostess, moved here from New York many years ago and had the foresight to anticipate the need for a modest hotel in the quickly-expanding town. Although she has a Mexican business partner, Susan personally manages the hotel and welcomes guests. Los Milagros has the warmth and intimacy of a B&B. However, breakfast is not included, nor needed with so many restaurants near by. When you enter into the hotel's secluded inner courtyard, enclosed by white-washed walls, it is hard to realize you are so close to the non-stop action in town. A handsome stone fountain highlights the garden along with a pretty sitting area shaded by an umbrella. At the end of the courtyard there are steps leading up to a rooftop terrace. Most of the guestrooms are small, but their size is reflected by their reasonable rate. All the rooms are meticulously clean and pleasantly decorated. If you want more spacious accommodations and are willing to pay a bit more, the master suite on the top floor is especially nice. In addition to the hospitality, one of the nicest aspects of Los Milagros is that you have no need for a car since it only a few minute's walk from the hotel to restaurants, boutiques, bars, and the colorful marina. *Directions:* Located in town center, 4 blocks northwest of the Marina, on Matamoros (between Cardenas & Niños Heroes).

LOS MILAGROS
Owner: Sandra Scandiber
Matamoros 116
Los Cabos–Cabo San Lucas
Baja California Sur, 23400, Mexico
Tel: (624) 143-4566, Fax: (624) 143-5004
12 Rooms, Double: $80–$125*
*Breakfast not included
Open: all year, Credit cards: MC, VS
Region: Beach-Baja California

Stretched along the splendid coast between San José del Cabo and Cabo San Lucas there is a breathtaking choice of sumptuous hotels, most of which are very, very expensive. However, there is one remarkable exception: the Cabo Surf, which is not only well priced, but also has a fantastic location. This was previously a private home, which perhaps accounts for its privileged position on the bluff overlooking Acapulquito, a world-class surfing beach. The original house, an attractive white-stucco building, has a reception area, a small parlor, and a large open lounge extending out to a spacious terrace restaurant-bar partially covered with a thatched roofed. Here guests sip a cool drink or dine to the sound of the surf while enjoying an incredible view of the sea. In this main building you find two very spacious guestrooms with great balconies and lovely views. The other guestrooms are located in an adjacent, two-story wing. Those on the top floor have the choice views, my favorites being rooms 3 and 4. Tall palms dot the grounds and nestled on a terrace is an idyllic swimming pool with an infinity edge creating the illusion that the water blends into the sea. Lounge chairs dot the lawn around the pool where you can relax and watch some of the finest surfers in the world. NOTE: this hotel has been remodeled since our last visit. *Directions:* The hotel is signposted near km. 28 on the coastal highway between San José del Cabo and Cabo San Lucas.

CABO SURF HOTEL
Owner: Mauricio Balderrama
Carretera Transpeninsular, Km. 28
Playa Acapulquito, Baja California Sur
Los Cabos–San José del Cabo, 22676, Mexico
Tel: (624) 142-2666, Fax: (624) 142-2676
19 Rooms, Double: $310–$1320*
*Breakfast not included
*Service: $4 a day, Tax: 12%
Open: all year, Credit cards: all major
Different World
Region: Beach-Baja California

The Casa del Mar (located in a gated community surrounded by luxurious condominiums) is one of the deluxe hotels that dot the coast between Cabo San Lucas and San José del Cabo and, although it rivals the others in beauty, the cost of the rooms is substantially less. Looking like a lovely hacienda, the pastel ochre-colored building is accented by Moorish arched windows, wrought-iron lamps, a stone-framed doorway, and a circular fountain in front accented by colorful tile. This old-world effect is reinforced by the splendid Spanish-style interior garden courtyard, complete with a stunning stone fountain in the center, which is surrounded by an upper gallery supported by pillars. At the far end of the courtyard, a series of open arches artistically frames a gorgeous picture of tropical gardens, splendid swimming pool, swaying palms, and the deep-blue sea. The swimming pool is like a lake, dropping by a gentle waterfall from one level to the next. A path leads to a wide stretch of beach where there is a second swimming pool and beach club. The guestrooms exude great quality and are very attractively appointed with wrought-iron headboards, wicker furniture, colorful ceramic lamps, and exceptionally large bathrooms. Some of the rooms are located in two adjacent buildings, but my favorites are those in the main house, looking over the gardens to the sea. *Directions:* Located at Km 19.5. Watch the kilometer signs along the highway.

CASA DEL MAR
Manager: Oscar Ornelas
Carretera Hwy, Km 19.5
Los Cabos–San José del Cabo
Baja California Sur, 23400, Mexico
Tel: (624) 145-7700, Fax: (624) 144-0034
31 Rooms, Double: $290–$550*
*Breakfast not included: $18
*Service: 10%, Tax: 12%
Open: all year, Credit cards: all major
Region: Beach-Baja California

For a charming, intimate hotel in the heart of San José del Cabo, you can do no better than Casa Natalia, which boasts a restaurant so outstanding that guests from many of the super-exclusive resorts nearby come here to dine. The hotel is owned by Nathalie and Loic Tenoux, from Luxembourg and France respectively, who combine the colorful ambiance of Mexico with the quiet elegance of Europe in their small inn. From the street you see a simple, squarish, beige-colored building and it is not until you step inside that the appeal of the hotel is revealed. After passing through the foyer, you come to a small sitting area to the left with white slipcovered sofas splashed with color by brightly embroidered pillows and colorful ceramics set on simple wooden tables. A shuttle is available to the Beach Club, their beachfront restaurant, and pool. Guestrooms are in several buildings forming one side of a walled garden, which features an especially attractive half-circle swimming pool embraced by tall palm trees. All of the individually decorated bedrooms exude a charming Mexican ambiance with loomed fabrics, embroidered pillows, hand-crafted wooden furniture, hand-carved sconces or lamps, original artwork, and luxurious amenities. No detail has been overlooked to pamper guests. All of the guestrooms have balconies with hammocks and the two suites have Jacuzzi tubs. *Directions:* On main street in downtown San José del Cabo.

❄ ☕ 🔥 💳 🏨 ☎ @ W ‖ 🚭 ✿ ≈ 🖼 🏹 ⚓ 🏃 🐎 🚶

CASA NATALIA
Owners: Nathalie & Loic Tenoux
Boulevard Mijares no. 4
Los Cabos–San José del Cabo
Baja California Sur, 23400, Mexico
Tel: (624) 146-7100, Fax: (624) 142-5110
16 Rooms, Double: $250–$395*
2 Suites: $395–$465*
*Service: 15%, Tax: 13%
Open: all year, Credit cards: all major
Different World
Region: Beach-Baja California

El Encanto Inn is located in the heart of San José del Cabo, the most picturesque town in the Los Cabos area. Your hostess, Blanca Pedrin Torres, was born just a few doors away and is exceptionally familiar with the area—knowing the best places to go and what to see. In addition she lived in California for many years and speaks fluent English. The hotel had a simple beginning with a few modest rooms facing onto a narrow garden. In 2003 the hotel built a new addition across the street and evolved from its humble beginnings into a really classy small hotel. If you are looking for value, the original rooms are nice and still available, however for charm the new poolside suites (although more expensive) are what we would recommend. As you step into the entry hall, you immediately slip back in time with arched doorways, terra cotta floor, handsome antique tables, wrought iron chairs, an elaborate candelabrum, oil paintings, huge potted ferns, dramatic mirror and a massive chandelier. Just beyond the reception you come to a lush manicured garden. Here you find a palapa bar, a bougainvillea laced galleria, a pretty stone fountain and a lovely swimming pool. The new poolside suites, all of which are spacious and very attractively decorated, face the garden. An added bonus is an adorable little chapel—a perfect place for a wedding. *Directions:* Located in town center, between Oberegón & Comonfort, three blocks northwest of Central Plaza.

EL ENCANTO INN
Owner: Blanca Pedrin Torres
Calle Moreles 133
Los Cabos–San José del Cabo
Baja California Sur, 23400, Mexico
Tel: (624) 142-0388, Fax: (624) 142-4620
29 Rooms, Double: $89–$240*
*Breakfast not included
*Service: $7 a day
Open: All year, Credit cards: MC, VS
Region: Beach-Baja California

When Las Ventanas al Paraiso opened it doors to guests in the late 1990s, it joined the elite group of opulent hotels stretching across the tip of the Baja Peninsula. This deluxe inn is housed in a simple beige, flat-roofed building, which blends tastefully with the desert landscape, the starkness of which is relieved by majestic towering palm trees and a garden of cactus. A palapa-style thatched roof protects the lobby, which otherwise is open to the fresh sea breezes. The grounds are fabulous and highlighted by a stunning, lakelike swimming pool dropping gently from one terrace to the next in a series of waterfalls. At the bottom level there is an open-air grill by the swimming pool for casual dining. For dining in style, there is an elegant, formal dining room nearby. From the swimming pools and restaurants there is a splendid view of the deep-blue sea as the waves roll in to the creamy-sand beach. The richly appointed, lavishly decorated guestrooms, with their softly curved adobe walls, are a sensual delight. The suites overlooking the sea are spectacular, with marble bathrooms, the finest linens, sumptuous furniture, handsome fabrics, a fireplace tucked in the corner, a telescope for watching the whales go by, a little plunge pool, and a balcony that is so spacious and tastefully appointed that it seems like an outdoor living room. *Directions:* Located on the parkway between San José del Cabo and Cabo San Lucas, at Km 19.5.

LAS VENTANAS AL PARAISO
Manager: Christian Tavelli
Carretera Hwy, Km. 19.5
Los Cabos–San José del Cabo, Baja
California Sur, 23400, Mexico
Tel: (624) 144-2800, Fax: (624) 144-2801
61 Rooms, Double: $725–$5900*
*Breakfast not included
*Service: 15%, Tax: 12%
Open: all year, Credit cards: all major
Different World
Region: Beach-Baja California

When wealthy sports fishermen discovered Cabo, the One & Only Palmilla was the first luxury hotel built, and remains as the grand dame of them all, exuding a quiet, old-world elegance. After an extraordinary renovation, the Palmilla reopened with 57 new rooms, including two superb beachfront villas, a second swimming pool geared for families, a swimming beach, and a gorgeous spa. The hotel is currently going through more renovations. Surrounded by manicured grounds, the low-rise building has a Spanish feel with its white façade, red-tiled roof, watchtower, arches, and dramatic stone fountain at the entrance. The hotel sits on a gentle rise overlooking the sea, a setting enhanced by splendid gardens. Comfortable lounge chairs are strategically positioned on the lush green lawn dotted by tall, swaying palms where you can relax in utter tranquility overlooking the surging sea. A path winds down to the beach, which has secluded nooks for sunbathing cleverly tucked in amongst the boulders. The luxurious guestrooms offer the ultimate in good taste. The suites with large terraces overlooking the coast are especially outstanding. Golfers will enjoy the Jack Nicklaus golf course next door. *Directions:* The hotel is signposed near km. 7.5 on the coastal highway between San José del Cabo and Cabo San Lucas.

❄ ✀ 💳 ☎ 🏋 @ 🍸 P 🍴 ✿ ≈ 🏄 ⛵ ⚓ 🏃 👥 🏇 🚤

ONE & ONLY PALMILLA
Manager: Edward T. Steiner
Carretera Hwy, Km. 7.5
Los Cabos–San José del Cabo
Baja California Sur, 23400, Mexico
Tel: (624) 144-5000, Fax: (624) 144-5100
172 Rooms, Double: $650–$3100*
*Breakfast not included
*Service: 15%, Tax: 12%
Open: all year, Credit cards: all major
Different World
Region: Beach-Baja California

For years the Costa Maya, a pristine stretch of beach and jungle, was little known except for ardent divers and snorkelers seeking the cheapest possible accommodations. Basic hotels are still the norm; but, happily, a few new places are popping up for those who want to enjoy this unspoiled natural paradise now in total comfort. One of the best is the Balamku, built by Carol and Alan Knight, who moved to Mexico from Canada, discovered the Costa Maya, and built a small hotel. Reception is in the main house where guests enjoy breakfast, relax, or browse through the rich collection of books about the area. The tastefully furnished guestrooms featuring Mayan art are right on the white sand beach in clusters of whimsical, white, round cottages, each topped with a thatched roof. The architecture is appealing and ecologically designed for minimal impact on the environment. In most of Costa Maya there is no electricity. However, there is an abundance of power here due to a large solar system and the clever use of a quiet windmill. In front of the hotel is a shallow beach where sea grass, an important part of the ecosystem of the reef, is cleaned each day. Just offshore is the second largest coral reef in the world. Free kayaks are available for guests to paddle out to explore this wonderland. Breakfast is the only meal served, but this is no problem as Mahahual, with its restaurants and shops, is closeby. *Directions:* Located about 6 km south of Mahahual.

■ ⚲ @ W P ⚑ ⊥ 👥 🐎 🦆

BALAMKU
Owners: Carol Tumber & Alan Knight
Mahahual–Costa Maya
Quintana Roo, 77940, Mexico
Tel: (983) 839 5332
9 Rooms, Double: $80–$85*
*Includes breakfast & taxes
Open: all year, Credit cards: none
Region: Yucatán Peninsula-Costa Maya

Upon arriving at the Mayan Beach Garden, Marcia and Kim Bales warmly welcome you like members of the family. Lasting friendships are often formed, departing guests giving hugs and promises to soon return. This tiny inn, snuggled on a sandy beach between the sea and jungle, is located in Costa Maya, a remote, newly developing coastal area south of Riviera Maya. Kim (who before retirement built huge apartment complexes) used his skills to build this delightful, tiny hotel. Marcia is an artist, as well as a software designer, so her talents added greatly to the style and design. Not a deluxe hotel, but instead a simple place offering great comfort, including super mattresses and wonderful home-cooked meals. The spacious, nicely decorated, solar-powered guestrooms are divided into two buildings that stagger back from the sea, cleverly designed so that each cabaña has its own private terrace shaded by a a large deck inspired by Mayan architecture. There are also three beach view rooms with private decks and elevated beds that allow you to view the sea from bed. You are literally on the beach—just steps from the Caribbean. Beyond the classically sandy beach the turtle grass grows in its natural setting—the environment is the highest priority. The hotel is close to the Sian Ka'an Biosphere and there is an excellent guide who can help you discover this amazing nature preserve. You can explore the world-class coral gardens. Directions: Located about 6 km south of Mahahual.

❋ ☛ ⚞ ☕ ⚟ CREDIT 🐾 @ W ☉ P ⚟ 🚭 ⚞ ⚟ ⚓ 🏃 🐎 ⚟

MAYAN BEACH GARDEN
Owners: Marcia & Kim Bales
21.5 km. N Rio Indio - Uvero Carretera
Mahahual–Costa Maya
Quintana Roo, 77940, Mexico
Tel: 983-132-2603 (Mexico), Cell: 206-905-9665 (USA)
3 Rooms, Double: $72–$147*
3 Suites: $120–$165*
*Tax: 12%
Minimum Stay Required: In high season
Open: all year, Credit cards: all major
Region: Yucatán Peninsula-Costa Maya

      Hotel Descriptions

Dolphin Cove Inn is a gem. A real discovery if you are looking for a well-priced, charmingly decorated place to stay with breathtaking views that can't be surpassed anywhere in Mexico, not at any price. Enhanced by impeccably groomed gardens and brilliant displays of bougainvillea, the bedrooms are nestled in clusters of white buildings hugging a steep hillside next to the world-class Las Hadas Resort. Dolphin Cove Inn is a select group of 50 suites (from studios to three bedrooms), which are run like an intimate hotel within a large complex called PlayaSol Manzanillo. Every room has either a balcony or terrace capturing a romantic panorama of the deep-blue bay backdropped by green volcanic hills. Every suite has a well-equipped kitchenette, a bathroom decorated with hand-painted Talavera tiles, colorful hand-loomed fabrics, and enchanting headboards carved by the Tarascan Indians. If you are economizing, the studios are fabulous, but the one-bedroom suites with huge terraces are exceptionally appealing and offer outstanding value. A maze of staircases laces the property, leading to the swimming pool and, just below, a beach. The main attraction at Dolphin Cove is just relaxing: reading a novel, sleeping late, taking a swim, a quiet stroll on the beach. However, golf and tennis are readily available. Note: Dolphin Cove's many steps make it unsuitable for those with a walking problem. *Directions:* Adjacent to Las Hadas hotel.

❄ 🍽 🏋 💳 🍴 @ W ♈ 🍴 🚭 ⚓ 🏃 📷 ⛳ ⚓ 🏃 🏄

DOLPHIN COVE INN   ***Cover painting***
Manager: Isiss Alvarez
Av. Vista Hermosa SN
Manzanillo, Colima, 28860, Mexico
Tel: (314) 344-1515, Fax: (314) 334-1689
50 Rooms, Double: $110–$210*
*Tax: 17%
Open: all year, Credit cards: MC, VS
Different World
Region: Beach–Pacific Coast

When we first visited and fell in love with Las Hadas many years ago, it was a small hotel, comprised of just a cluster of low cottages snuggled around a pristine, palm-ringed beach. Over the years the hotel has grown and can no longer be classified as the small, intimate type of property we normally feature. Nevertheless, it holds a secure niche in our hearts, and still has the same romantic features that captivated us so long ago. The architecture is pure fantasy, with whitewashed walls, whimsical turrets, jaunty spires, and ornate domes, reflecting the romantic concept of a Moorish village. Cobblestone pathways shaded by palm trees meander through the property where fountains, statues, fragrant flowers, and walls draped with bougainvilleas make every stroll a delight to the senses. The accommodations reflect a subdued elegance with shades of white predominating, punctuated by accents of color. The enormous, free-form swimming pool with its swinging bridge set new standards of opulence when the hotel first opened. The hotel has a marina, ten tennis courts, and an 18-hole, Pete Dye championship golf course. But, in our appraisal, one of the most outstanding features of Las Hadas is its beach—one of the finest, gentlest beaches I have ever seen for children—which fringes a private cove where the swimming is sublime. *Directions:* Coming south from Manzanillo airport, turn right at the Peninsula de Santiago and follow signs to the hotel.

LAS HADAS
Manager: Carlos Arellano
Av. Los Ricos s/n
Manzanillo, Colima, 28200, Mexico
Tel: (314) 331-0101, Fax: (314) 331-0121
233 Rooms, Double: $190–$1015*
*Breakfast not included
*Tax: 17%
Open: all year, Credit cards: all major
Region: Beach–Pacific Coast

Meson Doña Paz, a very special hideaway north of Manzanillo, was the home of the developer of the community of Isla Navidad, which features the beautiful Grand Bay Hotel. In this gated, deluxe complex is a superb 27-hole golf course, a marina, a number of homes, and condominiums. Meson Doña Paz is secreted down a small road that passes by the Grand Bay Hotel and continues on to its own secluded cove, complete with its own beach, swimming pool, and dock. The structure is so impressive that it is hard to believe this was once a private home. You enter into a spectacular three-story house with reception area, lounge, meeting rooms, and restaurant, all fabulously decorated. This is flanked by two adjoining buildings with 11 guestrooms and two suites. The gracious staff strives to make you feel at home, except here you have your own chef and waiters to take care of you. Although there is a menu, the chef is happy to cook whatever you desire, and usually the daily menu consists of his suggestions or perhaps suggestions you made the day before. You also have your choice of locations for dining: on the beach, on the jetty, near the pool, or on the terrace. Tennis courts are on site with golf, fishing, and boating available nearby. You have all the benefits of a large property, but the charm and service of an intimate small hotel. *Directions:* From the Manzanillo airport turn left onto the highway. Go north to the 53.5 kilometer marker and follow signs the Grand Bay Hotel.

MESON DOÑA PAZ
Manager: Jorge Garibay
Rinconada del Capitan s/n, Costa Alegre
Manzanillo–Isla Navidad, Colima, 28830, Mexico
Tel: (314) 337-9000, Fax: (314) 337-9018
13 Rooms, Double: $250–$600*
*Breakfast not included: $12
*Tax: 17%
Open: all year, Credit cards: all major
Region: Beach–Pacific Coast

The Balboa Club used to be a private club, an exclusive place that the wealthy called home when they flew into Mazatlán on their private planes to fish or hunt or relax by the sea. Not that it was ever opulent. Quite the contrary: it always had an understated, casual air—just a simple, two-story lodge built around an inner garden courtyard with a swimming pool, and an open air dining room and lounge looking out to the sea. The Balboa Club is being renovated with new bathrooms, room decor and updated exteriors. The staff is very friendly, the food excellent, and the air-conditioned guestrooms are comfortable with tiled floors, large marble bathrooms, and balconies or terraces. Be sure to ask for an ocean view. There is a faded, dated, nostalgic charm to the property and, if you like small, low-rise hotels, this one is a winner. It also boasts a prime location facing one of Mazatlán's loveliest stretches of beach where the gentle surf is usually safe for swimming. With beachfront property so precious and high-rise hotels in every direction, it is quite amazing that the Balboa Club still exists. Plans are underway to turn the property into a timeshare and they are slowly updating the hotel. We highly recommend it for those looking for an intimate, old-fashioned, small hotel with low room rates. When making reservations, be sure to specify the Balboa Club and not the Balboa Towers next door. *Directions:* Located in Zona Dorada, about midway on Las Gaviotas Beach.

❄ 🏊 🖭 ☎ Ⓨ P ‖ ≈ ⚓ 🛶

BALBOA CLUB
Manager: Jose Luis Olguin
Avenida Camaron Sabalo
s/n Zona Dorado
Mazatlán, Sinaloa, 82110, Mexico
Tel: (669) 913-0193, Fax: (669) 914-4389
40 Rooms, Double: $95–$150*
*Breakfast not included
*Tax: 17%
Open: all year, Credit cards: all major
Region: Beach–Pacific Coast

For many years the once-elegant historic center of Mazatlán was neglected and gradually became rundown. Happily, this is rapidly changing. Today you see historic buildings renovated, houses repainted, the Cathedral freshened, cafes opening, art galleries popping up, and most dramatic of all, the remarkably lovely Teatro Ángela Peralta restored to its original grandeur. With the rejuvenation of the city center, hotels and bed & breakfasts are also appearing to accommodate travelers who want to experience a bit of "old Mexico" instead of staying at huge resorts. One of the best of these is the Casa de Leyendas B&B, which opened in 2005 after a top to bottom restoration of the home of one of Mazatlán's most honored citizens, Dr. Hector Gonzales Guevara. The B&B has the best of all worlds—it is tucked in the historic section, yet within easy walking distance to the beach. However, it is your American hosts, Sharon & Glenn Sorrie, who make a stay the Casa de Leyendas special. Their motto is "Your comfort is our number one priority" and they do indeed make that happen. The amenities are amazing for such moderately-priced rooms: a tiled swimming pool in the garden courtyard, free telephone calls to the United States, complimentary wireless internet, an honor bar where guests just leave a note for drinks, free laundry service, cooking classes, and Spanish classes taught three times a week. *Directions:* Ask for directions when making your reservation.

CASA DE LEYENDAS B&B
Owners: Sharon & Glenn Sorrie
Venustiano Carranza #4
Centro Histórico
Mazatlán, Sinaloa, 82000, Mexico
Tel: (669) 981-6180 or (602) 445-6192 (USA)
Fax: 602-412-3338, Toll Free: 866-391-2301
6 Rooms, Double: $89–$125
Open: all year, Credit cards: MC, VS
Region: Beach–Pacific Coast

Only 20 minutes away from Mazatlán the charming Hacienda Las Moras is gracefully tucked into the tranquil foothills of the Sierra Madre mountains on an immense, 2,500-acre ranch. Michael Ruiz, a designer and builder, bought the abandoned 19th-century plantation and restored everything with taste, preserving all the architectural heritage of the original home. The main hacienda has a wide veranda stretching across the front and a cozy, rustic ambiance inside, with a low, beamed ceiling, thick stuccoed walls, terra-cotta floors, accents of antique furnishings, beautiful old mirrors, sofas and chairs with colorful hand-woven fabrics, and oil paintings adorning the walls. On a terrace behind the hacienda is a large, beautiful swimming pool with lounge chairs strategically set to capture unobstructed views of the rolling hills. The charming open-air restaurant stretches along the end of the pool. All of the 11 spacious guestrooms are exceptionally appealing and feature the finest of Mexican artisanship, with hand-crafted wood furniture, beautiful loomed fabrics, rich terra-cotta floors, and large bathrooms with Talavera tiles. Tennis courts and bikes are available and if you want to explore the countryside, the ranch has a stable of horses. Rates include all meals and activities. *Directions:* From Mazatlán, take Hwy 15 libre toward Culicán. After 9 km, turn right toward La Noira. Go about 9 km and turn left at the sign to the hacienda.

HACIENDA LAS MORAS
Owner: Michael Ruiz
Cocoteros no. 1, Rincon de las Palmas
Mazatlán, Sinaloa, 82110, Mexico
Tel & Fax: (669) 914-1346
11 Rooms, Double: $280*
*Service: 15%, Tax: 17%
*Includes 3 meals
Open: all year, Credit cards: all major
Region: Beach–Pacific Coast

Pueblo Bonito-Emerald Bay is a 258-unit timeshare property, which we don't normally feature in our guides, however it is operated as a hotel, with the guestrooms rented out in the owners' absence. It is a wonderful choice for those looking for a stunning, deluxe hotel with a beautifully trained, welcoming staff. The attractively decorated guestrooms are spread out on 20 acres of manicured gardens in a stand of 150-year-old mangrove trees. Stretching in front is a wide sandy beach that is great for walking, but not good for swimming. All the rooms have a balcony or terrace, usually with a view of the ocean. The architecture of the pretty, soft-yellow buildings seems to be a modern interpretation of an old Mexican hacienda, a style enhanced by tall pillars and wicker furniture set on wide verandas. The foyer is built as a rotunda with light streaming through a skylight to illuminate a large fountain. From the lobby, the property steps gently down to the sea with waterfalls, ponds, manicured gardens, and outstanding swimming pools beautifying the landscape. The dining room is exceptionally lovely, with tall windows opening to the terrace and walls and furniture in soft shades of white, accented by potted plants. *Directions:* Go north from Mazatlán on the coast road—you see a sign to the hotel about five minutes after the road loops around the yacht harbor.

❄ ✈ 💳 ☎ 🛗 🏋 🍸 P 🍴 ≈ 🎣 ⛵ ⚓ 🏊 🏇 🚣

PUEBLO BONITO-EMERALD BAY
Manager: Roberto Tussi
Av. Ernesto Coppel Campana 201
Zona Cerritos
Mazatlán, Sinaloa, 82110, Mexico
Tel: (669) 989-0525, Fax: (669) 988-0718
258 Rooms, Double: $150–$260*
*Breakfast not included
*Tax: 17%
Open: all year, Credit cards: all major
Region: Beach–Pacific Coast

The Villas at Estrella del Mar fills a much-needed niche in Mazatlán—a city best known for its huge high-rise hotels and vast number of time-share complexes. We were thrilled to discover an outstanding small beachfront hotel—a perfect choice for those who crave the tranquility of pristine beaches, blissful seclusion, and top notch accommodations. The hotel is part of an exceptionally well-planned, 816–acre, gated community called Estrella del Mar, located south of Mazatlán that features private homes, townhouses, condominiums and a Robert Trent Jones Jr. 18-hole championship golf course. When the developers bought the land, it included a small hotel that was originally the private home of Art Linkletter, the charming host of two of America's longest-running TV shows. The hotel sits right on the beach. And, what a beach it is! A wide expanse of creamy beige sand that stretches for over three miles—it seems you can walk forever in both directions. The origional hotel had 21 rooms and more rooms, a restaurant, and a top notch spa are being added. The old and new sections of the hotel are seamlessly blended together, maintaining the original hotel's quiet charm with Mexican-style furnishings and quality throughout. As an extra bonus, all are welcome to use Estrella del Mar's golf course, call for tee times. A shuttle service is available to Mazatlán. *Directions:* 10 minute drive from the airport. Ask hotel for directions.

VILLAS AT ESTRELLA DEL MAR
Manager: Pat Butler
Camino Isla de la Piedra Km. 10
Mazatlán, Sinaloa, 82110, Mexico
Tel: (669) 982-3390, Toll Free: (800) 967-1889 (USA)
67 Rooms, Double: $149–$219*
*Breakfast not included
*Tax: 18%
Open: all year, Credit cards: all major
Region: Beach–Pacific Coast

The most attractive section of Mérida is the very heart of the old city, where the cathedral looms over the picturesque central square. Just steps away, you find the Caribe Hotel, which enjoys the prime hotel location in town. To add to its appeal, the hotel faces onto a small plaza, the Parque Hidalgo, dotted by shade trees. The building is attractive with tall windows opening onto wrought-iron balconies that reflect its Spanish heritage. Within, the old-world appeal continues with stone arches accentuating handsome black-and-white marble floors. In the traditional Colonial style, the hotel wraps around a central courtyard where a series of arches supports a gallery above. Another of the hotel's pluses is its restaurant, El Rincon, which features regional specialties. When the days are warm, guests also enjoy a light meal or cool drink outside on the plaza. The decor in the guestrooms is rather bland, but everything is fresh and tidy. For a moderately priced hotel in such a good location, it is a good value. Another bonus of the Caribe is that it has a small swimming pool tucked on its rooftop terrace, a pleasant place to take a dip and relax after a day of sightseeing. There is a wall surrounding the terrace with arched windows through which you can view the cathedral and square. *Directions:* Located less than a block from the main square. The streets are all numbered—odd numbered streets in one direction, even-numbered in the other.

HOTEL CARIBE
Manager: Jorge Torre Loria
Calle 59 no. 500 (corner Calle 60)
Mérida, Yucatan, 97000, Mexico
Tel: (999) 924-9022, Fax: (999) 924-8733
53 Rooms, Double: $49–$84*
*Breakfast not included: $5
Open: all year, Credit cards: all major
Different World
Region: Yucatán Peninsula-Archaeological Area

Located just a couple of blocks off the main square, the Casa del Balam offers a nostalgic charm. This small hotel is so closely interwoven with the beginning of tourism in the Yucatán that it could not help winning a place in our hearts. Casa del Balam was built in the early 1900s as the private home of the Barbarchano family, pioneers of tourism. It all began when Señor Barbarchano, as a young man, picked up a number of guests from a ship and took them to see some Mayan ruins, originating the idea of sharing the Yucatán's wonders with non-archaeologists. Now, three generations later, the Barbarchano family operates many of the region's buses and tour companies and owns the majority of the hotels in prime locations, including this one in the heart of Mérida. There is nothing fancy or flashy about the Casa del Balam—this is just a good, old-fashioned hotel that has excellent management and exudes the faded glamour of bygone days. The best feature is the interior courtyard, highlighted by a stone fountain and surrounded by greenery and tables and chairs. Although there is a restaurant, you can be served in the courtyard, which is more romantic. All of the rooms are comfortable so there's no need to splurge on a suite. I particularly liked 203 and 204, large rooms with wrought-iron headboards. *Directions:* Just two blocks off the main square. The streets are all numbered—odd-numbered streets in one direction, even-numbered in the other.

❄ 🏊 💳 ☎ 🚻 @ W Ⓨ P 🍴 🚭 🏊 🏞 🐾 ♿ ⚓ 🏌

HOTEL CASA DEL BALAM
Owner: Doña Carmen Barbachano
Calle 60 no. 488 (corner of Calle 60 & Calle 57)
Mérida, Yucatan, 97000, Mexico
Tel: (999) 924-2150, Fax: (999) 924-5011
*42 Rooms, Double: $85–$117**
*9 Suites: $100–$160**
**Breakfast not included: $9*
**Service: 15%, Tax: 17%*
Open: all year, Credit cards: AX, MC, VS
Different World
Region: Yucatán Peninsula-Archaeological Area

One of the pleasures of traveling on the Yucatán Peninsula is the opportunity to stay in one of the beautifully restored haciendas dotted throughout the area. A gem in this collection is the superbly restored, award-winning Hacienda Xcanatún. Built in the mid-18th century, the hacienda was once used to produce sisal, known as "green gold" for the fortunes it made local families. When the sisal market collapsed, the property was abandoned for many years until the present owners purchased it and began an arduous five-year restoration project. The result resembles a work of art, as the owners used only the region's best master craftsmen and materials. The spacious guestrooms are richly decorated, many with antiques, and have incredible bathrooms featuring hydrotherapy Jacuzzi bathtubs complete with a waterfall. Each room is unique; some hacienda-style with wide, covered terraces outside, while others enjoy romantic private gardens with outdoor Jacuzzis. The grounds include acres of lush tropical gardens, a large fishpond, two swimming pools and a full service spa. The hotel's very popular restaurant, the Casa de Piedra, offers gourmet cuisine that fuses French techniques with regional Caribbean ingredients. Mérida has much to offer culturally, yet is an oasis for pure relaxation. This hacienda is also a great starting point for exploring the incredible Mayan sites. *Directions:* About 12 km north of Mérida on the highway to Puerto Progreso.

HACIENDA XCANATÚN
Owners: Christina Baker & Jorge Ruz Buenfil
Calle 20 S/N, Comisaria Xcanatún
Mérida, Yucatan, 97302, Mexico
Tel: (999) 941-0213, Fax: (999) 941-0319
5 Rooms, Double: $245–$270*
13 Suites: $270–$340*
*Service: 5%, Tax: 17%
Open: all year, Credit cards: all major
Different World
Region: Yucatán Peninsula-Archaeological Area

For visitors to the rich archaeological sites of the Yucatán, the trip frequently begins in Mérida, a major airline hub. From its outskirts, Mérida first appears to be a rather scruffy, sprawling, unappealing city, but don't let this put you off. At its core, Mérida's colonial heritage shines through. Like most of the cities founded by the Spaniards, there is a very grand cathedral in the center facing a lovely, tree-shaded park (zócalo) surrounded by handsome 17th-century buildings. Two blocks from the park sits the La Mision de Fray Diego, an intimate, appealingly appointed, charming inn that we just love. Although its street isn't one of the prettiest in Mérida, just a few minutes' walk takes you to the center of all the activity. You enter into the hotel's delightful courtyard, which is as pretty as can be with a fountain in the middle, an exuberant display of flowers and greenery, and a statue of Fray Diego, the Catholic brother for whom the hotel is named. The reception area and restaurant face this patio. A few more steps bring you to a second patio, this one highlighted by a lovely swimming pool surrounded by a garden. The guestrooms wrap around this courtyard in a three-storied, colonnaded wing enhanced by a wrought-iron balcony. All of the fresh-looking, uncluttered guestrooms are equally pleasing and provide modern amenities. *Directions:* Two blocks from the zócalo on Calle 61, #524, between Calle 64 and Calle 66 in Downtown.

※ ⚞ ▭ ☎ ⌶ P ⅋ ≈

LA MISION DE FRAY DIEGO
Owner: Jorge Torre
Calle 61 no. 524
Mérida, Yucatan, 97000, Mexico
Tel: (999) 924-1111, Fax: (999) 923-7397
26 Rooms, Double: $90–$150*
*Breakfast not included: $6
*Tax: 17%
Open: all year, Credit cards: all major
Different World
Region: Yucatán Peninsula-Archaeological Area

For those who want to the romance of staying in a hacienda, yet prefer the city over the countryside, you are in luck. In 2005, a stunning hotel opened in Mérida near the town center. This 19th-century nobleman's home is a handsome, one-story, hacienda painted deep Mayan red highlighted by crisp white detailing. Step inside and be instantly whisked back to another era with beautiful tile floors, an abundance of antiques, wood-beamed ceilings, thick adobe walls, and stone arches. It is not until you continue on to the inner courtyards with lush, tropical foliage and beautiful gardens that the timeless grace of the hacienda is revealed. Five-meter high limestone walls wrap around the entire property, secreting within a hidden oasis. Stone fountains, sun-drenched courtyards, manicured gardens, lily ponds, palm trees, cool breezeways, and a lovely two-story arcaded gallery create a wonderland. Starring in the center of the garden is a dazzling swimming pool. The beauty here is that its glamour is not skin-deep. In the guestrooms colonial ambiance prevails but amenities are the best of the today's world: handmade antique-style beds with ultra-comfortable mattresses, the finest of imported linens, high-speed internet access, satellite TV, direct dial telephones, and mini-bars. There is no restaurant; but for guests who want to dine in, meals can be arranged. *Directions:* Ten blocks from the main square on Calle 59, #615a, between Calle 80 and Calle 82.

THE VILLA @ MÉRIDA
Manager: Stuart Oli
Calle 59, # 615a, (between calle 80 & 82)
Mérida, Yucatan, 97000, Mexico
Tel: (999) 928-8466, Fax: (999) 928-8467
7 Rooms, Double: $265–$295
Open: all year, Credit cards: all major
Different World
Region: Yucatán Peninsula-Archaeological Area

Casa Vieja is perfectly situated on a quiet side street in the popular district of Polanco, within walking distance to many sites of interest. Avenida Masyrik (often known as the Rodeo Drive of Mexico) is just a block away, plus Chapultepec Park and Avenida Reforma, both well worth visiting, are within walking distance, while the historical central part of the city is an easy taxi ride away. Casa Vieja, an ochre-colored, two-story mansion, draped with ivy and enhanced by blue trim, oozes Mexican charm. It doesn't look like a hotel at all, but rather like a very old, enchanting private hacienda. Inside, brilliantly-colored stucco walls, cheerful bouquets of flowers, beautiful ceramic vases, tinkling fountains, masterful craftsmanship, original Mexican paintings, sculptures, Mexican folk craft, beamed ceilings and hand-crafted quarrystone floors harmonize to create a magical old-world mood. Each sumptuously decorated, luxurious suite is unique and complete with every amenity imaginable, including a kitchenette. Rooms are very spacious, especially the two-bedroom Lolita Suite, named after the famous owner of the hotel. The top floor overlooks the street and features an open terrace restaurant/bar with excellent cuisine, as well as a meeting/entertainment room off to one side. *Directions:* Centrally located a block from Av. Masyrik in Polanco. Turn on Eugenio Sur and the hotel is less than one block before the Chapultepec Park.

❄ 🏂 CREDIT ☎ ⛾ 🍴

CASA VIEJA
Manager: Martin Morales
Eugenio Sue 45, Colonia Polanco
Mexico City, D.F., 29230, Mexico
Tel: (55) 5282-0067, Fax: (55) 5281-3780
10 Rooms, Double: $300–$950*
*Breakfast not included
*Tax: 17%
Open: all year, Credit cards: all major
Region: Central–Colonial City

La Casona is a treasure—a charming, beautifully managed small hotel nestled in a lovely residential area. Staying here, you would never believe you were in the world's second-largest city: instead, you feel as snug as can be, pampered with such loving attention that you feel like a guest in a private home. Indeed, facing a quiet street with a tree-lined parkway in the middle, the pretty, two-story, pink hotel looks like a charming private residence. Inside, the ambiance continues, with an intimate lounge with lovely slip-covered sofas and chairs, a grand piano in the corner, soft lighting, bouquets of fresh flowers, and nicely framed paintings decorating the walls. The bedrooms too look like those in a private home. Each is individually decorated, but all exude the understated elegance reminiscent of a bedroom in an English country estate. Rooms are not large but adequate in size and have all the most modern conveniences. La Casona has a musical theme throughout and the bedrooms each display a musical instrument. The hotel has a cute restaurant with checked tablecloths, humorous paintings of dogs in fancy dress, and an exterior courtyard with fountain for outdoor dining in balmy weather. La Casona is not in the center of town, but taxis quickly whisk you to wherever you want to go, then after all your sightseeing you have the pleasure of returning to your oasis of comfort. *Directions:* Four blocks south of the Reforma, one of Mexico City's main boulevards.

❄ ☕ ⚕ 💳 ☎ 🍸 @ W P 🍴

LA CASONA
Manager: Ines Macedo
Durango No. 280 at Cozumel, Colonial Roma
Mexico City, D.F., 06700, Mexico
Tel: (55) 5286-3001, Fax: (55) 5211-0871
29 Rooms, Double: $140–$200*
*Tax: 17%
Open: all year, Credit cards: all major
Different World
Region: Central–Colonial City

If you want to sample of bit of Mexico's rich historic past, the Hotel de Cortés is your best bet. In fact, it is the only choice for accommodations in a building that dates back to the 17th century. Now part of the World Hotels chain, this hotel is well located just across from the Alameda Park and only steps from the Palace of Fine Arts, the hotel is a richly adorned, baroque stone building constructed in the early part of the 17th century as a hospice for the Order of the Augustinians. From the beginning, the monastery welcomed weary friars who used this as a resting place on their journeys. Over the handsome stone entry is a charming carving of Santo Tomás de Villanueva, patron of the needy, shown bestowing his gentle blessing on all who enter. Inside, the most inviting feature of the Hotel de Cortés becomes immediately evident: the building is constructed around an exceptionally cheerful interior courtyard adorned by a central fountain, flowers, trees, and potted plants. There is an indoor restaurant but on sunny days the sheltered patio is the heart of the hotel where guests dine at colorfully set tables. Most of the bedrooms overlook the courtyard and are appropriately simple in their decor. This is not a deluxe hotel: the guestrooms are plain but very pleasant and the bathrooms are a bit dated—but spotlessly clean. *Directions:* Located on the corner of Hidalgo Avenue and Reforma Boulevard, in front of Alameda Park.

HOTEL DE CORTÉS
Manager: Sebastian Rincon Gallardo
Av. Hidalgo 85, Colonia Guerrero
Mexico City, D.F., 06300, Mexico
Tel: (55) 5518-2181, Fax: (55) 5512-1863
29 Rooms, Double: $120–$220*
*Breakfast not included
*Tax: 17%
Open: all year, Credit cards: all major
Region: Central–Colonial City

We normally feature small hotels, especially those secreted off the beaten path. The Hilton Aeropuerto hotel, with 129 rooms and smack in the middle of Mexico City's airport, certainly doesn't fit our usual criteria. However, by any standards this hotel is a real winner; especially if you are overnighting in Mexico City and have an early-morning flight. Few cities can boast of a hotel truly inside an airport, which is exactly where you find this Hilton. When the elevator doors open, you enter into a grand lobby, charming in its simplicity. No clutter here—just a large open room with green-marble floor, a sitting area accented by modern sofas and chairs, a bar tucked into one corner, and, along one side, a restaurant, discreetly cordoned off by potted palms. The most special feature of the decor is a wall of glass overlooking the airport runways. This foyer has an air of tasteful simplicity, with one dramatic accent of a huge bouquet of colorful fresh flowers on a table in the center of the room. Wide hallways carpeted in a deep-green color, which complements the green marble in the foyer, lead to the beautifully equipped guestrooms. Be sure to request one overlooking the runways for the fun of watching the endless parade of planes taking off and landing just below your window. *Directions:* Go to the "F" sign in the airport lobby and take the escalator up one floor, then the elevator marked to the hotel.

HILTON AEROPUERTO
Manager: Omar Santillanes
Benito Juárez International Airport
Mexico City, Distrito Federal, 15620, Mexico
Tel: (55) 5133-0505, Fax: (55) 5133-0500
129 Rooms, Double: $160*
*Breakfast not included
*Tax: 17%
Open: all year, Credit cards: all major
Region: Central–Colonial City

Mexico City abounds with excellent hotels in all price categories, but many of them lack personality. Not so the Imperial Hotel, which makes a statement from first glance. The hotel is wedged between two intersecting streets that form a pie-shaped piece of land with the Imperial proudly dominating the scene—a crisp-white, five-story building with a jaunty tower at the corner. It is hard to believe that in 1904, when the hotel was first opened by President Porfirio Díaz, this was the tallest building in the city. It is still impressive with a stately, old-fashioned elegance displayed in its series of tall arched windows shaded by formal dark-green awnings and matching dark-green, wrought-iron railings that wrap around the hotel. Inside, the traditional, old-world ambiance continues. The foyer is extremely dramatic with a huge crystal chandelier suspended from a soaring ceiling and a white marble floor with a staircase sweeping up to a balcony that overlooks the entrance. Galleries enwrap each floor, like a series of wedding cakes, with a huge glass skylight at the top. The guestrooms are all similar in decor with modern furnishings. The prize rooms are those tucked into the rounded front corner of the hotel. The Imperial Hotel is in a central location, well situated for sightseeing. If you like walking, you can see many of the sights on foot. *Directions:* Located on one of Mexico City's finest avenues, the Paseo de la Reforma.

IMPERIAL HOTEL
Manager: Alberto Valle Sanchez
Paseo de la Reforma 64
Mexico City, D.F., 06600, Mexico
Tel: (55) 5705-4911, Fax: (55) 5703-3122
65 Rooms, Double: $70–$120*
*Breakfast not included: $9
*Tax: 17%
Open: all year, Credit cards: all major
Different World
Region: Central–Colonial City

For location, the Hotel Majestic just can't be beat—not at any price. It overlooks Mexico City's colorful zócolo (main square), national palace, and spectacular cathedral. However, it is not just location that makes the Majestic such a winner: it brims with character. From the moment you walk into the lobby, which glows with soft light, you are transported back to another era. Here you find a handsome red-tile floor, a beamed ceiling, arched coves, intimate sitting niches, elaborate bouquets of fresh flowers, potted palms, a stone fountain, and richly-hued mosaics—predominantly blue and white with a touch of yellow. These beautiful mosaic tiles are the hallmark of the Hotel Majestic and richly enhance the staircases, hallways, and public rooms. You reach the guestrooms, which are simple with a 1930s-style decor, by an old-fashioned elevator or up a winding staircase. Don't expect luxury, but the rooms are very comfortable and have air conditioning, security boxes, mini-bars, cable TVs, and telephones. Be sure to ask for a room overlooking the zócolo. The Majestic's renowned restaurant, the Terraza, located on the seventh floor, has a stunning balcony around two sides, which affords a prime view of the cathedral. A bountiful buffet breakfast (included) is served here each morning. Although not super-deluxe, this Best Western hotel offers incredible value and is one of our personal favorites. *Directions:* On a corner overlooking the main square.

HOTEL MAJESTIC
Manager: Jaime Escudero Garcia
Madero 73, Centro
Mexico City, D.F., 06000, Mexico
Tel: (55) 5521-8600, Fax: (55) 5512-6262
85 Rooms, Double: $75–$220*
*Tax: 17%
Open: all year, Credit cards: all major
Different World
Region: Central–Colonial City

Mineral de Pozos, a once–booming silver and gold mining town, is located within an hour's drive of such colonial jewels as San Miguel de Allende, Guanajuato, and Querétaro. In the early part of the 20th century the town was abandoned and lay dormant until recently rediscovered by an ever growing number of artisans and expatriates. A transplant from New Mexico, your charming hostess Susan Montana, fell in love with Pozos' laid-back charm and bought property on the main square. All that was left standing of the original mansion was a splendid façade. This was enough for Susan who visualized a romantic boutique style hotel. Using highly skilled local workmen whom she oversaw with a passion for perfection, she created a romantic, colonial-style inn, blending so perfectly into its surroundings that it looks centuries old. Susan's skills as an interior designer are obvious in the architectural details, the décor of the rooms, and the gorgeous gardens. The restaurant, "Gallery" is delightful and the food delicious. When weather is warm, meals are served outside on the patio. There are five guestrooms. Ask for one of the two suites: they are worth the splurge. Our favorite is suite number one, which has a four poster, queen-sized bed with a hand-carved headboard and a cozy sitting area in front of stone arched windows framing a delightful view. Horseback riding can also be arranged. *Directions:* In the center of town, facing the plaza with the church.

CASA MONTANA
Owner: Susan Montana
4A Jardín Principal
Mineral de Pozos, Guanajuato, 37910, Mexico
Tel: (442) 293-0032, Fax: (442) 293-0034
5 Rooms, Double: $105–$110*
*Tax: 17%
Open: all year, Credit cards: MC, VS
Region: Central–Colonial Town

One of the most recent hotels to open in the historic center of beautiful Morelia is La Casa de Las Rosas, conveniently located less than two blocks from the main plaza and steps from the Jardín de Las Rosas. This is not your normal commercial hotel, but rather an intimate, friendly, boutique style inn. Dating back to the 18th century, this grand old mansion now houses not only a tiny hotel but also a charming small restaurant. The hotel has only four guestrooms, predominantly spacious suites with several rooms. Modern wood paneling on some walls blends with other walls of exposed stone. Each guestroom has its own personality with furnishings to accent its motif. One of my favorites is the Suite Angeles with accents throughout of angels. Another guestroom, named for the Monarch Butterfly, has butterflies hand-painted on the headboard and the walls. Each of the suites has a fireplace and all modern amenities such as air conditioning, internet access, refrigerator, cable television, DVD, piped-in music, and safe deposit box. The bathrooms are particularly handsome with white marble walls and white tieback shower curtains. Extra niceties to make guests feel at home are bathrobes, slippers, and complimentary fruit. Original artwork, handmade furniture, antiques, and cozy gardens add to the ambiance of understated elegance. An extra convenience is an adjacent parking garage. *Directions:* From the west end of the plaza, take Guillermo Prieto north.

LA CASA DE LAS ROSAS
Manager: Raymundo Chavez Rodriguez
Guillermo Prieto 125 Centro Historico
Morelia, Michoacán, 58000, Mexico
Tel: (443) 312-4545, Fax: (443) 312-3867
4 Rooms, Double: $224–$324*
*Service: 8%, Tax: 17%
Open: all year, Credit cards: all major
 Region: Central–Colonial Town

Hotel Los Juaninos' central location, right across from the plaza and the cathedral, is perfect for exploring the streets of Morelia. This small boutique hotel with 33 rooms, once the Episcopal palace and then the Royal Hospital of San Juan de Dios, opened its doors in 1986, with major renovations taking place in the late 1990s. The lobby is enhanced by stained-glass windows, beamed ceiling, stone arches, numerous religious icons, floral bouquets, Victorian-style furniture, and a huge basket of colorful glass balls. A steel, freestanding elevator dominates the end of the entrance hall, but there is also a handsome curved stairway whose stone steps are well worn from centuries of use. The spacious bedrooms feature vaulted, wood-beam ceilings, wood floors, and lace curtains. One of our favorites, 214, is a junior suite with a view of the cathedral. Each floor looks out over a central courtyard, hacienda style, with wide passageways lined with finely carved doors and doorways framed in stone. On the rooftop, La Azotea, a renowned gourmet restaurant and bar with excellent regional cuisine, offers live music on weekends and lovely views of the plaza and church. Adjacent to the restaurant is an appealing small lounge, solely for the enjoyment of hotel guests. Morelia has many museums and fine examples of colonial architecture to discover, as well as markets where local handicrafts are sold. *Directions:* Overlooking the cathedral.

LOS JUANINOS
Owner: Lorena Morales
Morelos Sur 39
Morelia, Michoacán, 58000, Mexico
Tel & Fax: (443) 312-0036
30 Rooms, Double: $170–$300*
*Breakfast not included: $15
*Tax: 15%
Open: all year, Credit cards: all major
Region: Central–Colonial Town

For those who prefer the friendliness of a bed & breakfast over the formal atmosphere of a hotel, Quinta Torcasa is an excellent choice. The property, perched on the hillside above the lovely colonial town of Morelia, is adjacent to one of Mexico's finest hotels, Villa Montaña. Opened in the spring of 2005, Quinta Torcasas is named for the tiny village where your gracious host, José Cacho Vega, was born. José is a passionate collector of antiques and handicrafts and sells an assortment of his eclectic treasures in a shop in front. Behind the shop, wooden doors open unto the gardens and a swimming pool highlighted by centuries-old stone arches. All the bedrooms have wood-burning fireplaces and are chock full of antiques. Three of the guestrooms are in a separate house complete with living room, dining room, and kitchen. These guestrooms can be individually rented, or the house can be rented in its entirety. A path leads upward to my favorite two guestrooms. One of these, "Inchatiro", has a spacious bedroom with a cozy sitting area in front of the fireplace. My other favorite, "La Tiendita" (tiny shop), has a large living room with walls lined with antique shelving plus a separate modestly sized bedroom. The Quinta Torcasa's greatest asset is José, who loves to share his profound knowledge of Michoacán and takes great delight in helping guests plan their sightseeing. *Directions:* In the hills above the city. Ask for directions.

QUINTA TORCASAS
Owner: José Cacho Vega
Patzimba 590-A
Morelia, Michoacán, 58000, Mexico
Tel: (443) 314-6553
6 Rooms, Double: $140*
*Includes full breakfast & taxes
Open: all year, Credit cards: all major
Region: Central–Colonial Town

Snuggled on a hillside overlooking Morelia lies one of our favorite inns, the charming Villa Montaña Hotel & Spa. For many years it has been known as one of the finest small hotels in all of Mexico. The entrance sets the mood of refinement and good taste with an enormous stone fireplace, massive oil paintings, exuberant bouquets of fresh flowers, an antique reception desk, and a huge wrought-iron chandelier. The magic continues in the parklike grounds, which are stunning: everywhere you look there are treasures—from whimsical fountains to romantic statuary—all lovingly chosen by the artistic owner whose passion for handicrafts and antiques is obvious in every tiny detail. Brick pathways lace the property, leading to the 36 suites, each different in layout and distinct in design with wood furniture, handcrafted accessories, and fine European antiques. The ceilings are vaulted with thick wood beams and supported by carved columns. Fireplaces make the rooms cozy at night in winter, while sunny afternoons can be enjoyed poolside with a beautiful panoramic view of the city of Morelia below. The gourmet restaurant features both international and local dishes, with a wonderful ambiance and fine cuisine. On balmy evenings dinner is served outside on a terrace with an incomparable panorama. Other amenities include a tennis court, tours to nearby colonial towns, and a golf course nearby. *Directions:* In the hills above the city. Ask for directions.

VILLA MONTAÑA HOTEL & SPA
Manager: Ana Compeán
Patzimba 201, Colonia Vista Bella
Morelia, Michoacán, 58090, Mexico
Tel: (443) 314-0231, Fax: (443) 315-1423
13 Rooms, Double: $210–$290*
23 Suites: $290–$490*
*Breakfast not included: $13
*Service: 7.5%, Tax: 17%
Open: all year, Credit cards: all major
Different World
Region: Central–Colonial Town

The Virrey de Mendoza, a wonderful hotel exuding old-world refinement and understated elegance, has an unparalleled location looking across the picturesque Armas Square to Morelia's exquisite cathedral. The original building was a simple stone home constructed in the 16th century but over the years it was greatly enhanced and became one of the most magnificent mansions in town. The hotel is built around an attractive three-story arcaded courtyard crowned by a beautiful large stained-glass skylight. The lobby has an air of stately grandeur, with a handsome Oriental carpet accenting a gorgeous parquet floor, a huge bouquet of flowers, fine oil paintings, potted palms, soft lighting, a grand piano, and intimate groupings of leather sofas and chairs. There is a romantic, formal dining room with rich paneling halfway up the walls, a beamed ceiling, and antique-style chandeliers. The rather compact standard bedrooms are all pleasantly decorated with traditional-style furniture and tasteful artwork. The suites are more spacious and many are decorated with lovely antiques. The quietest bedrooms overlook the interior courtyard, but those facing the street, although noisier, have more sunlight. For a splurge, request one of the five suites that face the cathedral—these have incredible views of the cathedral. At night, when the cathedral is gently illuminated, these suites are truly magical. *Directions:* Facing the cathedral, across Armas Square.

HOTEL VIRREY DE MENDOZA
Manager: Letica Pina Morfin
Av. Madero 310
Morelia, Michoacán, 58000, Mexico
Tel: (443) 312-0633, Fax: (443) 312-6719
41 Rooms, Double: $161–$207*
*Service: 15%
Open: all year, Credit cards: all major
Different World
Region: Central–Colonial Town

If you are looking for luxurious accommodations without sacrificing one iota of charm, the Camino Real is an incomparable choice. Not only is this spectacular hotel a real beauty, but it also boasts the finest location in town—between two of Oaxaca's prime targets: the zócalo (main square) with its gorgeous cathedral and the lovely Santo Domingo. This former convent of Santa Catalina dates back to the 16th century, when it was constructed for the Dominican nuns. Happily, nothing has been over renovated: the building has been tenderly restored, preserving its stunning architectural features and authentic grace while subtly adding deluxe amenities. Time slips by as you step into the first romantic garden courtyard, bound by massive arched colonnades. Quiet tiled corridors enhanced by faded original frescoes lead to two additional sun-drenched courtyards: one features a pretty stone fountain where the nuns used to do their washing, while the other has a lovely swimming pool. The guestrooms vary in style and size due to the age of the building, but all are most appealing and decorated with great taste using native weavings, hand-loomed fabrics, and colorful Mexican tiles in the bathrooms. As would be expected in a luxury hotel, all rooms are air-conditioned and offer all modern amenities. The hotel also offers live entertainment on the weekends. *Directions:* On Calle 5 de Mayo, one block south of Santo Domingo.

CREDIT @ W P

CAMINO REAL OAXACA
Manager: Omar Gil Celis
Calle 5 de Mayo No. 300
Oaxaca, Oaxaca, 68000, Mexico
Tel: (951) 501-6100, Fax: (951) 516-0732
*85 Rooms, Double: $268–$363**
*6 Suites: $413–$428**
**Breakfast not included: $17.50*
**Service: 15%, Tax: 18%*
Open: all year, Credit cards: all major
Different World
Region: Central–Colonial Town

The Casa Cid de León is a mirror of the vibrant personality of owner/operator Lety de Cid de León and indeed, each of the four suites follows a theme taken from some aspect of, or time in, Lety's life. The decoration and design are at once eclectic but delicate, and sophisticated. Lety cares profoundly about her small bed and breakfast and takes great care in selecting only the finest linens and top-quality furnishings, and ensuring that fresh flowers abound in all the rooms. You could literally spend days in your room and still be discovering something new. If you are traveling with family, Lety can certainly accommodate you, as a couple of the rooms offer additional space or a connection with other rooms. The hotel has three floors, with the third being a rooftop terrace that serves as the dining room, lounge and bar. Although there is no restaurant on the premises, Lety has made arrangements with a couple of restaurants close by that deliver anything on their menus. Casa Cid de León is located right in the heart of downtown Oaxaca, making it perfect for exploring this truly wonderful city. There are so many markets and shops in Oaxaca and nearby, that staying somewhere right in the middle is extremely convenient. *Directions:* The hotel is easy to find. It is on one of the major streets (Morelos) in downtown Oaxaca. Two blocks from the square.

CASA CID DE LEÓN
Owner: Leticia de Cid de León
Avenida Morelos 602
Oaxaca, Oaxaca, 68000, Mexico
Tel: (951) 514-7013, Fax: (951) 514-0414
4 Suites: $200–$230*
*Tax: 18%
Open: all year, Credit cards: all major
Region: Central–Colonial Town

The Casa Conzatti, a mustard-colored colonial-style building, is a moderate-sized hotel on the edge of the historic section of Oaxaca. The hotel was the home of Cassiano Conzatti, a renowned Italian botanist who lived in Oaxaca at the end of the 19th century. Grateful for his remarkable work, the city named the garden where he did his research Jardín Conzatti. The Casa Conzatti faces the park and has a roof garden overlooking it. Like so many of the properties in Oaxaca, it reflects its early heritage with massive wooden beams, arched passageways leading to the guestrooms, and thick 200-year-old wooden double doors giving onto a central courtyard. To the right as you enter is a popular restaurant with tables and chairs overflowing into the patio, a very popular place to eat with the locals. Rustic wooden furniture and rich-colored fabrics decorate the bedrooms, all of which offer many amenities such as hairdryers, room safes, cable TV, air conditioning, and telephones with modem ports. The master suites have the added bonus of Jacuzzi tubs. Care has been taken to preserve all the architectural details of the colonial era to maintain the historic flavor of Oaxaca while offering a high level of comfort. The Casa Conzatti's sophisticated ambiance and similarly decorated rooms give it more of a commercial air than some of the other hotels we feature in Oaxaca. *Directions:* Three blocks from Santo Domingo Church, facing Conzatti Park.

CASA CONZATTI
Manager: Marco Díaz Hermández
Gómez Farias, 218
Oaxaca, Oaxaca, 68000, Mexico
Tel: (951) 513-8500, Fax: (951) 515-0777
45 Rooms, Double: $100–$213*
*Breakfast not included
*Tax: 17%
Open: all year, Credit cards: all major
Region: Central–Colonial Town

Superbly located in the heart of town, the Casa Oaxaca offers an old-fashioned style of personal service and a sophisticated, gentle refinement—far beyond what you would expect in such a tiny hotel. This simple, unadorned, bright-blue, stucco house is typical of the buildings found throughout Oaxaca. The heart of the hotel is its open garden courtyard, which is surrounded by a white columned arcade. Whereas most of Oaxaca's courtyards exude a cheerful, colorful, busy ambiance with many potted plants and fountains, Casa Oaxaca's is much less cluttered and, with its dazzling white walls, carefully placed accent trees, and rattan tables and chairs, has an almost Oriental look. In fact, throughout the hotel there is a most refreshing, minimalist, modern simplicity. The guestrooms have modern furnishings and white walls accented by well-framed photographs of Indian villages. Most of the guestrooms have doors opening onto the courtyard, but the suite faces a second patio with swimming pool. The hotel has an excellent, intimate restaurant where the talented chef, Alejandro Ruiz Olmedo, upon sufficient prior notice, will prepare a menu of your choice. Like the décor in the rest of the hotel, the small restaurant has a delightfully fresh look, with white walls and modern furnishings. A continental breakfast including homemade breads is served each morning in the tranquility of the courtyard. *Directions:* Four blocks from the square.

CASA OAXACA
Manager: Alejandro Ruiz
Calle Garcia Vigil 407
Oaxaca, Oaxaca, 68000, Mexico
Tel: (951) 514-4173, Fax: (951) 516-4412
5 Rooms, Double: $165–$224*
2 Suites: $300–$360*
*Service: 15%, Tax: 18%
Open: all year, Credit cards: all major
Different World
Region: Central–Colonial Town

Just before Christmas in 2000, your gracious young host, Ernesto Suárez, opened the doors of Casa San Felipe, a new hotel in Oaxaca. "New" isn't exactly the proper word since the hotel is within a centuries-old, Spanish-style home built around a central courtyard. This small hotel, with a brick-red stucco façade and doors and windows framed in white stone, faces a busy, one-way street, about five blocks from the zócalo (main square). Double wooden doors lead into a small, simple courtyard with walls painted a cheerful butter yellow and with green plastic chairs surrounding small tables. Potted palms and red geraniums add color. The guestrooms open off the courtyard, some on the ground level and others off an upper gallery with a wrought-iron railing. The junior suites are extremely spacious, but even the standard rooms are pleasant. Windows are insulated by double glass but for the greatest quiet, request accommodations upstairs away from the street. All of the bedrooms are nicely decorated in a tasteful, uncluttered, attractive style. They have fresh white walls, wrought-iron and wood headboards, good lighting, hand-loomed fabrics, and original paintings by local artists. This is a simple hotel, but provides great value for the amenities offered such as internet connections in all the rooms, excellent bathrooms, and air conditioning. *Directions:* From the main square, go four blocks on Av. Hidalgo and turn right on Xicotencatl.

CASA SAN FELIPE
Owner: Ernesto Suárez
Xicotencatl No. 212, Col. Centro
Oaxaca, Oaxaca, 68000, Mexico
Tel: (951) 514-8801, Fax: (951) 514-8802
8 Rooms, Double: $110–$200*
*Breakfast not included
Open: all year, Credit cards: MC, VS
Region: Central–Colonial Town

The Hacienda Los Laureles is located on the outskirts of Oaxaca about a 10-minute taxi drive from the heart of town in an area called San Felipe del Agua. You would never know you are in a separate village since Oaxaca is so spread out that the various neighborhoods blend together. It is great fun to be in the center of town where you can explore the fascinating city on foot. However the Hacienda Los Laureles has much to offer: it is a beautifully run, lovely old hacienda with excellent food, friendly service, spacious guestrooms, a mini-spa, exercise room, and a swimming pool. Also offered are Eco-Historic Tours and private Oaxaca style cooking classes in the garden. Wide verandas wrap around a large, beautifully tended garden shaded by centuries-old trees and accented by colorful beds of flowers. Facing the garden is a charming restaurant where meals are served outside on balmy days. If your main purpose for coming to Oaxaca is to visit the archaeological sites of Mitla, Monte Albán, and Yagul, then the hacienda makes an especially appealing choice for accommodations since after a day of exploring the ruins, you can return to the peace and quiet of Los Laureles for a relaxing swim and excellent dinner. The hotel is the dream of well-known hotelier, Peter Kaiser, who after years of operating hotels for some of Mexico's finest hotel chains, opened his own boutique hotel. *Directions:* Ask the hotel to fax you detailed instructions.

HOTEL HACIENDA LOS LAURELES SPA
Owner: Peter Kaiser
Hidalgo 21
Oaxaca, Oaxaca, 68020, Mexico
Tel: (951) 501-5300, Fax: (951) 501-5301
23 Rooms, Double: $190–$370*
*Breakfast not included: $12–$20
*Service: 15%, Tax: 18%
Open: all year, Credit cards: all major
Region: Central–Colonial Town

The Hostal de La Noria has a prime location just two blocks from the zócalo (main square). From first glance, you see that this handsome, deep-pink-colored 17th-century mansion with white trim and wrought-iron balconies oozes authentic, old-world charm. You walk through the front door into a charming courtyard framed by white marble columns supporting a series of arches. Here you find a flower-bedecked fountain in the center surrounded by many potted plants and attractive wrought-iron tables shaded by white awnings with pretty lacy trim. Guests can dine in the courtyard but there is also a cozy inside dining room with a ceramic tiled floor, beamed ceilings, hanging chandeliers, and attractive French-style chairs. The food is delicious and not expensive. The guestrooms, off the courtyard, have no air conditioning and the decor is a bit dated but all of them are spotlessly clean and comfortable, with many amenities such as marble bathrooms, hairdryers, cable TV, and direct-dial phones. My favorite, 206, a junior suite, is an especially attractive corner room. It has very appealing wood furniture hand-carved by artisans from the state of Michoacán and is further enhanced by light streaming in from windows on two sides. If you are looking for a hotel right in the heart of town with a wonderful faded old-world charm, you'll love the Hostal de La Noria. *Directions:* From the zócalo take Av. Hidalgo for two blocks. The hotel is on a corner on the left.

HOSTAL DE LA NORIA
Manager: Manuel Franco Trueba
Av. Hildago 918
Oaxaca, Oaxaca, 68000, Mexico
Tel: (951) 501-5400, Fax: (951) 516-3992
50 Rooms, Double: $130–$250*
*Breakfast not included: $7.50 to $10.50
Open: all year, Credit cards: all major
Region: Central–Colonial Town

The Parador del Dominico is a well-located hotel that can be depended upon for quality and service. The hotel rooms are all similar in style and furnishings and, although it is perhaps not quite as quaint as some of our other hotel recommendations in Oaxaca, it has the advantage that you are assured of consistent standards whatever room you are in. The guestrooms are furnished in a typical hotel style, with wooden headboards, writing tables, and chests of drawers. All offer air conditioning, good lighting, nice bathrooms, mini-bars, satellite TV, direct-dial phones, and room service. Facing onto one of Oaxaca's main streets, the hotel looks the same outside as so many of the town's colonial-era buildings: an unadorned, one-story, colorful, stuccoed building with windows and doorway bound by stone and an entrance enhanced by antique wrought-iron light fixtures. Not until you step inside does the personality of the hotel appear. The enclosed interior courtyard has a pretty zigzag-patterned brick floor, an old stone well, potted plants, and even a large old shade tree. A contemporary wooden bar tucked against one wall of the courtyard provides refreshments to guests sitting at the wrought-iron tables and chairs. There is also a restaurant at the front of the hotel with yellow walls. *Directions:* From the square go east 4 blocks on Av. Hidalgo to Pino Suárez. Turn left and go to # 410.

PARADOR DEL DOMINICO
Pino Suárez 410
Oaxaca, Oaxaca, 68000, Mexico
Tel & Fax: (951) 513-1812
32 Rooms, Double: $130–$160*
*Breakfast not included
Open: all year, Credit cards: all major
Different World
Region: Central–Colonial Town

Palenque is a "must-see" site for all who are enthralled by Mayan ruins, so it is not surprising that the Chan-Kah Resort Village (the closest good place to stay near the ruins) is extremely popular—with both individual travelers and tour groups. Although the hotel is usually bustling with activity, it exudes the personal intimacy of a family-owned hotel. When you first arrive, the Chan-Kah appears to be a normal hotel—but just wait! This is a very special property within 50 acres of ecological reserve: a lush jungle paradise with the Michol River winding through it. Best of all, the rooms are in individual cottages tucked artfully around the grounds. Except for the suites, all of the rooms are identical in configuration. The décor is simple, but the rooms themselves are really nice with two walls of windows looking out to the dense foliage, two double beds, a stone floor, writing desk, chairs and table, a large bathroom, and a wonderful covered porch with two comfortable rocking chairs. If possible, be sure to request one of the rooms snuggled deepest in the jungle, such as 35, 36, 40–45, and 63–74. All of these are very special, but my very favorite is room 39. When you stay here you feel like Tarzan, high in a treehouse in the jungle. The hotel also has three stunning lagoon-type swimming pools. *Directions:* Follow signs for the ruins. Before you arrive, the hotel is prominently marked on the left side of the road.

❄ ⚄ 📟 ☎ P ‖ ≈

CHAN-KAH RESORT VILLAGE
Manager: Roberto Romano Huerta
Km 3, Carretera Ruinas, Zona Arqueológica
Palenque, Chiapas, 29960, Mexico
Tel: (916) 345-1100, Fax: (916) 345-0820
77 Rooms, Double: $120–$330*
*Breakfast not included
Open: all year, Credit cards: all major
Region: Southeast–Archaeological Area

The Casa de La Real Aduana, a charming boutique hotel that opened in 2004, is the creation of two artists, Gemma Macouzet and Didier Dorval, who have exquisitely restored one of Pátzcuaro's beautiful historic buildings into an intimate, exclusive, small hotel. Also on the premises is La Folia Arts Center where concerts, exhibits, and workshops are organized, along with a permanent international exhibition of photography, painting and sculpture. The Casa de La Real Aduana was built in the 16th century as a magnificent residence for the Spanish noblemen who were responsible for the Royal Customs during the Colony period. The hotel has a prime location in the heart of Pátzcuaro, half a block from the stunning Plaza Vasco de Quiroga, one of the most beautiful plazas in Mexico. The individually appointed guestrooms reflect the artistic talent of the owners—each is exquisitely decorated with antiques as well as modern pieces of art. Most of the guestrooms are named after famous composers. One of them is named for the Dorvals' good friend Hugh Pissarro, a French painter who is the grandson of the great impressionist Camille Pissarro. A royal breakfast is served each morning in the lovely dinning room that displays such a rich selection of art that, like the rest of the house, you feel as if you are in a fine gallery. Dinner available with 24 hour advance notice. *Directions:* Ask hotel for directions.

CASA DE LA REAL ADUANA BOUTIQUE HOTEL
Owners: Gemma Macouzet & Didier Dorval
Ponce de Leon 16
Pátzcuaro, Michoacán, 61600, Mexico
Tel & Fax: (434) 342-0265
4 Rooms, Double: $240–$295*
1 Suite: $275–$340*
*Service: 6%
Open: all year, Credit cards: none
Region: Central–Colonial Town

If you are looking for a moderately-priced place to stay in Pátzcuaro, yet don't want to sacrifice charm, La Casa Encantada makes an outstanding choice. Housed within an 18th-century adobe mansion—located just a block from Pátzcuaro's magnificent Plaza Don Vasco de Quiroga—La Casa Encantada contains eleven guestrooms facing two enclosed, lush garden patios. Each of the guestrooms is individually decorated; all exude a cozy, Mexican ambiance with hand-loomed fabrics, terracotta floors, Talavera tiles, beam ceilings, wrought iron accents, handmade furniture, and local handicrafts. The amenities far exceed what one usually expects in a B&B. All the guestrooms have at least one king-sized bed, a fireplace or wall heater, cable TV, wireless internet connection, down pillows, and heated mattress pads (a great bonus since nights in Pátzcuaro can be very chilly). A picture-perfect, colorful Mexican kitchen opens onto a pretty dining room where a bountiful breakfast (which varies each morning) is served. There is also a comfortable living room with a fireplace where guests can relax and share the highlights of their sightseeing adventures. Your gracious hostesses, Victoria Ryan and Cynthia de la Rosa, are exceptionally knowledgeable about the region and can recommend outstanding local guides to help you explore this fascinating part of Mexico, rich in history, art, wonderful churches, archaeological sites, and handicrafts.

LA CASA ENCANTADA
Owners: Victoria Ryan & Cynthia de la Rosa
Dr. Coss #15
Pátzcuaro, Michoacan de Ocampo, 61600, Mexico
Tel: (434) 342-3492 or (619) 819-8398 (USA)
11 Rooms, Double: $90–$135*
*Tax: 17%
Open: all year, Credit cards: none
Region: Central–Colonial Town

Dating back to the 17th century, the handsome Hotel Mansión Iturbe has a rich history. In 1830, it was given as a dowry gift by Francisco de Iturbe to his daughter, Paca, when she married Francisco de Arriaga y Peralta; and the home has been in the same family ever since. It has now been converted into a small hotel, but the interior still reflects its past grandeur. As is typical with these beautiful Colonial buildings, the house sits directly on the street with many of the rooms facing onto an interior garden courtyard with a galleried walkway on the second level. Inside, the Spanish-style décor features heavy carved furniture and walls painted in deep tones of mustard yellow and red. The hotel's most outstanding attribute is its unsurpassable location—it is absolutely center stage, overlooking Pátzcuaro's stunning Plaza Vasco de Quiroga, without a doubt one of the most beautiful squares in Mexico. Best of all, in three bedrooms facing the plaza you can open wide your French doors and step out onto a small wrought-iron balcony to savor the ever-changing scene before you. Although less spacious than the others, but in my opinion the best, ask for 11, 12, or 14 (12 is smaller, but has the same view). To make reservations in English, it is best to contact the hotel via email or fax. All rooms have central heating. *Directions:* Facing Plaza Vasco de Quiroga square.

HOTEL MANSIÓN ITURBE
Owner: Margarita Pedraza Arriaga
Portal Morelos 59, Plaza Vasco de Quiroga
Pátzcuaro, Michoacán, 61600, Mexico
Tel: (434) 342-0368, Fax: (434) 342-3627
14 Rooms, Double: $80–$185*
*Tax: 17%
Open: all year, Credit cards: all major
Different World
Region: Central–Colonial Town

The most recent addition to the enticing selection of fine accommodations in Pátzcuaro is the lovely La Siranda Casa-Hotel. The owners, Manuel Rodriquez Arriaga & Isabel Lange, purchased the property in the early 1990s with the idea of some day opening a tiny, exquisite hotel exuding the coziness, privacy, and charm of a bed and breakfast. The dream of an inn was delayed for ten years while they traveled the world as Manuel pursued his diplomatic career. Upon returning to Mexico, the 16th-century house was tenderly renovated and beautifully refurbished by Isabel using their personal collection of furniture, antiques, and artwork collected from their years abroad. As characteristic of colonial-style buildings, the beauty of the home is secreted behind massive wooden doors that front the street. The magic begins as you step into an intimate garden courtyard, flanked by five deluxe suites, tastefully decorated and radiating obvious top quality in every detail. Breakfast and dinner (dinner by prior request) are served in an elegant dining room that overlooks a second tranquil garden. A large separate garden is ideal for reading under the shade of the trees or sunbathing by the pond. A fully equipped business room is available for those who might need to work during their stay or organize a business meeting on the premises. *Directions:* Located half a block off the Plaza de Don Vasco de Quiroga.

LA SIRANDA CASA-HOTEL
Manager: Magdalena Torres
Dr. Coss 17
Pátzcuaro, Michoacán, 61600, Mexico
Tel: (434) 342 6717
5 Rooms, Double: $230–$260*
*Tax: 17%
Open: all year, Credit cards: VS
Region: Central–Colonial Town

The beach at Playa del Carmen is truly spectacular—a long stretch of sand whose beauty is enhanced by the crystal-clear, turquoise sea. It is no wonder that Playa del Carmen is so popular and that many large, rather bland hotels have sprung up to cater to the influx of tourists who come for fun and sun. What is appealing about Mosquito Blue (located in the center of town, steps from the many colorful shops and restaurants) is its intimate size and abundance of personality. Although not right on the sea, it is very close—just one-and-a-half blocks away. You enter into a gallery-like lobby with walls accented by paintings done by local artists. The ambiance is a blend of Polynesian, Mexican, and Mediterranean. A color scheme of white, blue, and yellow, lush gardens, palm trees, colorful flowers, carved mahogany furniture, and intimate courtyards add to the appeal. There are two swimming pools. The most dramatic of these is highlighted by a two-story, open-air, thatched roof lounge. Some of the guestrooms face onto the street and these can be noisy at night, especially because of the popularity of the hotel's colorful bar. We suggest you request a deluxe room (the standards are pretty snug) facing the courtyard. Many of the guestrooms have king-sized beds as the hotel caters to adults (no children under 16). *Directions:* Located on Calle 12 that dead-ends at the ocean, and just off Av. 5, the pedestrian-only main street of town.

MOSQUITO BLUE
Manager: Anola Girondin
Calle 12, between Av. 5 & 10
Playa del Carmen–Riviera Maya
Quintana Roo, 77710, Mexico
Tel: (984) 873-1335, Fax: (984) 873-1337
46 Rooms, Double: $213–$351*
*Tax: 12%
Open: all year, Credit cards: all major
Different World
Region: Beach-Caribbean Coast–Riviera Maya

Newly opened in 2002, The Tides brings new heights of luxurious, understated elegance to the Riviera Maya. There is nothing ostentatious about this gorgeous small property: in fact, there is very little about the hotel that hints of any commercialism. No signs boldly point the way; only a privileged few who have secured a reservation in advance will ever find their way to this intimate hotel secreted down a gravel lane in a lush wooded park that stretches to the beach. Once you arrive you are greeted personally by either the exceptionally gracious manager, Nicolás Dominguez, or one of his able assistants. Paths meander through the property to the guestrooms, each an individual villa tucked into the rich foliage with a small private pool in front and beautiful private terrace, your own romantic hideaway. The décor of the bedrooms reflects the kind of quiet simplicity that exudes top quality and refinement. Nothing is cluttered or busy. You have just a king-sized bed with sumptuous linens, a soaring thatched ceiling, beautiful hardwood floors, a cabinet hiding television, stereo, and VCR, and a top-of-the-line bathroom with a second shower in the garden. Paths wind down to a splendid stretch of white-sand beach where a beautiful pool and restaurant with gourmet dining complete the scene of perfection. If that is not enough, there is also a spectacular spa. *Directions:* About 8 km north of Playa del Carmen.

❇ ☕ 🛏 CREDIT ☎ Ⴑ P ⑂ ⚘ ≈ ⚓ 🐎 ⚓

THE TIDES
Manager: Nicolás Dominguez
Playa Xcalacoco, Playa del Carmen–Riviera Maya
Quintana Roo, 77710, Mexico
Tel: (984) 877-3000, Fax: (984) 877-3009
29 Rooms, Double: $468–$1680*
*Service: 10%, Tax: 12%
Open: all year, Credit cards: all major
Different World
Region: Beach-Caribbean Coast–Riviera Maya

The Camino Real Puebla, situated in the historic center of the beautiful city of Puebla, is housed within a beautiful convent dating back to 1593. It was built by the local priest, Don Leonardo Ruiz de la Peña, to fulfill a promise he made to the Virgin for saving his life after a flood ravaged the city. The Convent of Immaculate Conception allowed into the order only girls who came from families of a pure Spanish bloodline. Their fathers had to pay to have them accepted, and this accounts for why the rooms in the hotel vary so in size—the girls from wealthy families received the largest rooms (these are now the suites), while those whose fathers were less affluent received smaller quarters (now the standard rooms). A few of the guestrooms have some of the original 16th-century frescoes and four have amateurish but quite interesting paintings on the walls that were done by soldiers who were barracked here in 1865. On the rooftop is a Jacuzzi pool and terrace with a great view of the city. My favorite guestroom, 407, is a standard room but quite special and private, with a door opening onto this terrace. The hotel is built around various interior courtyards, the main one enhanced by a large fountain in the middle and surrounded by an arcaded portico, a favorite place to dine on balmy days. There are two dining rooms plus a cozy bar. *Directions:* Just a few blocks from the cathedral, on Calle 7 Poniente, between 16 de Septiembre and Calle 3 Sur.

CAMINO REAL PUEBLA
Manager: Mr. Alvaro Narvaez
Calle 7 Poniente 105, Centro Histórico
Puebla, Puebla, 72000, Mexico
Tel: (222) 229-0909, Fax: (222) 232-9251
*84 Rooms, Double: $140–$500**
**Breakfast not included*
**Tax: 17%*
Open: all year, Credit cards: all major
Region: Central–Colonial Town

The Hotel Colonial, with a prime location one block from Puebla's main square, dates back to 1668 when it was built as a Jesuit monastery. Not only is the mustard-yellow building with white trim and wrought-iron balconies attractive; but it also has another great bonus: it faces onto a pretty cobblestone, pedestrian-only street adorned by a fountain and shade trees. The hotel is not deluxe or sumptuous, but it exudes a quiet air of quality. Officially designated as a three-star hotel, in our estimation the Hotel Colonial soars far above this rating. You enter into a spacious reception foyer whose vaulted ceilings, arched doorways, thick walls, and handsome stone floors attest to the building's origins. The hotel is built around a central courtyard where meals are served at tables with handsome wood and leather chairs. A lovely antique stone fountain accents one of the walls and the room is gently illuminated by an exceptionally pretty domed skylight, which has colorful Talavera tiles dividing the sections of glass. Talavera tile is also used on the staircase that leads up to the guestrooms, which are surprisingly spacious and pleasantly decorated in a simple way. Best of all, most of the guestrooms have a small wrought-iron balcony where you can step out and enjoy the view. If you are looking for quality and location at a reason price, you can do no better than the Hotel Colonial. *Directions:* One block east of the main square.

HOTEL COLONIAL
Manager: Maria Luisa Ortiz de Montellano
4 Sur 105
Puebla, Puebla, 72000, Mexico
Tel: (222) 246-4612, Fax: (222) 246-0818
66 Rooms, Double: $59–$59*
*Breakfast not included
Open: all year, Credit cards: all major
Region: Central–Colonial Town

The Mesones Sacristía Puebla are two historic houses that are managed as one hotel by your hosts, the Espinosa family, who have been antique dealers for four generations. With a talent for decorating, accentuated by a fine collection of antiques and religious artwork, they have created two charming, boutique-style hotels. Both are tiny, but the intimate size allows for personal attention. Both are located in Puebla's centro histórico and are within walking distance of each other. The closest to the town's fascinating main square, is the hotel on 6 Sur, which is built around a colonial-style courtyard where tables are gaily set with colorful linens for dining. This restaurant is well known for its fine Pueblan cuisine and the adjacent bar is also a favorite with locals. The hotel on 9 Oriente, an aristocratic home dating back the 16th century, is a bit farther from the main square, but it is quieter since there is no restaurant or bar with live music until the wee hours. The guestrooms in both properties are individually decorated, and each has its own distinct personality. A combination of antique and modern furnishings lends an eclectic, comfortable ambiance. When making reservations, ask more information about each hotel's location and special merits; then decide whether you want the property on 6 Sur or the one on 9 Oriente. *Directions:* After choosing your accommodations, ask for detailed driving instructions.

MESONES SACRISTÍA PUEBLA
Manager: Leobardo Espinosa
6 Sur 304 and 9 Oriente 16
Puebla, Puebla, 72000, Mexico
Tel: (222) 242-3554, Fax: (222) 232-4513
*15 Rooms, Double: $110–$200**
**Service: 10%*
Open: all year, Credit cards: all major
Region: Central–Colonial Town

Puerto Escondido, long a favorite destination for surfers and those seeking a laid-back beach vacation, is far removed in mood from the upscale resort of Huatulco, a deluxe resort on the coast about 115 kilometers to the east. The beach at Puerto Escondido is very nice, punctuated with outcroppings of rocks that add interest to the long stretch of sand where snack bars and simple restaurants offer refreshment. Not fancy, yet very comfortable, with a prime location just across the road from the beach, the Hotel Santa Fe suits the casual air of the town. It exudes the traditional Mexican flavor with its peach-toned stucco building topped by a heavy red-tiled roof, accents of wrought-iron, arched walkways, staircases punctuated by colorful Talavera tiles, and inner garden courtyards ablaze with brilliant bougainvillea and palms. The guestrooms are on various levels of terraces that are joined by meandering, attractive tiled staircases. The simple rooms have wooden furniture and are decorated with Mexican-style fabrics. There are also a few bungalows that offer kitchenettes, but in our estimation, the regular bedrooms are more inviting. The attractive, palapa-style, open-air restaurant overlooks the beach. There are two swimming pools, each in its own well-kept garden courtyard, around which are placed comfortable lounge chairs shaded by palm trees. *Directions:* Located toward the west end of the beach that stretches below the town.

HOTEL SANTA FE
Owner: Victor Manuel Lepe Ramírez
Blvd Zicatela y Calle del Morro
Puerto Escondido, Oaxaca, 71980, Mexico
Tel: (954) 582-0170, Fax: (954) 582-0260
60 Rooms, Double: $126–$525*
*Breakfast not included
Open: all year, Credit cards: all major
Different World
Region: Beach–Pacific Coast

The Ceiba del Mar Spa Resort returns renovated and glamorous, now with fewer rooms, yet each is much more spacious and enhanced to a new level of 5-star luxury. We think it will appeal to many of you looking for a pretty beachfront property away from the crowds. From the moment you enter into the low-rise reception area with its thatched roof and open-air reception lounge, it is obvious from the very attractive furnishings that good taste abounds. A huge, wrought-iron chandelier dominates the room, which is furnished with handsome sofas, chairs, and tables brought from Guadalajara. The guestrooms are located in eight three-story buildings that form a loop around two swimming pools. Each of the buildings is fresh and pretty, with white stucco walls, wood trim, and a thatched roof. All guestrooms are attractively decorated and offer every amenity. One of my favorites, 1832, has an especially romantic view of the turquoise sea. In addition to the swimming pools, each building has a rooftop garden with a Jacuzzi pool for guests. You also find a spa, beauty parlor, bikes for guests, an exercise room, and even a library where guests can check out books or videos for use in the VCRs in the rooms. However, during the day one certainly wouldn't want to sit inside and watch movies with that glorious white-sand beach stretching in front of the hotel! *Directions:* Just at the north end of Puerto Morelos. Well marked with signs.

❋ ◾ 🎿 💳 ☎ ⛷ Υ P ‖ ❀ ≈ ⛷ ⚓ 🚣

CEIBA DEL MAR SPA RESORT
Manager: Juan Mudespacher
Costera Norte Lt. 01 SM 10 MZ 26, Riviera Maya
Puerto Morelos–Riviera Maya
Quintana Roo, 77580, Mexico
Tel: (998) 872-8060, Fax: (998) 872-8061
88 Rooms, Double: $371–$998*
*Service: 5%, Tax: 12%
Open: all year, Credit cards: all major
Different World
Region: Beach-Caribbean Coast–Riviera Maya

The lavish, Moroccan-style Casa Velas is located within Marina Vallarta, a beautiful Marina development close to the airport. Though it primarily appeals to those looking for an escape from the hustle and bustle of the city, just minutes away are Puerto Vallarta's wonderful restaurants and nightlife. An 18-hole golf course drapes itself around the hotel, providing privacy and solitude. The hotel's enclosed lobby features tropical plants and pleasant seating arrangements, and adjoining it in the rear is a sitting area—the lobby bar, overlooking the swimming pool. The pool area is the highlight of the hotel: it is surrounded by lush gardens and tall, majestic palms and is set with very comfortable lounge chairs and white-canopied tents that offer shade from the tropical sun. Next to the pool is the gourmet restaurant El Candil, which serves wonderful blends of Mexican and international cuisine. The rooms are spacious and tastefully decorated, with separate sitting areas and in some cases terrace Jacuzzis. Amenities include a gymnasium, tennis courts, and jogging and biking trails; while the marina nearby is great for walking, admiring boats from around the world, and enjoying the shops, cafés, and restaurants. *Directions:* Located a few minutes from the airport. Follow signs south to Puerto Vallarta and take the Marina Vallarta exit. Signs will lead you to the hotel.

CASA VELAS
Manager: Philip Vidal
Calle Pelicanos 311, Marina Vallarta
Puerto Vallarta, Jalisco, 48354, Mexico
Tel: (322) 226-6688, Toll Free: (866) 612-1097 (USA)
67 Rooms, Double: $420–$1770*
*Tax: 17%
*All inclusive hotel
Open: all year, Credit cards: all major
Different World
Region: Beach–Pacific Coast

Puerto Vallarta's beaches are jammed with high-rise resorts catering to those seeking action. If instead you prefer an intimate hotel that exudes refinement, old world charm, genuine hospitality, and outstanding quality, the Hacienda San Angel reigns supreme. The hotel is not on the beach, but rather tucked up behind the church on a cobbled street in the heart of the Old Town. This gem was originally the private home of your hostess, Janice Chatterton. When she left Northern California and moved permanently to her Mexican hideaway, she began to expand her property. The first purchase was an adjacent lot where her dogs could romp. Gradually she added nearby houses, and her home just grew and grew, becoming the perfect size for a small hotel. Four houses (Casa Bursus, Casa San Angel, Casa La Joya and Casa Las Campanas) have been cleverly melded into a work of art, abounding with exquisite antiques that are beautifully displayed throughout the inn. Series of small patios and secluded terraces, enhanced by fountains and lush gardens, are tucked throughout the hacienda. There is also a delightful restaurant and three swimming pools. The rooms vary in size from small to exceptionally grand in scale, but all have outstanding amenities such as fine linens with handmade lace, down pillows and wonderful mattresses. *Directions:* Ask for detailed instructions.

HACIENDA SAN ANGEL
Owner: Janice Chatterton
Miramar 336, Col. Centro
Puerto Vallarta, Jalisco, 48300, Mexico
Tel: (322) 222-2692, Fax: (322) 223-1941
11 Rooms, Double: $315–$745*
10 Suites: $570–$1390*
*Service: 5%, Tax: 17%
Minimum Stay Required: 3 nights
Open: all year, Credit cards: all major
Region: Beach–Pacific Coast

Verana is a truly unique resort: a secluded hotel that has an intriguing blend of primitive simplicity and subtle sophistication. A 25-minute drive south from the Puerto Vallarta Airport to the tiny fishing village of Boca de Tomatlán, a half-hour boat ride to Yelapa, followed by a 20-minute hike up a mountainous path through the jungle bring you to a nondescript gate with a small sign, "Verana." As you turn back and look down across the dense foliage, you get a breathtaking view of blue sea with a crescent of beach edged by the colorful village of Yelapa. The hotel has just eight guesthouses, six in individual cottages and two sharing one house. Each is unique in style and eclectic in furnishings—some are ultra-modern, some cozy with antique accents—but each is extremely appealing to the eye. All of the houses have a close-to-nature mood, but my favorite, the Palapa, is really special. It is like luxury camping, with waist-high stone walls, no windows at all, various levels of sitting and sleeping areas, a large terrace, and a shower open to the stars. In addition to the Jungle Spa reserved for overnight guests, the hotel offers a striking indoor-outdoor rustic-meets-modern spa on the cliffs below the hotel. Meals are served on a terrace overlooking the bay. Guests enjoy relaxing by the stunning pool, which seems to float over the jungle. All meals are included for an additional $80 p/p per day. *Directions:* The hotel will pick you up by boat at Tomatlán.

VERANA
Owners: Veronique & Heinz Legler
Playa Yelapa, Puerto Vallarta, Jalisco, 48300, Mexico
Tel: 866-687-9358, Toll Free: (866) 687-9358 (USA)
Cell: (322) 227.5420
8 Rooms, Double: $320–$480*
*Service: 10%
Minimum Stay Required: 5 nights
$80 pp/per day for all meals
Open: Nov 1 to Jul 6, Credit cards: MC, VS
Different World
Region: Beach–Pacific Coast

At the end of an 18-kilometer dirt road, hugging the length of a rocky promontory, is the gorgeous Posada de Las Flores (sister hotel to the Posada de Las Flores in Loreto). The setting is stunning and the hotel brilliantly designed to maximize bay and water views. Standard rooms are in a cluster of buildings overlooking an attractive rock and cactus garden, while spacious junior suites are found in a one-story building that stretches across a low bluff right at the water's edge. Each suite has a private patio and stone arches in front, which frame a marvelous view of the sea. Definitely splurge and request one of these suites; they are so special that you will be disappointed if you don't. The suites have terracotta tile floors, a small sunken sitting area in front of a closed-off fireplace, and large picture windows capturing a magnificent sea view. Coffee and sweet cakes are set out each morning on tables just outside each guestroom. Wrapping around the hotel, a stone terrace set with comfortable teak lounge chairs shaded by white umbrellas looks out to the turquoise-blue water of the bay. Down from the guestrooms is a charming outdoor bar and restaurant with tables set under a protective palapa. On the other side of the restaurant is a beautifully landscaped pool whose water seems almost an extension of the bay. *Directions:* Located 48 km north of Mulegé, 54 km south of Santa Rosalia. Watch carefully for the hotel sign at Palo Verde.

POSADA DE LAS FLORES
Owner: Giuseppe Marcelletti
Punta Chivato, Baja California Sur, 23880, Mexico
Tel: (615) 155-5600, Fax: (619) 872-0781
20 Rooms, Double: $100–$240*
8 Suites: $240–$450*
*Tax: 12%
*Includes breakfast, lunch & dinner
Closed: Sep 9 to Oct 10, Credit cards: VS
Region: Beach-Baja California

Less than an hour's drive south of Cancún (yet light years away in mood), the Maroma is an intimate, luxurious, beachfront hotel where the pampered guests are known and greeted by their first name. The owners consider the Maroma their home: a home with guestrooms for visiting friends, which is how the tale began. In 1980, your delightful hostess, Sally, made a brief trip from Chicago to Cancún. While there, she fell in love with the gentle beauty of the Caribbean and with José Luis Moreno, who took her to see a gorgeous property he owned with dense jungle growing to the edge of an endless stretch of stunning white-sand beach. Sally and José Luis married and their hideaway cottage grew into a permanent residence, always filled with friends. When rebuilding after a devastating hurricane in 1988, it seemed the perfect opportunity to add more bedrooms and transform Maroma into a hotel. Guestrooms are individual in decor, yet all exude a quiet, tasteful, rustic appeal, with native handicrafts used throughout. Hammocks swing lazily from the porch or balcony, enticing one to forget the cares of the world. The beach is superb and studded by small palapas, which shade comfortable lounge chairs. Nearby you find a lovely swimming pool, an open-air restaurant, and an elegant, gourmet restaurant with truly outstanding food. *Directions:* Included in the room rate is a transfer from the Mérida airport. If driving, ask for detailed instructions.

❄ ⚐ 🅲🆁🅴🅳🅸🆃 P ⑂ 🐾 ⚐ ⊥ ⚓

MAROMA
Owners: Sally & José Luis Moreno
Punta Maroma–Riviera Maya
Quintana Roo, 77501, Mexico
Tel: (998) 872-8200, Fax: (998) 872-8220
36 Rooms, Double: $510–$2010*
*Breakfast not included
*Service: 10%, Tax: 12%
Open: all year, Credit cards: all major
Different World
Region: Beach-Caribbean Coast–Riviera Maya

Casa de Mita is truly a treasure. Tucked on a small peninsula about half an hour's drive north of Puerto Vallarta, next door to the super-deluxe Four Seasons Hotel, the intimate, tastefully decorated Casa de Mita offers not only a gorgeous white-sand beach and a lovely swimming pool, but also fabulous dining and genuine warmth of welcome. Best of all, the rate is extremely fair—in our estimation, one of the best values in Mexico. This delightful small inn is owned by Marc Lindskog, your charming host, who fell in love with Mexico many years ago and has made it his permanent home. The hotel has just eight guestrooms, each individual in size and decoration. All are oceanfront and have handcrafted furniture, custom original artwork, beautiful tiled bathrooms with huge showers, and terraces overlooking the sea. The pool, positioned by the beach, is the heart of the hotel. Next to the pool is the restaurant where three wonderful meals a day (included in the room rate) are served. Several choices of entrée are available and there is even a special pastry chef. Marc wants each guest to truly feel like a friend in his home, so even drinks are included in the room rate. In addition, each guestroom has a refrigerator stocked with complimentary cold drinks. There is a minimum three-night stay, but you will quickly decide that this is too short. *Directions:* Airport transfers available. If driving, call for directions.

❄ ☕ 💳 @ W ♗ P ♚ ≋ 🏹 ⛵ ⚓ 👤 👥 🏇 🤿

CASA DE MITA
Owner: Marc Lindskog
Playa Careyero, Puerto Vallarta
Punta Mita, Nayarit, 48324, Mexico
Tel: (329) 298-4114, Fax: (329) 298-4112
6 Rooms, Double: $445–$635*
2 Suites: $525–$735*
*Tax: 18%
Minimum Stay Required: 3 nights
*Includes all meals
Open: all year, Credit cards: all major
Different World
Region: Beach–Pacific Coast

The luxurious Four Seasons is larger than hotels we normally feature, but there is no way we could possibly not share this gem with you. Although it has many guestrooms, the ambiance is one of a small, intimate, boutique hotel. We love it! Don't expect to drop by to "take a look"—security is absolute. You must have a reservation to be admitted through the front gates. This is to protect the privacy of the guests, many of whom are very high-profile. However, the joy is that, once you enter the property and drive through the spectacular manicured grounds, you receive such a warm reception that it would seem you are in a small, family-run hotel. You feel the mood of refined luxury, ultimate quality, and superb décor as soon as you enter. The reception area extends on to become a beautiful lounge with a peaked palapa-style ceiling and a color scheme of creamy beiges and whites accented by a few well-placed sculptures and splendid bouquets of fresh flowers. The guestrooms continue the same degree of quality and refinement. However, my absolute favorites are the rooms in small cottages right on a tiny, palm-studded beach with a crescent of sand just outside your door. Sports are a big deal here, with world-class golf courses, tennis, and all water sports instantly available. *Directions:* Drive north from Puerto Vallarta following signs to Punta Mita. You cannot miss the dramatic entrance to the hotel on the right-hand side of the road.

FOUR SEASONS
Manager: Dennis Clark
Bahía de Banderas, Puerto Vallarta
Punta Mita, Nayarit, 33734, Mexico
Tel: (322) 291-6000, Fax: (322) 291-6060
146 Rooms, Double: $590–$4400*
*Breakfast not included
*Service: 15%, Tax: 17%
Open: all year, Credit cards: all major
Different World
Region: Beach–Pacific Coast

La Casa de La Marquesa, located in the heart of Querétaro, is an enchanting, 18th-century palace, richly embellished with an ornately sculpted roofline, windows framed by lavishly carved stone, a family crest above the door, and wrought-iron wall lamps. The legend goes that the original owner fell in love with a beautiful nun who asked him to build the most sumptuous home in Querétaro, La Casa de La Marquesa. You would almost think you have stepped into the palace of a Moorish prince: graceful arches, colorful tiles, wrought-iron balconies, potted plants, enormous chandeliers, giant floral bouquets, lace curtains at the windows, antique furniture, and a dramatic staircase create a mood of amazing splendor. The hotel is built within two lovely homes across the street from each other. Guestrooms are found in both, but those in the second home exude more of an antique ambiance in their furnishings. Snuggled in the courtyard of this second house there is an absolutely charming restaurant with deep-blue walls, an arched colonnade, potted plants, bright-red geraniums, wrought-iron tables, and, in the center, a romantic stone fountain adorned by a gigantic bouquet of fresh flowers. This lovely property is owned by the exceptionally charming Maria del Carmen Gonzalez Cosio de Urquiza, who runs her small inn like a fine home and overlooks no detail in assuring guests' comfort. *Directions:* In the historic center. One block west of Jardín Obregon.

LA CASA DE LA MARQUESA
Manager: Juan Pablo Urquiza
Madero 41, Querétaro, Queretaro, 76000, Mexico
Tel: (442) 212-0092, Fax: (442) 212-0098
25 Rooms, Double: $170–$240*
*Breakfast not included
*Tax: 17.5%
Open: all year, Credit cards: all major
Region: Central–Colonial Town

Although this is a sprawling urban area, you find at Querétaro's center a rich colonial heritage—beautiful churches, centuries-old buildings, tree-lined streets, and pretty little squares replace the modern buildings on the outskirts of town. The Mesón de Santa Rosa, built in the 1700s for horsemen, sits in the heart of the historic center and its romantic charm is immediately apparent. As you enter the lobby there is an intimate, antique-filled parlor to your left and ahead a positively delightful courtyard surrounded by red walls laced with greenery and with a vine-covered trellis above to filter the bright sun. Enhancing the scene are potted plants, tables set with fine linens, and a lovely old stone fountain. Many Spanish-style mansions have not just one, but a series of courtyards; and such is the case with the Mesón de Santa Rosa, where you discover a delightful tile-lined swimming pool, surrounded by potted plants and accented by colorful geraniums, tucked into another courtyard. Most of the simply furnished guestrooms face onto this courtyard and are a bit dark because there is not much sunlight coming through the windows. Another wonderful feature of this small hotel is that just across the street is Independence Square, a jewel of a little park surrounded by charming, arcaded old buildings. *Directions:* In the historic center, facing Independence Square.

MESÓN DE SANTA ROSA
Manager: Marco A. Del Prete
Pasteur Sur 17, Centro Histórico
Querétaro, Queretaro, 76000, Mexico
Tel: (442) 224-2623, Fax: (442) 212-5522
22 Rooms, Double: $120–$190*
*Breakfast not included
*Tax: 17.5%
Open: all year, Credit cards: all major
Region: Central–Colonial Town

The East Cape forms the southeast corner of the Baja Peninsula. For years this desert paradise was rarely visited except by a few intrepid sportsmen (such as Bing Crosby) who flew in by private plane for some of the most extraordinary fishing in the world. If you are looking for a secluded, friendly hotel with a spectacular natural setting, the Rancho Leonero, perched on a low bluff overlooking the Sea of Cortez, is a real find. This is not a fancy hotel, nor does it pretend to be one. If you want posh accommodations, there are plenty of these in Los Cabos. John Ireland, your charming host, bought the property in the early 1980s, and built this small hotel. About 90% of the guests come for the incredible fishing. Boats leave from the pier below the hotel to prow the waters for game fish—the marlin here can exceed 1,000 pounds (high fishing season is mid-March through September). Fishing from a kayak is another option that looks like fun. However, you don't need to be a fisherman to enjoy your stay here. A pristine sand beach stretches forever in front of the hotel with crystal clear water that provides excellent snorkeling. The hotel offers various accommodation—our favorites are the ocean-view thatched cottages. *Directions:* Directions: From Los Cabo Airport, go north on Hwy 1 toward La Paz. At Km 103 (just south of Buena Vista) turn right off Hwy 1 and and follow signs to Rancho Leonero, which is about 8 km farther on a gravel road.

RANCHO LEONERO
Owners: John & Jennifer Ireland
Rancho Leonero, Baja California Sur, 23310, Mexico
Tel: (760) 438-9205 (USA), Fax: (760) 438-184 (USA)
35 Rooms, Double: $150–$250*
*Service: 10%, Tax: 12%
Open: all year, Credit cards: MC, VS
Different World
Region: Beach-Baja California

Only those who love to explore off the beaten path have probably ever heard of Real de Catorce, a once thriving silver mining town. Long forgotten, it has become slightly better known after the "The Mexican", a movie with Julia Roberts and Brad Pitt, was filmed here. The approach to the town is intriguing—a cobbled stone road winds up into Sierra Madre Mountains, ending at the Ogarrio tunnel. After traversing this 2.3-kilometer-long passage, the ghost town appears before you, nestled in a pocket of the high, desolate mountain canyon. Most of the buildings have crumbled, but there are several hotels, restaurants, shops, and the stunning church of San Francisco. Our favorite hotel is the simple but quite delightful Mesón de la Abundancia, owned by Thomas Peter and his wife, Petra Puente. Housed in an 18th-century stone mansion, the hotel exudes a rustic charm. Its attractive small restaurant serves amazingly good food. Not much English is spoken either in the restaurant or at the reception, however, the staff is accommodating and friendly. The guestrooms, each with a private bathroom with plenty of good hot water, are located up and down various staircases. All are attractive with hand-loomed fabrics and accents of Mexican artifacts. One of the nicest, number 11, is a spacious guestroom with a king-sized bed and a tiny balcony. *Directions:* Exit the tunnel and follow the one-way road. The hotel is on your right, between El Jardín and the church.

MESÓN DE LA ABUNDANCIA
Owners: Petra Puente & Thomas Peter
Calle Lanzagorta 11
Real de Catorce, San Luis Potosi, 78550, Mexico
Tel: (488) 887-5044, Fax: (488) 887-5045
12 Rooms, Double: $85–$120
Open: all year, Credit cards: all major
Region: Central–Colonial Town

You will instantly fall in love with Casa Felipe Flores—a jewel that oozes old world Mexican charm. For many years, your gracious hosts, Nancy and David Orr, used this centuries-old mansion as a second home. Upon moving nearly full time to San Cristóbal de las Casas, they purchased the house next door as a personal residence and converted their original home into an outstanding bed & breakfast. This romantic inn, with white-washed exterior accented by wrought-iron sconces and thick terracotta roof, is ideally located in the historic heart of town (about a eight-minute stroll to the central plaza). From the street you enter a flower-filled courtyard, off of which is a cozy dining room where guests enjoy breakfast in front of an open fireplace, a superbly decorated living room where guests are welcome to browse through the rich selection of books, and two of the five guestrooms. Steps away is another garden courtyard where two more guestrooms are located (the fifth guestroom is one floor up, accessed by a circular wrought-iron staircase). Two of the bedrooms are quite snug. The best choice is number 3, a large, extremely attractive, twin-bedded room. However, no matter which bedroom you choose, each has a cozy wood-burning fireplace, private bath, and is tastefully decorated with colonial-style furnishings, hand-loomed fabrics, and lovingly-selected Mexican artifacts. *Directions:* Located 4 blocks southeast of the plaza.

■ 🏃 @ W P 🚭

CASA FELIPE FLORES
Owners: Nancy & David Orr
Calle Dr. Felipe Flores 36
San Cristóbal de las Casas
Chiapas, 29230, Mexico
Tel & Fax: (967) 678-3996
Cell: (967) 107-7533
5 Rooms, Double: $95–$125*
*Service: 10%, Tax: 2%
Open: all year, Credit cards: none
Region: South-Colonial Town

The Casa Vieja is a well managed, very friendly, moderately sized hotel with an excellent location in the historic section of town, just a short walk to the central plaza. The exterior exudes a rustic charm with its creamy white façade, enhanced by blue trim and accented by a red-tiled gable roof. You enter into a reception area with a small lounge to the right where comfortable chairs are clustered beneath an antique wall clock. Although the original adobe brick home dates back to 1740, its layout is contemporary with exterior wooden staircases and guestrooms opening onto walkways that wrap around three garden courtyards with pastel peach-colored stucco walls laced by ivy. The restaurant, which serves very good meals, faces onto one of the prettiest of these courtyards that is highlighted by a Talavera tile fountain. A glass roof covering the courtyard allows meals to be served in the garden even on chilly days. The standard guestrooms are modestly decorated with traditional Mexican-style dark wood furniture and colorful fabrics. All of the guestrooms are reasonably priced, but without a doubt, the two suites (48 and 49) offer one of the best values in San Cristóbal. Be sure to request one of these spacious rooms— each has a king-sized bed, comfortable sitting area, Jacuzzi tub, and pretty view. The small difference in price is well worth the splurge. *Directions:* Located 4 blocks northeast of the Plaza.

HOTEL CASA VIEJA
Manager: Javier Espinosa
Calle Maria Adelina Flores 27
San Cristóbal de Las Casas
Chiapas, 29230, Mexico
Tel: (967) 678-5223, Fax: (967) 678-6386
40 Rooms, Double: $50–$85*
*Breakfast not included
Open: all year, Credit cards: MC, VS
Region: South-Colonial Town

If a larger, traditional hotel with more amenities appeals to you, the Flamboyant Español is an excellent choice (part of the Holiday Inn chain). The location is perfect—surrounded by shops and restaurants, just steps from the central plaza. Its single-story façade is painted yellow with bright blue trim. From the street, you walk through a pink foyer accented with colorful Talavera tile into a charming, arcaded courtyard with flowers, trees, fountains, and cozy sitting nooks. The restaurant stretches out into a patio, enclosed in glass to protect against chilly days, yet capture the sun and beauty of the garden. This is the oldest section of the building that dates back to the 17th century. Pathways lead from the main courtyard to two newer sections of the hotel that are cheerfully painted in rich tones of pink and yellow. Each of these has a galleried, two-level walkway supported by columns that wraps around its central courtyard. The stunning gardens throughout are one of the most outstanding features of the hotel. The gardeners must be masters since each picture-perfect garden is manicured to perfection. Flowers, trees, fountains, wrought-iron fixtures, terracotta pots, and sculptures of doves complete the enchanting scene. The guest rooms vary in size, but all are pleasantly similar in décor with colorful bedspreads and Mexican-style wooden headboards and desks. One of our favorites is room 333. *Directions:* Located 2 blocks north of the plaza.

FLAMBOYANT ESPAÑOL
Manager: José Angel Leon Reynaga
Calle Primero de Marzo 15
San Cristóbal de las Casas
Chiapas, 29220, Mexico
Tel: (967) 678-0045, Fax: (967) 678-0159
100 Rooms, Double: $90–$140*
*Breakfast not included
Open: all year, Credit cards: MC, VS
Region: South-Colonial Town

If you have a deep interest in the culture of the indigenous people of Chiapas, make a beeline for Na Bolom. For many years—before there were scarcely any hotels in San Cristóbal—Na Bolom (House of the Jaguar) is where archaeologists, researchers, writers and artists lived when in town. At that time this wasn't a hotel at all, but rather the home of two fascinating people: Frans Blom, an anthropologist who came from Denmark, and Trudy Duby, a photographer and journalist from Switzerland. They arrived independently in Chiapas in the mid-1940s, met, and fell in love. Their home became (and still is) a museum, abounding in paintings, local crafts, photographs, and an extensive collection of artifacts which they collected during their extensive travels to jungle villages and archaeological sites. Frans and Trudy are gone, but their home (now a non-profit foundation) is open to paying guests, not only anthropologists and archaeologists who still make up most of the clientele, but also to any traveler who seeks the romance and rich ambiance of this fascinating guest house. There is a Bohemian air throughout. Some of the guestrooms face onto enclosed, colonnaded courtyards, while others are in separate cottages that are tucked in amongst the trees in the parklike gardens. Dinner is a festive affair with the guests sitting at one large wooden table, enjoying a hearty, family-style meal. *Directions:* Located 9 blocks northeast of the plaza.

 @ W P ¶

NA BOLOM
Manager: Rachel James
Avenida Vicente Guerrero 33
San Cristóbal de las Casas
Chiapas, 29220, Mexico
Tel: (967) 678-1418, Fax: (967) 678-5586
11 Rooms, Double: $90–$110
5 Suites: $110–$135
Open: all year, Credit cards: MC, VS
Region: South-Colonial Town

The Parador San Juan de Dios, which opened as a hotel in 2003, is the creation of Marío Uvence Rojas, one of the directors of the Na Bolom foundation. It is located on the edge of town (about a 30-minute walk to the central plaza), but for those who like to be removed from the action, it has the advantage of a quiet, park-like setting. With cable television and direct dial phones, the parador offers some of the most deluxe accommodations in town and, as such, is one of the most expensive places to stay. Entering through the gate of the thick adobe walls that enclose the property, you come into a beautifully manicured, delightful courtyard, wrapped by low-rise, very attractive, white-washed buildings with rustic red-tile roof. One houses an attractive restaurant that looks out to a second garden where tables are set for dining when the weather is warm. There are two large apartments furnished with antiques. These apartments have a kitchen and a bedroom accessed by a circular staircase. The remaining accommodations do not have kitchens but have a separate sitting area (mostly with built–in concrete furniture) and an adjoining, quite small, bedroom. Original artwork and colorful, hand-loomed fabrics on the cushions and bedspreads add to the decor. One of the most outstanding attributes of the hotel is your sweet, exceptionally gracious hostess, "Gina", the owner's lovely daughter. *Directions:* Located on the edge of town, northeast of the plaza.

PARADOR SAN JUAN DE DIOS
Owner: Mario Uvence Rojas
Calzada Roberta no. 16
San Cristóbal de Las Casas
Chiapas, 29229, Mexico
Tel: (967) 678-1167
11 Rooms, Double: $140–$480*
*Breakfast not included, Add 15% if paying by credit card
Open: all year, Credit cards: all major
Region: South-Colonial Town

If you are looking for a posh resort with all the amenities, don't read any further. But if you are young at heart, have a passion for the wonders of nature, long to see huge whales up close (maybe even kiss one), and don't mind roughing it, then Campo Cortez affords an unforgettable experience. If you go to see the whales at San Ignacio Lagoon, your only choice of accommodation is at a tent camp, of which Campo Cortez is one of about four. You'll find no telephones, running water, electricity, or comfy beds with fine linens. All accommodations are basic. To add to the experience, unless you fly in on a charter or your own plane, the access is formidable—a two-hour drive along a gravel, wash-board-like, bumpy road. But you will quickly forget all of this when the first mother whale pops her head up beside the boat and introduces you to her baby. All meals (simple but hearty and good), beverages, two whale watching trips a day, kayaking, and nature walks are included in the price. Because the camp is small and everyone eats family style, a house party atmosphere prevails and usually everyone quickly becomes friends. Campo Cortez is owned by Johnny Friday and Maldo Fischer. Johnny was filming in San Ignacio in 1989 when he first met Maldo, a local fisherman and whale–watching guide. They became fast friends and started Campo Cortez to share the wonders of this lagoon with others. *Directions:* Directions will be provided when you reserve.

CAMPO CORTEZ
Owners: Marie Dalcourt & Johnny Friday
San Ignacio Lagoon, Baja California Sur,
23930, Mexico
Tel: (760) 721-8433 (USA), Fax: (866) 352-8838 (USA)
15 tents, Double: $370*
*Tax: 10%
Minimum Stay Required: 2 nights
*Includes all meals & 2 whale watches daily
Open: late-Dec to mid-Apr, Credit cards: none
Region: Whale Watching-Baja California

As is typical of many buildings in Colonial Mexican towns, an inconspicuous door leads directly from the street into the building. However, once you step inside a totally different world awaits you: the romance of Old Mexico with lush gardens, arcaded walkways, patios, fountains, and cozy shaded nooks. Casa Luna Quebrada is the second B&B in San Miguel de Allende that the clever American-born owner, Dianne Kushner, has created. Her original property, named Casa Luna Pila Seca, is located just two blocks away. Both 18th-century restored mansions exude a happy, relaxed, colorful personality and are decorated with a whimsical Mexican charm. Because it is newer and smaller, the sister property, located on Quebrada Street, is our choice. Each of the twelve guestrooms is decorated in a theme to match its name (such as Tree Tops and Sunset Room) and each has a fireplace and two beds that can be used as twins or converted into one king-sized bed. The mansion abounds with antiques and has thick adobe walls, many of which are painted with richly-hued colors. Beam ceilings, hand-loomed fabrics, carved chests, pretty mirrors, and fanciful Mexican artifacts displayed throughout add to the cozy ambiance. However, it is the staff that makes Casa Luna exceptionally outstanding. Guests rave about the personal attention they receive here. *Directions:* Located 4 blocks west of the main square, between Calle Umaran and Pila Seca streets.

CASA LUNA QUEBRADA
Owner: Dianne Kushner
Quebrada #117
San Miguel de Allende, Guanajuato, 37700, Mexico
Tel: (210) 200-8758 (USA) or (415) 154-4059
Fax: (415) 152-1117
10 Rooms, Double: $140–$160
2 Suites: $166–$176
Open: all year, Credit cards: none
Region: Central–Colonial Town

If you are looking for an impeccably kept bed and breakfast with romantic charm, lovely gardens, gorgeous swimming pool, unbeatable location, and warmth of welcome, you will find nowhere better than the Casa Schuck Boutique B&B. It is truly a jewel, with amazingly low rates for such quality. Like so many beautiful old colonial homes, the exterior gives little hint of the beauty inside, but behind the thick front door you discover a charming, flower-filled garden courtyard whose lower terrace accesses some of the guestrooms and a dining room. If you are staying for a while, I recommend requesting one of the upstairs suites, which are exceptionally spacious, some with large balconies, others a terrace, and definitely a bargain. All the rooms face the courtyard and have high beamed ceilings and working fireplaces. My favorite is the suite just above the swimming pool. Speaking of swimming pools, this one is really a dream: cozily tucked into an old stone wall and bounded on one side by a carved balustrade, it is enhanced by masses of potted geraniums, has a dear statue of Mary and baby Jesus, and, to top it off, is guarded by a friendly lion sculpture. The Casa Schuck is a rare find for those looking for charm, quality, and location. *Directions:* Located 4 blocks southeast of El Jardín (the main plaza). There is an excellent map on their website.

CASA SCHUCK BOUTIQUE B&B
Owner: Susan Cordelli
Garita 3-Centro
San Miguel de Allende, Guanajuato, 37700, Mexico
Tel: (415) 152-0657, Cell: (937) 684-4092 (USA)
10 Rooms, Double: $169–$249
Add 5% fee if paying by credit card
Open: all year, Credit cards: MC, VS
Region: Central–Colonial Town

Tucked in the hills above San Miguel de Allende, La Puertecita has an air of seclusion yet is within walking distance of town (though you might want to take a cab for your return uphill). La Puertecita is a contemporary stucco-and-stone building accented by a series of arches that form a canopy stretching over the parking area. You can see from the outside that everything is meticulously kept, but it is not until you walk down the steps into the hotel that its lush beauty is revealed. The property slopes gently down a wooded hillside, accented by terraces and lovely gardens. The especially attractive restaurant not only serves fabulous cuisine, but is perfectly positioned to take the ultimate advantage of this beautiful landscape. One of the two swimming pools is near the restaurant on a terrace surrounded by gardens. The accommodations are found in various buildings, some in condominium apartments, which offer more space, including kitchenettes. However, my favorite by far is a romantic little cottage tucked away all by itself. It looks like a fairy-tale house with its white-stuccoed façade laced with ivy and climbing roses, a red-tiled overhang above the entrance, a carved wooden door, a whimsical circular window, and even its own little birdbath. Inside, the décor is most attractive, with a terracotta floor, handsome carved headboard, rustic wood furniture, and hand-loomed fabrics. *Directions:* Ask for driving instructions.

LA PUERTECITA
General Manager: Donato Ortega
Santo Domingo 75
San Miguel de Allende, Guanajuato, 37740, Mexico
Tel: (415) 152-5011, Fax: (415) 152-5505
32 Rooms, Double: $250–$500*
*Breakfast not included
*Tax: 17%
Open: all year, Credit cards: AX, MC, VS
Region: Central–Colonial Town

Villa Rivera, wonderfully located for exploring the streets and central plaza of San Miguel de Allende, is situated just a block from the town's famous Arcángel Church and surrounded by shops, boutiques, and great restaurants. This intimate, well-run hotel, blending contemporary elements and rustic furnishings, was previously a private residence and reflects the homey ambiance of its heritage with just 12 guestrooms. The heart of the inn is a perched garden terrace highlighted by beds of well-tended flowers, mature shade trees, and a delightful swimming pool. This terrace is snuggled into the walls that back up to the Arcángel Church and captures fabulous views of the town and church towers. Facing onto this appealing garden is a charming restaurant serving a fusion of Italian and Mexican cuisine. The guestrooms on the upper floor of the hotel give splendid views of the church and town, while the other bedrooms are well situated next to the pool and garden. Most rooms have a fireplace. The owners have lovingly decorated each room in a personal style with a liberal use of local handicrafts. San Miguel de Allende, registered as a national monument, has been superbly preserved as the thriving silver town it once was. It is one of Mexico's loveliest colonial cities, with its old mansions and flower-filled patios making strolling along the winding cobblestone streets a delightful activity in itself. *Directions:* One block from the main square.

VILLA RIVERA
Owner: Jesús Manuel Calvo
Cuadrante 3
San Miguel de Allende, Guanajuato, 37700, Mexico
Tel: (415) 152-0742, Fax: (415) 152-2601
12 Rooms, Double: $180–$242*
*Breakfast not included: $10
*Tax: 17%
Open: all year, Credit cards: all major
Region: Central–Colonial Town

Founded in 1605, San Sebastián del Oeste is an extremely picturesque village tucked high in the mountains with narrow cobblestone streets lined by white adobe houses with rustic red-tiled roofs. This remote, long-forgotten hamlet was once the most important silver and gold mining town in the state of Jalisco. It is accessible by charter flight from Puerto Vallarta or a very difficult 2½-hour drive along a gravel, one-way, twisting road (impossible to drive in the rainy season). However, for those who love the adventure of getting off the beaten path and discovering a tiny village untouched by time, this one is a jewel. Surprisingly (considering San Sebastián del Oeste's seclusion) there is an appealing, reasonably priced place to stay here—Hotel El Pabellon Mexicano, a white, one-story structure with tile roof, facing the central plaza. Originally this was a "counting house" where the miners brought their gold and silver. The simple, tastefully decorated guestrooms are built around a central garden courtyard. All have beamed ceilings, terracotta floors, bathrooms with Talavera tiles, and beds topped by hand-loomed spreads. Our three favorite guestrooms (Membrillo, Tejocote, and Ciruela) have the added bonus of shuttered French windows that face the plaza. A charming rustic ambiance prevails throughout, with Mexican artifacts and leather chairs brightened by gaily colored throw pillows. *Directions:* Located 64 km northeast of Puerto Vallarta.

HOTEL EL PABELLON MEXICANO
Lopez Mateo #1
San Sebastián del Oeste, Jalisco, 46990, Mexico
Tel: (322) 297-0200
11 Rooms, Double: $40–$55
No English spoken
Open: all year, Credit cards: none
Region: Inland–Pacific Coast

Of all the alluring haciendas in the Yucatán, the Hacienda Santa Rosa is perhaps the prettiest—an appealing 17th-century building, delightfully decorated in blues, reds, and ochres. The first thing you see as you drive up is the owner's mansion, enhanced at the front by a long row of arches, which form a romantic veranda. On arrival, you are cordially welcomed with a glass of fresh juice and a refreshing cold towel. As you step inside, years seem to slip away—the antique furnishings re-create to perfection the ambiance of a wealthy plantation owner's home. The luxurious guestrooms, in various buildings around the property, live up to all expectations: each has its own personality, but all have tremendous charm. The suites have individual plunge pools adorned with floating flower petals. The most unusual accommodation is a Mayan-style, thatched-roof cottage where the king-sized bed is suspended from the ceiling like a hammock. The lovely young girls in native costume who care for the rooms create incredible designs with the flowers that adorn the robes, the towels, the bed linens, the baskets of shampoos and lotions, the bathmats, the dishes—everything is magic. The food is delicious and dining a special treat in an open-air porch with the jungle almost at your fingertips. *Directions:* 70 km from Mérida airport. Because maps are inaccurate we suggest you arrange a transfer from the airport. Otherwise, ask for detailed driving instructions.

❄ ⚓ 💳 ☎ Υ P ⑪ 🌿 ≋ 🐎

HACIENDA SANTA ROSA
Manager: Szilvia Ori
Mérida, Santa Rosa, Yucatán, 97800, Mexico
Tel: (999) 923-8089, Fax: (999) 923-7963
11 Rooms, Double: $302–$572*
*Breakfast not included: $15
*Service: 5%, Tax: 17%
Open: all year, Credit cards: all major
Different World
Region: Yucatán Peninsula-Archaeological Area

La Casa de Maty is a charming hotel in Tapalpa, a picturesque village perched 1,950 meters-above sea on a plateau surrounded by pine-clad forests. Many tourists have never heard of Tapalpa, yet it is well known to Mexicans who arrive in droves on weekends to enjoy its tranquil beauty and breathe its crystal clear cool mountain air. If you would like to discover a truly unspoiled 17th-century village imbued with the flavor of old Mexico, Tapalpa will delight you. An appealing place to stay is La Casa de Maty. It has a perfect location on the street that runs just below the church. An extra advantage to staying here is that the church spires mark your way as you drive into town. The hotel is immediately appealing: a white-washed, two-story building facing right onto the street with rustic red tiled roof, wood shuttered windows, and wrought iron embellishments. You step inside to the reception area. Just beyond is a captivating courtyard with a centuries-old adobe brick tower and a garden highlighted by a stone fountain. The guestrooms seem to be more recently built than the main part of the hotel, but they maintain the same traditional rustic architectural style with terra cotta floors, adobe walls, beamed ceilings, local pine furniture, and cozy, wood burning fireplaces which are welcome on chilly nights. *Directions:* Tapalpa is located 140 km south of Guadalajara in the Sierra Madre Mountains.

LA CASA DE MATY   **New**
Manager: Salvador Hernandez
Matamoros 69, Col. Centro
Tapalpa, Jalisco, 49340, Mexico
Tel: (343) 432-0189
Toll Free: (800) 223-7627, Fax: none
14 Rooms, Double: $80–$100*
*Breakfast not included
Open: all year, Credit cards: MC, VS
Region: Central–Colonial Town

We have explored the quaint cobbled streets in Taxco many times looking for a charming small boutique hotel. Since Taxco is so picturesque and is a favorite destination for travelers, we have broadened our spectrum and suggest the Hotel Agua Escondida. Its setting cannot be surpassed—right in the heart of colorful Taxco, facing directly onto the main square with all the silver shops and sightseeing attractions within walking distance. The exterior of the hotel reflects its 18th-century heritage with white-washed thick adobe walls, stone portals, and a typical Mexican red-tiled roof. Because this historic building spreads up a hill and dates back many centuries, the guestrooms vary in size and are located on many levels that are accessed through a maze of hallways. Request one of the larger guestrooms with a good-sized bathroom, everything seems to be priced the same. The décor, although simple, reflects the hotel's Colonial heritage with terracotta floors, wrought iron fixtures, colorful hand-woven fabrics, and carved wood furnishings. Meals are served in the Hacienda Restaurant, but be sure also to go to the El Terraza bar on the rooftop terrace where you can enjoy a cold drink, a cup of coffee, dessert or a glass of wine along with a stunning view. There is also a swimming pool tucked up amongst the rooftops. *Directions:* Located on the northeast corner of the main square.

HOTEL AGUA ESCONDIDA
Manager: Julian Brito Cuevas
Plaza Borda No.4
Taxco, Guerrero, 40200, Mexico
Tel: (762) 622-1166 or (762) 622-0726
Fax: (762) 622-1306
30 Rooms, Double: $83–$97*
2 Suites: $95–$108*
2 Cottages: $117-$163*
*Breakfast not included: $5
Open: all year, Credit cards: all major
Different World
Region: Central–Colonial Town

The 17th-century Hacienda Temozón is a superb hotel with the warmth and charm of a private home, which is exactly what it once was. Not only is it convenient to the Mérida airport (about a 45-minute drive), but it also makes an excellent hub for exploring some of the Yucatán's most popular archaeological sites. Using the Hacienda Temozón as your home base, you can visit off-the-beaten-path Mayan ruins, convents, stunning old haciendas, and breathtaking cathedrals—the possibilities are endless. The hacienda has been renovated with meticulous care and love, maintaining its marvelous features such as soaring ceilings, wood beams, thick walls, sweeping verandahs, lovely tiles, and arched windows. However, all the creature comforts have been added: air conditioning, direct-dial phones, mini-bars, the finest linens, excellent mattresses, beautiful decor, and wonderful bathrooms. Many of the guestrooms have an individual plunge pool, and the Presidential Suite even has a private swimming pool. In addition, there is a huge, 48-meter pool with a swim-up bar. A floodlit tennis court is tucked into the estate's old stockyard and, for joggers, a path leads through the hacienda's 37-hectare garden. The Hacienda Temozón has more guestrooms than its "sister" hacienda-hotels, but it maintains the same intimacy, charm, and incredible service. *Directions:* 35 km south of Mérida. Ask for directions when making reservations.

HACIENDA TEMOZÓN
Manager: Herman Reeling Brouwer
Km 182, Carretera , Mérida-Uxmal
Temozón, Yucatán, 97825, Mexico
Tel: (999) 923-8089, Fax: (999) 923-7963
28 Rooms, Double: $302–$667*
*Breakfast not included: $15
*Service: 5%, Tax: 17%
Open: all year, Credit cards: all major
Different World
Region: Yucatán Peninsula-Archaeological Area

A visit to Teotihuacán (in its prime one of the largest cities in the world, surpassing even Rome) makes a splendid introduction to the ancient history of Mexico. You can see the site as a day trip from Mexico City. However, the best way to explore Teotihuacán is to spend the night at the Villa Arqueológica Teotihuacán, an attractive, low rise, hacienda-style hotel located within easy walking distance of the ruins. By mid-morning, hoards of tourists begin to arrive, but if you are staying nearby, you can have an early breakfast and be at the gates when the archaeological site opens at 8 am and roam the ruins in blissful solitude. Villa Arqueológica Teotihuacán is an appealing, efficiently run hotel with a friendly staff. You enter into a courtyard with handsome stone fountains, wrought-iron lamps, arched doorways, potted plants, and benches ornamented with colorful Talavera tiles. The guestrooms wrap around a second garden courtyard highlighted by an especially pretty swimming pool. The modest-sized guestrooms are nicely decorated in a Mexican motif with rustic, wooden furniture. When the weather cooperates, meals are served on the terrace overlooking the swimming pool. At other times, guests dine in a very pleasant restaurant where a beamed ceiling, tiled floor, and colorful paintings and ceramics decorating the walls create a welcoming ambiance. *Directions:* On the cobblestone access road to the ruins, near Gate 1.

VILLA ARQUEOLÓGICA TEOTIHUACÁN
Manager: Guy Charles Faure
San Juan Teotihuacán
Teotihuacán, Mexico, 55800, Mexico
Tel: (555) 836-9020, Fax: (594) 956-0244
39 Rooms, Double: $87–$100*
*Breakfast not included
*Service: 15%
Open: all year, Credit cards: MC, VS
Region: Central–Archaeological Site

The intimate Hacienda San José exudes charm and offers incredible service. What a surprise to find luxurious accommodations so far off the beaten path. Although, as you drive to the hotel it seems very remote (near Tixkokob, the hammock capital of the Yucatán), this is actually a great location for visiting the colonial city of Mérida and taking trips to see the many rich archaeological sites nearby. However, you might not want to stray from this alluring, utterly romantic property. The rooms all exude a quiet elegance and are appropriately decorated with simple furnishings of the very highest quality. Many of the bedrooms have a private plunge pool, but in addition there is a dramatic, large swimming pool with a very special bottom coating that makes the water shimmer like the sea. When restoration began on this abandoned sisal property, the hacienda was no more than a shell; but lots of money and, more importantly, impeccable taste have transformed it into a dream of a small hotel, while avoiding over renovation. Although offering the ultimate in luxury, the colorful old hacienda and its surrounding buildings still ring true to their romantic origins. As you dine exquisitely on the terrace with large arches opening to the gardens, you feel as pampered as the owners of this wealthy sisal plantation must have felt so long ago. *Directions:* About 45 minutes east of Mérida. Ask the hotel for detailed instructions.

❄ ✧ 🖃 ☎ Ⴘ P ⊩ ✿ ≈ 🐎

HACIENDA SAN JOSÉ
Manager: Veronique Timsonet
Mérida, Tixkokob, Yucatan, 97470, Mexico
Tel: (999) 910-4617, Fax: (999) 923-7963
15 Rooms, Double: $302–$730*
*Breakfast not included: $15
*Service: 5%, Tax: 17%
Open: all year, Credit cards: all major
Different World
Region: Yucatán Peninsula-Archaeological Area

Perhaps you have never heard of Tlaxcala—it isn't well known as a tourist destination; but you should put it on your priority list of places to see. If you like colonial towns, you will be instantly captivated: Tlaxcala is a real jewel. Happily, it also has an excellent hotel, the Posada San Francisco, which exudes great old-world ambiance and charm. Its location is perfect, facing onto the gorgeous Plaza de la Constitución, one of the most beautiful in all of Mexico, and, in keeping with the other architectural masterpieces that line the square, the oldest sections of the Posada San Francisco date back to the 16th century. It is a two-story, handsome stone building with arched windows and doorway. Whereas the exterior has a somber appeal, as soon as you enter into the large lobby, formerly an interior courtyard, the mood changes to a joyous one with bright-yellow walls, a terracotta floor, a fountain, bouquets of flowers, and sun streaming in through a ceiling of stained glass. An arched passage leads to an inviting restaurant with dark-green wicker tables and chairs, bright-yellow table linens, yellow walls, and a skylight for its ceiling. (Another restaurant upstairs overlooks the plaza.) As you continue on, you come to a garden courtyard and a large swimming pool, around which you find most of the guestrooms. Rooms on the first floor have French doors opening to the pool area and those on the second floor have balconies. *Directions:* Facing the main square.

POSADA SAN FRANCISCO
Manager: Minerva Flores Mendez
Plaza de la Constitución 17
Tlaxcala, Tlaxcala, 90000, Mexico
Tel: (246) 462-6022, Fax: (246) 462-6818
68 Rooms, Double: $110–$145*
*Breakfast not included
Open: all year, Credit cards: all major
Region: Central–Colonial Town

Libusche and Juerg Wiesendanger left successful careers in Zurich and moved to Mexico with the goal of creating a small, deluxe inn offering fine food and accommodations. They built their dream a ten-minute drive from the quaint town of Todos Santos, taking great care not to disturb the natural beauty of the pristine freshwater lagoon and untouched nature they found. The restaurant, headed by a top-notch chef, serves a creative blend of Mexican and Swiss cuisine in an attractive dining room with potted plants, a whimsically painted fireplace, windows capturing a view of the sea. Most guests perfer to dine outside either on the bar terrace looking out to the cacti and palm trees or on the whale deck overlooking the tropical gardens, lagoon and the Pacific ocean with its magnificent sunsets. Seven guestrooms, located in two adjacent buildings, are all beautifully appointed and have excellent bathrooms. The décor takes advantage of the beautiful Mexican fabrics but the fine linens and pillows were brought from Switzerland. The Honeymoon Suite has a large private terrace and cozy patio with hot tub for two. The two junior suites each offer a romantic outdoor Jacuzzi. All rooms have air conditioning, CD players, refrigerators, and even binoculars—but no TVs or telephone. Guests enjoy a large salt-water swimming pool and birdwatchers in particular delight in the estuary, which is a natural sanctuary. *Directions:* Ask for directions.

※ ▄▇ 'Ϋ@W Ⴤ P ¶ Ⓢ ❀ ≋ ⟆ ⊥ ⵓ ⵚ ⵞ

POSADA LA POZA
Owners: Libusche & Juerg Wiesendanger
Todos Santos, Baja California Sur, 23305, Mexico
Tel: (612) 145-0400, Fax: (612) 145-0461
4 Rooms, Double: $195–$240*
4 Suites: $275–$480*
*Service: 4%, Tax: 13%
Minimum Stay Required: 2 nights
Open: all year, Credit cards: MC, VS
Region: Beach-Baja California

When you arrive at the Todos Santos Inn, you will be warmly greeted by your gracious host, John Stoltzfus. During a weekend trip to southern Baja, John was introduced to Todos Santos, a tiny, low-key village in Mexico with old-world character, lovely weather, art galleries, great restaurants, colorful boutiques, low-cost real estate, and a beach nearby. He was drawn immediately to the town; so much that he left the hustle and bustle of Los Angeles, purchased the Todos Santos Inn and moved in just four months later. The building was originally a 19th-century hacienda built in the middle of town and the former owner had transformed the derelict, but once-grand, old brick home into a charming small inn. The two standard guestrooms are in the original part of the house, while the other six are air-conditioned garden suites located in two buildings built with such skill that you would never know they were new. All of the spacious rooms exude great taste with terracotta floors, beamed ceilings, hand-carved furniture, heavy French doors, Oriental rugs, antique prints on the walls, great bathrooms accented with Talavera tiles, and very comfortable beds. New additions include a heated swimming pool (exclusively for guests), and the La Copa Bar & Resturant nestled in the lush tropical gardens (enjoyed by guests and locals). Breakfast is included. *Directions:* Three blocks off the main square.

TODOS SANTOS INN
Managers: John Stoltzfus & Todd Schaefer
Calle Legaspi #33
Todos Santos, Baja California Sur, 23305, Mexico
Tel & Fax: (612) 145-0040
8 Rooms, Double: $125–$225*
*Tax: 12%
Open: all year, Credit cards: MC, VS
Different World
Region: Beach-Baja California

If you yearn for a thatched hut facing an idyllic white-sand beach studded with coconut palms, the Cabañas La Conchita is your dream come true. However, this bit of paradise is not for everyone: you must be young at heart and have a bit of a bohemian spirit since the guestrooms have no phones, no air conditioning (ceiling fans in 6 rooms), and the lights (which are generated from a solar panel) come on only briefly for a couple of hours in the evening. The flip side is that when you arrive at the Cabañas La Conchita, you leave the real world far behind and fall into a routine of pure bliss, doing nothing more than reading a good book, napping under the palapa on the beach, swimming in the crystal-clear turquoise water, and enjoying evenings by candlelight. This tiny, romantic hotel is owned by Cynthia James and Jorgé Rosales, who originally intended it to be their vacation hideaway; but people kept begging to rent space on their beach, so the idea of a proper inn just evolved. Gifted local craftsmen built the beautiful thatched-roofed cottages. The simple guestrooms exude the perfect blend of comfort, style, and simplicity—thanks to Cynthia's artist's eye for color and fabrics. All the cottages are steps from the sea, but the prize is number 1, right on the beach. *Directions:* Just south of Tulum archaeological site. At the junction to Cobá, turn left to the beach and at the end of the road turn right. The hotel is 1 km down on the left.

🖥️ 🏄 P ⅋ 🏛 👫 🐴 ⚓

CABAÑAS LA CONCHITA
Owners: Cynthia James & Jorgé Rosales
5 Km, Carretera Tulum-Boca Paila
Tulum–Riviera Maya, Quintana Roo, 77780, Mexico
Tel: (888) 903-9512, Fax: (984) 871-2092
8 Rooms, Double: $140–$200*
*Includes breakfast & all taxes
Open: all year, Credit cards: none
Different World
Region: Beach-Caribbean Coast–Riviera Maya

The Haciendia Uayamón offers outstanding charm and ultimate luxury. This sumptuous hacienda has a wide, sweeping staircase leading up to a romantic veranda framed by high, open arches. Doors lead into several intimate parlors decorated with antiques, beyond which you find an enchanting dining room with large windows looking out to trees and a decorative round pond. Pathways lead from the main house through the jungle-like estate to the suites tucked about the property in brightly hued cottages. These at first appear to be basic, but looks deceive; inside, you find tasteful, appropriately simple furnishings of the finest quality. Excellent decor and quality can be found in many hotels but it is all the extra loving details that raise this hacienda to a whole new level of splendor—particularly the flowers, which decorate everything, from the bathroom toiletries, which are lavished with miniature flower designs, to the bathrobes, towels, and sheets. The bed linens appear to have delicate floral embroidery, but in fact these are fresh flowers. Other luxurious touches include an enormous, outdoor, king-sized sofa and a romantic plunge pool sprinkled with fragrant petals. There is also a gorgeous swimming pool tucked into the crumbling ruins of the old machine house. The best surprise of all comes with nightfall when all the paths are lined with what seem to be thousands of candles. Pure magic! *Directions:* Ask for detailed driving instructions.

❄ 🏊 💳 ☎ P ⫪ ≈

HACIENDA UAYAMÓN
Manager: Claudia Raymondi
Km 20, Carretera Campeche
Uayamón, Campeche, 24530, Mexico
Tel: (981) 819-0335, Fax: (999) 923-7963
12 Rooms, Double: $302–$509*
*Breakfast not included
*Service: 5%, Tax: 17%
Open: all year, Credit cards: all major
Different World
Region: Yucatán Peninsula-Archaeological Area

Uruapan is well known as the avocado capital of the world, but the congested downtown area is not too pretty and lacks any historical ambiance. However, the pine-covered hills surrounding Uruapan are lovely and on the outskirts of town is a real prize—the 1315-acre Eduardo Ruiz Parque Nacional, a wooded natural preserve with countless sparkling clear springs that form the source of the Cupatitzio River. The Hotel Mansión has a prime setting just on the edge of the park, capturing views of it from the large windows of the charming dining room. The architecture of the mansion mimics the colonial style and has a charming rustic appeal. Mexican handicrafts and regional artwork decorate the walls and are used throughout in the furnishings. The bedrooms are spacious, bright, and cheerful, with large windows looking out to the garden, and all have fine, very attractive, dark-wood furniture hand-painted with birds and other popular native motifs. All the rooms have satellite TVs, telephones, safes, hairdryers, and radios. The hotel, which wraps around a splendid central garden highlighted by a very large swimming pool, is justifiably famous for its gardens, which are outstanding—no matter what the season, you find gorgeous beds of flowers and hanging plants everywhere. The flower theme continues throughout the hotel with fresh flowers in all the rooms. *Directions:* On the northwest edge of town, next to the Parque Nacional.

HOTEL MANSIÓN DEL CUPATITZIO
Owner: Judith Ochoa De Monroy
Calz. de la Rodilla del Diablo No 20
Uruapan, Michoacán, 60030, Mexico
Tel: (452) 523-2060, Fax: (452) 524-6772
53 Rooms, Double: $130–$190*
4 Suites: $210–$400*
*Breakfast not included: $11
*Tax: 17%
Open: all year, Credit cards: all major
Region: Central–Colonial City

The Lodge at Uxmal is blessed with an unsurpassable location, just across from the archaeological site. However, location is not all this hotel has to offer; it's a real charmer in every way. Your introduction begins when the receptionist, dressed in colorful Mayan costume, welcomes you in an open-air, thatched-roof palapa. The Mayan theme continues in the cluster of five two-story, brightly colored, thatched-roof buildings that house the guestrooms. All of the accommodations are appointed with materials of the finest quality throughout. The woodwork is especially remarkable—highly polished hardwood floors, beautiful cabinetry, and handsome louvered plantation shutters. My favorite rooms are the corner units and my favorite buildings are those overlooking the lakelike swimming pool (there is a second pool located near the restaurant). Because of its strategic location so close to the ruins, the Lodge is naturally a target for busloads of tourists who come to eat lunch in its open-air restaurant. This is really no problem, since if you have a room overlooking the pool, you are ensured tranquility. In addition to being such a lovely small hotel, the Lodge has another super advantage: you can visit Uxmal first thing in the morning before the buses arrive then return to the hotel in the heat of the day to relax by the comfort of the pool. *Directions:* The inn is directly across from the entrance to the ruins.

❄ 💻 🛎 💳 ☎ @ W Ÿ P ⫩ ≈ 🖼 ⚲

THE LODGE AT UXMAL
Manager: Mr. Luis Maldonado
Archaeological Park
Uxmal, Yucatán, 97844, Mexico
Tel: (998) 884-4512, Fax: (998) 884-4510
30 Rooms, Double: $250–$394*
10 Suites: $290–$490*
*Tax: 17%
Open: all year, Credit cards: all major
Region: Yucatán Peninsula-Archaeological Area

For those who want to delve in depth into the rich history of the Spanish conquest of Mexico, then Veracruz, which still exhibits its Spanish heritage, is a key city to visit. It was here that Cortés landed in 1519 and, after burning his ships to discourage his soldiers from trying to return home, made his first settlement in the New World. The best place to stay in town is the Fiesta Inn, which opened in 2001, a modern, four-story hotel whose architecture conveys a vague Spanish feel with its stucco walls, red-tiled roof, and balconies. Inside, the hotel exudes a quiet, soothing, contemporary ambiance with cream-colored marble floors, indirect lighting, tasteful furnishings, and fabrics in tones of creams and rusts. You enter into a spacious lobby with a restaurant to the right offering a choice of quick buffet-style meals or à-la-carte menu selections. The hotel caters both to businessmen with its business center and conference facilities, and to families with its beautiful large swimming pool and children's playroom. Even though the Fiesta's amenities are first-rate, its finest attribute is its setting. Not only are you just steps from most of the major sights in town, but you are also right on the promenade that runs along the waterfront—a prime location that offers splendid views from many of the bedrooms (be sure to ask for a room with a balcony that looks out to the harbor, such as 426, 428, or 430). *Directions:* In the historic center, next to the bay.

FIESTA INN
Manager: Solange Coral
General Figueroa 68, Paseo del Malecón
Veracruz, Veracruz, 91709, Mexico
Tel: (229) 923-1500, Fax: (229) 923-1509
90 Rooms, Double: $155–$225*
*Breakfast not included: $11
Open: all year, Credit cards: all major
Region: Southeast–Colonial Town

Most tourists who are attracted to Villahermosa have a very special interest in archaeology, since it is conveniently close to the extraordinary archaeological site of Palenque and has two excellent archaeological museums. One of these, Parque Museo de la Venta, is located within a pretty park that also has an outdoor museum displaying colossal Olmec stone carved heads. This is one of the prettiest parts of Villahermosa and, happily, the most charming hotel in town, the Hotel Cencali, is nearby. Although of contemporary construction, the hotel uses a brilliant Mayan color scheme and in the lobby huge, bold murals of Indian mythology cover the walls, surrounding an intimate sitting area. Steps lead down to a lower level where you find the dining room, La Isla, its walls of glass looking out to a particularly delightful swimming pool in a lush, jungle-like setting, with mango, cocoa, and palm trees stretching to the edge of Las Ilusiones Lagoon. (This is the same lagoon that meanders through the park where you find the Olmec carved heads.) All of the attractive guestrooms are spacious and similar in décor, with built-in headboards, color-coordinating drapes and bedspreads, good lighting, and comfortable beds. By far the most attractively located bedrooms are those in the back with a balcony overlooking the lagoon (such as rooms 229, 231, 233, 235, 237). Be sure to ask for one of these. *Directions:* Facing the lagoon near Parque Museo de la Venta.

❄ ☕ 🛵 💳 ☎ P ∥ 🏊

HOTEL CENCALI
Manager: Jorge Bacha Padilla
Juárez #105 Col. Lindavista
Villahermosa, Tabasco, 86040, Mexico
Tel: (993) 315-1999, Fax: (993) 315-6600
160 Rooms, Double: $100–$112*
*Tax: 17%
Open: all year, Credit cards: all major
Region: Southeast–Archaeological Area

If you don't care about luxury hotel amenities and the idea of a tiny, very simple hotel overlooking one of the world's most exquisite beaches sounds appealing, you will fall in love with Al Cielo. It is a miracle that along the famed Riviera Maya, where ocean-front land is so precious with large, luxury hotels dominating the scene, that such a jewel as Al Cielo could possibly exist. The hotel, right on the beach only steps from the turquoise sea, consists of four guestrooms within two cream-colored buildings that are joined by a porch with a rough-hewn log railing. Each house has one moderately sized guestroom on each of two levels. The interiors reflect rustic appeal with dark, polished wood walls and floors in the bedrooms and bathrooms. The wood is complimented by white mosquito netting gracefully draping the comfortable beds and by filmy, white curtains accenting the louvered windows. There is no air conditioning, but gentle sea breezes cool the room naturally. A romantic "Robinson Crusoe" mood prevails. Shoes seem totally inappropriate with bare feet the more desirable mode. The white, sugary soft sand beach in front of the hotel is one of the world's finest. Dotting the beach are the hotel's own adorable little palapas, accented by colorful gauze curtains. You never need to roam from this paradise— Al Cielo has its own open-air restaurant right on the beach. *Directions:* Ask for detailed directions when making reservations—it's a bit tricky to find.

AL CIELO
Owner: Andres Olavarrieta
118 Km Carretera Cancún (near Playa del Carmen)
Xpuha Beach–Riviera Maya, 77710, Mexico
Tel: (984) 840-9012
4 Rooms, Double: $190–$350
Minimum Stay Required: 3
Open: all year, Credit cards: none
Different World
Region: Beach-Caribbean Coast–Riviera Maya

Until the Chicanná Ecovillage opened in 1995, there weren't any good accommodations near the newly accessible, fascinating archaeological treasures of Río Bec. In fact, the roads in this remote area were so bad that one had to be truly motivated to dare to make the trip. All that has changed. The roads are good and a few more hotels are coming on the scene, but none can surpass the central location of the Chicanná Ecovillage. The developers indeed displayed great foresight in putting such excellent accommodations in an area where there was no tourism and is even now almost unknown. This is not a deluxe, trendy resort; nor is it meant to be. Instead, what you find is a pleasingly casual complex of pastel-hued, thatched cottages tucked in a jungle-like setting. Some of the cottages are one-story with two guestrooms, others are two-story with four guestrooms. There is no air conditioning, just ceiling fans, and rooms on the upper level have more of a breeze. Each spacious bedroom is nicely furnished, has a very good bathroom, comfortable beds, and its own private deck or terrace. Paths meander about the property, one of them going to a small swimming pool, which has real allure for guests after a day of sightseeing. This is a casual hotel—no need to dress up for dinner in the thatched-roofed restaurant. *Directions:* On 186, between Escárcega and Chetumal, just west of Xpujil.

CHICANNÁ ECOVILLAGE
Manager: Richardo Trueba
Km. 144, Carretera Escárcega-Chetumal
Xpujil, Campeche, 24000, Mexico
Tel: (981) 811-9191, Fax: (981) 811-1618
32 Rooms, Double: $80–$100*
*Breakfast not included
Open: all year, Credit cards: all major
Region: Beach-Caribbean Coast–Riviera Maya

Rio Bec Dreams offers simple accommodations in a convenient spot for visiting the extraordinary group of Mayan ruins that dot the Rio Bec area. Your hosts, Diane Lalonde and Richard Bertram, tired of the bitter cold winters of Canada and settled in the Yucatán in 2000. They bought 50 hectares of jungle along highway 186 and built the hotel. "Hotel" is really not the accurate term since the rooms are each in separate cottages. Four of these are called "Jungalows" and share a bathhouse with shower, toilets, and wash basin. They are tastefully furnished, but would appeal only to those on a really tight budget. We only decided to include the Rio Bec when they embarked upon a plan to add four cabanas with private bathrooms. A jungle path leads to the thatched hut cottage which has a screened-in porch, two nice-sized bedrooms, and a tiled bathroom. It is attractively furnished with native materials and handicrafts. Richard, who was a contractor in Canada, built the cottages. Diane's talents as a passionate gardener and a wonderful cook add to what makes Rio Bec Dreams special. The meals she serves in the open-air, palapa-style restaurant attract many guests who just come to dine. Diane and Richard have extensive knowledge of the Yucatan area and can help with itinerary planning and guided trips. However, if you want the amenities of a hotel, this would probably not be your spot. *Directions:* Directly on highway 186 at the 142 kilometer.

🏊 @ W P ⑪ 👫

RIO BEC DREAMS
Owners: Diane Lalonde & Richard Bertram
Carretera 186, Escarcega-Chetumal Km. 142
Xpujil,Calakmul, Campeche, 24000, Mexico
Tel: (982) 103-8794, Cell: (982) 103-8794
4 Jungalows, 3 Cabanas, price per person:$50–$85*
*Breakfast not included: $15
*Service: 10%, Tax: 15%
Open: all year, Credit cards: none
Region: Beach-Caribbean Coast–Riviera Maya

This wonderful hotel, located in the rather less-visited town of Zacatecas, may well be the most spectacular boutique hotel in all of Mexico. It was built within an old stone bullring just on the outskirts of the historic central area of this once-thriving mining town. Today the town is delightful, with narrow, winding streets lined with recently restored colonial classic buildings. The small chain of Quinta Real hotels prides itself on offering very personalized service, gourmet cuisine, and fine examples of hotel design and architecture. Each property is unique, with this impressive hotel certainly being the most extraordinary of the group. The architect was a master at combining old and new: built into the surrounding walls of the bullring are the bedrooms, the lobby, and a gourmet restaurant, all situated to take in the wonderful views of this ancient structure. Even more unique is the bar, situated on the ground level looking out over the ring, which uses what were once the bullpens for small sitting areas. Dining at any Quinta Real restaurant is always a pleasure; but the view, the setting, and, of course, the cuisine, make this dining experience truly wonderful, especially when the ring and its walls are lit up at night. The Quinta Real is so special that it definitely warrants a splurge when visiting Zacatecas. *Directions:* Located 8 blocks from the center of town, in the old bullring facing the aqueduct.

QUINTA REAL ZACATECAS
Manager: Carlos Fernandez
Av. Rayon 434
Zacatecas, Zacatecas, 98000, Mexico
Tel: (492) 922-9104, Fax: (492) 922-8440
49 Rooms, Double: $262–$855*
*Breakfast not included: $15
*Tax: 17%
Open: all year, Credit cards: all major
Different World
Region: Central–Colonial Town

Amuleto is truly a gem: a tiny romantic hotel tucked high on a densely wooded hillside at the south end of Zihuatanejo overlooking La Playa Ropa beach. Only a few thatched roofs peek out of the trees to announce its location. Although a delightfully rustic ambiance prevails with the use of local hardwoods, terracotta floors, Talavera tiles, wood beams, thatched roofs, Mexican furnishings, handcrafted fabrics, and lacey crocheted hammocks, the hotel exudes luxury and elegance. There are six beautifully decorated suites, four with their own plunge pools. The two larger suites have very private outdoor showers and one has a roof top deck where you can watch the cruise ships come into the bay and anchor. All the rooms are equipped with air conditioning, but the high palapa thatched roofs and the sea breezes cool the rooms in all but the hottest weather. Sitting just below the bar and restaurant, an infinity swimming pool, which has a breathtaking view, seems to blend seamlessly into the distance blue water of the ocean. If you are feeling energetic, a 25-minute walk downhill takes you to La Ropa beach, but you will probably want to hale a taxi for the 5-minute ride back home. Amuleto has an excellent restaurant where each year a guest-chef displays his talents. The owner, Ricardo Teitelroit, and his wife are both natives of Brazil and can often be found in the hotel. *Directions:* At the south end of Zihatanejo Bay. Ask for directions.

AMULETO
Owner: Ricardo Teitelroit
Calle Escenica # 9, Playa La Ropa
Zihuatanejo, Guerrero, 40880, Mexico
Tel: (755) 554-6200 or (213) 280-1037 (USA)
6 Rooms, Double: $350–$660*
*Tax: 17%
Open: All year, Credit cards: all major
Region: Beach–Pacific Coast

Casa Buenaventura, a contemporary white stucco building facing the road is an upscale bed and breakfast built into the hillside above Playa La Ropa—about a 5-minute walk down the road to the beach. It is not until you enter through the wrought-iron entrance and climb up the steps to the reception that the charm of the property is revealed. Mexican touches such as a red–tiled roof, Talavera plates on the walls, and polished terracotta floors add charm. There are seven bedrooms. One is located on the first level, near the swimming pool and dining room. Ascending the circular staircase, you reach six more guest rooms, all with sitting areas, full baths, and terraces with the proverbial hanging hammocks. Some bedrooms have a king-size bed; others have two double beds. The furnishings in all of them remind you of the tasteful simplicity of old Mexican-style houses. Although the rooms have ceiling fans and no air conditioning, the bay brings cool, fresh sea breezes. All rooms come equipped with a mini-bar filled with complimentary bottled water and soft drinks and have pretty views out over the rooftops to the Bay of Zihuatanejo. The blue-tiled pool on the terrace invites you for a refreshing dip and is also a good spot for watching the tropical sunsets. Breakfast is included and features fresh-squeezed juice, assorted tropical fruits, granola, yogurt, eggs, breakfast meats, and Mexican favorites. *Directions:* Located above Playa La Ropa.

CASA BUENAVENTURA
Owner: Elia Laura Rodriquez
Carretera a Playa la Ropa
Zihuatanejo, Guerrero, 40880, Mexico
Tel: (755) 554-2855, Fax: (755) 554-9377
7 Rooms, Double: $120–$235*
*Service: 10%, Tax: 17%
Lunch & dinner on request
Open: all year, Credit cards: none
Region: Beach–Pacific Coast

Located just a short walk from the beach, Casa Frida is an intimate bed & breakfast with a casual, bohemian charm, tucked away in a corner of Barra de Potosi, a tiny fishing hamlet south of Zihuatanejo. Your gracious hosts are Annabella Martinez, a Mexican actress, and her husband, François Heritier, a specialist in Mexican culture. A high wall wraps around the small, lush garden complex, which consists of two-storied, orange stucco cottages with thatched roofs. Displayed throughout are photos and memorabilia of Diego Rivera's wife, Frida, which set the theme for the inn. Annabella is exceptionally artistic and has skillfully combined brightly painted wooden furniture, cheerful hand-loomed fabrics, colorful ceramics, and whimsical handicrafts to create a setting so Mexican in flavor that it looks like a stage set. The guestrooms all have king-size beds and bathrooms decorated with Talavera tiles. Ocean breezes and ceiling fans cool the open–air guestrooms. Our favorite is the bedroom on the top floor of the cottage overlooking the swimming pool. The beds come equipped with mosquito netting that can be tucked in at night. Hammocks beckon you to take a nap or spend a lazy afternoon with a good book. A breakfast of fresh juice, a mixed fruit plate, croissants, and coffee or tea is included in the room rate. Lunch and dinner are offered by reservation. *Directions:* Located south of Zihuatanejo. Ask for directions when making reservations.

🖥 ⚙ P ⫪ ≈ ⊥ 🐎

CASA FRIDA B&B
Owners: Annabella Martinez & François Heritier
Barra de Potosi
Zihuatanejo, Guerrero, 40880, Mexico
Tel: (755) 556-3944
3 Rooms, Double: $90
Open: Nov to Apr 15, Credit cards: none
Region: Beach–Pacific Coast

This lovely all-suite hotel, featured in the movie "When a Man Loves a Woman", is built into the rocks of a tiny peninsula that juts into Zihuatanejo Bay. A short walk down a small lane leads to Zihuatanejo's superb La Ropa Beach. La Casa Que Canta (the house that sings) derives its name from the musical sounds of the sea, and each of its suites is named for a Mexican song. The air-conditioned guestrooms all have unique personalities, privacy, serenity, and stunning views. All have terraces, ceiling fans, a mini-bar filled with complimentary bottled water, soft drinks and beer, and a marble bathroom with double sink and walk-in shower. Some have private pools and the proverbial hammock. The textured walls are painted a wonderful terracotta color. Furnishings for the hotel were collected from the finest artisans throughout Mexico. The palapa roof, typical of this tropical area, is outstanding by its size and shape. Meandering stairs lead from the lobby to the restaurant below, past the beautiful infinity pool, and down to a saltwater pool on the ocean level. Special features of the hotel include beautiful designs crafted from fresh flower petals and leaves that the maids create on the bedspreads and a wonderful gift shop in the lobby. Breakfast and lunch are reserved exclusively for guests, while dinner is open to all by reservation. *Directions:* On a rocky promontory above Playa La Ropa.

LA CASA QUE CANTA
Managers: Ana Maria Frias & Teresa Arellano
Carretera a Playa la Ropa
Zihuatanejo, Guerrero, 40880, Mexico
Tel: (755) 555-7000, Fax: (755) 554-7900
25 Rooms, Double: $490–$885*
2 houses also available for rent*
*Breakfast not included: $22
*Service: 10%, Tax: 18%
Open: all year, Credit cards: all major
Different World
Region: Beach–Pacific Coast

If you yearn for a secluded, supremely luxurious hideaway just steps from one of Mexico's finest beaches (Playa La Ropa), nothing can surpass El Murmullo, a sister hotel of the beautiful La Casa Que Canta. This tiny, four-guestroom, boutique-style hotel looks like something featured in Architectural Digest—a cluster of pastel peach-colored towers topped by palapa roofs, snuggled on a private rocky outcrop overlooking the ocean and the beach. There is no hint that El Murmullo is a hotel. Even when you step through the massive wooden doorway it seems you might have inadvertently entered an exquisite private residence—perhaps one owned by royalty. With a dedicated staff that even includes a chef to serve a maximum of eight guests, you will be totally pampered from the moment you arrive. Each of the beautifully decorated, romantic guestrooms opens fully to the sea breezes and has a private terrace or garden and its own plunge pool. There is also a spectacular infinity swimming pool tucked into the rocks where the water seems to blend seamlessly into the blue of the sea. Although you probably won't want to stray from your personal paradise, all the facilities of La Casa Que Canta are available to the guests of El Murmullo, including its spa, swimming pool, restaurant, and gift shop. *Directions:* Take the small lane next to La Casa Que Canta. Just before you come to the beach, El Murmullo is on the right.

※🔲🛏🕿@W ⌇ P🚭⚱🛶⚓🏌🐎🚣

EL MURMULLO DE LA CASA QUE CANTA
Managers: Ana Maria Frias & Teresa Arellano
Camino Escenico a Playa La Ropa
Zihuatanejo, Guerrero, 40880, Mexico
Tel: (755) 555-7030, Fax: (755) 554-7900
4 Rooms, Double: $660–$1000*
*Breakfast not included
*Service: 10%, Tax: 17%
Open: all year, Credit cards: all major
Different World
Region: Beach–Pacific Coast

Over a rough road, fifteen minutes from Ixtapa-Zihuatanejo International Airport and five minutes from the fishing village of Barra de Potosi, is the Hotel Las Palmas, a romantic hideaway owned by Shari and Scott Crawford who, while on an around-the-world tour, conceived the idea of leaving their careers in Phoenix and opening a small luxury hotel. After a visit to Playa Blanca, they knew they had found the perfect secluded spot and commissioned one of Zihuatanejo's premier architects to build their dream. The design is excellent, featuring a thatched palapa roof and high ceilings that allow ocean breezes to cool you as you enjoy the quiet evening. The four downstairs bedrooms are air-conditioned, while ceiling fans and sea breezes cools the ones upstairs. The rooms all come with king-sized beds and wooden shutters to keep out the early-morning light and the afternoon sun. All bedrooms face the ocean and you can watch the sunset from your private deck. The practically deserted beach in front of the hotel is glorious and you can walk endlessly in either direction, often without seeing another soul. Although the surf here is treacherous for swimming, this is not a problem as there is a gorgeous infinity swimming pool that sits just below the outside dining room. This hotel is for adults only. Breakfast is included in the room rate, and lunch and dinner can be had upon request. *Directions:* Ask for directions when making reservations.

HOTEL LAS PALMAS
Managers: Josefina Sanchez & Ricardo Garcia
Calle Playa Aeropuerto, Playa Blanca
Zihuatanejo, Guerrero, 40880, Mexico
Tel: (755) 557-0634, Fax: (602) 253-3487 (USA)
6 Rooms, Double: $225*
*Tax: 17%
Open: all year, Credit cards: none
Region: Beach–Pacific Coast

When one heads to the tropics for a vacation, falls in love with the sun and sea, then contacts the home office to tell them, "I'm never returning!" the Aussies say, "He's gone troppo." This is how the outstanding small hotel, La Quinta Troppo, acquired its name. This charming hotel offers guests eight uniquely decorated rooms filled with colorful Mexican art and handicrafts. All the bedrooms offer something special: some have balconies, one a private garden, and another a beautiful bath with two showerheads and a headboard painted by local artisans; while others have a magnificent view of Zihuatanejo Bay. No matter which room you choose, you will be pampered from the time of your arrival when you are greeted with a complimentary margarita and taken to your lovely room where you find cotton robes and slippers. Each night when you return to your room, you will find the bed turned down and fresh towels supplied. The hotel exudes a tropical luxury with every detail well-thought-out to make your stay memorable. The lap pool, with its pre-Hispanic-style fountains, is located in the terrace garden and is a perfect place to relax after a full day on the beach. The rates include a wonderful tropical Continental breakfast. The hotel has no TV, but does offer guests the use of a dedicated computer and has wireless internet. Kids over age 15 are welcome. *Directions:* La Quinta Troppo is located on the hillside above the sea, a five-minute walk to La Ropa Beach.

❄ ☕ 🍴 ▦@ P ≋ ⬍ 🧍 🐎 ⛵

LA QUINTA TROPPO
Owner: David Ferguson
Camino Escenico a Playa la Ropa
Zihuatanejo, Guerrero, 40880, Mexico
Tel: (755) 554-3423, Fax: (755) 554-7340
8 Rooms, Double: $275–$340*
*Service: 10%, Tax: 17%
Open: all year, Credit cards: all major
Different World
Region: Beach–Pacific Coast

The Villa del Sol, which began in the late 1970s as the dream of a German engineer, Helmut Leins, evolved over the years to become one of Mexico's finest boutique hotels. The property remained under Helmut's loving care until 2007 when it was acquired by the Kor Hotel Group, a luxury hotel operator. In the beginning the hotel consisted of just a small cluster of casitas on Zihuatanejo's splendid beach, Playa la Ropa, but it slowly grew. In addition to more rooms and an adjacent condominium complex, all the amenities of a deluxe hotel were added, including four swimming pools, tennis courts, a spa, and a fitness center. There are now 70 rooms and suites, all splendid in décor and with Mexican-style furnishings. Although all the guestrooms are special, the beachside ones, some with terrace and private pool overlooking an expansive view of the bay, are choice. But for that special occasion, the upgrade is well worth it. Playa la Ropa, right outside your door, is perfect for long evening walks or morning jogs. Villa del Sol also offers gourmet cuisine, lunch on the beach with linen tablecloths and the sand at your feet, to casual and fine dining in the evenings at sunset. Zihuatanejo, with its beachside cafés, restaurants, and market, is just a few minutes' ride away by taxi and is well worth a visit. No hotel in Zihuatanejo can surpass the Villa del Sol's prime location, right on the best section of the unrivaled Playa de Ropa beach. *Directions:* Directly on Playa La Ropa.

THE TIDES
Manager: Carlos Blanco
Playa la Ropa, P.O. Box 84
Zihuatanejo, Guerrero, 40895, Mexico
Tel: (755) 555-5500, Fax: (755) 554-2758
70 Rooms, Double: $264–$1280*
*Breakfast not included: $15
*Service: 5%, Tax: 17%
Open: all year, Credit cards: all major
Different World
Region: Beach–Pacific Coast

The Villa Carolina, a well-designed, family-owned, all-suite, small luxury hotel, is located on the hillside above Zihuatanejo's most popular beach, Playa La Ropa. Guests use a special exit from the hotel to walk down the road that leads to this superb beach. The architecture creates a sense of space in the seven sienna-colored, thatched-roofed, split-level, fully-equipped suites. Each suite has a king-size bed and a sitting area where you can catch the local news on CNN, enjoy a video from the office selection, or listen to music on the cassette player. All the tastefully decorated rooms have high ceilings, fans, and air conditioning; along with full marble bathrooms, fully-equipped kitchens, and safe-deposit boxes. Each master suite has a partial ocean view, separate bedroom with terrace, dining area with kitchen, private Jacuzzi, dining area, a hammock, lots of sea breeze, and ample space to move around. The garden suites, located in front of the swimming pool, are large and beautifully appointed. Guests can relax by the pool and, in the afternoon, enjoy hors d'oeuvres and a drink. Breakfast and lunch are offered from 8:30 am to 4:30 pm. If you really want something really special, ask about the Grand Suite, a gorgeous, large suite crowning the top level of the hotel. *Directions:* Located on the hill above Playa La Ropa. Within walking distance to the beach.

VILLA CAROLINA
Manager: Tim Conti
Carretera a Playa la Ropa
Zihuatanejo, Guerrero, 40880, Mexico
Tel: (755) 554-5612, Fax: (755) 554-5615
6 Rooms, Double: $169–$350*
*Breakfast not included: $10
*Tax: 17%
Open: all year, Credit cards: MC, VS
Region: Beach–Pacific Coast

When visiting Mexico's incredible Monarch butterfly sanctuary, Rancho San Cayetano is definitely the place to stay. But don't limit your visit to migration time—the Rancho San Cayetano offers a tranquil retreat year round. The hotel has a superb setting in 12 parklike acres that encompass manicured gardens, exotic trees, wide expanses of lawn, and even a river cutting a gorge through the grounds. This delightful inn, reminiscent of a mountain lodge with large windows accenting walls of stone and wood, also hints of a Mexican hacienda in the verandas that stretch in front of the rooms. The main building houses the reception office, a lounge with a huge stone fireplace accented by tiles, and a cozy dining room. The guestrooms are decorated in a rustic style: brick and exposed-stone walls, beamed ceilings, and tiled floors are enhanced by hand-loomed fabrics, local artwork, and attractive wooden furniture. In addition to the standard guestrooms there are three separate cottages, my favorite being the Casita de Adobe, a romantic 100-year-old adobe cottage with a cozy, wood-burning stove and a terrace overlooking the river running far below in a deep ravine. All the rooms are decorated by your charming hostess, Lisette, who also creates the exceptionally delicious meals. Pablo Span is marvelous at helping guests plan their excursions. *Directions:* Just outside town on the road to Huetamo. Ask for detailed instructions.

HOTEL RANCHO SAN CAYETANO
Owners: Lisette & Pablo Span
Km 2.3, Carretera a Huetamo
Zitácuaro, Michoacán, 61500, Mexico
Tel: (715) 153-1926, Fax: (715) 153-7879
Cell: (715) 115-6517
9 Rooms, Double: $130–$130*
3 Suites: $190–$300, 3 Cottages: $190–$300*
*Breakfast not included: $17
*Service: 15%, Tax: 17%
Open: all year, Credit cards: MC, VS
Region: Central–Near butterfly sanctuaries

Index

414   *Index*

Index

KAREN BROWN wrote her first travel guide in 1976. Her personalized travel series has grown to 17 titles, which Karen and her small staff work diligently to keep updated. Karen, her husband, Rick, and their children, Alexandra and Richard, live in a small town on the coast south of San Francisco.

CLARE BROWN was a travel consultant for many years, specializing in planning itineraries using charming small hotels in the countryside. Her expertise is now available to a larger audience—the readers of her daughter Karen's travel guides. When not traveling, Clare and her husband, Bill, divide their time between northern California, Colorado, and Mexico.

JANE STEVENSON DAY, Ph.D., is a Mesoamerican archaeologist. She served for many years as Chief Curator at the Denver Museum of Natural History where she holds the title of Chief Curator Emeritus. Jane is also an adjunct professor in Archaeology/Museum Studies at several universities in the Denver area. Jane is an immensely popular lecturer in the Denver community and has led many museum trips to various archaeological sites around the world. She lives in Denver, Colorado, and has four daughters residing nearby.

JANN POLLARD, the artist of all the beautiful cover paintings in the Karen Brown series, has studied art since childhood and is well known for her outstanding impressionistic-style watercolors. Jann has received numerous achievement awards and her works are in private and corporate collections internationally. She is also a popular workshop teacher in the United States, Mexico and Europe. *www.jannpollard.com*. Fine art giclée prints of her paintings are available at *www.karenbrown.com*.

BARBARA MACLURCAN TAPP, the talented artist who produces all of the hotel sketches and delightful illustrations in this guide, was raised in Sydney, Australia where she studied interior design. Although Barbara continues with architectural rendering and watercolor painting, she devotes much of her time to illustrating the Karen Brown guides. Barbara lives in Kensington, California, with her husband, Richard, and is Mum to Jono, Alex and Georgia. For more information about her work visit *www.barbaratapp.com*.

Karen Brown's World of Travel

A FREE KAREN BROWN WEBSITE MEMBERSHIP IS INCLUDED WITH THE PURCHASE OF THIS GUIDE

$20 Value – Equal to the cover price of this book!

In appreciation for purchasing our guide, we offer a free membership that includes:

- The ability to custom plan and build unlimited itineraries
- 15% discount on all purchases made in the Karen Brown website store
- One free downloadable Karen Brown Itinerary from over 100 choices
- Karen Brown's World of Travel Newsletter—includes special offers & updates

Membership valid through December 31, 2010

To take advantage of this free offer go to the Karen Brown website shown below and create a login profile so we can recognize you as a Preferred Customer; then you can utilize the unrestricted trip planning and take advantage of the 15% store discount. Once you set up an account you will receive by email a coupon code to order the free itinerary.

Go to *www.karenbrown.com/preferred.php* to create your profile!

Karen Brown's
2010 Readers' Choice Awards

Most Romantic
Hotel Las Palmas
Zihuatanejo

Warmest Welcome
Playa Azul
Cozumel

Greatest Value
Quinta Don Jose
Guadalajara - Tlaquepaque

Splendid Splurge
Las Mañanitas
Cuernavaca

Be sure to vote for next year's winners by visiting
www.karenbrown.com